THE CASE FOR COLONIALISM

THE CASE FOR COLONIALISM

BRUCE GILLEY

Published by New English Review Press
a subsidiary of World Encounter Institute
PO Box 158397
Nashville, Tennessee 37215
&
27 Old Gloucester Street
London, England, WC1N 3AX

Cover Art & Design by Kendra Mallock

ISBN: 978-1-943003-89-1

Library of Congress Control Number: 2023945417

First Edition

This book is dedicated to my colleagues who stood strong in the face of censorship, especially:

Nigel Biggar
Jeremy Black
Niall Ferguson
Peter Wood
Steve Balch
Mukui Waruiru
Tendai Ruben Mbofana
Wanjiru Njoya
Sumantra Maitra
Helen Andrews
Noah Carl
Peter Boghossian
Andrew Nathan
Tirthankar Roy
Zareer Masani
S.G. Cheah
Collin McMahon
Frances Widdowson
Jay Bergman
Seiuli Fa'auliulito Meni
Joy Zhu
Peter Baehr
Nirmal Dass
Jayant Bhandari
Marcel Yabili
Christopher Hallpike

Permission is gratefully acknowledged for permission to use material from the following articles: "The Case for Colonialism" (2017) and "A Response to My Critics" (2021), *Academic Questions* (National Association of Scholars); "The Challenge of the Creative Third World" (2015), *Third World Quarterly*; "The Case for Colonialism in the Middle East" (2022), *The Caravan Notebook* (Hoover Institution Press, Stanford University); "King Hochschild's Hoax" (2023) and "Stoned in America" (2022), *The American Conservative;* "Review of Nigel Biggar, Colonialism: A Moral Reckoning"(2023), *Aristotle Public Policy Foundation*; "A History of Colonialism that's More Angry than Accurate" (2022), *Washington Examiner*; "Thank Britain for the 'People's Republic of Malaya' We Never Knew" (2022), *History Reclaimed*; "A Big Dose of Colonialism is Needed to Save Yemen" (2019), *The Article*; "Chinua Achebe on the Positive Legacies of Colonialism" (2016), *African Affairs* (Oxford University Press); "V.S. Naipaul's Reckoning with Empire" (2018), *The Open Magazine*; and "Elegy for a Colonial Perspective" (2009), *Far Eastern Economic Review.*

CONTENTS

Foreword

As a black person—in fact, not just a black person, but someone born under colonial rule—the thought of "a case for colonialism" was supposed to spook me.

When Dr. Bruce Gilley sent me a copy of his book, *The Case for Colonialism*, my natural reaction should have been rage at the sheer audacity of the man in pushing for colonialism.

I could have easily branded him all sorts of names—from an unrepentant racist to someone still hungover from the privileged position whites gained from colonialism.

Yet, that is not the case. I am not offended! Not only that, but I actually share his views on colonialism to the full!

That may come as a shock to many; however, the most articulate and well-researched points raised by Dr. Gilley in his book are already shared by a growing number of black Africans, who now appreciate how colonialism was actually better than the "independence" of which we attained.

Dr. Gilley brilliantly captures the essence of how the foundations of a modern advanced Africa were actually laid during the colonial period.

This was a time of phenomenal development and civilization for the African people.

The ability to read, write, and engage in meaningful economic, political and social participation was brought by colonialism.

In fact, never has the black African been more empowered than during this time in our history. Never has the continent been more developed than during colonialism.

This is when my own country, Zimbabwe (then known as Rhodesia), was crowned the "jewel of Africa" on account of the massive advancements in all sectors of the economy, including agriculture, manufacturing, and retail.

Our fathers and mothers enjoyed very high standards of living, having received the best education and training in various professions.

Yet, under "independent governments" our countries have all but collapsed—with the numerous gains experienced during colonialism undone and virtually destroyed.

From the "bread basket of Africa," my own Zimbabwe has been reduced to a basket case—riddled with corruption and gross mismanagement.

Under colonialism, merit took center stage in appointments—in stark contrast to today, where to whom one is related, or connected to, gets them top positions. As a result, the country's infrastructure, agriculture, industries, and our livelihoods have all been run into the ground.

This is a sentiment shared widely across many people—as much as it enrages the ruling elite.

In his book, Dr. Gilley perfectly brings to light what made colonialism such a phenomenal success, and why we have failed as black Africans in governing ourselves.

This is a must-read for everyone—more so, those who have previously harbored misconceptions about colonialism, which has all along been incorrectly painted as an evil thing, driven by pure greed and racial hatred.

The Case for Colonialism beautifully unravels such lies and inaccuracies, whilst unpacking the truths—which we now also appreciate as black Africans.

Colonialism actually did much good to us—a fact proven by my own abilities to even write this testimony.

All I can say is "thank you" to Dr. Bruce Gilley for his bravery, for it could not have been easy, in a supposedly "politically correct" world to write this book.

—Tendai Ruben Mbofana
Social justice advocate, writer, researcher, and social commentator

Introduction

FOR MORE THAN a century after the discovery in the early 1700s of the headwaters of the Niger river in the highlands of northwest Africa, the consensus among European geographers was that it flowed north, ducked under the Sahara desert, and emptied into the Mediterranean Sea.[1] A minority faction believed it flowed east into darkest Africa and joined the Congo river. No one could be sure because Africa was impenetrable and dangerous.

A great race began to find the outlet of this great river. Various expeditions toiled in the nether regions of a continent still largely unknown. In 1795, the Royal Geographical Society sent a Scotsman to solve the mystery. He set out from the northwest African coast, was imprisoned and robbed by the locals and ended up back where he started. One local emir patiently explained to his alarmed people that this oddly pale man was a species of fish looking for tributaries of his home river. Not until 1830 did one intrepid English explorer finally realize that the Niger took a sharp right at Timbuktu and tore southwards, emptying into a swampy delta in the crotch of the continent. The outlet was just 150 miles east of a trading port that the Portuguese called "The Lakes" (Lagos).[2]

The British realized this could make Lagos a commercial dynamo. They stepped up attacks on Spanish and Portuguese slavers in the area. The problem was that poisoned arrows flew in every direction among the feuding tribes of the Lagos delta. Every time the British tried to sign a treaty with one chief, he would be ousted or skewered by another. After a particularly nasty coup against the legitimately enthroned King of Lagos in 1845, the British received letters requesting help from both the ousted king as well as the chief of the tribe that had given him refuge. "We request that you would take Lagos under your protection, that you would plant the English flag there, and that you would re-establish me on my rightful throne," the king proposed. The protective chief chimed in to "humbly request that the Queen should take possession of this town, and that she should place some person of authority here, which would greatly contribute to our safety and the welfare of this country at large."[3]

In 1851, after offering amnesty to the pretender and being refused, the British and their African allies stormed the town and restored the legitimate king. From this beginning, the colony of Lagos would expand into the greatest British colony in Africa, and eventually the gargantuan independent country of Nigeria, today with 225 million souls.

The 19th century period of Europe's economic rise and subsequent expansion coincided with the deterioration of rival empires in the non-Western world. These empires had lorded it over subject peoples based on little more than force and spectacle. But the Industrial Revolution and the rapid spread of communications and knowledge in Europe undermined their claims to rule. The alternative to European colonial rule was not a merrie land of milk and honey but a toxic mix of rival European armies, feuding local chiefs, unscrupulous arms dealers, and dishonest commodity brokers. "Changes were bound, in the nature of things, to come; we could not have resisted external influences much longer and, even if some had wished to do so, the effect of education, which too must have come to us before long, would have forced a general tidying up," recalled one Nigerian man, Ahmadu Bello, born in 1909.[4]

The northerly regions of what became Nigeria, for example, were a stew of collapsing Muslim empires and feuding chiefs that were vulnerable to rival French and German interests alongside various importunate missionaries, concession-seekers, and adventurers. Flora Shaw, a fearless English woman who travelled solo in the region, wrote in the London *Times* of the "frightful slavery" and tyranny of the local Fulani rulers who had controlled the region for more than a century. This made other Arab and black slaving empires in east Africa look like "a mere bagatelle."[5] A Royal Niger Company was given a charter by the British in 1886 to oversee trade along the Niger river (an area twice as big as France, with 35 million inhabitants). It soon found itself engaged in quasi-governmental functions. It ran public services, freed slaves, and maintained peace. Its chief physician introduced the treatment for leprosy. Company-protected church missions offered a refuge for slaves whose masters had died, or to local chiefs who found themselves fleeing the tip of a poisoned arrow.

In 1903, a local British commander, Frederick Lugard, marched north with a force composed mainly of Hausa Africans. He relieved the Royal Niger Company of its duties. The British "conquest" if it can be called that, was remarkably easy since local peasants were all too ready to swap the degrading rule of their emirs for the protection of the British. Journalist Shaw was so impressed that she married Lugard and wrote the first account of the amalgamation of the region under British rule.[6] She called it a "new India."

A blind Islamic cleric and part-time ventriloquist tried to raise a rebellion against British rule in the town of Satiru in 1906. But the local emirs, and even a few distant ones, rallied around the British. After that, British rule consolidated with such speed that the entire region was left mostly in the hands of native administrators. "There was no ill-will after the occupation. We were used to conquerors and these were different; they were polite and obviously out to help us rather than themselves," Bello wrote. Like many locals, he sought work with the native administration, becoming the equivalent of a district commissioner in 1934. The British "made no drastic changes, and what was done came into effect only after consultation," he recalled. In 1959, on the eve of independence, Bello assumed the premiership of northern Nigeria in the aptly named Lugard Hall of the regional capital. A few years later, he became independent Nigeria's first premier.

Until very recently, world history has been a history of empires, meaning nations and states that extended their governance systems over others. The European versions were unusual in that they comprised several empires rather than one and varied widely in time and place. By far the biggest was the British empire followed by the French. The other significant ones were the Spanish, Portuguese, Dutch, and Belgian. But as a general rule, these colonial empires came from the same civilization, and thus we can speak of "European colonialism" in Africa, Asia, the Middle East, and Latin America as a coherent whole.

Confining ourselves only to the post-Napoleonic empires, one half of the member states of today's United Nations and one half of the world's population live in countries that came under European colonial rule at some point from the 19th to the 20th centuries. The 17 biggest of these contain 3 billion people, or 85% of the population of these roughly 80 states. They are the four successors states to British India, India (which is the colossus with 1.3 billion or nearly half of the colonial total), Pakistan, Bangladesh, and Burma/Myanmar; the three largest states of east sub-Saharan Africa, Tanzania, Uganda, and Kenya; the other three giants of sub-Saharan Africa, Nigeria, the Congo, and South Africa; the four successors to the main Dutch, Spanish, British, and French colonies in Southeast Asia, Indonesia, the Philippines, Malaysia, and Vietnam; and the three behemoths of north and Muslim Africa, Morocco, Algeria, and the Sudan.

This post-Napoleonic period of European colonialism should be divided from the preceding 300-odd years of European empires because it marked a shift in power and purpose for Europe. In the British case, the first phase began with Ireland in 1603, Jamestown in 1607, and Bermuda in 1609. The grander post-Napoleonic phase began with the Cape of Good Hope (1814), Singapore (1819), and Burma (1824). What distinguishes these two eras is not just the different European powers (Spain, for instance, largely disappeared as a serious colonial player as Latin American areas became independent while Germany was only a participant in the second), but more importantly, the different ideas and institutions that came with European colonialism. While the word "colonialism" initially connoted the settlement of people, in the course of the 19th century, it came to connote more the settlement of ideas and institutions—in particular liberal toleration, political representation, the rule of law, property rights, and the security of borders. It was these Enlightenment ideas and institutions, far more than soldiers and administrators, that colonized the world. Sending settlers, building a fort, or establishing a silver mine were now disparaged as "mere" imperialism. The term "colonialism" represented a more elevated vocation in which improving the lives of subject peoples through a transfer of liberal norms and impersonal governance institutions were the goals.

Another reason for distinguishing these two periods is that the 19th century was the final and most potent phase of what economic historians call "the great divergence" between the West and the Rest.[7] The Europe that was colonizing now was a vastly more advanced civilization, measured in terms of its material and organizational capacities, than the Europe of the first colonial era, when Europeans were often as primitive as the native peoples they encountered. This mattered because the legitimacy of colonial rule in this era was founded not just on the civilizing ideas and institutions of the modern state but also on the material advantages that came with being integrated into the global economy created by Europe.

Very few major areas of the world were not touched by this colonialism because the "push" factors emanating from Europe were almost always reciprocated by even stronger "pull" factors emanating from the colonized themselves. The Sultan of Brunei, for instance, installed an English traveler, James Brooke, as the rajah of his chaotic province of Sarawak (in today's Malaysia) in 1841, after which order and prosperity improved to such an extent that even once a British protectorate was established there in 1888, the Sultan preferred to leave it under Brooke family control until 1946.[8] Brooke family rule in Sarawak showed how a culturally-informed external actor could gain legitimacy by delivering good governance—in this case an end to piracy, head-hunting and slavery as well as expanded foreign trade and wage labor opportunities. European rule was established with remarkable ease throughout the world because local elites believed that on balance, it would be better than the alternatives—the "preservers," "facilitators," and "collaborators," as the Stanford political scientist David Abernethy called them, far outnumbered the "resisters."[9] For most colonized peoples, especially women and marginalized groups, European rule was an opportunity more than a threat.

Countries that were not subject to colonial rule in this second era—like China, Ethiopia, Liberia, Libya, Saudi Arabia, Thailand, Haiti, and Guatemala—provide a measure of comparison to help identify what, if anything, were the distinctive effects of colonialism. The famous paired comparisons of colonized versus non-colonized countries like Belize-Guatemala, Jamaica-Haiti, Malaysia-Thailand, Kenya-Ethiopia, Liberia-Ghana, or Pakistan-Iran provide one approach. These comparisons suggest that the only thing worse than being colonized was not being colonized. The main countries that were never European colonies—especially China, Ethiopia, Iran, Thailand, and Nepal—or whose colonial experiences ended before the modern colonial era—Brazil, Mexico, Guatemala, and Haiti—are hardly compelling as evidence that not being colonized was a boon.

Areas that were colonized drew in colonial powers not just because of the weakness of their institutions and societies but also because there was a vacuum of governance in the face of modern pressures that Western colonialism could fill. In India, which looms large in the "might have been" debates, the Muslim Mughul empire had collapsed just as European trading interests arrived. The Persian king Nader Shah issued a common Persian-Indian currency at the end of 1739 after defeating the Mughul army, indicative of his plan to incorporate the area into his Iranian empire. Some Indian nationalists opine that Persian rule would have been preferable.[10] But as the British historian Michael Axworthy noted, "the massacre of perhaps 30,000 people perpetrated by

Nader while he was in Delhi would hardly have been an auspicious curtain-raiser for permanent Persian rule there."[11] When Nader returned home, he gouged out his son's eyes, castrated his military commander, and had eight merchants who had purchased a royal carpet chained together by the neck, thrown into a pit, and burned alive. Thousands more perished in his various pogroms. To the Hindu on the street, the arrival of the British East India Company must have seemed a godsend.

Moreover, there is no reason to believe that the various feuding Hindu princes of the subcontinent would have magically come together to form a tolerant and civic republic absent colonial rule and every reason to believe that the region would have become one giant failed state. As Karl Marx wrote: "The question, therefore, is not whether the English had a right to conquer India, but whether we are to prefer India conquered by the Turk, by the Persian, by the Russian, to India conquered by Briton."[12] In 1858, a year after a small group of native soldiers mutinied against, and a larger group of soldiers, princes, and commoners rallied around the British, India was reorganized into a fully-fledged colony.

~

The case for European colonialism is simple. It is the case for humanity itself, for the ways that human beings have always acted rationally to better their situations in life, and those of their children. It is the case for having a teacher, a coach, or a model. It is the case for having opportunity. It is the case for peace, progress, and running water. It is the case for living in a place where life is better and escaping from a place where life is worse. It is the case for human agency and freedom. In short, it is the case for a humble submission to the facts of life rather than the worked up intellectual fantasies of the scholar class.

All of this should not be controversial. Indeed, up to around 1945, it wasn't. The first critiques of colonialism were hardly scathing, indeed they were not even anti-colonial.[13] "The contact with white races cannot be avoided, and it is more perilous and more injurious in proportion as it lacks governmental sanction and control," wrote the English economist John Hobson in 1902. Attacks on colonial rule were "ethically indefensible," he assayed, because they ignored what would almost certainly have happened without European rule: "If organized Governments of civilized Powers refused the task, they would let loose a horde of private adventures, slavers, piratical traders, treasure hunters, concession mongers, who, animated by mere greed of gold or power, would set about the work of exploitation under no public control and with no regard to the future." To allow this would be "a barbarous dereliction of a public duty on behalf of humanity and the civilization of the world." Hobson argued for a "sane and legitimate" colonialism that served the broad interests of both colonized and colonizer.[14] The disasters of "free" states like Haiti (which threw off its French colonial rulers in 1803 and promptly descended into two centuries of chaos), Hobson noted, showed that ordered and coordinated European colonial rule was better in most cases than a mad scramble.

Hobson's generation sought a liberal colonialism that responded to rising expectations of economic development and political opportunity in the colonies. His idea that colonies should be treated as trusteeships reflected the spirit of the Berlin Conferences of 1884-5 where the Germans had forged a cross-European agreement on the need to put native interests at the center of colonial policy.[15]

Not surprisingly, the most forceful advocates of Western colonialism were the colonized themselves. A lawyer from India working in South Africa wrote of his pride in fighting for the British during World War I, a war that he hoped would "bind closer still the different parts of the mighty empire of which" the Indian community was "so proud."[16] When this lawyer returned to India, he was disgusted by the backwardness of his homeland and called for an acceleration of colonial development and progress. Gandhi later donned native garb and claimed to be a spiritualist challenging the empire. But his whole life and mental make-up was a testament to the benefits of colonialism.

This generation of native officials and businessmen who had risen up in colonial society knew that they would be in no position to take over for a very long time. They wanted to inherit the colonial state and economy, not destroy it. Most leading nationalists did not believe in outright independence. Ho Chi Minh in Vietnam and Ferhat Abbas in Algeria both hoped for a continued French condominium, while Patrice Lumumba praised Belgian rule in the Congo. The challenge, as they saw it, was how to enjoy the stabilizing role of an external governing power while unlocking the benefits of empire. That is why the former colonies of the defeated Ottoman empire were put under the control of European countries as League of Nations "mandates" after World War I.

The Second World War changed everything. The Anglo-American Atlantic Charter of 1941 promised "the right of all peoples to choose the form of government under which they will live." Western powers were exhausted from a second sapping world war centered in Europe. They were ready to throw in the towel. Countries like Lebanon and India that became independent as a direct result of the war styled themselves liberators of colored people everywhere. In 1946, at the foot of an active volcano on the island of Java, Dutch officials signed an agreement with the leaders of a republican movement left over by the invading Japanese army. Both sides rejected "a return to colonialism." When crowds waving Dutch flags gathered outside the local governor's house in Medan on the east coast of northern Sumatra the following year demanding independence, the governor applauded their moral courage and noted that the Netherlands was "not interested in a return to colonialism." "The meeting ended with three cheers for Queen Wilhelmina, for Sumatra's east coast, and for the restoration of law and order," the London *Times* reported.[17]

India tabled a resolution at the United Nations in 1947 demanding that all European colonies be put under UN control as a prelude to rapid decolonization. "It can't hurt to ask!" became the motto for disgruntled native politicians everywhere. To their surprise, the colonial rulers usually said, "Yes." The reason was not noble anti-colonial "resistance" but ignoble European resignation. A by-product of the two world wars was a deep turn inwards for Europe. Material deprivation and national confidence were at a low point. Among the many targets of the emotional response to the devastations of war were overseas colonies, often seen as a conceit for nations that could no longer keep their own houses in order.

Anti-colonialism had begun in Europe in the early 1900s and simmered away in cafes and fringe groups in the inter-war period, goaded on by the Leninist anti-colonialism of revolutionary Russia. The radical anti-colonialists of the Left were soon joined by radical anti-colonialists on the Right. The Nazis had seen themselves as freeing Germany from the "colonial" rule of the Treaty of Versailles. Like so many anti-colonial fanatics, Hitler wanted to purify his culture of the depredations of liberal civilization.[18] He pledged to turn Germany away from the cosmopolitan mission of "overseas policy" in Africa and Asia and to a recessive project of "land policy" in Central Europe. He courted like-minded ethnic chauvinists in the colonies like the Mufti of Jerusalem and members of the Congress Party in India who sought to free themselves from the odious rule of liberal civilization. They streamed to Berlin during Hitler's failed march on Europe for tips on how to seize power from decrepit liberal institutions and purge their countries of unwanted races.

After the war, this illiberal ideology of anti-colonialism was exported with a missionary zeal to the colonies by European intellectuals of both Left and Right. Egypt's leader Gamal Nasser employed ex-Nazis in Cairo to fan the flames of anti-colonialism throughout the Middle East. This new anti-colonialism offered natives a magical explanation of everything they disliked about modern life and a utopian promise of paradise if only the yoke of colonialism could be lifted. The European ideologues, whether Nazis or Leninists, preyed upon these impressionable minds, celebrating when they set up political movements outside of the normal parties and groupings of colonial politics. The illiterate and poor masses whose uplift was a long-term work in progress were offered a shortcut to modern life tinged with the thrill of racist appeals. The BBC's *Listener* magazine noted in 1957 that colonialism had become "the commonest term of abuse nowadays throughout more than half the world."[19]

The Soviets rechristened their People's Friendship University in Moscow as Patrice Lumumba University in 1961 to train Marxist revolutionaries and terrorists. Most of the graduates were spurned as Soviet stooges. But in the international propaganda war, it made Moscow seem a friend of black and brown people everywhere. An American envoy on colonial affairs warned Washington that it too needed to rally to the cause of decolonization lest it appear "a conspirator on the side of imperialism instead of a champion of independence."[20]

Once the United States and Soviet Union began vying for the affections of anti-colonial agitators, there was no will power in European capitals to remain. The French praised their war-time leader, Charles de Gaulle, for rapidly extricating their country from colonial wars, "delivering the country at whatever price," in the words of prime minister Edgar Faure, "from a malady that was consuming it."

In the span of three decades—roughly 1945 to 1975—the world system oversaw the mass production of 100-odd countries with little more than a flag and a Government House to their names. The new United Nations became what the American scholar Jeffrey Herbst called a "decolonization machine" as it stamp-pressed nation after nation into being.[21] The Oxford philosopher John Plamenatz warned in 1960 that "foreign rulers ought to see to it that, when they withdraw, the passive and inarticulate do not fall victims to a ruthless minority of exuberant patriots."[22] Yet, this is precisely what happened in most places. Civil war, political tyranny, and economic collapse spread from one major country to another, including to 11 of the Big 17 mentioned above: Pakistan,

Bangladesh, Burma, Tanzania, Uganda, Nigeria, the Congo, Vietnam, Morocco, Algeria, and the Sudan.

There was no end of devastating accounts of life after colonialism published in the 1970s, known as the "forgotten decade" in development circles. Guinea's first president Ahmed Sékou Touré declared himself "The Terror of International Imperialism, Colonialism, and Neo-Colonialism" and proceeded to carry out regular public hangings of cabinet ministers—58 in one session alone in 1970.[23] Given the proximity to the colonial era, it was easy to blame these disasters on "the legacies of colonialism," even if non-colonized places like Ethiopia and Iran were experiencing similar traumas, while many former colonies like Singapore, Malaysia, Botswana, and Belize got along just fine with "the legacies of colonialism" because their leaders made better choices. This pat phrase —"the legacies of colonialism"—would have enduring appeal to anti-colonial intellectuals. It had no statute of limitations because to deny oneself this intellectual cop-out was to force oneself into mature thinking.

One would think that the humanitarian catastrophe that was decolonization would have revived positive assessments of colonialism, and a rueful regret about anti-colonialism and decolonization. Far from it. As time went by, these ideologies went from strength to strength. So rarified and detached from historical reality did this thinking become that a new piece of jargon was invented: post-colonialism. Having opposed colonial rule, and driven colonial rulers out, the thought leaders of Third Worldism were left with nothing to think about. Agog at the devastation throughout the Third World, and unwilling, as the African novelist Chinua Achebe put it, to examine "the chaotic jumble of tragic and tragi-comical problems we have unleashed on ourselves," Western intellectuals and their Third World imitators invented a make-believe world called "post-colonialism" that was entirely insulated from reality. In this cuddly world of post-colonial thought, they would preen and posture with dense jargon about obscure topics and theories of cause and effect.

No amount of decolonized disaster seemed sufficient to jolt this intellectual mindset from its reveries. Successive genocides in Zanzibar, Cambodia, Bangladesh, Rwanda, and Sri Lanka left little impression on the bright minds of post-colonial theory. Nor did Zimbabwe's downward spiral after decolonization in 1980, South Africa's after 1994, or Hong Kong's after 1997. Calling these human tragedies "the cost of progress" became untenable. So did explanations of them in terms of "the legacies of colonialism." But a persistent and trained blindness afflicted the intellectual classes.

~

The island of Zanzibar (off the east coast of Africa) became independent from Britain in 1963. It had a carefully designed constitution with elections that were contested by ethnically mixed parties that balanced the interests of the Arab and black populations. It offered a pathway forward, a rare place where independence might lead to a decent life. Barely a month after Prince Philip presided over independence ceremonies, a black-led rebellion led to the massacre of Arab and South Asian civilians and the flight of most non-blacks from the island. One of the two black rebel leaders, both of whom had moved to the island from the mainland in colonial times because of its opportunities, declared that God had called upon him to massacre Arabs. He later proudly described in his memoirs how he ordered his thugs "to fire in all directions and to kill whatever came before them—men, women, children, disabled persons, even chickens and goats."[24] A U.S. diplomat stationed on the island described black gangs going house to house with machetes.[25] An Italian film crew recorded the blood-letting from the air.[26] Only 1 in 10 of the criminals who took part in the revolution were from Zanzibar, despite attempts to portray it as a local uprising against colonial legacies.[27] Over just two days, between 5,000 and 10,000 people were murdered. A further 20,000 "stooges" were imprisoned, while 100,000 mostly middle class and wealthy people fled the island—so 43% of the population was either killed, imprisoned, or exiled.[28]

One Arab member of the revolutionary government claimed the revolution was driven by the popular desire to "achieve a genuinely free society—free from the shackles of slavery, of feudal landlordism, and of colonial humiliation" and that it "shook the entire imperialist camp as a devastating blow to their well-planned post-colonial strategy for East Africa."[29] It could come as a surprise only to the most pickled progressive mind that these high ideals were a fraud in practice. Communist friends arrived in this new "people's republic" offering state repression and poverty. An East German attempt to move the urban population into ten-story concrete apartment blocks with identical sizes and layouts was spurned by the "workers and peasants" who preferred traditional huts with courtyards for communal cooking and rooms for extended families.[30] The clove and coconut palm sectors were nationalized and then collapsed. The two black leaders of the revolution were soon gone: one expelled back to Africa for his genocidal appeals and the other assassinated in 1972. For the next forty years, a human disaster unfolded on the island that would leave it shattered and destitute. In the words of an American historian, the revolution led to "confiscations, shortages, surveillance, and fear." It "swept away much of the substance of the legal, bureaucratic order of the colonial state." The new regime "sat atop an extensive, East German–trained security apparatus and was able to rule by personal decree."[31]

Despite official attempts, abetted by Western intellectuals, to uphold the myth of a virtuous anti-colonial revolution on Zanzibar, folk memories remember nothing but horror. On the adjoined island of Jongowe, a militia arrived in 1969 and arrested the village leaders of the local Tumbatu people as traitors, taking them back to Zanzibar and executing them all. School-children, including those whose parents had been executed, were then forced to attend a rally to denounce them. As the son of one recalled: "There was one rally song and banner which directly supported their execution; it read: 'Slaughter, slaughter, slaughter all the traitors. Slaughter, slaughter, slaughter all the Tumbatu and their leaders.' Imagine me, forced to attend this rally, chanting along with a banner urging that my father and all my village's leaders be slaughtered."[32]

One of the Arabs who fled this post-colonial disaster was the writer Abdulrazak Gurnah. He eventually found a cozy position as a professor of literature in Britain. At first, he was honest about the horrors of the revolution, commenting in his 1996 book, *Admiring Silence,* on "the incompetence of the [revolutionary] authorities, their mindless bullying, the endless fiascos, their irrational vengefulness."[33] But when he was awarded the Nobel Prize for literature in 2021, the commendation stressed "his uncompromising and compassionate penetration of the effects of colonialism." Gurnah, who was nothing if not a clever publicist, warmed to this anti-colonial reading of his life and works. The insistence by the mavens of the Nobel committee that the disaster that became Zanzibar was a result of "the effects of colonialism" became Gurnah's calling card. Nothing to do with the anti-colonialism in Egypt that had animated the Arab elites to push for independence; nothing to do with the anti-colonialism in Kenya, Tanganyika, and Uganda that had stirred the black revolutionaries who arrived on the island to unleash violent mayhem; nothing to do with the anti-colonialism of the Soviet bloc whose comrades provided toxic "aid;" nothing to do with the anti-colonialism of the Western intellectual establishment that stared agog as the disaster unfolded without supporting those calling for intervention and stabilization to save lives. No, none of that. The blame must be laid at the feet of Prince Philip and all he represented.

It is staggering to learn that even today the Zanzibar revolution is an official holiday and a source of pride to the majority black population on the island. Academics, meanwhile, churn out books on the revolution with chapters on "the ambiguities of remembrance," "the reconstructed self," and "patterns of interpretation" as if they are contributing to a symposium on Baudelaire.[34]

One is hard-pressed to identify a "peak crazy" moment in the intellectual mania that was anti-colonialism, decolonization, and post-colonialism. Faced with no dissenting opinions, this broad mesh of ideology began to think of itself as natural and uncontestable. Even as post-colonial disasters like Zanzibar were unfolding in the 1960s and 1970s, the intellectual apparatus of anti-colonial thought grew stronger not weaker. Seminal books that would become bibles to generations of university students—Frantz Fanon's *Wretched of the Earth* (1961), Walter Rodney's *How Europe Underdeveloped Africa* (1972), Edward Said's *Orientalism* (1978)—were published even as the premises of their arguments were collapsing in the real world. If colonialism had been such a terrible thing, as these books claimed, then formerly colonized places should have sprung to vigorous life the moment the colonizers were sent packing. Even allowing for a seemly pause to recover from the alleged traumas of colonialism, it should not have taken more than a decade or so for the fruits of decolonization to be harvested. Germany and Japan, after all, had been laid waste by the war and were quickly becoming democratic and wealthy by the late 1950s. Zanzibar should not have been far behind. Next would come a world-beating Pakistan and an India attracting back generations of its migrants ("Who wants to live in Manchester when we can live in Mumbai?"), followed by economic miracles from Lebanon to Lesotho.

But what if....what if the whole intellectual apparatus of anti-colonial thought was one big error? What if the problems in the Third World were a result not of colonialism but of anti-colonialism, and of a rushed termination of the colonial project? What if the *mission civilatrice* and the White Man's Burden were precisely what the developing world desperately needed? The West is nothing if not prone to "critical thinking," especially about orthodoxies. Even as intellectuals and public leaders lived in mortal fear of uttering anything outside the orthodoxy, dissent began to appear on the margins. "There has been far too much sackcloth and ashes, and I think it has done a great deal of harm," said longtime British colonial civil servant Sir Alan Burns in 1947.[35]

Like all intellectual movements, the renewed case for colonialism had early traces. Two works in the 1970s were seminal. The Oxford professor Ronald Robinson wrote a seemingly innocent article on the "Non-European Foundations of European Imperialism" in 1972.[36] Rejecting the dominant idea of colonialism as an illegitimate imposition upon the colonized, Robinson argued that colonialism was more often a cooperative endeavor. His book chapter was a small crack that would eventually cause a key plank of the anti-colonial platform to splinter and collapse. The more that scholars looked into the question of indigenous "agency," the more they saw the awful truth: even if they could not yet bring themselves to say that European colonialism was legitimate, as time passed, it became impossible to call it strictly illegitimate. A much later book by the Swiss economic historian Bouda Etemad neatly began with the question: "How did they do that?"[37] In his study of how European colonization happened, Etemad documented the extraordinary extent to which very few Europeans were actually involved. Most of the colonizing was done by natives. A whole new vocabulary arose to explain how and why the colonized seemed so darned content with colonialism: "instrumentalism," "strategic engagement," "exchange relations," and sometimes even that poisoned term "collaboration."

No less subversive to the anti-colonial creed was the Nigerian writer Wole Soyinka's charge in 1975 that anti-colonial bombast about The Horrors of the White Man with his running water and railways was a demeaning creed of what he called "neo-Tarzanism."[38] All those progressives promising to "decolonize" African literature and replace it with some supposed "African tradition" were generating images little different from "the traditional Hollywood image of the pop-eyed African in the jungle," he wrote. Those Western anthropologists in Africa showing up at the local Festival of the Arts with their tape recorders to capture an "authentic" African idiom were in cahoots with neo-Tarzanian locals fresh off a flight from Boston with a quick wardrobe change into local garb. Oil rigs and railways were just as African as wooden gourds, Soyinka insisted. Thatched huts and bonga fish? Give me stained glass and the suffocating exhaust of a motor boat instead, he responded. The anti-colonialists had outdone their colonial tormentors in terms of racism, exoticization, and degradation. Those post-colonial thinkers who espied a "Christian-colonialist conspiracy" behind every aspect of modern society were engaged in a fantasy. Such allegations were "facile cover-up expressions for the lack of a painstaking concern for truth," he charged.

A sharp repudiation of the anti-colonial mindset came in 1979 when Singapore's foreign minister, Sinnathamby Rajaratnam, told the UN general assembly that Third World leaders had developed a tendency "to adopt the vices of their former imperial masters while carefully eschewing some of their virtues." Third World failures, he declared, were "largely self-induced." He continued: "To reverse this drift towards disaster, it is necessary for the Third World to recognize that it has and it is committing errors—instead of attributing its difficulties to its imperial past and to the machinations of the rich advanced nations."[39]

More broadly, the notion that Third World countries were hapless victims of "structural conditions" rather than of their own mismanagement lost credibility. The common refrain, for example, that Zambia's development was "undermined by the dramatic fall in worldwide copper prices"[40] after 1975 became untenable. Instead, studies showed that inefficient production by the state copper company, macroeconomic policy mistakes, an over-expansion of the public sector, and a harmful policy response of increased nationalizations and controls were mainly to blame.[41] Zambia's economic decline began in the late 1960s, *before* the copper crash, while Chile, another copper-dependent developing country, managed prudently and thrived. The notion of the culpability of the West, which Puchala identified as a key tenet of "Third World thinking," could not survive the daily evidence of Third World misrule.[42]

By the 1980s, Third Worldism was on its way to being discredited. I recall sitting in a lecture room at the University of Toronto listening to my Marxist professor extolling the benefits of radical policies for the Third World, finding it more amusing than serious. We were assigned to read the 1981 book *Global Rift: The Third World Comes of Age* by the Greek socialist Leften Stavrianos which, among other things, praised China's Cultural Revolution as a great boon to the peasantry. Unbeknownst to the aptly named Leften, those lucky peasants were in the process of throwing off the shackles of Maoist collectivism just as he was writing his book.

If a beginning of the shift can be seen, it was the tragic reminder at the 1983 meeting of the anti-colonial Non-Aligned Movement in New Delhi. Three weeks before the summit, inter-ethnic election violence in India claimed the lives of between 1,600 and 5,000 East Bengali migrants in an Assamese town with the cruelly ironic name of Nellie.[43] As the delegates gathered for their ritual denunciations of colonialism, the Nellie Massacre outside the conference windows told a story of the problems of anti-colonialism. Even for a group so obsessed with blaming the West, it was hard to ignore the reminder that most depredations were self-inflicted.

The 1980s was the decade when the former colonies showed the first signs of reclaiming the colonial structures their leaders had destroyed: market economies, political democracy, the rule of law, property rights, freedoms, and foreign investment and trade. In a now-classic paper on economic development, the Burmese economist Hla Myint had advocated export-led policies that "in their technical properties, may not be very different from those of the colonial governments in the past."[44] Those lessons were hitting home by the 1980s. At the time that Myint wrote, in 1958, South Korea's economy was the same size as Peru's, while Taiwan's was the same size as Egypt's. In the following decades, South Korea and Taiwan pursued colonial-style policies of export-development and financial and economic integration with the West, while Egypt and Peru pursued anti-colonial protest. By 1982, South Korea's economy was more than twice as large as Peru's, while Taiwan's was 70% larger than Egypt's. Today, Taiwan and South Korea have per capita levels of GDP that are four times higher than their anti-colonial counterparts. Throughout the Third World, other countries like Kenya and Chile that also rejected the prescriptions of the *dependistas* became richer than their neighbors.

A small trickle of dissident literature challenging anti-colonial orthodoxies became a stream. Some of the first "wound literature"—memoirs of the horrors of decolonization—began to appear from some surprising sources. The Congolese scholar Albert Tshibangu-Wa-Mulumba disturbed the French world by publishing *Hommage à la colonisation* [*A Tribute to Colonialism*] in 1987, saying that the precious legacies of colonialism—especially the rule of law and a non-tribal political sphere—had been destroyed by Africans themselves, drunk on revolutionary idealism. Africa could never thrive until it reclaimed the colonial trajectory, he argued.

Broader critiques of Third Worldism were made in this decade, such as the Venezuelan diplomat Carlos Rangel's 1986 book, *Third World Ideology and Western Reality,* that urged developing countries to reclaim the Western liberal heritage. A more devastating critique of Third Worldism was offered by the French scholar Pascal Bruckner in his book of the same year, *The Tears of the White Man*, that described the effects of Western intellectual pandering to Third World anti-colonialism, suggesting it reflected a deep-seated racism about the inability of black and brown peoples to run modern countries, as captured in the book's subtitle, *Compassion as Contempt*.

By the 1990s, the backlash against anti-colonial madness was in the full swing throughout the former colonies, even if academics in the West dug in like terriers to defend their tired old positions. It did not take a Ph.D. to realize that the countries which had preserved their colonial legal orders, economic systems, bureaucracies, and political pluralism were the ones that were doing better. In Southeast Asia, Singapore and Malaysia carried on the colonial system with great success while anti-colonialists laid waste to Burma and former French Indo-China. Across the Middle East, anti-colonial movements destroyed millions of lives from Algeria to Lebanon while a few beacons of stability like the United Arab Emirates and Israel took over colonial mandates to create decent societies. Africa was no different: grotesque human suffering at the hands of anti-colonial movements from Ghana to Mozambique leavened by adherence to colonial systems of law and market economies in places like Botswana and South Africa. Apartheid South Africa served as a model of a modernized African state, and over 100,000 black Africans a year applied to migrate there during the 1980s.[45] Countries like India that had spent forty years trying to build socialism and Marxist secular societies finally did a U-turn, liberalizing both economy and society after running into a brick wall (in India's case with a currency crisis in 1991).

In this post-Cold War decade, the intellectual turn against anti-colonialism was more prominent. Now that the Soviet world order was revealed to be a hollow shell of repression and starvation, all those post-colonial countries with Lenin Universities and Friendship Farms realized they had been sold a false bill of goods. For the first time, serious empirical work appeared showing the economic and social benefits of Western colonialism and the capitalist economies and plural societies it had encouraged.

Two works by economists published in 1999 were the first to gather together long-term data to show the economic benefits of colonialism. Cambridge economic historian David Fieldhouse, born in India to missionary parents, showed that the main gift of colonialism was to have conjoined backward areas to the world capitalist system. Post-colonial leaders had a choice: either embrace or spurn that legacy. Incorporation into the world economy as exporters of raw materials had provided the first step in domestic industrialization, to be followed, if leaders adhered to good governance and investment, to export-based economic success. The economic benefit of colonialism was simple, Fieldhouse argued: for the first time in world history, "wealth" was something that accumulated and could be sold, which translated into social benefits.

The 1990s also saw the first serious attempts at the statistical modelling of colonial legacies. The American economist Robin Grier found that British colonies, mainly because of their educational systems, generated sustained growth for their colonies. Across all colonies, those that were held for longer did better. Without investigating more precise mechanisms, Grier could state that his findings were a rejection of "a crude form of exploitation theory."[46] It was the first scientific refutation of three decades of anti-colonial dogma dressed up as "social science." And because "economic growth" was always the driving engine of other good outcomes—health, education, the rule of law, social equality, good governance, etc.—it had more than passing significance.

Grier's findings would be reproduced by dozens of others over the coming decades. Two Dartmouth economist scholars, for example, noted that islands offered an almost perfect natural experiment in colonialism's effects because their discovery by Europeans was sufficiently random that they should not have been affected by the "pull" factors that made some places more likely to be colonized at certain times and in certain ways. In their study of the effects of colonialism on the income levels of people on 81 islands, they found "a robust positive relationship between colonial tenure and modern outcomes." Bermuda and Guam were better off than Papua New Guinea and Fiji because they were colonized for longer. The costs of anti-colonialism in Cuba were shocking: comparable islands had income levels roughly ten times that pitiful island.[47]

The way was being cleared. Stanford political scientist David Abernethy, in his magisterial account of the year 2000 on European global expansion, ended his book with the conclusion that depending on how you weighted different factors, there was a plausible weighting in which "the case for colonialism is strong."[48] The breakthrough into open dissent came in 2003 when the distinguished British historian Niall Ferguson published *Empire: How Britain Made the Modern World*. Like Fieldhouse, he argued that economic and political modernization could not have happened without colonialism. The British empire brought the English language, property rights, banking, the rule of law, Christian ethics, a limited state, representative government, civil society, and the idea of liberty to places that would have at best concocted some debased local interpretation of these things in the absence of direct colonial rule. The liberal rule of empire meant that when empire fell short of its high ideals it was subject to scathing critique on the home front, which rather proved its advantages. Just as Marx had failed to realize that the parliamentary reports into factory conditions that he devoured in order to stand up his criticism of capitalism were themselves the reason that capitalism would survive, critics of colonialism who spent many delightful hours parsing the lurid details of colonial crimes found in the public records, failed to understand that it was precisely the liberal civilization that so diligently investigated and corrected such crimes that was why it was of such benefit to the colonized. Post-colonial tyrants tended to just dump the bodies in the river and deny anything had happened.

Ferguson was accused by the American historian Frederick Cooper of the cardinal sin of "imperial nostalgia" which he defined as "a longing for the days when responsible, honest white men ruled." Ferguson also committed the graver error of ignoring "how gender and class played out in relation to race."[49] In other words, Ferguson left them speechless. The cat was out of the bag. After Ferguson, one could in polite conversations for the first time talk about "the debate on colonialism." The eminent British historian Jeremy Black published *The British Empire: A History and a Debate* in 2011.

Serious thinkers began to return to the basics. The American philosopher Christopher Morris wondered in a 2006 essay why critics of colonialism never paid attention to the evidence of illegitimacy, repression, exploitation, racism, and violence in independent states. "All systems of governance involve some kind of 'domination,'" he noted. One could not deny that in principle, good colonies could be more ethical forms of domination than bad states. In practice, it did not take a trained statistician to see that many were. "Nice empires are 'not so bad,'" Morris wrote, "and empires are not harder to justify or to legitimate than states."[50]

The post-9/11 world also spurred some serious criticisms of Edward Said's sacred anti-colonial text, *Orientalism*.[51] While Said's book was mainly about knowledge rather than governance, he had argued that the West's curiosity about other areas "fatally tended towards the systematic accumulation of human beings and territories." In other words, obscure scholarship on the religions, art, literature, cultures, and histories of places like Syria and China would cause countries in Europe to itch for foreign conquest. The flowering of "Orientalist" scholarship, according to Said, could "elucidate subsequent developments," in particular the rise of an "explicitly colonial-minded imperialism." And so "every European, in what he could say about the Orient, was consequently a racist, an imperialist, and almost totally ethnocentric."[52]

In 2007, a Pakistani scholar writing under the pseudonym Ibn Warraq published *Defending the West: A Critique of Edward Said's Orientalism.* Warraq pointed out the many logical contradictions in Said's theory. His insistence that all Orientalist knowledge was false and distorted sat uneasily with his simultaneous claim that this knowledge was so excellent that it helped Europeans to dominate foreign cultures. In addition, Said argued that all claims of "true" knowledge are narratives, which begs the question of how something can be false. The main empirical problem for Said's theory was that it could not account for Germany. It was like a theory of war that could not account for peace. Said recognized "the great scientific prestige that accrued to German scholarship by the middle of the nineteenth century." Even by 1830, he wrote, German scholarship "had fully attained its European preeminence."[53] If so, we should have observed a cohort of German politicians and diplomats brined in Orientalist learning demanding overseas expansion. The problem was that German officials, like German capitalists, did not lift a finger for colonialism. Both groups demeaned such acquisitions as a waste of time. "Said very conveniently leaves out the important contributions of German Orientalists, for their inclusion would destroy—and their exclusion does indeed totally destroy—the central thesis," wrote Warraq.[54] Perhaps, Warraq joked, the German scholars were secretly in the pay of imperialists in Britain and France.

The flinty professor Said variously excused, defended, and apologized for his theory's inability to grapple with the German case. The obfuscations came fast and furious: actually the Brits started Oriental studies not the Germans; the Germans had no unified state or foothold in the Orient to carry out their imperialism; all this talk of finding the "truth" about the relationship between scholarship and empire is a delusion of modern thinking that postmodernists like himself have been sent to correct; perhaps the theory is wrong, for which he apologizes; he is not sure but promises to return to the German case in his later book *Culture and Imperialism* (1993), which he never does. And so on and so on. After Warraq and others, much less was heard about Professor Said.

The renewed concerns with democracy in the 2000s were also captured in new studies of the positive democratic legacies of colonialism.

To be colonized in this 19th to 20th century era, was to have much better democratic prospects, according to a statistical study of 143 colonial episodes by the Swedish economist Ola Olsson.[55] His research, as well as that of the Danish political scientist Jacob Hariri in a statistical study of 111 countries, also found the obvious counterpart conclusion: to not be colonized because of the existence of militarily or politically strong pre-modern state, or to be only symbolically ruled by Europeans piggy-backing on traditional institutions rather than replacing them, was to be more likely to be saddled with a dysfunctional state and political system later on.[56] The "tidying up" of personalistic and autocratic traditional rulers that Ahmadu Bello anticipated coming from European colonialism was essential to the emergence of a truly sovereign and democratic people. That, in turn, was the basis for better economic and social development.

I began paying attention to new research on colonialism in the 2010s while teaching a course on Africa. Having been sniffed at by scholars for decades, those colonial roads, railways, power plants, irrigation canals, water systems, and sewage facilities were suddenly back in vogue.[57] One intellectual chestnut of anti-colonial ideology after another was crushed in the maw of empirical research: that the Europeans had "carved up" Africa and created states with "artificial borders,"[58] for instance; or that the British in India had caused famines.[59]

The boiler of dissent against anti-colonial dogmas, in order words, was about to steam. My little contribution of 2017, deviously published in the reliably anti-colonial *Third World Quarterly*, was called "The Case for Colonialism." The lid blew off.

As I describe in Chapters 2 and 5, the backlash against my article was fierce. The most delightful attack came from a lecturer in education and international development at University College London who promised: "If a student had submitted such a piece to my undergraduate module, they would have received a very poor, if not a failing, grade."[60]

But the backlash should not obscure the equally strong support. A Harvard professor wrote to me to say that my article "was bound to written by someone given the accumulated evidence" of recent scholarship. A Nigerian woman, alarmed by the backlash, asked: "Why are academics so quick to silence anyone who points out the positive side of colonialism?" The colonialists had done some good things, she noted, like educating women and ending human sacrifice. "As much as I am not ignoring or downplaying the damaging impacts of colonialism, it is important to make clear that not everything about it was evil."[61]

Several times after 2017, I started and stopped writing a comprehensive manuscript on the case for colonialism. Such a vast subject seemed impervious to the sorts of evidence-based arguments I could live with. All the while, I was writing shorter pieces on specific episodes, places, and aspects of colonialism. At a certain point, I realized that the outlines of a book were taking shape in those essays. It seemed an easy proposition to turn them into a book. But as I revisited each essay, there were gaps and confusions that needed fixing. The result was that wholly new chapters emerged with some arguments changed completely and everything much elaborated. All I can say in good faith is that the result you are holding in your hands represents for me the most empirically robust discussion of the debate on colonialism that your humble servant could achieve. Greater minds than mine are needed to carry on the research. I lay down my pen, exhausted by this unexpected direction in my career, and prepared to stand by what I have written here, no matter the cavils to come.

Endnotes:

1 Rufane Shawe Donkin, "A Dissertation on the Course and Probable Termination of the Niger," *Quarterly Review* (1829).
2 Archibald Hamilton, *The River Niger and the Progress of Discovery and Commerce in Central Africa* (1862); Bishop Crowther, "Notes on the River Niger," *Proceedings of the Royal Geographical Society of London* (1876/77).
3 Sir Alan Burns, *A History of Nigeria* (8th edition, 1972), 119, 121.
4 Alhaji Ahmadu Bello, *My Life* (1962), 19.
5 "The Niger-Sudan Campaign," *The Times* (London), February 17, 1897.
6 Flora Louisa Shaw, *A Tropical Dependency: An Outline of the Ancient History of the Western Soudan, with an Account of the Modern Settlement of Northern Nigeria* (1905).
7 Kenneth Pomeranz, *The Great Divergence: China, Europe, and the Making of the Modern World Economy* (2000).
8 John Henry Walker, *Power and Prowess: The Origins of Brooke Kingship in Sarawak* (2002).
9 David Abernethy, *The Dynamics of Global Dominance: European Overseas Empires, 1415-1980* (2000), 272-273.
10 Sanjay Subrahmanyam, "Un Grand Dérangement: Dreaming an Indo-Persian Empire in South Asia, 1740-1800," *Journal of Early Modern History* (2000), 337-378.
11 The estimate comes from a Persian manuscript translated into French and then into English. See: William Jones, *The History of the Life of Nader Shah, King of Persia* (1773). Axworthy cites the figure as reliable. Michael Axworthy, *The Sword of Persia: Nader Shah, from Tribal Warrior to Conquering Tyrant* (2009), 213.
12 Karl Marx, "The British Rule in India," *New York Daily Tribune*, June 25, 1853; also see *Karl Marx on Colonialism and Modernization* (1968).
13 Bernard Porter, *Critics of Empire* (1968).
14 John Hobson, *Imperialism: A Study* (1902, 1948 edition), 243-244.
15 Bruce Gilley, *In Defense of German Colonialism* (2022), 25-40.
16 Ashwin Desai and Goolam Vahed, *The South African Gandhi: Stretcher-Bearer of Empire* (2015), 53.
17 "Dutch Enter Tjilatjap," *The Times* (London), August 4, 1947.
18 Bruce Gilley, *In Defense of German Colonialism* (2022), 201-230.
19 British Broadcasting Corporation, "The Revolt Against Colonialism." *The Listener*, August, 1957.
20 Mason Sears, *Years of High Purpose* (1980), 82.
21 Jeffrey Herbst, *States and Power in Africa* (2000), 257.
22 John Plamenatz, *On Alien Rule and Self-Government* (1960), 90.
23 Martin Meredith, *The Fate of Africa* (2005, 2011 edition), 164, 272.
24 John Okello, *Revolution in Zanzibar* (1967), 151.
25 Donald Petterson, *Revolution in Zanzibar: An American's Cold War Tale* (2002), 3-4, 94-95.
26 Gualtiero Jacopetti and Franco Prosperi (Directors), *Africa Addio* [*Farewell Africa*] (1966).
27 Roman Loimeier , "Memories of Revolution: Zur Deutungsgeschichte einer Revolution (Sansibar 1964) [Memories of Revolution: On the Interpretation of a Revolution (Zanzibar 1964)]," *Africa Spectrum* (2006).
28 A.M. al-Barwani, *Conflicts and Harmony in Zanzibar: Memoirs* (1996), 35, 150.

29 Abdulrahman Muhammed Babu, "The 1964 Revolution: Lumpen or Vanguard?" in Abdul Sheriff and Ed Ferguson (eds.) *Zanzibar under Colonial Rule* (1991), 220.
30 Garth A. Myers, "Making the Socialist City of Zanzibar," *Geographical Review* (1994).
31 G. Thomas Burgess, *Race, Revolution, and the Struggle for Human Rights in Zanzibar: The Memoirs of Ali Sultan Issa and Seif Sharif Hamad* (2009), 23.
32 Makame Ali Muhajir and Garth Andrew Myers, "Uncommon Misery, Relegated to the Margins: Tumbatu and Fifty Years of the Zanzibar Revolution," in William Cunningham Bissell and Marie-Aude Fouéré (eds.), *Social Memory, Silenced Voices, and Political Struggle: Remembering the Revolution in Zanzibar* (2018), 208.
33 Abdulrazak Gurnah, *Admiring Silence* (1996), 150.
34 William Cunningham Bissell and Marie-Aude Fouéré (eds.), *Social Memory, Silenced Voices, and Political Struggle: Remembering the Revolution in Zanzibar* (2018).
35 Sir Alan Burns, *Colonial Civil Servant* (1949), 317.
36 Ronald Robinson, "Non-European Foundations of European Imperialism: Sketch for a Theory of Collaboration," in Roger Owen and Bob Sutcliffe (eds.), *Studies in the Theory of Imperialism* (1975).
37 Bouda Etemad, *Possessing the World: Taking the Measurements of Colonisation from the Eighteenth to the Twentieth Century* (2007).
38 Wole Soyinka, "Neo-Tarzanism: The Poetics of Pseudo-Tradition," *Transition* (1975).
39 Sinnathamby Rajaratnam, Speech By Mr S. Rajaratnam, Minister For Foreign Affairs, at the 34th Session of the United Nations General Assembly, September 24, 1979, National Archives of Singapore, Document Number: SR19790924s.
40 Chris Alden and Sally Morphet, *The South in World Politics* (2010), 77.
41 Howard White, "Zambia in the 1990s as a Case of Adjustment in Africa," *African Development Review* (1997).
42 Donald Puchala, *Third World Thinking and Contemporary International Relations* (1998).
43 Makiko Kimura, *The Nellie Massacre of 1983* (2013).
44 Hla Myint, "'The "Classical Theory' of International Trade and the Underdeveloped Countries," *Economic Journal* (1958), 336.
45 Aurelia Wa Kabwe-Segatti. "Reforming South African Immigration Policy in the Post Apartheid Period (1990–2010)," in Aurelia Wa Kabwe-Segatti and Loren Landau (eds.), *Contemporary Migration to South Africa* (2011).
46 Robin Grier "Colonial Legacies and Economic Growth," *Public Choice* (1999), 323.
47 James Feyrer and Bruce Sacerdote, "Colonialism and Modern Income: Islands as Natural Experiments," *Review Of Economics and Statistics* (2009), 248.
48 Abernethy, *The Dynamics of Global Dominance*, 403.
49 Frederick Cooper, "Empire Multiplied: A Review Essay," *Comparative Studies in Society and History* (2004), 248-249.
50 Christopher Morris, "What's Wrong with Imperialism?" *Social Philosophy and Policy* (2006), 165.
51 Robert Irwin, *For Lust Of Knowing: The Orientalists and Their Enemies* (2006).
52 Edward Said, *Orientalism* (1978), 123, 32.
53 Ibid., 18, 19.
54 Ibn Warraq, *Defending the West: A Critique of Edward Said's Orientalism* (2007), 44.
55 Ola Olsson, "On the Democratic Legacy of Colonialism," *Journal of Comparative Economics* (2009).
56 Jacob Hariri, "The Autocratic Legacy of Early Statehood," *American Political Science Review* (2012).

57 David Donaldson, "Railroads of the Raj: Estimating the Impact of Transportation Infrastructure," *American Economic Review* (2018); Mattia Bertazzini, "The Long-Term Impact of Italian Colonial Roads in the Horn of Africa, 1935–2015," *Journal of Economic Geography* (2021); Ambe Njoh and Fenda Akiwumi, "The Impact of Colonization on Access to Improved Water and Sanitation Facilities in African Cities," *Cities* (2011); Pierre Lanthier, "From the Raj to Independence: British Investment in the Indian Electricity Sector," *Utilities Policy* (2014).
58 Camille Lefebvre, "The Decolonization of a Commonplace: The Artificiality of African Boundaries: How a Colonial Intellectual Legacy became the Banner of Anti-Colonialism," *Revue d'Histoire des Sciences Humaines* (2011).
59 Tirthankar Roy, *Natural Disasters and Indian History* (2012); "Were Indian Famines 'Natural' Or 'Manmade'?" *London School Of Economics and Political Science: Department Of Economic History Working Papers* (2016).
60 Rebecca Schendel, "Our mission to speak truth to power is under threat," *University World News*, January 19, 2018.
61 Folasade Lamikanra. "Dare We Make a Case for Colonialism?," *Conatus News*, October 13, 2017.

PART I

The Article and Its Aftermath

CHAPTER ONE

The Case for Colonialism

FOR THE LAST hundred years, Western colonialism has had a bad name. Colonialism has virtually disappeared from international affairs, and there is no easier way to discredit a political idea or opponent than to raise the cry of "colonialism." When South African opposition politician Helen Zille tweeted in 2017 that Singapore's success was in part attributable to its ability to "build on valuable aspects of colonial heritage," she was vilified by the press, disciplined by her party, and put under investigation by the country's human rights commission.

It is high time to reevaluate this pejorative meaning. The notion that colonialism is always and everywhere a bad thing needs to be rethought in light of the grave human toll of a century of anti-colonial regimes and policies. The case for Western colonialism is about rethinking the past as well as improving the future. It involves reaffirming the primacy of human lives, universal values, and shared responsibilities—the civilizing mission without scare quotes—that led to improvements in living conditions for most Third World peoples during most episodes of Western colonialism. It also involves learning how to unlock those benefits again. Western and non-Western countries should reclaim the colonial toolkit and language as part of their commitment to effective governance and international order.

There are three ways to reclaim colonialism. One is for governments and peoples in developing countries to replicate as far as possible the colonial governance of their pasts—as successful countries like Singapore, Belize, and Botswana did. The "good governance" agenda, which contains too many assumptions about the self-governing capacity of poor countries, should be replaced with the "colonial governance" agenda. A second way is to recolonize some regions. Western countries should be encouraged to hold power in specific governance areas (public finances, say, or criminal justice) in order to jump-start enduring reforms in weak states. Rather than speak in euphemisms about "shared sovereignty" or "neo-trusteeship," such actions should be called "colonialism" because it would embrace rather than evade the historical record. Thirdly, in some instances it may be possible to build new Western colonies from scratch.

Colonialism can return (either as a governance style or as an extension of Western authority) only with the consent of the colonized. Yet, now that the nationalist generation that forced sudden decolonization on hapless populations has passed away, the time may be ripe. Sèbe has documented how the founding figures of Western colonialism in Africa (such as Livingstone in Zambia, Lugard in Nigeria, and de Brazza in Congo) are enjoying a resurgence of official and social respect in those countries now that romanticized pre-colonial and disappointing post-colonial approaches to governance have lost their sheen.[1] As one young man on the streets of Kinshasa asked Van Reybrouck in his seminal 2010 book on the Congo: "How long is this independence of ours going to last anyway? When are the Belgians coming back?"[2]

Three Failures of Anti-Colonial Critique

The case for the past record of Western colonialism—usually referring to British, French, German, Belgian, Dutch, and Portuguese colonies from the early nineteenth to mid-twentieth centuries—rests on overturning two distinct lines of criticism: that it was objectively harmful (rather than beneficial); and that it was subjectively illegitimate (rather than legitimate). There is, in addition, a third line of criticism that merits revision: that it offends the sensibilities of contemporary society.

The objective cost/benefit approach identifies a certain need of human flourishing—development, security, governance, rights, etc.—and asks whether colonialism improved or worsened the objective provision of that need. One main challenge of this research is to properly enumerate the things that matter and then to assign them weights, which presumably vary with time and place. In a brutally patriarchal society, for instance, access to justice for women may have been more important than the protection of indigenous land rights (which may be part of that patriarchy), as Andreski argued was the case for women in northern Nigeria under colonialism.[3]

A second challenge is measuring the counterfactual: what would likely have happened in a given place absent colonial rule? Many research designs, for instance, control for variations in colonial rule itself and for a variety of other factors that coexisted with colonialism (such as cultural norms, geography, population, disease burden, etc.). But they do not control for the presence or absence of colonialism (for instance, in a highly cited study by Acemoglu and colleagues).[4] To construct such a counterfactual requires measuring not just global social, economic, and technological trends but also the likely course of indigenous development, of regional factors, and of an ungoverned non-colonial encounter with the West. Countries that did not have a significant colonial history—China, Ethiopia, Liberia, Libya, Saudi Arabia, Thailand, Haiti, and Guatemala, for instance—provide a measure of comparison to help identify what if anything were the distinctive effects of colonialism. So too does research into pre-colonial histories that, almost by definition, reveal comparatively weak institutions, divided societies, and subsistence economies, for instance in Biber's study of pre-colonial Namibia.[5]

Noting some of these complexities, Abernethy summarizes the objective cost/benefit question as follows: "[I]n times and places where colonial rule had, on balance, a positive effect on training for self-government, material well-being, labor allocation choices, individual upward mobility, cross-cultural communication, and human dignity, compared to the situation that would likely have obtained absent European rule, then the case for colonialism is strong. Conversely, in times and places where the effects of foreign rule in these respects were, on balance, negative compared to a territory's likely alternative past, then colonialism is morally indefensible."[6]

Beyond these requirements, there is a list of simple epistemic virtues. Non-biased data and case selection, for instance, requires that evidence be gathered in a way that does not confirm the hypothesis at stake. Any claim about, say, the level of colonial violence, requires not just assumptions about the scale of violence that would have occurred absent colonial rule but also a careful measure of that violence relative to the population, security threat, and security resources in a given territory. One is hard-pressed, to take a prominent example, to find such care in measurement in the vast critical scholarship on the British counterinsurgency campaign against the Mau Mau in Kenya from 1952 to 1960, especially in the scolding work of Elkins.[7] Daniels argues that "[h]ad the British left Kenya to the Mau Mau, there would have been anarchy and further civil war, perhaps even genocide."[8] Just as many Kenyans joined the Kikuyu Home Guard and the special prison service for the rebels as joined the insurgency, and the independent Kenyan government has long applauded the historic contribution of the British in suppressing the movement.[9] At the very least, it is incumbent on scholars to show that the brutalities unleashed by the British in this campaign were not the likely result of a proportionate response given the context and scale of the threat. If this supposedly solid case is wobbly, what does it tell us about the lesser "violence" often cited as invalidating colonialism?

Perhaps the most egregious violation of epistemic virtues is internal coherence (or non-contradiction). Eminent scholars repeatedly make the logically contradictory claim that colonialism was both too disruptive and not disruptive enough, whether with regard to boundaries, governing institutions, economic systems, or social structures, as evidenced in the short space of just two pages by Young.[10] Africanists in particular applaud the work both of Herbst, who argued that colonialism did too little state-making, and Young, who earlier argued that it did too much.[11] New territorial boundaries are criticized for forcing social integration while old ones are criticized for reinforcing tribalism, a contradiction noted by Lefebvre.[12] Marxist scholars found colonialism at fault when it did not invest in public health and infrastructure (showing a callous disregard for labor) and when it did (in order to exploit it).[13] Colonialism is ascribed near-magical powers to sweep away everything good in its path (like tribal chiefs or ethnic identity) and with equally magical powers to make permanent everything bad in its path (like tribal chiefs or ethnic identity).

Finally, there is the simple epistemic virtue of falsification. This is most pointed in the treatment of what was undoubtedly a benefit of colonialism: the abolition of slave-trading. Anti-colonial critics squirm and fuss over this issue because it puts the greatest strain on their "colonialism is bad" perspective. The result is a constant stream of revisionism: it did not happen fast enough; there were mixed motives; not all colonial officials supported it; former slaves remained poor and former slave owners remained rich; it should never have existed in the first place.[14]

Of course, not all research falls afoul of the basic prescriptions above. Research that is careful in conceptualizing and measuring controls, that establishes a feasible counterfactual, that includes multiple dimensions of costs and benefits weighted in some justified way, and that adheres to basic epistemic virtues often finds that at least some, if not many or most, episodes of Western colonialism were a net benefit, as the literature review by Juan and Pierskalla shows.[15] Such works have found evidence for significant social, economic, and political gains under colonialism: expanded education; improved public health; the abolition of slavery; widened employment opportunities; improved administration; the creation of basic infrastructure; female rights; enfranchisement of untouchable or historically excluded communities; fair taxation; access to capital; the generation of historical and cultural knowledge; and national identity formation, to mention just a few dimensions.[16]

This leads to the second failure of anti-colonial critique. Given that objective costs and benefits varied with time and place, another approach is simply to defer to the judgements of those affected. The subjective legitimacy approach asks whether the people subject to colonialism treated it, through their beliefs and actions, as rightful. As Hechter showed, alien rule has often been legitimate in world history because it has provided better governance than the indigenous alternative.[17]

Yet anti-colonial critics simply assert that colonialism was, in Hopkins's words, "a foreign imposition lacking popular legitimacy."[18] Until very late, European colonialism appears to have been highly legitimate and for good reasons. Millions of people moved closer to areas of more intensive colonial rule, sent their children to colonial schools and hospitals, went beyond the call of duty in positions in colonial governments, reported crimes to colonial police, migrated from non-colonized to colonized areas, fought for colonial armies, and participated in colonial political processes—all relatively voluntary acts. Indeed, the rapid spread and persistence of Western colonialism with very little force relative to the populations and geographies concerned is *prima facie* evidence of its acceptance by subject populations compared to the feasible alternatives. The "preservers," "facilitators," and "collaborators" of colonialism, as Abernethy shows, far outnumbered the "resisters," at least until very late: "Imperial expansion was frequently the result not just of European push but also of indigenous pull."[19] In Borneo, the Sultan of Brunei installed an English traveler, James Brooke, as the rajah of his chaotic province of Sarawak in 1841. Order and prosperity expanded to such an extent that even once a British protectorate was established in 1888, the Sultan preferred to leave it under Brooke family control until 1946.[20]

Sir Alan Burns, the governor of the Gold Coast during World War II, noted that "had the people of the Gold Coast wished to push us into the sea there was little to prevent them. But this was the time when the people came forward in their thousands, not with empty protestations of loyalty but with men to serve in the army ... and with liberal gifts to war funds and war charities. This was curious conduct for people tired of British rule."[21] In most colonial areas, subject peoples either faced grave security threats from rival groups or they saw the benefits of being governed by a modernized and liberal state. Patrice Lumumba, who became an anti-colonial agitator only very late, praised Belgian colonial rule in his autobiography of 1962 for "restoring our human dignity and turning us into free, happy, vigorous, and civilized men."[22] Chinua Achebe's many pro-colonial statements, meanwhile, have been virtually airbrushed from memory by anti-colonial ideology.[23] The few scholars who take note of such evidence typically dismiss it as a form of false consciousness.[24]

The failure of anti-colonial critique to come to terms with the objective benefits and subjective legitimacy of colonialism points to a third and deeper failure: it was never intended to be "true" in the sense of being a scientific claim justified through shared standards of inquiry that was liable to falsification. The origins of anti-colonial thought were political and ideological. The purpose was not historical accuracy but contemporaneous advocacy. Today, activists associate "decolonization" (or "postcolonialism") with all manner of radical social transformation, which unintentionally ties historic conclusions to present-day endeavors. Unmoored from historical fact, postcolonialism became what Williams called a metropolitan *flaneur* culture of attitude and performance whose recent achievements include an inquiry into the glories of sadomasochism among Third World women and a burgeoning literature on the horrors of colonialism under countries that never had colonies.[25]

This third failure of anti-colonial critique is perhaps most damaging. It is not just an obstacle to historical truth, which itself is a grave disservice. Even as a means of contemporary advocacy, it is self-wounding; for it essentially weaponizes the colonial past, as the gradually imploding postcolonial South African state's persecution of Helen Zille shows. "What a meta-narrative of anti-colonial sentiment can render invisible are ways in which people made claims on new possibilities without deploying either anti- or pro-colonial idioms," Englund writes in his study of colonial-era newspapers in Zambia. "To devote all scholarly attention to the question of how different actors during this period sought to end colonial rule is to succumb to a limiting meta-narrative of anti-colonialism, one that allows no conceptual space between colonial and anti-colonial agendas, and thereby keeps other possibilities inaccessible to the scholarly and moral imagination."[26]

The Costs of Anti-Colonialism

It is hard to overstate the pernicious effects of global anti-colonialism on domestic and international affairs since the end of World War II. Anti-colonialism ravaged countries as nationalist elites mobilized illiterate populations with appeals to destroy the market economies, pluralistic and constitutional polities, and rational policy processes of European colonizers. In our "age of apology" for atrocities, one of the many conspicuous silences has been an apology for the many atrocities visited upon Third World peoples by anti-colonial advocates.[27]

Few cases better illustrate this than Guinea-Bissau and its anti-colonial "hero" Amilcar Cabral. In launching a guerrilla war against Portuguese rule in 1963, Cabral insisted that it was "necessary to totally destroy, to break, to reduce to ash all aspects of the colonial state in our country in order to make everything possible for our people." He took aim at a successful colonial state that had quadrupled rice production and initiated sustained gains in life expectancy since bringing the territory under control in 1936.[28] Cabral, in his own words, was "never able to mobilize the people on the basis of the struggle against colonialism."[29] Instead, he secured training and arms from Cuba, Russia, and Czechoslovakia and economic assistance from Sweden.[30] The resulting war killed 15,000 people (out of a population of 600,000) and at least as many civilians, and displaced another 150,000 (a quarter of the population).

Once "liberation" was achieved in 1974, a second human tragedy unfolded, costing at least 10,000 further lives as a direct result of conflict. By 1980, rice production had fallen by more than 50 percent to 80,000 tonnes (from a peak of 182,000 tonnes under the Portuguese). Politics became a "cantankerous din of former revolutionaries" in the words of Forrest.[31] Cabral's half-brother, who became president, unleashed the secret police on the tiny opposition—500 bodies were found in three mass graves for dissidents in 1981.[32] A tenth of the remaining population pulled up stakes for Senegal.[33] The Cabralian one-party state expanded to 15,000 employees, ten times as big as the Portuguese administration at its peak.[34] Confused Marxist scholars blamed the legacies of colonialism or the weather or Israel.[35]

Things have gotten worse. Guinea-Bissau has a more or less permanent UN peacekeeping force and continues to suck up millions in aid as the "continuadores de Cabral" squabble under what the World Bank calls "continuing political disarray."[36] Today, in per capita terms, rice production is still only one-third of what it was under the Portuguese despite forty years of international aid and technological advances. The health transition, meanwhile, slowed considerably after independence. By 2015, the average Guinea-Bissauan was living just fifty-five years, meaning gains of just 0.3 years of extra life per year since independence, less than half of the 0.73 extra years of life per year being gained in the late colonial period. What might have become a prosperous and humane Macau or Goa of Africa is today a cesspool of human suffering. Western and African anti-colonial scholars continue to extol Cabral's "national liberation" ideas.[37] But actually existing Guineans may be asking: when are the Portuguese coming back?

Guinea-Bissau seems like an extreme case. It is not. Of the eighty countries that threw off the colonial "yoke" after World War II, at least half experienced similar trauma while most of the rest limped on. For sixty years, Third World despots have raised the specter of recolonization to discredit democratic opposition and ruin their economies. Yet there is virtually nothing written about most of these postcolonial traumas since, as Igreja notes, it still assumed that anti-colonial movements were victims rather than victimizers.[38] Scholars in full Eurocentric mode prefer to churn out books on colonial atrocities or to suggest that "colonial legacies" have something to do with the follies and body blows inflicted on these countries by their anti-colonial leaders.[39]

To be sure, just as the colonial era was not an unalloyed good, the independence era has not been an unalloyed bad. A few postcolonial states are in reasonable health. Those whose moral imaginations were not shrouded by anti-colonial ideology had the most productive encounter with modernity, emerging as leaders of what W. Arthur Lewis called the "creative" Third World.[40]

But most of the rest remained stuck in anti-colonial "protest" identities with dire consequences for human welfare. A sobering World Bank report of 1996 noted: "Almost every African country has witnessed a systematic regression of capacity in the last thirty years; the majority had better capacity at independence than they now possess."[41] This loss of state capacity was no trifle; it meant the loss of tens of millions of lives. And it is not getting better. For instance, only thirteen of 102 historically developing countries are on track to have high state capacity by the year 2100, according to Andrews and colleagues. The people of Bangladesh will have to wait another 244 years at their current rate to reach a high capacity state.[42] Would it have taken Britain, even in some adjusted role (as discussed below), until the middle of the twenty-third century to institute good government in this former province of Eastern Bengal?

The airport in French colonial Ivory Coast, 1950s. Credit: Edna Schaus Sorensen and Clarence W. Sorensen Collection, University of Wisconsin-Milwaukee Libraries.

In international affairs, meanwhile, otherwise liberal and democratic states like India, Brazil, and South Africa continue to style themselves as enemies of Western colonialism. As Chatterjee Miller shows, the foreign policies of these former colonies continue to be driven by a sense of victimhood and entitlement rather than rational self-interest or global responsibility.[43] This means that every time the world is desperate for a coordinated response to a human, political, or security catastrophe—in Sri Lanka, Venezuela, or Zimbabwe for instance—the voices of anti-colonialism intercede to prevent action. As it turned out, the most serious threat to human rights and world peace was not colonialism—as the United Nations declared in 1960—but anti-colonialism.

Chatterjee Miller argues that it is the responsibility of the West to be "sensitive" to these anti-colonial viewpoints. An alternative view is that it is the responsibility of the West to help these nations kick the habit. After all, Britain's rise is surely inseparable from the ways that it embraced and celebrated its colonizers from the Romans through to the Normans. If anti-colonial sentiments had gone unchallenged in Britain, the country today would be a backwater of druid worshippers.

Resurrecting Colonial Governance

Even as intellectuals have continued to plough the anti-colonial furrow since the end of the Cold War, many countries have changed their domestic governance to replant the seeds of "colonial governance." This agenda has many things in common with the "good governance" agenda: economic liberalization, political pluralism, and administrative streamlining have replaced the socialist road in most countries. But the colonial governance agenda is distinct from the good governance agenda in two respects.

First, the colonial governance agenda explicitly affirms and borrows from a country's colonial past, searching for ideas and notions of governmentality. As Burton and Jennings note, "In the first decade or so after independence ... East African governments often adopted or adapted both administrative structures and ideological concepts from their colonial predecessors in order to create quite successful forms of governance—certainly by regional standards."[44] In many cases, colonial bureaucrats and police were rehired by the newly independent governments.

Reclaiming this colonial trajectory abandoned at independence is key to the colonial governance agenda. No less an anti-colonial "hero" than Chinua Achebe ended his days with a memoir that explicitly affirmed the positive contributions of colonialism to governance in his native Nigeria: "[I]t is important to face the fact that British colonies were, more or less, expertly run," he wrote.[45] What was important about Achebe's "articulation of the unsayable," as Msiska called it, was his rediscovery of "the colonial national formation as a habitable community."[46] This had concrete implications for how to organize the civil service, how to manage federalism, and how to promote education. As with democratic episodes in a country's past, colonial episodes become an attic to ransack in search of a livable past. This also underscores the importance of reinvesting in a non-biased historiography of colonialism so that the colonial periods are seen not as objects of resistance but as fruitful sources of creativity.

Secondly, and related, the colonial governance agenda recognizes that the capacity for effective self-government is lacking and cannot be conjured out of thin air. The lack of state capacity to uphold the rule of law and deliver public services was the central tragedy of "independence" in the Third World, as a few voices like Plamenatz and Barnes warned at the time.[47] To reclaim "colonial governance" means increasing foreign involvement in key sectors in business, civil society, and the public sector in order to bolster this capacity. In 1985, for instance, the Indonesian government fired all 6,000 government inspectors at the Jakarta port of Tanjung Priok and replaced the corrupt and inefficient customs service with the Swiss firm SGS. The Swiss rebuilt the customs service, handing back partial control in 1991 and full control in 1997.[48] Indonesia's exports boomed. Civil society and successful policy reforms, meanwhile, improve faster with the presence of international civil society actors, as they did in the colonial era, as shown by studies of environmental civil society.[49] Multinational corporations, moreover, can be tasked with public service provision near their facilities in direct imitation of colonial practices, as Hönke has documented.[50]

The colonial governance agenda embraces a cosmopolitanism—a civilizing mission—often lacking in the good governance agenda. Bain, for instance, admits the "grim reality" and "ghastly consequences" of decolonization.[51] Yet he simultaneously rejects the idea that the West has anything to offer, since this implies an imperial mission. This "uncritical critique of the liberal peace," as Chandler calls it, consigns Third World nations to the foibles and vagaries of "authentic" or "indigenous" practices, a *de facto* abandonment of hope in their self-governing capacities.[52] By contrast, the colonial governance agenda resurrects the universalism of the liberal peace and with it a shared standard of what a well-governed country looks like.

The Case for Recolonization

The second broad way to reclaim colonialism is to recolonize some regions. It may be that in some cases, only a formal share of sovereignty for Western countries can provide the mix of accountability and authority needed to build capacity in weak states. In Chesterman's oft-quoted phrase, the problem with modern state-building is not that it "is colonial in character; rather the problem is that sometimes it is not colonial enough."[53]

The World Bank and USAID, for instance, experimented with "co-signatory" arrangements in Liberia and Chad in the 1990s and 2000s where major government expenditures required the signatures of both domestic and external agents. In the Australia-led Regional Assistance Mission to Solomon Islands (RAMSI) or the UN's International Commission against Impunity in Guatemala (known by its Spanish acronym CICIG), key legal and police functions were handed over to external powers because of rampant corruption and criminalization of the state.

Sèbe calls this "cosmopolitan nation-building" because it represents an explicit rejection of the parochial myth of self-governing capacity that drove most postcolonial countries into the ground.[54] Rather than use an ever-expanding set of euphemisms that avoid the "c" word—"shared sovereignty," "conservatorship," "proxy governance," "transitional administration," "neo-trusteeship," "cooperative intervention"—these arrangements should be called "colonialism" because it would embrace rather than evade the historical record. As Ignatieff wrote in 2002: "Imperialism doesn't stop being necessary just because it becomes politically incorrect."[55]

While the conceptual abandonment of the myth of self-governing capacity is now mainstream, the challenges of making new forms of colonialism work are immense. There are three separate questions for policy-makers: (1) how to make colonialism acceptable to the colonized; (2) how to motivate Western countries to become colonial again; and (3) how to make colonialism achieve lasting results.

Any colonial relationship requires a high degree of acceptance from the local population. Perhaps this explains why post-Cold War interventions have sought to emphasize their participatory and consensual nature in contrast with an alleged illegitimate and coercively imposed colonialism.[56] This is another area where an accurate historiography of colonialism is sorely needed because, as noted, colonialism usually spread with a significant degree of consent from politically salient actors.

One lesson from colonial legitimation is that at least in the initial phases, legitimacy will be demonstrated not by the holding of a plebiscite or by the support of organized and broadly representative groups, but simply by the ability of the intervening state to win compliance from key actors and get the job done. Too often, critics of modern interventions have decried the lack of "accountability or representation."[57] Yet, it is precisely the absence of conditions for meaningful accountability or representation that makes intervention necessary in the first place, much as colonialism spread in order to better manage ungoverned encounters with the West. As Chesterman wrote: "If genuine local control were possible, then a transitional administration would not be necessary." The creation of accountable political power "may well be the end of the transitional administration," he writes, "but by definition it is not the means."[58]

To push the logic further, it is the intervening state, bound to act as a trustee, that has the capacity initially to choose a legitimate path forward. As in colonial times, foreign control by a liberal state with its own robust accountability mechanisms is the closest that a people with a weak state can come to "local ownership." The widespread support in Sierra Leone for the 1999 to 2005 British overhaul and rebuilding of the police force was explained by this externally created legitimacy with an explicit colonial vestige: "There has always been a soft spot for the British among Sierra Leoneans. That feeling has now come into full play, with public demands for the Brits to stay for as long as necessary, because of the helpless condition of the country," one local journalist noted.[59]

The legitimacy of a new colonialism will almost always require a local leader who is both domestically popular and a strong advocate of the colonial relationship. After initial skepticism, Liberia's energetic president Ellen Johnson Sirleaf championed the post-2005 Government and Economic Assistance Management Program (GEMAP) that gave extensive powers over spending and budgeting to external actors. As a result, Liberians generally welcomed GEMAP.[60] "Although some Liberian politicians see the plan as thinly veiled colonialism, it is wildly popular among those living on the rubbish-strewn streets of the capital," noted the *Times*. "We love GEMAP," Henry Williams, a shopkeeper, said to nods from the crowd at the counter. "It will stop the politicians from stealing from us."[61]

The dynamics of colonial legitimation moving forward are tricky because as a country "earns sovereignty" the legitimacy of the colonial relationship will decline if it is not constantly recalibrated and reaffirmed. As local institutions and norms improve, the colonial relationship will become more intensive but also more contested because of this more complex polity. Again, lessons from past colonialism are germane: "The central paradox of the process of colonial exit was that it coincided in most cases with the most active phase of colonial state-building," wrote Darwin.[62]

Very little attention is ever paid to the second challenge although it is arguably greater: how to motivate Western countries to become colonial. Despite cries of "exploitation," colonialism was probably a money loser for imperial powers. The Stanford economist Richard Hammond coined the term "uneconomic imperialism" to describe the ways that European powers embarked on ruinously costly and ultimately money-losing colonialism for largely non-economic reasons.[63] That is why they gave up their colonies so easily, as Wu also showed with regard to the Dutch surrender of Taiwan.[64] The benefits of empire were widely diffused while the costs were narrowly borne by the colonial power. As Kaplan wrote: "The real problem with imperialism is not that it is evil, but rather that it is too expensive and therefore a problematic grand strategy for a country like the United States."[65]

Australia's Lowy Institute for International Policy, for instance, calculated that the RAMSI program cost Australian taxpayers about $2 billion over its ten-year period, roughly the annual health and education budget for the capital city of Canberra or the equivalent of a year's economic output for every Solomon Islander. The institute described this as "a massive investment for a country where Australia's interests are limited."[66] The moment there was a whiff of Solomon Islander opposition using anti-colonial tropes, the Australians headed home.[67] A willingness to assume responsibility for the affairs of a foreign land will not come easily since Western governments are held closely to account for their spending and anti-colonial ideology can be easily mobilized. The UN, meanwhile, is not likely to step in with more "international administration" due to the enduring anti-colonialism of leading Third World states.[68] Collier's suggestion for expanded UN-led governance provision is impractical for this reason.[69]

To solve the incentives problem, Hechter has called for a "market in transnational governance" which we might call less euphemistically "colonialism for hire."[70] Colonial states would be paid for their services, an important motivator to be successful. The contractual motivation would also strengthen consent through periodic renegotiation of the terms. Properly designed, host countries would more than recoup those costs through higher foreign investment, lower external borrowing costs, and greater business confidence, benefits that were arguably more significant than improved governance in the colonial era.[71]

That still leaves the third question of whether new forms of colonialism would work. The salient point is simply to draw attention to the relevance of the colonial past to this question since the appropriate models for state building are probably not modern liberal ones but something else.[72] Whereas the number of post-Cold War interventions involving a share of sovereignty has been quite small, there were many episodes and types of colonialism from which to draw lessons. For instance, the largely successful resurrection of the state in Cambodia after a Chinese-imposed genocidal regime is not attributable to the UN-led reconstruction effort of 1992–1993. Liberal peacebuilding failed in Cambodia judged in terms of the intention to create a robust democracy or an independent police and army.[73] Rather what emerged was a successful semi-authoritarian polity with deep roots in the colonial past.[74]

One lesson from the colonial past is that the share of sovereignty needs to be substantial and thorough in most cases. If external actors are constrained to work with rotten local institutions, as Matanock has argued, then reforms will be difficult.[75] Remaking a local police force may be possible without a share of sovereignty. But cleaning out a thoroughly corrupt national criminal justice system requires external control. Again, the reason to reclaim the word "colonialism" is that it does not sidestep this important empirical insight.

The second lesson is what Lemay-Hébert calls "the centrality of the social," the centrality of a congruence between the values in the community and those of the state.[76] Liberal interventions fail, he argued, because of their aversion to the social. Colonial interventions, by contrast, may stand a greater chance of success because historically this "emphasis on the social" is what colonialism was good at: the dual mandate, indirect rule, minimal expatriate staffs, and customary law went hand-in-hand with the infrastructure of modernity (schools, universal laws, "Western" medicine, etc.). "Since gaining independence, Congo has never had at its disposal an army comparable in efficiency and discipline to the former [Belgian colonial] Force Publique," was Van Reybrouck's sad conclusion.[77] Maybe the Belgians should come back.

The Tale of Galinhas

Even with local legitimacy, Western will, and a good plan, the challenges of making new forms of colonialism work are immense. Leaders will need to come up with novel solutions to continued chaos and displacement caused by a century of anti-colonial policies. So here is a modest idea: build new Western colonies from scratch.

In 2009, the economist Paul Romer—who became the World Bank's chief economist in 2016—suggested that rich nations build "charter cities" in poor countries.[78] Under this model, largely empty land is leased to a foreign nation or group of nations so that their sovereignty allows a modern enclave to grow up, as was the case in Hong Kong. That tiny British colony, according to Romer, "did more to reduce world poverty than all the aid programs that we've undertaken in the last century."

New colonies solve the three challenges above nicely. For the local population, they are legitimate because citizens choose to move there, escaping worse situations and because their governments agree to the terms. They are potentially attractive to Western states because for conservatives they are low risk and self-financing while for liberals they are "acts of justice."[79] Finally, charter cities could be effective—which was Romer's main concern in developing the idea—because they have a blank slate to transplant home institutions without having to work with rotten local ones.

Back to Guinea-Bissau. Suppose that the government of Guinea-Bissau were to lease back to Portugal the small uninhabited island of Galinhas that lies ten miles off the mainland and where the former colonial governor's mansion lies in ruins. The annual lease would be $1 so that the Portuguese spend their money on the island and the Guinea-Bissau government is not dependent on a lease fee. Suppose, then, that the $10 to $20 million in foreign aid wasted annually on the country were redirected to this new offshore colony to create basic infrastructure. As part of the deal, the Portuguese would allow a certain number of Guinea-Bissau residents to resettle on the island each year. Portuguese institutions and sovereignty would be absolute here for the term of the lease—say ninety-nine years as was the case with the mainland parts of Hong Kong. A small European state would grow up on the African coast.

At sixty square miles Galinhas could, over time, easily accommodate the entire population of Guinea-Bissau. If successful, it would attract talent, trade, and capital. The mainland parts of Guinea-Bissau would benefit from living next to an economic dynamo and learning to emulate its success, while symbolically escaping from the half-century anti-colonial nightmare of Amilcar Cabral. The same idea could be tried all over the coastlines of Africa and the Middle East if successful. Colonialism could be resurrected without the usual cries of oppression, occupation, and exploitation.

A preposterous idea? Perhaps. But not so preposterous as the anti-colonial ideology that for the past hundred years has been haunting the lives of hundreds of millions of people in the Third World. A hundred years of disaster is enough. It is time to make the case for colonialism again.

Endnotes:

1 Berny Sèbe, "From Post-Colonialism to Cosmopolitan Nation-Building? British and French Imperial Heroes in Twenty-First-Century Africa," *Journal of Imperial and Commonwealth* (2014).
2 David Van Reybrouck, *Congo: The Epic History of a People* (2014), 255.
3 Iris Andreski, *Old Wives' Tales: Life-Stories from Ibibioland* (1970).
4 Daron Acemoglu, Simon Johnson, and James A. Robinson, "The Colonial Origins of Comparative Development: An Empirical Investigation," *American Economic Review* (2000).
5 Bruce Biber, *Intertribal War in Pre-Colonial Namibia* (1989).
6 David Abernethy, *The Dynamics of Global Dominance: European Overseas Empires, 1415–1980* (2000), 403.
7 Caroline Elkins, *Imperial Reckoning: The Untold Story of Britain's Gulag in Kenya* (2005).
8 Anthony Daniels, "Mau Mau Revisited," *New Criterion* (2005), 26.
9 Tim Stanley, "History Is Never Black and White," *History Today* (2012), 44; and Daniel Branch, "The Enemy Within: Loyalists and the War against the Mau Mau in Kenya," *Journal of African History* (2007).
10 Crawford Young, "The Heritage of Colonialism," in *Africa in World Politics* (2016), 11, 13; Jeffrey Herbst, *States and Power in Africa* (2000).
11 Crawford Young, *The African Colonial State in Comparative Perspective* (1994).
12 Camille Lefebvre, "We Have Tailored Africa: French Colonialism and the 'Artificiality' of Africa's Borders in the Interwar Period," *Journal of Historical Geography* (2011).
13 Elinor Burns, *British Imperialism in West Africa* (1927).
14 Suzanne Miers and Martin Klein, *Slavery and Colonial Rule in Africa* (1999); Philip Misevich and Kristin Mann, *The Rise and Demise of Slavery and the Slave Trade in the Atlantic World* (2016); Amalia Ribi Forclaz, *Humanitarian Imperialism: The Politics of Anti-Slavery Activism, 1880–1940* (2015).
15 Alexander De Juan and Jan Henryk Pierskalla, "The Comparative Politics of Colonialism and Its Legacies: An Introduction," *Politics & Society* (2017).
16 Matthew Lange, James Mahoney, and Matthias vom Hau, "Colonialism and Development: A Comparative Analysis of Spanish and British Colonies," *American Journal of Sociology* (2006); David Fieldhouse, *The West and the Third World: Trade, Colonialism, Dependence, and Development* (1999); Lewis Gann and Peter Duignan, *Burden of Empire: An Appraisal of Western Colonialism in Africa South of the Sahara* (1967); Ola Olsson, "On the Democratic Legacy of Colonialism," *Journal of Comparative Economics* (2009); James Midgley and David Piachaud, *Colonialism and Welfare: Social Policy and the British Imperial Legacy* (2011); Charles Amone and Okullu Muura, "British Colonialism and the Creation of Acholi Ethnic Identity in Uganda, 1894 to 1962," *Journal of Imperial & Commonwealth History* (2014).
17 Michael Hechter, *Alien Rule* (2013).
18 Anthony Hopkins, *The Future of the Imperial Past* (1997), 19.
19 Abernethy, *The Dynamics of Global Dominance*, 272–73, 264.
20 John Walker, *Power and Prowess: The Origins of Brooke Kingship in Sarawak* (2002).
21 Sir Alan Burns, *Colonial Civil Servant* (1949), 318.
22 Patrice Lumumba, *Congo, My Country* (1962), 12, 13.
23 Bruce Gilley, "Chinua Achebe on the Positive Legacies of Colonialism," *African Af-*

fairs (2016).
24 Waltraud Ernst and Biswamoy Pati, *India's Princely States: People, Princes and Colonialism* (2007); Benjamin Freud, "Organizing Autarky: Governor General Decoux's Development of a Substitution Economy in Indochina as a Means of Promoting Colonial Legitimacy," *SOJOURN: Journal of Social Issues in Southeast Asia* (2014); Sean Stilwell, "Constructing Colonial Power: Tradition, Legitimacy and Government in Kano, 1903–1963," *Journal of Imperial & Commonwealth History* (2011); Lea Ypi, "What's Wrong with Colonialism," *Philosophy & Public Affairs* (2013).
25 Adebayo Williams, "The Postcolonial Flaneur and Other Fellow-Travellers: Conceits for a Narrative of Redemption," *Third World Quarterly* (1997); Maneesha Deckha, "Pain as Culture: A Postcolonial Feminist Approach to S/M and Women's Agency," *Sexualities* (2011); Barbara Lüthi, Francesca Falk, Patricia Purtschert, "Colonialism without Colonies: Examining Blank Spaces in Colonial Studies," *National Identities* (2016).
26 Harri Englund, "Anti Anti-Colonialism: Vernacular Press and Emergent Possibilities in Colonial Zambia," *Comparative Studies in Society and History* (2015): 243.
27 Mark Gibney, Rhoda Howard-Hassmann, Jean-Marc Coicaud, and Niklaus Steiner, eds., *The Age of Apology: Facing up to the Past* (2008); Tom Bentley, *Empires of Remorse: Narrative, Postcolonialism and Apologies for Colonial Atrocity* (2016).
28 Robin Cohen, "The State in Africa," *Review of African Political Economy* (1976); Rosemary Galli and Jocelyn Jones, *Guinea-Bissau: Politics, Economics, and Society* (1987), 43; James Riley, "The Timing and Pace of Health Transitions around the World," *Population and Development Review* (2005).
29 John Cann, *Counterinsurgency in Africa: The Portuguese Way of War, 1961–1974* (1997), 24.
30 Martin Wolfers, "West African Leader Seeks Talks with Portugal," *Times* (London), October 26, 1971, 7.
31 Joshua Forrest, *Guinea-Bissau: Power, Conflict, and Renewal in a West African Nation* (1992), 50.
32 Galli and Jones, Guinea-Bissau: *Politics, Economics, and Society*, 98; Carlos Lopes, *Guinea-Bissau: From Liberation Struggle to Independent Statehood* (1987), 154.
33 Forrest, *Guinea-Bissau*, 97.
34 Avelino Teixeira da Mota, *Guiné Portuguesa*, 2 vols. (1954), 61.
35 Laura Bigman, *History and Hunger in West Africa: Food Production and Entitlement in Guinea-Bissau and Cape Verde* (1993); F.O.E. Okafor, "The PAIGC and the Economic Development of Guinea-Bissau: Ideology and Reality," *The Developing Economies* (1988).
36 Estanislao Gacitua-Mario, S. Aasland, H. Nordang, and Quentin Wodon, "Institutions, Social Networks, and Conflicts in Guinea-Bissau: Results from a 2005 Survey," in *Conflict, Livelihoods, and Poverty in Guinea-Bissau*, ed. Boubacar-Sid Barry (2007), 24.
37 Peter Mendy, "Amilcar Cabral and the Liberation of Guinea-Bissau: Context, Challenges and Lessons for Effective African Leadership," *African Identities* (2006); Amilcar Cabral, Dan Wood, and Reiland Rabaka, *Resistance and Decolonization* (2016).
38 Victor Igreja, "Frelimo's Political Ruling through Violence and Memory in Postcolonial Mozambique," *Journal of Southern African Studies* (2010).
39 Jacob Levy and Iris Marion Young, *Colonialism and Its Legacies* (2011); Lucy Mayblin, *Asylum after Empire: Colonial Legacies in the Politics of Asylum Seeking* (2017); William Miles, *Scars of Partition: Postcolonial Legacies in French and British Borderlands* (2014).
40 Bruce Gilley, "The Challenge of the Creative Third World," *Third World Quarterly* (2015).

41 African Governors of the World Bank, Partnership for Capacity Building in Africa: Strategy and Program of Action (1996), 5.
42 Matt Andrews, Lant Pritchett, and Michael Woolcock, *Building State Capability: Evidence, Analysis, Action* (2017), 20
43 Manjari Chatterjee Miller, *Wronged by Empire: Post-Imperial Ideology and Foreign Policy in India and China* (2013).
44 Andrew Burton and Michael Jennings, "Introduction: The Emperor's New Clothes? Continuities in Governance in Late Colonial and Early Postcolonial East Africa," *International Journal of African Historical Studies* (2007), 3.
45 Chinua Achebe, *There Was a Country: A Personal History of Biafra* (2012), 43.
46 Mpalive-Hangson Msiska, "Imagined Nations and Imaginary Nigeria: Chinua Achebe's Quest for a Country," *Journal of Genocide Research* (2014), 413.
47 John Plamenatz, *On Alien Rule and Self-Government* (1960); Leonard Barnes, *Africa in Eclipse* (1971).
48 David Liebhold, "Businesses Brace for Return of Customs," *Asian Business* (1997), 12.
49 Evan Schofer and Ann Hironaka, "The Effects of World Society on Environmental Protection Outcomes," *Social Forces* (2005).
50 Jana Hönke, "Multinationals and Security Governance in the Community: Participation, Discipline and Indirect Rule," *Journal of Intervention and Statebuilding* (2012).
51 William Bain, "For Love of Order and Abstract Nouns: International Administration and the Discourse of Ability," *Journal of Intervention and Statebuilding* (2009), 155, 157.
52 David Chandler, "The Uncritical Critique of 'Liberal Peace,'" *Review of International Studies* (2010).
53 Simon Chesterman, *You, the People: The United Nations, Transitional Administration, and State-Building* (2004), 12.
54 Sèbe, "From Post-Colonialism to Cosmopolitan Nation-Building?"
55 Michael Ignatieff, "Nation-Building Lite," *New York Times Magazine*, July 28, 2002.
56 Jeni Whalan, *How Peace Operations Work: Power, Legitimacy, and Effectiveness* (2014).
57 Philip Cunliffe, "State-Building: Power without Responsibility," in *State-Building: Theory and Practice*, ed. Aidan Hehir and Neil Robinson (2007).
58 Chesterman, *You, the People*, 239, 144.
59 Erlend Grøner Krogstad, "Local Ownership as Dependence Management: Inviting the Coloniser Back," *Journal of Intervention and Statebuilding* (2014), 115.
60 Louise Andersen, "Outsiders inside the State: Post-Conflict Liberia between Trusteeship and Partnership," *Journal of Intervention and Statebuilding* (2010).
61 Katharine Houreld, "World Turns Out to Hail Woman Who Carries Hopes of a Continent," *Times* (London), January 16, 2006.
62 John Darwin, "Exit and Colonial Administrations," in *Exit Strategies and State Building*, ed. Richard Caplan (2012), 29.
63 R.J. Hammond, *Portugal and Africa, 1815–1910: A Study in Uneconomic Imperialism* (1966).
64 Tsong-Min Wu, "A Re-Valuation of the Management of Dutch Taiwan," *Taiwan Economic Review* (2016).
65 Robert Kaplan, "In Defense of Empire," *Atlantic*, April 2014.
66 Jenny Hayward-Jones, *Australia's Costly Investment in Solomon Islands: The Lessons of RAMSI* (2014), 17.
67 Julien Barbara, "Antipodean Statebuilding: The Regional Assistance Mission to Sol-

omon Islands and Australian Intervention in the South Pacific," *Journal of Intervention and Statebuilding* (2008).

68 David Lake and Christopher Fariss, "Why International Trusteeship Fails: The Politics of External Authority in Areas of Limited Statehood," *Governance* (2014); Robert Murray and Aidan Hehir, "Intervention in the Emerging Multipolar System: Why R2P Will Miss the Unipolar Moment," *Journal of Intervention and Statebuilding* (2012).

69 Paul Collier, *Wars, Guns, and Votes: Democracy in Dangerous Places* (2009), 199–203.

70 Michael Hechter, "Alien Rule and Its Discontents," *American Behavioral Scientist* (2009).

71 Lance Edwin Davis and Robert Huttenback, *Mammon and the Pursuit of Empire: The Economics of British Imperialism* (1986).

72 Nicolas Lemay-Hébert, "Critical Debates on Liberal Peacebuilding," *Civil Wars* (2013).

73 Oliver Richmond and Jason Franks, *Liberal Peace Transitions: Between Statebuilding and Peacebuilding* (2009), ch. 1.

74 David Roberts, "Hybrid Polities and Indigenous Pluralities: Advanced Lessons in Statebuilding from Cambodia," *Journal of Intervention and Statebuilding* (2008); and John Tully, *France on the Mekong: A History of the Protectorate in Cambodia, 1863–1953* (2002).

75 Aila Matanock, "Governance Delegation Agreements: Shared Sovereignty as a Substitute for Limited Statehood," *Governance* (2014).

76 Nicolas Lemay-Hébert, "Statebuilding without Nation-Building? Legitimacy, State Failure and the Limits of the Institutionalist Approach," *Journal of Intervention and Statebuilding* (2009).

77 David Van Reybrouck, *Congo: The Epic History of a People* (2014), 470.

78 Paul Romer, "Why the World Needs Charter Cities," TED Talks, July 2009.

79 Christopher Freiman, "Cosmopolitanism within Borders: On Behalf of Charter Cities," *Journal of Applied Philosophy* (2013); and Rahul Sagar, "Are Charter Cities Legitimate?" *Journal of Political Philosophy* (2016).

CHAPTER TWO

How the Hate Mob Tried to Cancel Me

In 2012, I bought a copy of the late Nigerian author Chinua Achebe's last published book, *There Was A Country*, a memoir of the inter-ethnic Biafra War that killed between one and two million people in Nigeria between 1967 and 1970. I recall the moment, standing at the bookseller's table, when my eyes grew four sizes reading what Achebe had written:

> Here is a piece of heresy. The British governed their colony of Nigeria with considerable care. There was a very highly competent cadre of government officials imbued with a high level of knowledge of how to run a country. This was not something that the British achieved only in Nigeria; they were able to manage this on a bigger scale in India and Australia. The British had the experience of governing and doing it competently. I am not justifying colonialism. But it is important to face the fact that British colonies were, more or less, expertly run.

I was bowled over. As I read further, Achebe kept coming back to the British period with fonder memories and greater praise. His "articulation of the unsayable," as a Malawian scholar put it, was astounding coming from a man with totemic status in anti-colonial ideology. I went back and read everything he had written and said about colonialism. It turns out, he had been saying positive things from the start, as well as negative things. When I published "Chinua Achebe on the Positive Legacies of Colonialism" in *African Affairs* (the top peer-reviewed academic journal in the field) in 2016, I braced for a storm. There were a few critics. But mostly, I received thanks, especially from African intellectuals who were well aware of this great teacher's complex views.

A Masai tracker and a British civil servant attached to a colonial district officer's staff, Kenya. Credit: Kenya Information Services, National Archives (UK)

In the process of writing the Achebe article, I stumbled upon Sir Alan Burns. He was one of the last governors of the Gold Coast (later renamed Ghana). Then for ten years, until 1956, Burns was a member of the British delegation to the United Nations dealing mainly with colonial issues. His pugnacious defense of the colonial endeavor at the UN and in many writings (especially his 1957 *In Defense of Colonies*) made him a made-in-heaven object of the anti-colonial scorn that captured the world's intellectual imagination for the subsequent half century. Dinosaur. Reactionary. And of course: Racist.

As I dug deeper into Sir Alan's life, I found a well-liked and intelligent person who has been forgotten. I tracked down his family, a delightful bunch, scattered around the world. With their help, writing his biography became my major preoccupation. As I finished the research and prepared to write, I wanted to reformulate his thinking in a schematic way. We all want human dignity and flourishing. Why has a system that, by and large, provided more of this to subject peoples than they would otherwise have enjoyed (especially for women and non-dominant groups) and, importantly, was largely accepted as a result, been so roundly denounced? Why is the question of colonialism no longer a social scientific one and instead a doctrine to be hammered into the heads of undergraduates?

"The Case for Colonialism" was my answer. I approached the question in three ways. The "colonialism as history" section is mainly methodological: how do we set up a research design that is not juiced with anti-colonial (or pro-colonial) bias? The "colonialism as present" section was mainly a recounting of Guinea-Bissau and its astounding human tragedy after a Soviet-armed war against Portuguese rule. The "colonialism as future" section was about applying evidence-based lessons learned. Can we reclaim what Achebe called the "great human story" of colonialism's benefits while avoiding its pitfalls? If so, how?

Perhaps a more nuanced title would have been politic. Yet, I was reminded of the narrator in V.S. Naipaul's 1967 novel, *The Mimic Men*, who leads anti-colonial mobs to destroy a humane British colony in the Caribbean: "We wondered why no one had called our bluff. We felt our success to be fraudulent." It needed a straightforward title because I wanted to call the bluff: anti-colonial ideology is often logically incoherent and empirically false.

I first submitted the essay to the UK-based *Journal of Intervention and Statebuilding*. The editor, Nicolas Lemay-Hébert, was enthusiastic and asked me to bulk up the literature review before he sent it for peer review. "I really think it is a very powerful piece," he wrote to me. When the reviews came back, one was mostly positive and one was mostly negative, but both were stamped "Reject." As Lemay-Hébert later told me, he had argued for the piece to be published alongside critical responses. The question had gone to the journal's editorial board. They (correctly, as it turned out) anticipated a fury and decided it was not worth the grief. As he explained in an email to me: "I am sorry our reviewers and editorial board decided to play it safe, but I also understand their position (fear of political backlash)."

My next stop was the London-based *Third World Quarterly*, where I had previously published two peer-reviewed articles. The journal had been founded in 1979 to be "an open-minded and sympathetic search for establishing an international order based on justice" and "a forum for informed and reasoned debate." It had tilted far left for most of the time since, but its gentle Pakistani-born editor since 1990, Shahid Qadir, had remained adventurous. Too much for his own good as it turned out. The article went through the normal peer review process. As before, the two reviews were split, one positive and one negative. As before, the editor wanted to publish it. Unlike the first editor, Qadir did not run it through a political litmus test first. When the article appeared online, the fury was immediate and intense.

I was sitting in a coffee-shop with a recent Afghani refugee that my family was helping to resettle in Portland preparing to take him to a job interview, when I received a "high priority" email from an Australian colleague: "You are lighting up my Facebook page with hate mail. Well done mate!" Abdul, the father, saw my concern and gave me a questioning look. My reply was automatic: "Just like the fanatics you escaped from, Abdul!"

First, let me be clear that the article has generated a kind outpouring of support for my position on substantive grounds. That is, many scholars and friends have spoken out in favor of the proposition that a substantive body of empirical work generated over the last half century has validated the claim that colonialism's benefits usually exceeded its harms in most cases. And, just as important, it was supported more than opposed by host peoples. I have made many new friends in India, Africa, Southeast Asia, and the Middle East, and we are now working on several joint projects to summarize colonial contributions to human flourishing. A new friend in Guadeloupe stepped in to prepare a French translation. "The people of the Third World all thank you," a new friend in India wrote.

A second outpouring of support came from those who, while disagreeing to varying degrees with the substantive claims, vigorously defended the importance of the paper being published and debated. The paper quickly appeared on the syllabi of fall courses, often as an object of criticism but clearly filling a need. Graduate students at UC San Diego took it up as a case study of publishing controversial positions. Bloggers took up the questions of counterfactual history that it raises. The paper was read 16,000 times within weeks of appearing, becoming overnight the most widely read paper in *TWQ* history. As a leading medical researcher in the U.S. of South Asian heritage wrote to me, the suppression of heterodox ideas is "frightening if you think of the structure of scientific revolutions. What does this indicate for new theories, new knowledge, new ideas?"

Still, the hate campaign was Maoist in its ferocity. Words like "utter," "total" and "absolute" filled the soundings. Needless to say, with rare exceptions, critics did not engage the substantive findings of the paper. Who after all would really want to make an argument that Guinea-Bissau was better off without colonialism? Who would seriously argue that Hong Kong and Singapore are not great achievements of colonialism? Did I misquote Achebe? The serious critics wondered why I had not listed all the atrocities committed under colonial rule, of which there are many. It was for the same reason that I did not list all the atrocities committed before and after colonial rule: like it or not, the question facing most peoples was which rulers were less likely to commit atrocities. When they migrated en masse from non-colonized to colonized areas, they made a prudent choice in favor of regimes likely to commit less, and likely to investigate and punish those that occurred. For instance, after Belgian colonial rule began in the Congo in 1908, after the private fiefdom of King Léopold II, natives streamed into the colonial centers.

Two petitions gathered 16,000 signatures and more were coming in all the time. In part, such virtual flash mobs are becoming part of the discursive landscape of contemporary society. Much of this, I suspect, had nothing to do with me, my article, or even the question of colonialism. Powerful memes are used these days to generate data on users and to direct them to products and services. While my article was not clickbait, the response to it was.

Yet these were not just trolls and bots. They included hundreds of tenured professors at universities in Western countries whose professional and institutional charters insist on the protection of academic freedom and vigorous debate, especially when it comes to challenging orthodoxies. Indeed, these were for the most part the sort of people who spend their time looking everywhere for "hegemony" and insisting on the need for heterodox voices. Yet here they were with Pravda-like ferocity insisting on the completeness of their hegemony and the need to punish dissenting voices.

Noam Chomsky stepped in with a call for rebuttal not retraction. Yet his tolerance was too much for some. For a taste of the fanaticism, consider the following excerpt from an essay entitled "Moral paralysis in American academia" written for the *Al Jazeera* website by Hamid Dabashi, the Hagop Kevorkian Professor of Iranian Studies and Comparative Literature at Columbia University:

> [Chomsky] has as usual refused to denounce Bruce Gilley, offering his habitual bourgeois hogwash that the professor has the right to say what he said and that he too publishes things that offend peo-

> ple. This, of course, is highbrow gibberish - shifting the issue to the domain of censorship and freedom of speech…[Gilley] must be ostracized, publicly shamed and humiliated, and never ever called 'a colleague' who should be politely invited for a 'civilized debate'. Against that 'civilized' gathering of morally compromised scholars, I will proudly form a band of barbarian dissidents.

I encourage anyone concerned with liberal society to read his entire screed: it sends chills down the spine to think that a major U.S. university employs a person with such hostile views about a free society. It is incitement by any other name.

It was that sort of language that made me briefly lose confidence, apologize on my website, and ask the journal to withdraw the article. This was an act of self-censorship. It is what groveling teachers did in the Cultural Revolution, hurriedly writing obsequious letters of contrition and hoping to survive. Fortunately, the *Third World Quarterly* is party to the UK's Committee on Publication Ethics that prevents retraction for political reasons. I was grateful when they saved me from self-censoring. As a scholar of China, my teaching of the Cultural Revolution will never be the same. Taking my family out of Portland and over the Cascade Mountains for a holiday in Central Oregon, I felt like Captain von Trapp leading his family out of fascist Austria into Switzerland.

My home institution did not acquit itself well. This is not surprising. Whole departments—especially our new "School of Gender, Race, and Nations"—are already branded with a certain ideological stamp. The question for them is not whether but how to attack colonialism and "decolonize" everything they can lay hands on. Yet, in recent years, as the bioethicist Alice Dreger has written, this ideological branding has extended to universities as a whole. This creates problems when off-message faculty slip through the hiring and tenure process unnoticed and then go on to publish research with diverse viewpoints. My university's first response was to quote contract language to the effect that I could not be fired. When I self-censored, they rushed to thank me. It was no small irony that Portland State's president at the time was an exile of the Iranian Revolution who was saved from being returned to Iran by Jimmy Carter's amnesty for students studying in the U.S. You'd think he would have spoken up.

Predictably, the critics decided that I was a racist and white supremacist. This has become something of a compliment, as it was a compliment for a moderate liberal to be labelled a "commie" by a fanatic of the right during the Cold War. In today's coded language, a white supremacist is someone who believes that what Naipaul called the "universal civilization currently led by the West" is the cornerstone of global human flourishing. Count me in. Also count in hundreds of public intellectuals in the Third World who have long espoused a closer integration with the West as the best pathway to modernity. The Great Chief of Luanda told the governor of the Belgian Congo in 1959 to resist the "loud-mouthed minorities" who would "again plunge our country into the poverty and misery of the past" with their demands for sudden independence. I guess the Great Chief of Luanda was a white supremacist too.

Most of all, it was the intellectual vacuity of the mobs that surprised, and discouraged. The colonial encounter was huge, epochal, varied, and complex. To reduce it to a bumper sticker is worse than wrong, it is dull. Any great intellectual who actually lived through that period—like Achebe—rendered it in varied hues. They understood that it was not a tweet, an act; it was a confluence of world-historical forces that no one could control. The rise of the West; the Stone Age development of much of the Rest; the impossible interactions; the bitterness; the attempt to work together; the enduring rift. To say, as I did, that colonialism was mostly good, in the economic and social sense of the word, is merely to state the obvious. The University of Edinburgh's Neil Thin wrote that anti-colonial ideologues have lost the ability to actually learn from history—"appreciative history" as he calls it—so intent they are on whipping it into submission.

Intellectuals like Achebe always knew that there is a good chance they would not be alive but for the public health and nutrition improvements under colonialism. He was also deeply aware that it was the opportunities for publication, travel, income generation, and even residency in the West had made their intellectual vocation possible. There was a certain maturity and humanity in their thinking about colonialism. Yet, as time has passed, their children had become monomaniacal anti-colonial critics.

For radicals in the Third World, the psychological attractions of anti-colonialism are obvious. It builds group solidarity, offers a story of victimization and entitlement, and distracts attention from the business at hand. Yet this "protest" identity, as the black St. Lucian economist W. Arthur Lewis called it, has slowly been losing ground to what he called the "creative" identity that views the colonial past as a resource and a proud inheritance. That was the topic of my previous article in the *Third*

World Quarterly, "The Rise of the Creative Third World." I suspect that much of the vitriol this time was not just the fear of uncorking the bottle of research that shows the many benefits of colonialism. It was the fear that these "loudmouthed minorities" are no longer able to bully their kinsmen into silence on the question of colonialism.

These contradictions are nowhere better illustrated than in the person of Vijay Prashad, a devoted Communist from Bengal and professor of international studies at Trinity College in Connecticut. Prashad was the member of the *Third World Quarterly* editorial board who led the revolutionary uprising demanding that the article be airbrushed and all involved punished. "I told the managing editor that if [the journal] does not retract this essay, I will resign from the editorial board," he tweeted on September 11. After charges of censorship arose, he hummed and hawed. The *Third World Quarterly*, Prashad tweeted, "was started as an intellectual venue for anti-colonial thought, to build ideas against colonialism." He also said it was "the home...of values against this essay." The article could have been published elsewhere or sent to "the gutter." Later: "Our ideas must be debated, but not in terms set by the imperialist mindset. We must set the terms of the debate."

"We must set the terms of the debate." This was Lenin's view of the proper role of the party-run media. Like Dabashi, Prashad is happy to live in the West and make extensive use of its freedoms and its capitalist resources, all the while working feverishly to replace them with some failed experiment. The American magazine *The Weekly Standard* referred to the attacks on my article as the "thugs veto." The word "thug" comes from the Hindi word "thuggees" referring to the mobs who terrorized northern India after the collapse of the Mughal dynasty before British rule banned them in 1835 and created a stable framework for a new nation to emerge. India, of course, has been a major source of anti-colonial ideology since independence—it's biggest export to the West as the joke goes. But it is the heirs of the money-grubbing lower castes who rather liked colonial rule who now rule the roost in Delhi.

As it so happened, three weeks before my "viewpoint" essay was published in *Third World Quarterly*, the journal published a "viewpoint" essay by Prashad arguing that the term "imperialism" needs to be applied to all Western interactions with the Third World. When questions arose about whether my article had passed peer review, the publishers undertook a lengthy investigation and reported that "in line with the journal's policy" the article was put through double-blind peer review before being published. One would assume, therefore, that the same was true of Prashad's essay. The Connecticut chapter of the National Association of Scholars confirmed that Prashad's essay was published without peer review.

Not that this matters substantively. For a journal whose readers and reviewers generally lean far to the left, it probably would have been a mere formality. It is a wonderful irony that the same critics who reject science, objectivity, and empiricism (as Prashad does in his essay) as covers for "the imperial mindset," set such store by it when a heterodox opinion appears, and apparently give it little thought when a beloved comrade weighs in with another stirring denunciation of the West.

In the end, my essay was withdrawn because Indian anti-colonial fanatics made death threats against Qadir and his staff. This "suppression of research findings on blatantly political grounds" wrote the University of Buckingham historian and academic ethics specialist Geoffrey Alderman suggests "we have indeed stumbled into a very dark place." This is no understatement. "*L'affaire TWQ*" is about much more than one article. It is not even mainly about the substantive debate on colonialism, which reasonable people can disagree about. Rather, it is about a worrying loss of faith in the liberal and pluralistic norms that made the West. The rot is now so deep that that it extends well beyond the academy and into the virtual social spaces where, like it or not, most people's political views are formed.

In a strange way, then, "The Case for Colonialism" has unintentionally became a case for the recolonization of the West by its own liberal traditions. The pluralism, free inquiry, and reasoned debate on which Western civilization is built faces fanaticism from the Left that generates skepticism from the Right. The non-totalitarian center is shrinking. A very dark place indeed.

CHAPTER THREE

A Lecture*

In September 2017, my peer-reviewed article, "The Case for Colonialism," was published in an advance online version of the *Third World Quarterly*. The purpose of the article was to outline what I and many colleagues in the harder social sciences believe is the clear evidence for the benefits and legitimacy of the second phase of European imperialism, which ran from roughly the early-1800s to the mid-1900s. I also spent about half the paper discussing how those valuable lessons could be recovered by today's weak and failed states. A professor at Harvard's Kennedy School of Government wrote to me, saying that the thesis I advanced in the paper, "has been brewing for some time," as we gain more historical perspective on the human disaster that was decolonization.

One of the fairest criticisms of the paper is that it did not provide enough evidence for its claims about the objective benefits and subjective legitimacy of colonialism. To that end, I have since provided what is in effect the missing bibliography of the paper entitled, "Contributions of Western Colonialism to Human Flourishing: A Summary of Research," available on ResearchGate. I could easily spend this entire talk going through the rigorous social scientific research, which, in my mind, shows what should be a statement of the obvious: when a more advanced society is given the opportunity to diffuse its economic, technological, administrative, and educational systems to a less advanced society that by and large welcomes its presence, the results are so obviously good compared to what would otherwise have happened in that society that the only interesting questions are how large the positive ef-

* An earlier version of this chapter was given as a lecture at the Center for the Study of Western Civilization, Texas Tech University, November 27, 2018.

fects are.

From this research, we know that, in terms of body count, nothing comes close to anti-colonialism in terms of having cost lives and prevented lives. You simply have to do the math and compare trajectories in the late colonial period of the 1920s onward—when populations were growing, food supply expanding, life expectancy leaping upwards, government administration improving, wages and living standards bowling forward, and plans for self-government unfolding—and compare the widening gap of those trends with where most, but not all, former colonies ended up by, say, the late 1980s.

But I fear that such a talk would not change many minds because as I have come to realize, this is not really a scientific debate. Most anti-colonial critics will roll their eyes when you try to engage in them in questions of social scientific research because their real motivation is not getting history right, but getting the present right. Either they reject research findings as yet more evidence of Western imperialism and the need to "decolonize research" and replace it with some kind of ideologically progressive form of story-telling. Or they fear that formerly colonized peoples have such fragile psyches that they could not withstand an encounter with facts that make them uncomfortable.

You may have heard of the case of Helen Zille, the former premier of the Western Cape province in South Africa, who in 2018 was found guilty by the country's ethics board of improper conduct for tweeting, after a visit to Singapore, that South Africa should similarly build on the valuable inheritance of colonialism rather than trash it. South Africa provides a powerful image of this problem: it's twenty-five-year slow-motion collapse since the end of apartheid is closely linked to its inability to embrace its British colonial past. In 1993, the average Singaporean was 4.5 times wealthier than the average South African. Today, they are 7 times wealthier. In 1993, it took one Singapore dollar and 1.8 South African rand to buy a U.S. dollar using purchasing power exchange rates. Today, it takes just 84 Singapore cents to buy a U.S. dollar but 6.2 South African rand.

Such declines in living standards might not make great photos but they cost far more lives. The ethics board that censured Zille cited the mob attack on my article as evidence that the voicing of pro-colonial viewpoints should be curtailed. In her defense, Zille quoted no less an authority than Nelson Mandela citing the benefits of British colonialism. Clearly, these are lessons that the lawless and ignorant public prosecutor who found Zille guilty does not want to learn. Nor do most anti-colonial critics.

There is a second reason why I do not think it would be productive to go through the social scientific research on colonialism. We today live in a post-truth era in which social media, Wikipedia, and Google are more authoritative sources of information than robust research. It took David Donaldson of MIT ten years to research and publish his article in the *American Economic Review* showing that railroads in India had positive economic effects.[1] It takes any critic one second on Google to find the Congress politician Shashi Tharoor declaring in the *Guardian* that the railroads were "a colonial scam" that harmed Indians.[2]

So I am going to use this talk to engage in a more rhetorical and topical presentation so that, at the very least, the arguments for colonialism are made clear.

Baba of Karo

In 1887, a woman belonging to the Muslim Hausa ethnic group was born in the slave-based Sokoto Caliphate of what is today northern Nigeria. The Caliphate was a creation of the Fulani ethnic group which had defeated and subjugated rival tribes in a series of wars between 1804 and 1808, including the Habe branch of the Hausa to which the woman belonged. Fulani rule decayed with each successive ruler so that by 1886, when the British government gave a monopoly for trading in the region to the Royal Niger Company, the subject peoples of this empire were ready for a change. The Royal Niger Company found ready partners willing to sign treaties in exchange for liberation from Fulani autocracy. In 1899, the British government assumed control of the region from the Royal Niger Company, and in 1900 its troops—mostly black natives—arrived in this woman's village, named Karo, to assert their control.

"We Habe wanted them to come, it was the Fulani who did not like it," the woman, known as Baba, recalled. Why you might ask would an African woman welcome European colonization? Baba explained: "When the Europeans came, the Habe saw that if you worked for them, they paid you for it. They didn't say, like the Fulani: 'Commoner, give me this! Commoner, bring me that!' Yes, the Habe wanted them; they saw no harm in them."

Was this just an initial response that Baba of Karo later regretted? No, far from it. As she explained, life got immeasurably better after British colonization. The best thing the Europeans did was free slaves and depose indigenous tyrants. "The Europeans don't like oppression but they found a lot of tyranny and oppression here, people being beaten and killed and sold into slavery." For her personally, another benefit was the improved status of women. "In the old days if the chief liked the look of your daughter he would take her and put her in his house; you could do nothing about it. Now they don't do that."

Baba of Karo told her story over a six-week period in December 1949 and January 1950 to the English anthropologist Mary Felice Smith. The testimony was published as *Baba of Karo: A Woman of the Muslim Hausa* in 1954.[3] What are we to make of this first-hand account of an African woman's experience of the coming of colonialism? "It is strange that Baba welcomes the coming of the British," wrote a scholar from Niger in a 1994 essay.[4] Yet a moment's reflection shows why it made sense, he noted. Baba of Karo faced a concrete choice as a young girl between the relatively benign rule of the British and the fearsome rule of Fulani tyrants and the slave and wife-raiders they protected. So, he writes, it was not the British but the Fulani who were the "nasty Other."

In fact, the British never became the nasty Other for Baba or Karo. She was perfectly content in her cultural space, and the British protected and enlarged that cultural space by removing the threats to it from slave raiders and Fulani tyrants. The peace and security of British rule were the main changes that colonialism brought. Life went on more or less as usual in other respects, which is why no one thought of resisting the British. There was no tension in Baba's worldview between being pro-colonial and pro-Habe. Quite the opposite. The British facilitated the articulation of an authentic, living, and surviving Habe culture.

Why do I dwell at such length on the story of Baba of Karo? Because it is such a profound rebuke to the contemporary anti-colonial writers who presume to make the choices that women like Baba faced over a century ago. Among the widely circulated critiques of my paper, one was written by an American journalist who found some fake photos from King Léopold's Congo on the Internet and ramped up the outrage with claims that my paper amounted to Holocaust denial.[5] If you will indulge me, let us imagine a conversation between Baba of Karo and a composite of such writers who have attacked my paper whom I will call Edward of Boston.

Edward: Baba, how could you endorse a system that dismantled your governing institutions and replaced them with unaccountable alien rule?

Baba: Actually, Edward, our governing institutions even before the Fulani empire were more autocratic than anything the British imposed. In any case, like most colonized peoples, we lived under alien rule already when the Europeans arrived. Either a rival ethnic group, or a rival sub-group or faction were always in charge. Circa 1900, rule by the British—the most accountable political system in the world at the time—versus the caliphs of Sokoto. Hell ya!

Edward: But once you accepted British rule, self-government became impossible, whereas you could have slowly democratized the Sokoto caliphate.

Baba (eyes as big as saucers): The British began talking about preparing their colonies for self-government in the 1850s. The caliphate believed only in the rule of Islam. Colonialism was the pathway to self-government. Isn't that what happened in Boston too Edward?

Edward: What about the atrocities committed by colonial rulers throughout the 19th and 20th centuries—Amritsar, Namibia, Mau Mau, and in your country of Nigeria there were those 57 women traders shot dead by colonial police in 1929 over taxes? There are a lot of pictures and Wikipedia articles on the Internet.

Baba: I see how enlivened you are talking about atrocities, Edward. Why do you know so little about the atrocities in world history that did not involve Europeans? One reason is they are not recorded. You will find no pictures of them on the Internet, Edward, and no Wikipedia articles. We know about the frontier wars in British settlement colonies because they were recorded, investigated, debated, and yes, the atrocities were punished by the British. You liked the picture of severed hands in the Congo under King Léopold II, Edward. Have you seen the pictures of the piles of bodies in the eastern Congo under al-Zubayr and or the torched villages left in the Congo by Hamed ben Mohammed al-Murjebi (better known as Tippo Tip)? They were the most fearsome of the many Sudanese, Nubian, and Egyptian slave traders and ivory tyrants who terrorized the Congo before the relatively benign rule of King Léopold II. Would it surprise you Edward, to learn that most people welcomed King Léopold's rule, indeed it was this that explains how Tippo Tip, who began as governor of the king's eastern holdings, lost control?[6] Why are there only four books on Tippo Tip but at last count hundreds on Léopold II? Do you care about the actual history of people like my own?

Edward: But you keep changing the subject Baba. My subject is colonial atrocities.

Baba: My subject is saving human lives. Even when native atrocities were recorded somehow—like the Nama massacre of a fifth of the Herero population in today's Namibia in a single day on August 23, 1850 at a place now known as Murder Hill where women's feet were chopped off to obtain the copper rings they wore around their legs—you don't seem interested. Didn't you read what I told Mary Felice Smith about the constant warfare and murder my people faced under the Fulani? We did not have cameras like the Belgian lawyers investigating the atrocities of King Léopold's private fiefdom. In any case, I guess you would roll your eyes in boredom. And by the way, the suppression of the Mau Mau in Kenya and of the Women's War in Nigeria were both justified. The use of force was proportional to the threat. That's why most Kenyans and Nigerians supported the colonial governments, indeed did most of the restoration of order and prison work.

In any case, sorry to come back to counterfactuals Edward, but the Herero and Nama in Namibia, for example, were long-time rivals who were stockpiling arms for a war on each other at the time of the German settlement. Do you think they would have resolved their differences with a roundtable conference and knitting therapy? Yes, I am lucky. I was not a victim of a colonial atrocity or a colonial settlement war. I was, however, the victim of a Fulani atrocity after slave raiders carried off members of my family. Please read my book Edward. Even the libraries in Boston have copies.

Edward: Even, so, Baba, you seem to be engaging in a sort of morally cold-hearted cost-benefit analysis. That the good things that came with colonialism can offset the bad things.

Baba: I'm still not sure what the bad things are in my case Edward, but to give you the benefit of the doubt, let's throw some possible things out there: the humiliation and psychological harms of alien rule; the short-circuiting of our indigenous development path; the empowerment of "chiefs" with the backing of colonial coercion. Yes, perhaps these were harms in some cases. And when harms cross some threshold, they can never be justified by goods. But none of these, even if true, which I doubt, came close to that. Are you saying Edward, that the survival and longer-lives that my Habe people enjoyed after the British should be weighed against unaccountable chiefs or psychological harms that seemed mainly a concern of French-educated intellectuals?

Edward: Maybe you just have false consciousness Baba. You believed the British were legitimate rulers, rulers who had more of a right to rule your people than the feasible alternatives, because you really had no choice. You had a gun to your head and rationalized your behavior.

Baba: Didn't your professors ever teach you how demeaning it is to dismiss viewpoints your disagree with among common people as false consciousness? Maybe the silly little people like me could not think for ourselves, as you imply Edward. A whole generation of Western academics has dismissed voices like mine as false consciousness. But it was the elites who chose to invite and ally with the British in northern Nigeria. They had a choice to fight, but chose cooperation. The man who would become the premier of northern Nigeria at independence, also from a small tribe, wrote this of the coming of the British: "There was no ill-will after the occupation. We were used to conquerors and these were different; they were polite and obviously out to help us rather than themselves."[7]

Edward: OK, but really colonialism goes way further back, to the 16th through 18th centuries when the British were major slavers and their American, Canadian, Australian, and New Zealand settlers were massacring all and sundry. Shouldn't we throw this into the equation too?

Baba: Should we? And call them morally reprehensible for doing what every non-Western culture, including my own, was also doing at the time, simply without the technological and economic and organizational capacity of the West to make it work? These were frontier battles. Every empire—Ottoman, Qing, Russian, Japanese—was expanding its frontiers through warfare at the time: that's what empires did. The Zulus in southern Africa, the Maori in the south Pacific, the Bantu and Buganda in east Africa—I mean do you know how they came to occupy their "ancestral" homelands Edward? And not only in ancient times. The Maori of New Zealand massacred most of the 1,600 Moriori people on the Chatham Islands in a single invasion of 1835, and then claimed the islands as their ancestral homeland.

And where did the ideas for changes to those expansionist norms come from? Actually, from Europe: the Dutch lawyers who developed ideas of international law, the Quakers who led the push against slavery, the Scottish and English liberals who developed ideas of land rights. So you are appealing to norm shifts that came from the European colonizers themselves. It matters. It's not the same as burning down a fellow's house and then offering to rebuild it. A better analogy is the slum-lord who has a moral awakening and decides she is going to live better. She chooses to set higher standards for her rental units, fixing broken pipes and keeping heaters on. She advocates among her fellow slum lords to make this a norm. Eventually they make it a law. Are you telling me that she has no business claiming to have done good because she used to be a slum lord?

Edward: Ok, but in the end, they stole your money. They took your commodities. They locked you into economic dependency.

Baba: They paid us, as I told Mary Felice Smith. My family's children had job opportunities we could never have dreamed of. And by the way, you Marxists have a strange way of understanding economics. Commodities cannot simply be pulled from the Earth and deposited in a bank. If they could, resource-rich countries would all be rich. Nigeria has oil. It remains poor. Why? Because wealth comes from an economic system: free markets, the rule of law, global trade, corporate organization, social trust, investment certainty, worker training and education, infrastructure. Do you think this stuff just "happens" Edward? Do you have any idea why Boston is so prosperous? Because of the large number of clams in Boston harbor?

Edward: Baba, you are really flogging a dead horse here. I mean, nothing, nothing will ever convince most people that colonialism was a good thing.

Baba: Maybe. But truth matters to me, Edward, and it should matter to you too. And secondly, truth matters because it has lessons for today. Have you heard of Chinua Achebe? In his last book, he reminded his readers that Nigeria benefitted a lot from British colonialism and urged them to reclaim some of that past, like excellent administration and meritocracy in government and business.

Edward: I can't debate this any longer, I am late for a mental decolonization rally at the graduate student union.

Baba: Your mind has been colonized by half a century of gibberish about the evils of Western colonialism. A little decolonization of that material would be good for you.

Edward: (frowns angrily)

Baba: (smiles wearily)

Since 2017, I have had many debates of this sort. The critics have now retreated to calls for censorship with the claim that while they believe in free speech and academic freedom, they draw the line when it comes to research on colonialism that they believe is factually inaccurate and/or "violent and oppressive." The new terms they have invented are "academic integrity" and "academic monitoring" so that scholars with inappropriate ideological orientations, such as I, are put under the charge of scholars with advanced ideological views who seem mostly to be found in English departments. As a scholar of China, my teaching of Mao's Cultural Revolution will never be the same.

One obvious response to such charges is, to borrow John Stuart Mill's defense of liberty, that you will never really know whose arguments are factually correct and normatively defensible unless they are exposed to the strong gale of counter-argument.

The more substantive response is this: if factual or social scientific validity and normative defensibility are the standards by which we should judge scholarship on colonialism, then I submit that the problems of inaccuracy, misrepresentation, and ethical sophistry giving rise to scholarship that perpetuates violence and oppression against formerly colonized peoples lie, in the main, with the anti-colonial scholars who dominate the contemporary academy.

Testimonies

Several people from former colonial areas have written essays in support of my original article, which you can find on my website. One was written by a Nigerian women who is an educational consultant in that country. She called the mob attacks on my article a "bilious personification of anti-intellectualism." "Many Nigerians," she wrote, "see the colonial era as something of a golden age." The most lasting legacy, in her view, was the positive impact on education, which is the focus of her research. "Will I ever be able to publish my research?" she asked. "This is the fearful state that outraged mobs have put myself and others in. But I won't be intimidated. I will say what I believe to be true, no matter what."[8] The censorious Maoists have intimidated this Nigerian woman who is trying to resurrect the educational system of her country by recovering lessons from British colonial institutions so that young people there have a future.

The governor of British India visiting the workshops of the East India Railway Company in northeast India in 1897. Credit: The British Library.

In 2018, I received an email from a young Indian scholar studying for a graduate degree in Shakespeare in Texas. He wrote:

> My great grandfather, born to field laborers in Southern India, was...educated by Christian missionaries, Britishers, the very Colonizers I am supposed to hate. He was, having been so educated, commissioned by the British Government to found and run a high school in the village of his birth. His son, my grandfather, was the first of that village to complete high school, as well as to complete

> university. Moreover, he was employed by the British Government as a statistician, which was very prestigious in those days. My grandmother, similarly educated was able to go so far as a masters degree because of the educational system set up by the British. It is because of Colonialism that my family was educated, elevated far beyond the station of their birth, and it is because of this Colonialism that I am able to study Shakespeare at an American university, rather than labor in a field in India.

Both of these authentic voices from people in former colonized areas are being told by progressives mostly in the West that they need to shut up. I stand with the former.

Still, to Edward's point about flogging a dead horse, why should we really care? Many of my colleagues will say privately that they agree with me, but why enter into this fraught debate and risk being called a white supremacist or a Holocaust denier? It's not worth it. To some extent, I agree, and I think that pragmatism is the best way forward for many countries. "It's complex. It brings back bitter memories. The question is how to move forward." So, how to move forward? I think there are both intellectual and institutional prescriptions, but I put the most store by the former.

First and foremost, restoring colonial success requires coming to terms intellectually with the positive legacies of colonialism, as China did when it ousted the Maoists, and as Helen Zille urged on her countrymen. But this intellectual turn will require a massive Enlightenment. No less an otherwise reliable newspaper than the *Wall Street Journal* in 2018 carried an approving feature story on the "decolonization" of Belgium's Royal Museum for Central Africa.[9] According to the article, the "woefully dated statuary" and "exoticism" of the museum is being airbrushed in a makeover in which "colonial-era imagery" will be "countered" with new images showing "colonial-era oppression" and asserting, in the title of one statue, a "Burgeoning Congo" including a "robot used to control traffic in Kinshasa." Colonial "apologists" will be sent packing by the new museum and instead Belgian visitors will be abjectly told of the cruelty of their ancestors, and, by ascription, themselves and how, but for their meddling in central Africa there would have been a land of milk and honey.

The fact is that the Congo under al-Zubayr and Tippo Tip was doing anything but burgeoning. After the Belgians colonized the country in 1908, it entered into its only era of burgeoning, which lasted until so-called independence in 1960, under pressure from those who the Great

Chief of Luanda called "loud-mouthed minorities." This, by the way, according to the contemporary academy, makes the Great Chief of Luanda a white supremacist, a charge that I presume the old chief would have considered evidence of the inscrutable ways of the West.

And those robot-controlled intersections in Kinshasa? It's a story the Western liberal media loves and it repeats old tropes about an African renaissance. But it is more evidence of Africa imploding not burgeoning. They are designed to prevent bribery caused by mistrust between police and people. The robots cost $27,000 each and are paid for by foreign aid. They sidestep the issue of administrative capacity and state-society trust. A writer for the *Atlantic* calls them "a public relations stunt that turns attention away from serious growth and infrastructure issues in the city." They appeared after municipal elections were cancelled—"the flashy, modern way to distract the public from scrutinizing bad governance."[10]

So, the decolonization of the Royal Museum for Central Africa perfectly embodies the fatuous nature of anti-colonialism: a Belgian colonial state that made lives better for ordinary Congolese is being scrubbed from history and replaced by a robo-cop that symbolizes the tyranny and dysfunction of anti-colonial Congo and its guilt-ridden Western supporters.

Lands of Hope

The institutional fixes are more straight-forward. In 2016, a Danish aid worker in Nigeria rescued a boy who had been left to starve to death by the local community because they believed he was a witch. UNICEF estimates that in this one southwestern state of Nigeria, there are 15,000 children similarly abandoned by their parents as witches and 10,000 a year added to the streets nationwide.[11] The Danish aid worker got together with her local Nigerian colleagues and established the Land of Hope Children's Center in Nigeria for rescued children. The Nigerian government is unable and unwilling to act against this cultural practice. Exxon-Mobil has funded the Center along with a lot of international donors, and it is essentially playing the "colonial" role of filling in a governance deficit. There could be many more Lands of Hope with a re-engaged and explicitly colonial approach to these countries.

The borrowing and replication of governance functions embedded in a country's colonial past is one way that I suggested in my paper for re-colonizing the failing parts of the Third World. The other was for

Western governments to formally share some sovereign functions like public finance and law and order as has been successfully attempted in various African countries in recent years.

There is a third way. What do you think would happen if the British were invited back to rule a small parcel of land in Nigeria, somewhere where no one lived, just as Lagos, Singapore, Accra, Hong Kong, and Aden were sparsely-populated places until British colonialism turned them into humane, decent, and opportunity-filled places? This is the idea of a charter city suggested by Paul Romer back in 2009 in which the host nation would consent to hand over sovereignty for some fixed period, say 99 years, in order to stimulate development and diffusion of good governance. Over that period, people from the host nation who wanted to migrate to the charter city could do so at the discretion of its authorities.

Charter cities would be risky. Sir Paul Collier told a seminar at Oxford in 2018 convened to discuss my article "The Case for Colonialism" that the problem with charter cities is that if they do not work, local politicians will be blamed, and if they do, local politicians will also be blamed. This all stems from a fundamental problem: anti-colonialism has become so entrenched, not just in the Western academy, but in the politics of many failed states that nothing short of a Enlightenment that ushers in a productive encounter with the modern world will do. Charter cities are the developmental equivalent of a moon shot. Still, sometimes you reach the moon. The alternative makes it worth a try.

Endnotes:

1 Dave Donaldson, "Railroads of the Raj: Estimating the Impact of Transportation Infrastructure," *American Economic Review* (2018).
2 Shashi Tharoor, "'But What About the Railways?' The Myth of Britain's Gifts to India," *The Guardian*, March 8, 2017.
3 Mary Felice Smith, *Baba of Karo: A Woman of the Muslim Hausa* (1954), 66-68.
4 Chaibou Elhadji Oumarou, "One Speaks, Another Writes: The Oral Autobiography of a Hausa Woman (1877-1951)," *CEA Critic* (1994), 25.
5 Nathan Robinson, "A Quick Reminder Of Why Colonialism Was Bad: Ignoring or Downplaying Colonial Atrocities Is the Moral Equivalent of Holocaust Denial," *Current Affairs*, September 14, 2017.
6 Francois Renault, *Tippo Tip: Un Potentat Arabe en Afrique Centrale au XIXe Ciècle* (1987).
7 Ahmadu Bello, *My Life* (1962), 18-19.
8 Folasade Lamikanra. "Dare We Make a Case for Colonialism?" *Conatusnews.com* (Nigeria), October 13, 2017.
9 J.S. Marcus, "A Museum Rethinks Its Mission: After a Renovation, Belgium's AfricaMuseum Tries to Tell the True Story of Colonialism," *Wall Street Journal*, November 9, 2018.
10 Ed Yong, "The First Urban Case of Ebola in the Congo Is a 'Game Changer,'" *The Atlantic*, May 17, 2018.
11 Aleksandra Cimpric, *Children Accused of Witchcraft: An Anthropological Study of Contemporary Practices in Africa*, UNICEF Nigeria, April 2010.

CHAPTER FOUR

A Response to My Critics

On September 8, 2017, the *Third World Quarterly* published my article, "The Case for Colonialism," through its online platform in anticipation of its inclusion in a hard-copy edition at a later date. Within minutes of its appearance, a great controversy arose on social media. Over the ensuing weeks, half of the journal's editorial board resigned in protest and the editorial staff in London received credible death threats. On September 21, I assented to the withdrawal of the article in the interests of the physical safety of the journal's editorial staff. The article was reprinted in 2018 in *Academic Questions*, the journal of the National Association of Scholars, where it is the most read article in the journal's thirty-four year history.[1]

The article has its origins in 2012, when I stumbled upon the final book of Chinua Achebe while at an academic conference.[2] Achebe's many positive comments on colonialism led me to delve deeper into the legacy of this supposedly anti-colonial figure, resulting in an article which I later published in *African Affairs*.[3] It was while researching Achebe that I discovered the works of the British colonial official Sir Alan Burns, which led me to write a biography of him which was published in 2021.[4] I wrote "The Case for Colonialism" in order to frame the positive case that Burns made within a more general theory and body of evidence.

I submitted the article first to the *Journal of Intervention and Statebuilding*. The editor there, Nicolas Lemay-Hébert, gave it a desk approval and asked me to strengthen the policy-relevant aspects of the paper prior to sending it for peer review. The paper then received one positive and one negative review. Lemay-Hébert then asked his editorial board whether he should publish the paper and was told that it was too politically controversial to publish. The "fear of political backlash" determined the decision not to accept it, he wrote to me by email. I next turned to the *Third World Quarterly*. I had previously published two peer-reviewed articles in this journal, one of which took a clearly pro-colonial standpoint.[5] I first submitted it to a planned special issue on "the new imperialism." The special issue editors immediately rejected it because it took a positive, rather than negative, view of their chosen topic, even though their call for papers had not indicated that a particular normative perspective was required of submissions. The "range of theoretical and empirical viewpoints" that they had in mind, as they later explained, was limited to Marxism, post-colonialism, black Marxism, pan-Africanism, and "the revolutionary theory of Frantz Fanon and Che Guevara."[6]

After I failed to win consideration for inclusion in the special issue, the *Third World Quarterly* editor, Shahid Qadir, sent my article for normal peer review. It received one positive and one negative review. Qadir, as was his prerogative, decided to run it but as a "viewpoint" rather than "research" article, with my consent.[7]

In the subsequent years, the article has been the subject of countless essays, conference panels, seminar discussions, and journal articles. It is the ninth "most read" article in the *Third World Quarterly*'s forty-two-year history, even though readers can "read" only the withdrawal notice. Oddly, the *Third World Quarterly* began to allow authors to cite the original withdrawn article, albeit only critically and in a way that directs readers to the withdrawal notice rather than to the published version in *Academic Questions*, as, for example, in Fasakin's article continuing a long tradition of blaming colonialism for Africa's contemporary woes.[8] After a lifetime of writing as a journalist and academic, those eight-thousand words have come to identify me and to dominate my time in a way that I could never have imagined.

I have waited several years to respond to critics of the article, mainly in order to allow the dust to settle and for the best critiques to be lodged. Here, I will address only what I consider to be serious scholarly responses. This means I am not responding to the outpouring of emotionally-charged attacks on the article by reputable scholars, of which there are dozens. But they are a reminder of what I believe is the fundamentally ideological rather than scientific basis of my critics' complaints.

I find that my critics mostly misread my article, used citations they had not read or understood, failed to adhere to basic social scientific principles, and imposed their own interpretations on data without noting the possibility of alternatives. I note that a failure to adhere to academic standards, the main charge levelled against my paper, is rife among those who have levelled such charges. The use of their critiques to impose professional penalties and punishments on me as a scholar bespeaks the fundamental problems of ideological monoculture and illiberal censorship in academia today. I conclude that the problems of most research on the colonial past, roughly since 1950, are so deep-rooted that nothing short of a complete rewriting of colonial history under appropriate scientific conditions will suffice.

Definitions

I make clear in the article that I define "colonialism" as referring to "British, French, German, Belgian, Dutch, and Portuguese colonies from the early 19th to mid-20th centuries." This temporal separation of European expansion from the earlier fifteenth to early nineteenth century phase follows Abernethy who, along with others, argued that only in this second phase—which he dates to the 1824 Anglo-Burmese war—was formal "political control" the dominant mode of European empire while the industrial revolution made the modes and scope of empire qualitatively different from those in the first phase.[9] Klein is thus careless in claiming that my naming of Libya, Haiti, and Guatemala as countries that can be used as counterfactual examples to places that experienced modern colonialism was among my "errors."[10] Guatemala became independent in 1821, while Haiti revolted against French rule and was granted independence in 1825. Libya remained independent throughout the second phase of European colonialism until 1912, when Italy briefly laid claim to this fragment of the Ottoman Empire. I am therefore justified in citing these three, along with China, Ethiopia, Liberia, Saudi Arabia, and Thailand as countries that "did not have a significant colonial history," as I defined it.

Thus, while I believe that there is an equally compelling case for Anglo-settlement colonies in North America and the Antipodes, and for Spanish and Portuguese colonialism in the New World, those are separate historical issues and not my concern in this paper. I am also justified in excluding from my analysis the private estates in the Congo of the Belgian king Léopold II which he held from 1885 to 1908, until the area became a colony of Belgium. While general readers of my article, and undergraduate students, can be excused for this criticism, it is a puzzling mistake for credentialled scholars. Klein, for instance, in arguing against the use of corvée labor under colonialism writes of "Léopold's minions" as an example of such "colonial" practices.[11] Likewise, Brandon and Sarkar refer to "Belgian Congo under Léopold's rule" and "the trail of bloodshed that the small European nation left behind in the vast African country."[12] MacWilliam, too, complains that I make "[n]o mention ... of imperial Belgium's rule in the Congo Free State," which is true because there was no such thing.[13]

Klein, like others, cites the American journalist Adam Hochschild's 1998 book, *King Leopold's Ghost.* While carrying the subtitle, *A Story of Greed, Terror, and Heroism in Colonial Africa*, Hochschild acknowledged that control of the private plantation "was shared in no way with the Belgian government."[14] This was the same conclusion reached by an investigating magistrate at the time who wrote: "The state of Congo is no colonized state, barely a state at all but a financial enterprise."[15] The Belgian Congo came *after* Léopold's rule and the fifty-two years of this colony from 1908 to 1960 were the only period of good governance that this benighted region has ever known. This is not a technicality. Quite the opposite. The proposition that there was some feasible good governance model available to this region from indigenous sources is unsupported. The Batambatamba Afro-Arab slave traders of the area? The African warlord Msiri whose compound, decorated with human remains, was the inspiration, along with a similar compound of the king of Benin, for Conrad's *Heart of Darkness* (transposed onto a white trader to elicit the predictable outrage from white readers)? The feared Arab slavers Tippo Tip or al-Zubayr? Belgian colonization of the Congo in 1908 put an end to "independence" for the Congo and thank goodness for that. In making this small mistake, my critics open us to the wider world of their misunderstanding of colonial history.

The Unadorned Argument

I will begin by responding to critics of my core claim that European colonialism was objectively beneficial to colonized peoples. It is important to note that a grand total of 126 words were devoted to this topic, since much of the article's prelude is devoted to arguing that most research on colonialism falls afoul of basic principles of scientific research and thus does not "prove" anything about this most central of questions. By contrast, I wrote, "research that is careful in conceptualizing and measuring controls, that establishes a feasible counterfactual, that includes multiple dimensions of costs and benefits weighted in some justified way, and that adheres to basic epistemic virtues often finds that at least some if not many or most episodes of Western colonialism were a net benefit."

As I have often stated since then, the reference to just a few research works, including the overview article of Juan and Pierskalla,[16] was clearly insufficient to substantiate that claim, even as a review of literature. To that end, I have subsequently generated what is, in effect, the missing bibliography for that single paragraph.[17] It divides the topic into fifty-one subsections and runs to over forty pages, citing over five-hundred research books and articles. At over ten-thousand words, that bibliography could obviously not have been included, except as a separate article. Nonetheless, one response I commonly give to critics who argue that there is "no evidence" for the core claim of my article is: "Look at the bibliography."

To critics like Osterkamp, who complain that my article (and presumably, in his view, the bibliography as well) do not provide a thorough and balanced discussion of all research conducted on colonialism, I plead guilty as charged.[18] Such an article, in addition to being unfeasible, would have served no purpose other than add to the "it's complicated" intellectual approach that seems to be the only permissible alternative to the "it was evil" orthodoxy in the academy. If, after due consideration of evidence and logic, a scholar believes that colonialism was an unambiguously "good thing" in most times and places, then he needs to begin by making that case itself. My article does this. Indeed, if the main utility of my article has been to provide rhetorical cover for scholars who can thereby claim to be "moderates" on the question, I would consider it a worthy contribution.

Economics

Debates on the economic effects of colonialism occupy a large part of the criticism of my article. Thus, in two separate responses, Khan charges that colonial rule "impoverished" and "exploited" subject communities.[19] Others made the same claim: the economies of colonies were "exploited" and "underdeveloped" under colonial rule, often citing the Guyanese Marxist Walter Rodney,[20] also one of the authorities cited by Sultana in arguing that my article amounted to Holocaust denial.[21]

Part of the perennial debate here is simply the misunderstanding of economic growth by scholars whose worldviews are shaped by zero-sum Marxist approaches. Without "exploitation" and "profits," there can be no employment, wages, markets, and improvements in organization and technology. As the English economist Joan Robinson famously quipped, "the misery of being exploited by capitalists is nothing compared to the misery of not being exploited all."[22] That the re-issue of Rodney's book in 2018 was accompanied by introductory essays, not by economists, but by black Marxist activists in the United States, such as Angela Davis, speaks volumes about the ideological rather than scientific basis of claims of "exploitation" and "underdevelopment."[23]

More specifically, critics should simply refer to the mountain of evidence from serious economists showing the erroneous nature of both Rodney's specific claims about Africa, as shown in many regression studies beginning with the work of Grier,[24] as well as the more general claim first with respect to the granddaddy of them all, India, as shown repeatedly by the work of the acknowledged expert on that topic, Tirthankar Roy,[25] and to the colonial world taken as a whole as demonstrated by one study using islands as natural experiments.[26] Taylor writes: "[N]ot only should we not accept Gilley's general pro-colonial explanation of the poor performance of many post-colonial African nations since he provides us with no good reason to do so, we do have good reason to believe that their poor performance is a legacy of their colonial subjection."[27] Actually, we do not. If colonial subjection caused poor performance, then today's Ethiopia would be the economic miracle of Africa. Instead, the only semi-successful African economy ever was South Africa, until its system of white minority rule was hastily "decolonized" in the early 1990s and the country went into a tailspin.

I agree with Osterkamp that the long-form essay by Heldring and Robinson measures up well to the highest standards of scientific inquiry in reaching the conclusion that colonialism's overall effect on development in Africa was negative.[28] Though mainly a literature review and an interpretive foray, it provides a rigorous and logical counterargument to claims about colonialism's positive impact on development.

Although anti-colonial narratives have less traction in Asia because of the success of its former colonies, recent work that affirms the positive contributions of colonialism in Asia as well includes a study by Dell and Olken about Dutch sugar production in Java which concludes: "The establishment of a sugar processing infrastructure in colonial Java persistently increased industrialization, education, and household consumption in areas near government sugar factories, even after the factories themselves had disappeared. Similarly, villages forced to grow sugar cane for the Cultivation System have more schooling and manufacturing today ... the positive impacts on economic activity plausibly dominated [any negative effects] in the long-run."[29]

Kendhammer writes: "[W]hile some studies find that former British colonies have performed better economically and politically than others, virtually none find that colonial rule was itself an effective method of setting up long-term prosperity and stability."[30] While citing Grier incorrectly (his study makes a general claim about longer colonial rule in addition to the specific one about British rule), the "virtually none" citation is to Lange, and Kendhammer might have added the subsequent book on the subject.[31]

Several points are in order. First, let us agree that Lange's work is top-rate and scientific. Second, let us agree that other work that is top-rate and scientific reaches other conclusions. Third, if one were to pin such a sweeping statement about "virtually none" showing any positive effect to Lange's work, one would want to read it carefully. Lange's work looks only at variations within British colonialism: it has nothing to say about comparative colonialism much less colonialism versus non-colonialism. ("Since the analysis is limited to former British colonies ... further investigation is necessary if one attempts to generalize outside of the cases analyzed here."[32]) Nor does it consider the role of post-colonial policies in explaining contemporary conditions, a rather glaring omission. Moreover his theory does not work for India, which, depending on how you measure it, accounted for about 75 percent of British colonialism. Nor does it work for Botswana or Guyana, two of the four cases he chooses in the book to illustrate the uncertainties of his argument. Finally, the statistical model really just shows that African countries were six times more likely to be ruled indirectly than others,[33] and that such rule was associated with worse outcomes. Lange's work tells us nothing about colonialism. It does tell us about the challenges of development in Africa.

Kendhammer also cites the work of Ochonu in support of the statement that in "parts of West Africa, the tax burdens on farmers were so high in the 1930s they created a cycle of poverty and debt that keeps their descendants poor today."[34] In fact, Ochonu's book is about the inability of the colonial state to tax farmers during the Great Depression. Still, Kendhammer unintentionally provides a sterling example of the intellectual dead-end of colonial studies that offers scholars two options on every question. As I wrote: "Eminent scholars repeatedly make the contradictory claim that colonialism was both too disruptive and not disruptive enough." In this case: colonialism, according to Kendhammer, was bad because it did too much (like taxing effectively); or colonialism, according to Ochonu, was bad because it did too little (like failing to tax effectively). Tax well and you exploit and integrate into the imperialist economy; tax badly and you create patterns of disengagement from the state and the modern economy. Both are bad because both involve colonial rule. As Ochonu writes with puzzling logic: "British colonialism was just as disruptive to Africans' lives when it failed to exploit them as it was when it did."[35]

The same self-contradiction is embraced by Taylor, who writes that when Marxists criticize both an absence and a presence of colonial public health infrastructure "there is not even the appearance of contradiction." How so? Because the former is about missing "provision" while the latter is nefarious "use."[36] In other words, in Taylor's mind, colonial authorities should have gone around the world providing free healthcare and other public goods to alien peoples as a sort of quixotic humanitarian mission but should not have expected anything in return, such as the payment of taxes or even participation in the labor market. While Taylor is correct that there is no necessary contradiction in these claims, there is certainly a practical one.

Kendhammer is correct that I discount Crawford Young because he is an example of an eminent scholar whose claims about the colonial state are tied up in self-contradictions, although I refer not to his 1994 book but to a 2016 book chapter.[37] Taylor, too, rejects my interpretation of Young or others making similar claims, saying that it is consistent to assert that colonialists both disrupted too much (such as by "replacing Congolese institutions ... with Belgian ones") and disrupted too little (such as by failing to create a larger Belgian colonial state).[38] What these "Congolese institutions" with the capacity to govern central Africa were remain a mystery to me. So do Taylors' and Young's reasons for condemning the British for not trying to create larger units. Nigeria was the key example of doing just that, and its federation at independence was destroyed by Nigerians during a subsequent civil war.

Sometimes, my critics simply have a hard time coming to terms with the need for humans to earn their keep. Brandon and Sarkar, for instance, write darkly in their special issue, devoted to rebutting my article: "One of the driving forces of the colonial project at large was the extraction of natural resources and the cheap supply of precious commodities through the labour of the colonized."[39] I cannot think of a more noble aim. The comparative advantage of colonial areas was in resources and commodities and modernization entailed developing those advantages. To their second claim that in doing so, colonial rulers engaged in historically unique forms of brutal treatment of labor, we must distinguish two issues. The use of mandatory ("forced") labor in many colonies was intended as a replacement for taxation and was, of course, historically common in places where taxation was impractical. It may rub our modern sensitivities the wrong way, but this was the most fair and liberal means of providing for public services and infrastructure. Secondly, the "labour question" is whether under colonialism wages were generally rising and conditions of employment were generally improving. The work on wages in British Africa and India, and on employment law and unions shows the answer is "yes," most notably in the careful econometric work done on West Africa.[40]

Digging into their back issues, Brandon and Sarkar reprint twelve articles that they believe substantiate their claim of colonial labor failures. All of them are narrative histories or theoretical forays, rather than scientific inquiries with careful case selection, variable measurement, controls, and estimates. Moreover, most are written by avowed Marxists such as Vijay Prashad.[41] It is not clear what this is supposed to show. No doubt talking about one-hundred and fifty years of ruling half the globe with a rapidly modernizing global economy, diligent anti-colonial labour scholars can sniff out problems like truffle pigs.

One of the back issue articles they cite by Ian Kerr is explicitly written to reject anti-colonial dogmas, in this case, concerning circulating labor groups in India. "The ideal of a harmonious, stable, communitarian Hindu India living in a state of contentment until disrupted by Moslem invasions and British colonialism is a component of Hindutva ideology," Kerr wrote. Rather than singling out the colonial era, labor history in India "must be examined as a related activity."[42]

Junk Citations

This oversight by Brandon and Sarkar points up the common use of unread or misunderstood ("junk") citations by my critics.[43] This issue was reported by Ball in reference to science, where he quoted one study that showed that less than a quarter of citations used in physics were to work which the citing authors had read.[44] One thing that graduate students are supposed to learn is to avoid citing papers they have not read and citing them in a way that does not tell the reader anything about their methods or specific conclusions. "Don't accept a claim just because an authority asserts it," warned Booth and colleagues in their widely-used book on research methods.[45] Yet the practice of bombarding readers with a list of citations that supposedly provide evidence for a claim is widespread among my critics. Indeed, because of their careless nature, these citations are prone, as the Brandon and Sarkar case shows, to show the opposite of what is intended.

Klein, to take another example, writes: "The vast majority of employees of the colonial state were Africans, but those Africans did not necessarily work for colonial rulers because of affection for them (Lawrance, Osborn and Roberts, 2006)." I will return below to the substantive question. But what is this "Lawrance, Osborn and Roberts, 2006" that Klein cites as evidence without telling the reader anything about it? It is an edited collection for which Klein himself wrote the afterword. So by definition it does not take or show any one conclusion, separate from what Klein imposes on it. If there is a "corporate view" of the book, it is surely that of the editors who make clear in their introduction that Africans "used the new opportunities created by colonial conquest and colonial rule to pursue their own agendas even as they served their employers."[46] That certainly does not contravene my claim about the legitimacy of colonial rule.

Junk citations are also rife among the work of other critics. The article by Brandon Kendhammer is entirely made up of them[47] and, since it has been cited so widely by scholars demanding my head, it is worth considering each and every piece of evidence in detail. Granted, his is a newspaper opinion article rather than a scholarly critique. Still, it is worth delving into the volley of citations he uses to bludgeon the reader into acceptance of his claim that "thousands" of studies have reached a "resounding conclusion" of colonialism's harms.

1. Concerning living standards, the Frankema and Waijenburg paper that Kendhammer cites on real wage growth in British colonial Africa 1880 to 1965, which is meant to test the thesis that Africa suffered from impediments to growth due to geography and colonialism, shows instead that both are untrue: "Real wages increased during the colonial era in all of the countries we studied" and such growth rates "were in line and sometimes even outpaced the growth rate of real wages of unskilled workers in London during the nineteenth century."[48]

2. Concerning the rule of law, Kendhammer cites a Berinzon and

Briggs article that shows how seven former French colonies in West Africa retained different amounts of their French legal code from 1955 to 2013. If colonialism were harmful, then those that retained less would be better off. But the opposite is true. Senegal retained by far the most (48 percent) and was by far the best in terms of rule of law as measured by the World Bank governance indicators for 2013 (the year of the study). The correlation overall is 0.26 and rises to 0.93 without Guinea, an unusual case that was violently anti-colonial yet retained more of its colonial legal code by dint of the total dysfunction and aimlessness of the state. The other six countries line up perfectly: the less they retained in 2013, the worse their rule of law.[49]

3. Concerning historiography, Kendhammer suitably cites Frederick Cooper's work on the subject, which pioneered the pushback against anti-colonialism as the "True Cause against which opposition has no legitimate place."[50] Still, Cooper is hardly evidence of the vigorous contest of ideas about colonialism's outcomes because he expressly eschews that question in favor of an emphasis on the process of colonial rule.

4. The "reversal of fortunes" hypothesis than Kendhammer cites approvingly is about how extractive and closed-access political institutions are worse for development than entrepreneurial and open-access ones. No arguments there. What is in question, is whether European colonialism or pre-colonial legacies should be blamed for those institutions. The authors are unsure: European rule in places with extractive and closed-access systems, that had made those places relatively rich prior to the Industrial Revolution, "led to the establishment of, or continuation of already existing, extractive institutions in previously prosperous areas."[51] Either way, their paper implies that intrusive and disruptive colonialism was the best thing, hardly an argument against colonialism.

5. Kendhammer cites Vansina in support of the claim that "Central Africa lost as much as one-third of its population during the early years of colonial rule." Vansina's article is about the cosmology of the peoples of the Western Bantu language group, not about mortality rates relating to colonial rule. Kendhammer is referring to a single sentence where Vansina writes: "Central Africa may have lost half of its population and certainly more than one-third during the conquest."[52] Vansina's citation is to a section of a Harvard study concerning the Belgian Congo colony

founded in 1908.[53] That section is not about the entire swath of Central Africa from the Cameroons to Mozambique. Looking at the reference itself, Vansina himself has misquoted it. The report quotes an earlier report on the Belgian Congo of 1919 which claimed that the population "has been reduced one-half." It quotes this claim in order to state that it is almost certainly false. That is because population estimates for the Belgian Congo varied widely and remained pure guesswork. They were of "little value in drawing any precise conclusions." The only firm conclusion it reached was that population was not increasing. The causes were multiple, including sleeping sickness, inter-tribal warfare, poor nutrition, female trafficking, polygamy, and the working conditions for men in European industrial and commercial enterprises.[54] Kendhammer's vast condemnation of European colonialism as a near-genocidal enterprise thus refers to a study that reaches no such conclusion and, according to a review at the time in the *American Sociological Review*, "is not grounded in sentimental anti-imperialism" given the "not infrequent praise for good results accomplished."[55]

Health and Education

Economic development is closely linked to health and education. Here we see some uninformed attempts to discredit colonialism by taking absolute levels of health and education outcomes in the colonial period and comparing them to absolute levels today. Klein, for instance, writes: "At the time of decolonization, life expectancy in most African countries averaged around or a little above forty years. Today, most African countries have a life expectancy of over sixty years, often well over."[56] Again, while undergraduates may be forgiven, this is an unusual error for a credentialled expert. The standard for judging a governance system is not absolute differences across time—which will always, by definition, be improving because of technological advances and economic globalization—but comparative differences. Were these improving during colonialism faster or slower than the implied global or regional trendline, and what about the rate of improvement before and after the colonial era?

The evidence shows that health and education improved dramatically under colonial rule separate from the gains that would otherwise have happened as a result of technical advance and globalization. For instance, using 284 country-decades 1730 to 1970, Cappelli and Baten showed that British colonialism had a significant and positive effect on human capital as a result of their approach to education, while non-British colonies, taken together, did not (but also did not make it worse).[57] Since the British colonies accounted for three quarters of all the country-years of colonialism, this result has wide implications. Moradi, for instance, was able to construct time-series data on the height of army recruits in Kenya to tease out the distinctive contribution of colonialism. One finding was that "the nutritional status of cohorts born twenty years before and after colonization did not change significantly." The second was that during the colonial period, "expanding health infrastructure, slightly favoring the central region and urban areas, improved the nutritional and health status of most Kenyans." His conclusion: "the net outcome of colonial times was a significant progress in nutrition and health." While anti-colonialism is "fashionable," he noted, it is not supported by evidence.[58]

The governor of the British Gold Coast, Sir Alan Burns, greets players of a local soccer team competing in Victory in Europe Day celebrations in Accra in 1945. Africans fought for and contributed to the colonial war effort. Credit: British West Africa Photographic Service.

Other studies have found a uniform, positive, and large effect of all colonial empires on health and education. For instance, Calvi and Mantovanelli found in a study of 183 Protestant medical missions in 1908, sponsored by the colonial government in India (and located along colonial-built railway lines), that the presence of those missions generated durable long-term improvements in health for Indians through improved hygiene, health behavior, and nutrition.[59]

According to the theoretical model developed by Grossman and Iyigun, the gains in population size and health in the late colonial period created more "leisure" time for anti-colonial activism in Africa and Southeast Asia that may explain decolonization.[60] It is useful to pause to remind ourselves that the arguments I have made thus far in the paper have been described by critics as "Holocaust denialism." Klein also charges that I ignore the fact that "[c]olonial rulers ignored famines."[61] Actually, I did not ignore it. I denied it, at least insofar as I made a passing reference to the general colonial outcome of rising food supply and security and in giving, as an example, food supply under Portuguese rule in what became Guinea-Bissau. While famines occurred, they were never "ignored," even if contemporary critics find efforts insufficient. Tom Young writes: "Whatever we think about Gilley's article, then, the idea that colonialism can be summarized by reference to a gruesome picture of a Congolese peasant, a trite 'what if it happened to you,' scenario, and the cheap trick of its 'tantamount to' Holocaust denial is absurd."[62]

Self-Government

While many people assume that economic benefits dominate arguments for colonialism, it is the formation of states and preparations for self-government that dominated the self-understandings of colonial officials from at least the late nineteenth century onwards. Given that colonialism almost always intruded into alien empires, it enjoyed significant support from local actors. Resistance came from warlords and historic enemies of peoples placed under colonial protection. "In most colonial areas, subject peoples either faced grave security threats from rival groups or they saw the benefits of being governed by a modernized and liberal state," I wrote. Under those circumstances, "foreign control by a liberal state with its own robust accountability mechanisms is the closest that a people with a weak state [could] come to 'local ownership.'"

This is a fundamental point since many critics equate "colonialism" with "illegitimate and coercive rule by the white man." My claim took aim at a central article of faith of anti-colonialism and has thus been the subject of vigorous criticism. "European armies often marched uninvited into someone else's territories," wrote Klein. "[M]any colonial theorists talked about preparing Africans for self-government, but not much was really done."[63]

Again, "uninvited" and "not much" beg for some definition and historical context. What precisely are those words supposed to mean? Klein seems to imagine some UN-sponsored international treaty with agreed upon metrics and constant monitoring and intervention by armies of bureaucrats and advocacy organizations followed on social media. In a statistical study of 143 colonial episodes, the Swedish economist Ola Olsson showed the positive colonial contribution to democracy.[64] A counterpart study by the Danish political scientist Jacob Hariri in a study of 111 countries showed that not to be colonized was to be saddled with an autocratic political system later on.[65] In other words, merely being a colony resulted in a diffusion of democratic norms, laws, and institutions, quite aside from whether the personal efforts of colonial officials in pursuit of self-government met the exacting standards of later scholarly critics.

For that reason, it is puzzling that MacWilliam claims that my article dismisses democracy as a "lower priority"[66] because I note that in many countries "the capacity for effective self-government is lacking and cannot be conjured out of thin-air." To ensure "robust democracy," I argue, requires taking a step back from the feckless pluralism of post-colonial states and to bring in external institutions. Whatever the wisdom of my proposals, they certainly put democracy as one of the central goals of development.

A related issue is the formation of state borders. Lefebvre showed that in contrast to the "axiomatic" claim that African borders had been drawn by high-handed diplomats with no regard to local realities, in fact, there was significant local input and fieldwork done to draw boundaries that accorded with political and economic (but not ethnic) patterns.[67] The appeal by colonial critics to redraw borders along ethnic lines, she argued in a separate article, "had the paradoxical effect of erasing the history of African political structures and the role of the local populations in defining colonial boundaries" and reflected a mistaken and prejudiced view "that the essence of Africans is to be found in their ethnicity."[68] Thus, I wrote, Lefebvre had "noted" the self-contradictions of Africanists who criticize "[n]ew territorial boundaries ... for forcing social integration while old ones are criticized for reinforcing tribalism."

Taylor insists that I have misread Lefebvre: "At no point in her article does she hold that contemporary Africanists contradict themselves."[69] Indeed, the bulk of her article is devoted to the critics of colonial boundaries and their demeaning ethnic essentialism. She says these critics demonstrate "colonial prejudice" that "still haunts much of today's thinking about Africa."[70] In thus criticizing the critics of colonial boundaries as "colonial," Lefebvre exposes the contradictions of being an Africanist: you can be anti-colonial like her by rejecting primordialism, or you can be anti-colonial like those she writes about by embracing primordialism. Taylor is correct that I should not have written that this conclusion is "noted by" Lefebvre. A better phrase would be to say this contradiction is "highlighted by an examination of the work" of Lefebvre since the point being made is mine not hers. I hold, however, that it is a well-grounded and fair interpretation of her work, and that the general point that Africanists contradict themselves by holding two diametrically opposite viewpoints to both be "anti-colonial" remains true.

Other critics took up the "divide and rule" critique of colonial rule in rebutting my claims that colonialism advanced self-government and democracy. Khan, for instance, wrote: "The British exploited differences between the Hindu and Muslim communities in the sub-continent, creating deep resentments and divisions that persist today due to the 1947 Partition. Similarly, differences between the Hutus and Tutsis that led to the Rwandan genocide were created and exploited by Belgian colonizers."[71]

The old saw about "divide and rule" is indeed widely promoted by the likes of Khan who imagine their homelands as integrated, multi-ethnic utopias prior to the White Man. Others argue that existing divisions were institutionalized by colonial rule and but for colonial rule would not have erupted into inter-ethnic conflicts and later problems for democracy as they did. As Muslim League founder Maulana Mohammed Ali remarked during talks in London in 1930: "We divide and you rule. The moment we decide not to divide you will not be able to rule."[72] However, other scholars argue that this is not the case, and that colonial rule reduced, rather than worsened, this threat, and in turn made democracy more, rather than less, likely. In a recent paper making use of a novel experiment in three towns in Rajasthan, India, Latika Chaudhary and colleagues find that colonial institutions left stronger legacies of social cooperation than non-colonial ones.[73] From this latter viewpoint, the "divide and rule" critique of colonial rule was really just a form of nationalist rhetoric masquerading as a victimization claim.

Khan also stipulates a consensus where none exists. On the question of Rwanda and Burundi, for instance, Uvin concluded: "Burundians, Rwandans, and outside specialists of the region *disagree almost totally* on the nature of precolonial society ... [and on] the impact of colonization ... There is no scholarly consensus on answers to these questions."[74]

It is interesting to think that had Ethiopia been under any sustained colonial rule, anti-colonial scholars would by now have produced a vast corpus blaming ethnic conflict between the dominant Amhara and the minority groups like the Tigray and Oromo on the enduring malign legacies of colonial rule. Since no such cop-out exists, they must turn to what are better explanations: bad policies, such as the pastoral land policies in southern Ethiopia studied by Tache and Oba and bad governance, such as the failure to implement decentralization studied by Mengisteab.[75] Denied the "Colonialism Made Me Do It" explanation, scholars of Ethiopia instead provide more compelling explanations of that country's plight.

Colonial Violence

The study of violent encounters between colonial police or military forces and various native rivals forms a cornerstone of much anti-colonial historiography. Such encounters are usually highlighted in order to make the general claim that colonialism was illegitimate and criminal.

In the article, I make only a brief mention of colonial violence because, in most cases, I believe it was justified and in cases where it was not, it never rose to a level that rendered colonial rule, as such, illegitimate. In the oft-cited case of the Herero war against German colonial rule in German Southwest Africa from 1904 to 1906, for instance, the initial German response was justified and restrained.[76] Only later, with a shift in battle strategy on the ground under Lothar von Trotha, did the German campaign become unintentionally brutal. The changed strategy, wrote Kuss, "emerged entirely independently of any conscious decision for or against a strategy of concerted racial genocide." Trotha, she argued, "did not intend to bring about a situation in which the Herero would be subject to a slow death through adverse natural conditions."[77] In subsequent research, I showed that the loss of life in the Herero (and Nama) populations has been vastly exaggerated.[78]

Another example is the historiography of the Mau Mau rebellion in colonial Kenya in the late 1950s. As I wrote: "[A]ny claim about ... the level of colonial violence, requires not just assumptions about the scale of violence that would have occurred absent colonial rule but also a careful measure of that violence relative to the population, security threat, and security resources in a given territory. One is hard-pressed, to take a prominent example, to find a single example of such care in measurement in the vast critical scholarship on the British counter-insurgency campaign against the Mau Mau ... At the very least, it is incumbent on scholars to show that the brutalities unleashed by the British in this campaign were not the likely result of a proportionate response given the context and scale of the threat. If this supposedly solid case is wobbly, what does it tell us about the lesser "violence" often cited as invalidating colonialism?"

Taylor states that I provide "no reason" for my claims about scholarship on the Mau Mau and this in turn "sheds no light on the quality of the scholarship on other instances of colonial violence."[79] But I cite the work of Elkins as failing this minimal standard and use the glowing reception of her work as evidence that the standards of research on colonial violence are hopelessly unscientific and biased. Is this not a reason and does it shed no light? Were I writing today, I would add two later books that debunk the idea of a Mau Mau genocide through the use (not abuse) of primary sources.[80]

A failure to confront the "colonialism compared to what?" question is evident when critics cite "the Amritsar massacre."[81] For instance, the Library of Congress catalogue lists no fewer than thirty books written about the 379 people killed by a British detachment at Amritsar (or Jallianwala Bagh, India) in 1919. Much less, by contrast, is written about pre-colonial or post-colonial massacres in these countries, including those committed by government forces. It is not just that there have been several massacres at Amritsar both before and after colonial rule which took far more lives. The general question is: did tragedies like the one in 1919 become more or less likely as a result of British rule? Simply scouring colonial history for "bad stuff" proves nothing, and indeed the fact that colonial governments so scrupulously documented the "bad stuff" bespeaks an accountability and transparency that was missing before and after colonial rule. Scholars who prefer to spend many delightful hours at the Public Records Office at Kew rather than in the trying and dysfunctional conditions of archives in post-colonial countries (if they even exist and are accessible) are falling victim to a colonial archives fetish.

Kendhammer also states that 90 percent of Africa's conflicts are attributable to colonial rule while only 10 percent have their origins in the pre-colonial period. His junk citation here is to the work of Leonard and Strauss.[82] For a start, their explanation is threefold: colonialism, the post-colonial international system, and enclave economies, the latter two of which are not colonial legacies but legacies of Africa's encounter with the outside world. Moreover, only nine of the thirty-seven cases they consider have enclave economies. If colonialism created weak states via enclave economies, why didn't post-colonial rules change that? Scholars have so trained themselves in structural determinism that they dare not ask such questions.

In any case, Kendhammer misstates the *central claim* of Leonard and Strauss: they state that 90 percent of countries with ethnic conflicts, not 90 percent of ethnic conflicts, can "most often" be traced to colonial, not pre-colonial causes.[83] More important, he cites them without seeming to recognize that they merely assert this claim without any evidence, not even a junk citation to alleged evidence. To foreclose the discussion, they declare that "almost no contemporary conflicts correspond to ones found in precolonial times" and that attempts to show otherwise are "racist" and "offensive."[84] Much work has shown the opposite: the overwhelming causal role of pre-colonial ethnic formations ("tribalism") on contemporary African conflict, as in the work using a new dataset of pre-colonial formations constructed by Paine.[85]

This is in addition to the mainstream attention among conflict scholars to postcolonial decision-making by African elites. In other words, the "unsophisticated" and "racist" popular perception of Africa as wracked by pre-colonial tribalism and post-colonial corrupt rulers—notions that scholars take it upon themselves to beat out of their students—turns out to be a pretty good explanation. Klein writes that "[m]any of the students who enter our classes do so with ideas similar to Gilley's."[86] Perhaps we should give those students the podium and ask the professors to find a seat.

Concepts and Anchoring Vignettes

A common problem for historians and many social scientists is the failure to define concepts in a way that they could be properly measured. The sweeping and emotionally-charged denunciations of colonialism by many critics of my paper leave the reader puzzling about how they are defining their terms, what evidence they would use to measure them, and how they reach the conclusions they do. Klein, for example, offers a blanket summary of colonialism as "authoritarian, racist and often stagnant."[87]

If you are already predisposed to accept that characterization, I suppose you thump the desk with "Here, here!" and then cite Klein's article as "evidence" that colonial rule was authoritarian, racist, and often stagnant. If not, then you ask: "by what standard?" Compared to the pre-colonial era and the likely counterfactual (as shown in Ethiopia, Saudi Arabia, or Haiti)? Certainly not. Compared to what colonial powers could have achieved if they had tried harder or done a better job? Doubtful given the constraints of the era, which Klein seems to magically wish away with his calls for more spending, education, and intrusive governance. Compared to what came after colonialism? No, with very few exceptions. So what exactly does his statement mean?

If the history profession still considers itself a social science that approaches questions and makes claims based on logic, evidence, and shared standards of justification—as opposed to being a branch of literary theory devoted to moralizing and flights of emotional fancy—then his statement is false.

Similarly, Kendhammer, in a typical imputation, charges me with ignoring the "violence, discrimination, and repression" of colonial rule. I am not sure how to respond to such blanket indictments, except to say: please define your terms. A key role for the historian, or social scientist, is to ensure that concepts like "discrimination" do not become useless through free-form interpretation using modern norms. Gary King and colleagues, for instance, have shown the importance of using "anchoring vignettes" so that concepts have validity when used in social research.[88] In the case of studying forms of political rule that are a century or more in the past and involve cultural contexts none of us could imagine, anchoring a concept like "violence" or "discrimination" or "racism" takes on major significance.

To make an obvious point, most contemporary scholars in the social sciences and humanities consider their own liberal democracies to be rife with "violence," "racism," and "exploitation" by ruling systems. What possible chance is there that they could reach an objective assessment of colonial ruling systems?

Slavery

Klein allows that one of "the few things" I get right in my paper is that colonialism ended the slave trade and with it much of slavery itself,[89] recalling the folk memories he uncovered during his doctoral research in Senegal in the 1960s. British legal abolition of the slave trade came in 1807 and of slavery itself in 1834, so anti-slavery activism is one of the fundamental shifts that defined post-1824 colonialism that my paper defends. Actually, my claim in this paragraph is not so much about the ending of the slave trade—which is beyond dispute—but about how contemporary anti-colonial critics faced with this fact "squirm and fidget ... because it puts the greatest strain on their 'colonialism bad' perspective."

Khan, in her critique, illustrates the point. She insists that the claim that colonialism brought an end to slave-trading is "ridiculous" because pre-1824 colonialism was also responsible for its expansion: "Colonizers ... created the slave trade. Systematic decolonization and subsequent wars of independence eventually ended the slave trade."[90] She makes logical and empirical mistakes, both whoppers really. Early and late colonialism were different phenomenon, which, as a result, had different effects. As to the empirical question, in addition to being unsupported by any research I am aware of, her claim is flatly contradicted by that old friend of the historian: chronology. Most slavery had disappeared by the mid-nineteenth to late-nineteenth century as a result of imperial expansion. Independence did not come for a century. How can a cause come a century after an effect? Khan's claim here is simply untenable.

Oddly, one of the fidgeters I cite is Klein himself, who in an introduction to an edited volume with a co-editor wrote of the "flaws and hypocrisies of colonial policies" that "compromise with their principles" for a variety of practical reasons.[91] Although I did not cite these passages, they are indeed as good as any in showing the utopian and unrealistic ways that scholars approach questions relating to colonialism. What a luxury it is to sit in one's study poo-pooing the "compromises" and "flaws" of complex governance questions of two centuries ago, never admitting the possibility, much less adopting an analytical lens to understand normative judgements. Like Khan, Klein makes my point all too well.

Finally, Kendhammer, as well as Taylor, cites evidence on the negative consequences of the slave trade for Africa as an argument against colonialism, again either ignoring my focus on post-1824 colonialism or simply deciding that all alleged crimes of the West need to be thrown into the hamper when the argument requires it. Kendhammer again undermines his claim with a junk citation to Nunn and Wantchekon. Actually, their paper is not about the negative effects of only "the transatlantic slave trade," as Kendhammer writes, but the negative effects of "Africa's four slave trades (the transatlantic, Indian Ocean, Red Sea, and trans-Saharan) between 1400 and 1900," even though data is available only on the first two. Delving deeper, Kendhammer (and Taylor) misses the main finding: slavery explains almost nothing of contemporary social trust levels in Africa, despite the article's title "The Slave Trade and the Origins of Mistrust in Africa." The magnitude of negative effects of slavery is *very* small, ranging from a standardized coefficient of 0.10 to 0.16 (in other words, just barely below the average and well within the normal range of social trust in places *unaffected* by the slave trade). As the authors insisted heroically in an unpublished version of the paper: "These effects are not enormous, but they are not trivial either."[92] As to the strength of the relationship when controlling for other factors, it is indeed trivial. The contribution of slave exports to overall explained variation is between one and two percent, in effect a rounding error.[93] Again, junk citations intended to pummel the reader into agreement can go disastrously wrong in the hands of ideological reasoning.

Taylor cites a different work by Nunn on "A Model Linking Africa's Past to Its Current Underdevelopment."[94] It posits that the slave trade and colonial rule forced Africans out of productive labor and into unproductive activities like banditry, migration, and government jobs, which caused path-dependent effects on future development. I do not want to gainsay Nunn's rigorous and important paper, except to say that when he delved into the former (and allegedly worst) period, the effects turned out to be minimal. There is also, as mentioned, a robust econometric literature cited above showing the opposite. A World Bank study argued that, unlike India, Africa's "relative weakness or absence of states, classes, literacy and cities" in the pre-colonial period critically explained its inability to productively embrace and engage with colonial institutions.[95] Again, to make my main point without taking sides: claiming that my paper is "discredited" or "offensive" is to ignore the significant debates and research in which it is squarely situated.

Costs and Benefits

In assailing my reference to the "objective costs/benefits" approach, many critics fly off the handle. Brandon and Sarkar write: "How many miles of railroad built by the colonial powers or children educated in missionary schools equate to the worsening effects of the El Niño famines by imperial policies, the indignities produced through the application of scientific racism, or the systematic employment of torture in the Algerian War?"[96] Actually, I don't know, but it is a good question, especially once one discounts the reference to the work of the Marxist union activist Mike Davis claiming that nineteenth century global droughts were, in the mocking words of agricultural economist Vaclav

Smil, "murderous global conspiracies planned and executed by a small number of zealots from the smoggy capital of Victorian England."[97] My guess is that many colonial subjects would prefer the life-saving gains of education and infrastructure even after taking into account the indignities of petty racism or the excesses of justified counter-insurgency operations.

Critics like Kendhammer tend to use "cost-benefit analysis" as a byword for "cold-hearted and utilitarian calculations based on money" or some such vague characterization. They have little idea about this policy analysis method. If they understood it better, they would know that its main purpose is to elucidate the implications of different scope, weighting, and valuation strategies in policy analysis mainly for the purpose of stress-testing hypotheses and double-checking other methods. As I wrote: "One main challenge of this research is to properly enumerate the things that matter and then to assign them weights, weights that presumably vary with time and place." Critics studiously ignored my direct quotation from Abernethy that there is, at minimum, a plausible cost/benefit strategy under which "the case for colonialism is strong."[98] I can only assume that they worried that my argument might benefit from its clear appeal to such a reputable scholar. By rushing to the blackboard to scribble down the most outraged reference they can recall on the "costs" side, whatever its dubious quality, they make my point more eloquently than I could have.

Legitimacy

Khan prefaces her critique of my article to declare that it is "offensive."[99] I'm not sure what that means or why it is relevant. But one aspect of the article that clearly gave offense to anti-colonial critics was my claim that colonialism was by and large subjectively legitimate among the colonized. The reason this gave offense, I have since learned, is that many scholars define colonialism as illegitimate alien rule, thus foreclosing the empirical study of its legitimacy by definitional fiat. To even suggest that colonialism was sometimes or often empirically legitimate was, for these scholars, to debunk their preferred concept of colonialism altogether and thus to open their work to unwelcome scientific scrutiny. The relevant paragraph in the article read: "Millions of people moved closer to areas of more intensive colonial rule, sent their children to colonial schools and hospitals, went beyond the call of duty in positions in colonial governments, reported crimes to colonial police, migrated from non-colonized to colonized areas, fought for colonial armies, and participated in colonial political processes—all relatively voluntary acts. Indeed, the rapid spread and persistence of Western colonialism with very little force relative to the populations and areas concerned is *prima facie* evidence of its acceptance by subject populations compared to the feasible alternatives ... In most colonial areas, subject peoples either faced grave security threats from rival groups or they saw the benefits of being governed by a modernized and liberal state."

This general description was given personal testimony at an Oxford seminar on my paper held in 2018 where the former British colonial official in Sudan and Northern Rhodesia, Philip Bowcock, recalled his time as one of a mere handful of British colonial officers in Sudan: "If they did not want us, there is no way we could have been there. There were only 143 of us in Sudan. I slept outside at night. Anyone could have killed me easily. Instead, they welcomed us."[100]

The Malaysian Chinese writer S.G. Cheah wrote in response to my essay that her grandfather's decision to leave China for colonial Malaya was a deliberate endorsement of British colonialism over Manchu tyranny: "Modern day critics of colonialism over-emphasize their own frame of reference as they make their case, and in doing so, drown out the bulk of the voices of those who lived through that experience firsthand... When the question was asked of my father, why the Chinese immigrants did not have any qualms about 'shedding their Chinese identity' in favor of adopting the fashions and behaviors of the British, his answer, I paraphrase, was: 'The Chinese were more than happy to don themselves with Western clothing, because they saw it as a form of liberation after their horrific existence under the Manchu Emperor.'"[101]

My quotation of a young black man in Congo from van Reybrouck—"When are the Belgians coming back?" which he reports was "a widely heard lament" that he heard "countless times" when he was there in 2010[102]— has invariably been put into my mouth by critics like Brandon and Sarkar[103] as well as by my university's hysterical faculty union.[104] They clearly cannot face the fact that many former colonial peoples wish their countries could return to colonial rule. Colonial rule was for these people not some philosophical idea but a practical alternative that needed to be weighed against other practical alternatives and was often found less wanting in comparison. Such "dangerous thoughts" clearly need to be policed by the scolds in the faculty lounge lest they become widely known. The same response occurred when, during a talk, I cited the words of a woman belonging to the Habe sub-group of the Muslim

Hausas in the slave-based Sokoto Caliphate of the Fulani in what is today northern Nigeria on the coming of the British: "We Habe wanted them to come, it was the Fulani who did not like it," she recalled.[105] Bjerk charged me with ignoring the "complexity" of this response because the Fulani remained politically powerful under the British and slavery did not disappear at once.[106] But I never claimed otherwise, only that this reduced form under British colonialism was preferable to the Habe than its pre-colonial form. Why is that so hard to accept?

Klein admits that African support for colonial rule was another thing that I (sort of) got right. But he seems confused about the concept of legitimacy, which is simply the degree to which a political object is treated by those subject to its power as rightfully holding and exercising that power, a topic on which I have done conceptual and empirical research.[107] As an empirical concept, legitimacy: (1) admits of degrees; and (2) can be measured only through behavioral and attitudinal responses of the subjects themselves, who are alone in a position to judge in light of contextual factors.

While admitting that "the vast majority of employees of the colonial state were Africans" Klein hastens to add that "those Africans did not necessarily work for colonial rulers because of affection for them."[108] I am not sure what he means by "affection" but it is certainly not what I meant by "legitimacy." I doubt we would ever want people to "love" their rulers or hold them in "affection." They should love their families, their neighbors, and their gods. Africans may not have "loved" colonial rulers but they often treated them as legitimate—the preferable alternative compared to other feasible options.

Klein cites my discipline of political science to show how I "should know" that interests, not ideas, motivate individuals. Actually, that is not the only way political scientists view the world, even if it is the outlook of Marxists in our discipline. Legitimacy is not a rationalization of self-interest but a wholly different concept, embedded in ideas of fairness and truth that, if anything, define "self-interest" more than vice versa. While we are a long way from being able to measure levels of consent and legitimacy in various times and places during the colonial era, the fact that colonial rule existed in so many places with a trifling overall presence and even less coercive force and was staffed mostly by natives is *ipso facto* evidence of its legitimacy.

I am not the only scholar who sees substantial evidence of the legitimacy of colonial rule. It is a truism that colonial rule depended on native collaboration and cooperation, a theory first propounded by

Robinson faced with the brute fact that there were hardly any Europeans in most colonies relative to population and geography.[109] Yet anti-colonial scholars have been slow to admit the role of indigenous agency and to abandon their Eurocentric perspective on colonialism, preferring "helpless victims" rather than active participants, as the editors of one recent collection on various case studies of native collaboration argue.[110]

A soccer team in colonial Hong Kong, 1923. Credit: Frank and Frances Carpenter Collection, Library of Congress.

This leaves two issues: the balance of cooperation and coercion; and the extent to which cooperation was based on prudential and self-interested calculations or ethically-grounded moral evaluations. Scholars struggle to handle these issues in anything except impressionistic, untheorized, and ultimately ideological ways. Bührer and colleagues, for instance, insist confusingly that cooperation and coercion were "often two sides of the same coin" and that most cooperation was simply prudential. In those rare cases where cooperators "internalized colonial normative discourses,"[111] this too should be treated as coercion, but of the mind rather than the body. Thus, by definitional fiat they make impossible any finding of legitimacy. Other scholars can then junk cite their work as "evidence" that there was no legitimacy. Any suggestion to the contrary is "offensive."

Taylor charges that I misuse Hechter's analysis of the conditions under which alien rule can be legitimate. Hechter's work, I reported, showed that "alien rule has often been legitimate in world history because it has provided better governance than the indigenous alternative." I did not state that Hechter believes that alien rule has usually been legitimate, indeed he states clearly that he thinks it has not because of the very demanding conditions legitimacy requires for alien rule.[112] But his work is a theoretical not a general empirical study. Whether he is right about the empirical claim when applied to modern colonialism is separate from his theoretical analysis, which he illustrates with respect to three cases of legitimate alien rule, two of which are examples of British colonialism (in Hong Kong and Shanghai). Does this imply, as Taylor writes, that "the correct conclusion to draw from Hechter's work is thus that that colonial rule is almost always illegitimate?"[113] Hardly.

The general point is this: absent any minimally empirically robust general measurement of subjective legitimacy in the colonial era, we are left with the default assumption that given the ease of its spread and the minimal degree of coercion and coercive forces relative to time, population, and geography, the standing assumption must remain that colonial rule was highly legitimate, a fact reinforced by the tumult that followed colonial rule, especially in Africa. The only way to upset that conclusion, absent empirical evidence, is to rule out legitimacy by definition, and not surprisingly, this is precisely the strategy that scholars have adopted. Having definitionally ruled out the legitimacy of colonialism, scholars have to sweep under the carpet any unauthorized emanations of legitimacy from the colonized. This was my finding in a 2016 paper on the Nigerian novelist Chinua Achebe, whose naughty pro-colonial utterances have been studiously airbrushed from scholarly memory.[114]

Several critics were peeved by my quotation of the autobiography of Congo's first prime minister, Patrice Lumumba, published in French in 1961 just months before he was killed (and in English posthumously in 1962). In it, he praised Belgian colonial rule for "restoring our human dignity" and "turning us into free, happy, vigorous, and civilized men."[115] As someone celebrated as an anti-colonial hero in the contemporary academy, it is often forgotten that Lumumba was an active "collaborator" in Belgian colonial rule by any measure: a postal clerk, the head of a local trade federation, and an insider in colonial society as head of Stanleyville's Association des Évolués. His book was written in 1956, a year before anyone even talked about creating an independent country. Taylor insists that "there is considerable doubt as to whether it represents Lumumba's true views."[116] Where is the evidence of this "considerable doubt"? I know of none. While scholars have speculated about why Lumumba suddenly became an anti-colonial radical, no one doubts that he saw himself as a moderate and as a supporter of Belgian colonial institutions during the colonial era. As Catherine Hoskyns, who undertook a study of the first post-colonial Congo crisis for the Royal Institute of International Affairs in 1962 to 1964,[117] wrote reviewing the book: "Those who expect from it an exposition of the dynamic nationalism for which he is now the symbol will be disappointed. Lumumba at that time was a self-conscious évolué and an exponent of gradualism, much more concerned to mediate between the Belgian colonial system and the mass of Congolese peasants than to demand immediate independence."[118]

The Achebe and Lumumba examples highlight the trained incapacity of contemporary scholars to imagine, much less acknowledge, evidence of the subjective legitimacy of European colonial rule. With that as background, it is hardly surprising that they found my suggestion to the contrary to be "offensive."

Decolonization

Despite characterizing my article as "seriously flawed," Klein admits that, in addition to colonialism's role in the abolition of slavery, the participation of natives in colonial rule, and the many problems of post-colonial governments, another thing I got right was that "African nationalists often did not have massive support."[119] As Tom Young noted in passing, "This seems rather a lot to be right about."[120] Lumumba's party, for example, won only 24 percent of seats in the first election in Congo of 1960. Most Congolese, especially traditional leaders, saw him as a threat. But under pressure from the UN and the Cold War, the Europeans handed over power to such political neophytes with little knowledge of or support from the countries they claimed to represent. It was a disaster, not just in Africa, but also in South Asia, the Middle East, and Southeast Asia. Klein coyly allows that "a lot of unpleasant things have happened since the end of colonial rule."[121] Might we too be tempted to call this understatement about a half century of human misery caused by decolonization a form of Holocaust denial?

Kendhammer takes the normal route for scholars in blaming the disaster on colonialism. As he writes: "many of the post-colonial world's economic and political difficulties (including corruption, poor economic productivity and violence) are directly linked to colonialism and the geopolitical system it created." An ontological issue that none of my critics grapple with is that every historical phenomenon is by definition rooted descriptively in historical antecedents which, in the case of former colonies, are by definition colonial. So, yes, the post-colonial disasters are "directly linked" to the colonial era, just as the colonial era is "directly linked" to the pre-colonial era. That tells us nothing about causes, counterfactuals, and where the blame lies. My paper lays the blame for this disaster squarely on the nationalist leaders and their post-colonial leadership, as well as on Cold War pressures to decolonize.

Kendhammer offers two junk citations to bolster his claim. One is Nunn's 2007 paper discussed above which, as mentioned, hardly offers evidence for the depredations of colonial rule. The other is Bates' 2010 revision of his book *Prosperity and Violence*.[122] For the life of me, I cannot see how this reference substantiates Kendhammer's claim since it is a general study of state formation. More typically, Bates is a scholar whose work on Africa has repeatedly emphasized pre-colonial social structures and post-colonial policy choices—not colonialism—as determinative. His more pertinent book, on state breakdown in Africa after the colonial period, makes this clear: "When thinking about the origins of political disorder in Africa, I can find no way of analyzing the origins of insurrection without starting with the behavior of governments. The conditions that led to the breakdown of order in Africa include the authoritarian nature of its states and their rulers' penchant for predation."[123]

Khan is another critic who claims I get decolonization wrong because of my claim that it was "sudden." This is "empirically inaccurate," she insists, because India's independence "can be dated to the 1840s, when calls for independence from the British began" while "Algerian calls for independence from French rule date back to World War I." Thus: "This may be news to Gilley but decades of emancipatory struggles is not 'sudden.'" Note, first, her description of these struggles as "emancipatory," as if it is a truism that colonialism was oppressive and independence was freedom-giving. Putting that aside, my claim is that the process of going from colony to independent state was a sudden and largely unexpected movement in most places, whatever the decades of "calls" that preceded it. As noted, when Lumumba wrote his autobiography in 1956, no one was even talking about independence. Four years later, a country was birthed. The same story could be told of dozens of colonies. When Julius Nyerere testified at the United Nations in 1955, he estimated that Tanganyika would require another twenty years before it was ready for independence. Instead, it came like a firecracker in 1961. Throughout the 1950s, British policymakers talked of a renewal and expansion of empire, a fact too often obscured by the retrospective lens of knowing that this did not happen, as the papers in an edited volume by Lynn showed.[124] This may be news to Khan, but the view that decolonization was unexpected and sudden is the overwhelming consensus of those who were there.

Bring Back Colonialism

In my discussion of the three modes of reviving colonialism—through colonial governance forms, sovereignty-sharing with advanced countries, and the creation of charter cities—I make clear that the precondition for any such shift is "the consent of the colonized." Given my view that colonialism itself enjoyed considerable consent and legitimacy, this condition is not applied in order to make a break with the past but to be consistent with it. Khan, among others, rejects any such arrangements on the grounds of "the repressive nature of colonialism and the avenues it provides for gross violation of human rights." I am not sure which liberal and rights-abiding post-colonial states she has in mind, or why she believes that rule by advanced countries makes this less likely, but if she has in mind her native Pakistan, then I believe my case is made.

Others simply doubt whether the consent of the colonized could ever be secured, and I agree with them that this is a tall order, as it was in colonial times. As I write: "at least in the initial phases, legitimacy will be demonstrated not by the holding of a plebiscite or by the support of organized and broadly representative groups, but simply by the ability of the intervening state to win compliance from key actors and get the job done."

I cite the work of Sèbe[125] on "the resurgence of official and social respect" for "the founding figures of Western colonialism in Africa" to suggest that his concept of "cosmopolitan nation-building" that embraces the colonial past fits well with the revival of colonialism I am proposing. Several scholars, including Sèbe himself, have taken issue with my use of his work to reach conclusions not authorized by post-colonial groupthink. Sèbe, who declares my essay "deeply objectionable" on moral grounds, claims I make "selective use" of and "misrepresent" his article.[126] But his critique is not about my use of the facts he cites but only about reaching different conclusions about the implications, admittedly a distinction I could have made more clear. As he wrote: "While my research certainly offered an innovative framework of interpretation in an attempt to make sense of the resurgence of European imperial heroes in Africa, my argument that this new trend reflects a 'post-racial form of cosmopolitan nation-building' cannot be interpreted in any way as supporting, implicitly or explicitly, a 'case for colonialism.'"[127] I beg to differ. Khan charges that I ignore the "complex and multi-layered" conclusions reached by Sèbe and that my article "blatantly ignores postcolonial scholarship."[128] Again, if my error is to have reached conclusions that differ from those of Sèbe about the facts he uncovers, and in doing so steered clear of the jargon-ridden and ideologically-charged "post-colonial scholarship," then I plead blessedly guilty as charged.

Like other "studies" fields introduced in the 1960s with explicit and mandatory ideological doxologies, "post-colonial studies" is a field that lacks scientific conditions like falsifiability, openness to new data, and intellectual pluralism. Rodriguez too charges me with not adopting a post-colonial perspective, including the requisite denunciations of capitalism, pollution, and mental health issues in the West. "The problem with Gilley's case for colonialism is the lack of rigor, his inability or unwillingness to vigorously and transparently challenge his own beliefs, values, and fears—in a word, his perspective."[129] I will not claim to be superhuman in transcending my perspective. I would ask, however, whether the same strictures apply to my critics, including Rodriguez. Has he so fully internalized Third World victimology and hatred of the West (where he lives) that his own perspective, too, has become an obstacle to truth? Isn't the point of science to question perspectives?

Criticisms of my discussion of the human catastrophe that became Guinea-Bissau after the flight of Portuguese rulers are particularly instructive. MacWilliam charges that I fail to provide "any detail on its colonial condition" and do not consider the possibility that "the character of Portuguese colonialism had anything to do with" its anti-colonial disaster.[130] Actually I have quite a bit to say about its colonial condition, a full 433 words, practically a treatise given the word count limitations of the article. The direction of that discussion is made clear in those 433 words: Portuguese rule brought stability, new institutions, market relations, and growing health and food supply, all of which created a necessary beginning for any hopes of a viable country. It had ruled only since 1936, with a world war that delayed any efforts at governance until Portugal's First Development Plan of 1953. In the colony's budgets for 1952 and 1953, infrastructure accounted for 27 percent of spending, health for 25 percent, and police and military for 19 percent.[131] Portugal itself was an impoverished country at the time and was an authoritarian regime until 1974. This, MacWilliam argues, "would not seem to fit the description of liberal colonial governance." Why not? Despite the blanket description of "authoritarian regime," Portugal in the postwar era was characterized by plural institutions that laid the foundations for its successful transition to democracy. Given its small size, Portuguese Guinea had only a small advisory council to the governor rather than a legislature. It was run much like Hong Kong a generation earlier. I was quite intentional in choosing this colony because it was ruled by a relatively illiberal and poor European nation with a bad reputation compared to Britain and France. Choosing the Bahamas or Botswana would make the argument easy. Instead, I chose a hard case and found the case for colonialism no less compelling.

As to whether Portugal's comparatively executive-run and undemocratic rule of the colony in the 1950s explains the militancy of its opposition, much depends on how we explain the behavior of nationalist leader Amilcar Cabral. If he had grown up under the boot of Portuguese colonialists and faced repression, one might make a case. But none of that is true. I offer Chabal's description of his behavior:

> He was a Cape Verdean agronomist, born in Guinea in 1924, and educated in Portugal where he had been a brilliant student. He was at the time regarded as a young and promising engineer. He had published widely in his field and was highly regarded by his Portuguese colleagues. Unknown to them, however, he had steeped himself into political and social literature while a student in Lisbon. He had become thoroughly acquainted with the cultural movements (most notably Negritude) which had led so many privileged and educated young Africans to 'return to their African roots'. Unlike many, however, he had become determined to go beyond this cultural revolt and to seek an end to colonialism by political means.[132]

This speaks to a more general point about the dirty laundry of anti-colonial nationalists who despoiled the countries they claimed to "liberate." Most of their ideas and violence were hatched among radicals in Europe who exported anti-colonialism with a missionary vigor. The many scholars who celebrate the central role of Paris, Berlin, Moscow, and London in creating and exporting anti-colonial ideology reveal quite clearly its lack of indigenous roots. That many colonial subjects became addicted to claims that all would be paradise if they ousted colonial rulers was not a surprise. But blaming it on the colonial system itself is to get things exactly backward. MacWilliam is correct that I do not believe that "the character of Portuguese colonialism had anything to do with" its anti-colonial movement. If Portugal is at fault, it is the radicals in the cafes of Lisbon who should be blamed.

Academic Standards

While scholarly debate is central to the academic vocation, the critiques lodged against "The Case for Colonialism" discussed above have been used by scholars to seek to censor and punish me as a professional. While some of the critics make clear that they oppose such censorship, they contribute to an eco-system in which this is the predictable result. By engaging in such shoddy and erroneous critiques, they make it possible for others to claim that my article fails "academic standards." The main instances in which these criticisms have been used include:

(1) Farhana Sultana of Syracuse University, who started one of the petitions calling for the article to be retracted and for Princeton to revoke my Ph.D., cited the critiques by Khan and Kendhammer. She argued that it "downplayed or overlooked colonialism's legacies, cherry-picked data, was full of historical inaccuracies and misrepresentations, poorly researched, and distorted truths." As such, it was "hate speech" and "Holocaust denialism." In the future, "instruments and systems" should be put in place to silence people like me.[133]

(2) The publisher Rowman & Littlefield cited the critiques of Khan in order to justify a cancellation of a book series I was supposed to co-edit for them.[134]

(3) Hamid Dabashi of Columbia University citing the many critiques of my "shoddy scholarship" called for me to be "treated with utter disgust, with unsurpassed revulsion. He must be ostracized, publicly shamed and humiliated."[135] His ayatollah-like emanation is still difficult to credit.

(4) The chair of my home department, Melody Valdini, cited the work of Brandon and Sarkar as well as Rodriguez in an attempt to deny my post-tenure review in 2020, seeking to overturn a positive assessment by my senior colleagues. As she wrote citing Rodriguez: "The fundamental issue with Dr. Gilley's research is his lack of an open-minded, scientific approach."

(5) Kanika Batra of Texas Tech University cited the critiques of Khan and Kendhammer in an attempt to have a talk I was giving at Texas Tech cancelled.[136]

(6) The faculty union at my home institution led by "academic freedom" director Jennifer Ruth, a film studies professor, issued an official censure of my work, citing "the overwhelming consensus among our colleagues who are experts in history and political science that Gilley's research is not merely unpopular but rather discredited."[137] Ruth

and Penn State professor of English Michael Bérubé later published a book-length attack on me and other scholars who have dissented from their Maoist orthodoxies demanding that we be fired for violating "academic freedom."[138]

(7) Tanya Lyons of Flinders University, in introducing her two commissioned critiques of Klein and MacWilliam in the *Australasian Review of African Studies*, joined in efforts to have my article censored through one of many petitions, and "specifically advised our membership not to raise the metrics of the *TWQ* article or journal by clicking on their DOI or URL."[139]

Summary of Lessons

The response to "The Case for Colonialism" is a black eye for the academy. In addition to censorious petitions, no-platform attempts, and professional punishments, scholars who took up the task of rebutting the arguments proved only how deeply the problems the paper addresses reside. Those scholars who insisted on rebuttal engaged in dishonest and shoddy engagement with the question, showing their motivations were no different from those acting as outright censors. If this is the "scholarly" response that anyone pointing out anomalies in the anti-colonial paradigm is likely to receive, how can scholars of colonialism in good faith consider anything that they write to be scientifically valid? The field has become a cult, not a place of science. Those not willing to participate in the cult will choose other subjects. And the human costs of anti-colonialism will continue to be borne by those least able to respond.

Endnotes:

1 Bruce Gilley, "The Case for Colonialism," *Academic Questions* (2018).
2 Chinua Achebe, *There Was a Country: A Personal History of Biafra* (2012).
3 Bruce Gilley, "Chinua Achebe on the Positive Legacies of Colonialism," *African Affairs* (2012).
4 Bruce Gilley, *The Last Imperialist: Sir Alan Burns' Epic Defense of the British Empire* (2021).
5 Bruce Gilley, "The Challenge of the Creative Third World," *Third World Quarterly* (2015).
6 John Narayan and Leon Sealey-Huggins, "Whatever Happened to the Idea of Imperialism?" *Third World Quarterly* (2017).
7 Bruce Gilley, "How the Hate Mob Tried to Silence Me," *Standpoint*, November 27, 2017.
8 Akinbode Fasakin, "The Coloniality of Power in Postcolonial Africa: Experiences From Nigeria," *Third World Quarterly* (2021).
9 David Abernethy, *The Dynamics of Global Dominance: European Overseas Empires 1415-1980* (2000), 81.
10 Martin Klein, "A Critique of Colonial Rule: A Response to Bruce Gilley," *Australasian Review of African Studies* (2018), 40.
11 Ibid., 43.
12 Pepijin Brandon and Aditya Sarkar, "Labour History and the Case against Colonialism," *International Review of Social History* (2019).
13 Scott MacWilliam, "Africa's Past Invented to Serve Development's Uncertain Future," *Australasian Review of African Studies* (2018), 15.
14 Adam Hochschild, *King Leopold's Ghost: A Story of Greed, Terror, and Heroism in Colonial Africa* (1998), 87.
15 Félicien Cattier, *Étude sur la situation de l'État indépendant du Congo* (1906), 341.
16 Alexander De Juan and Jan Kenryk Pierskalla, "The Comparative Politics of Colonialism and Its Legacies: An Introduction," *Politics & Society* (2017).
17 Bruce Gilley, "Contributions of Western Colonialism to Human Flourishing: A Research Bibliography," ResearchGate, Version 3.0 (2020).
18 Rigmar Osterkamp, "A Sober View of Bruce Gilley's 'The Case for Colonialism,'" *CCR Spectrum* (2021).
19 Sahar Khan, "The Case Against 'The Case for Colonialism,'" *CATO Institute Commentary*, September 19, 2017; Sahar Khan, "Libertarians Shouldn't Accept the Case for Colonialism," *CATO Unbound*, October 9, 2017.
20 Walter Rodney, *How Europe Underdeveloped Africa* (1974).
21 Farhana Sultana, "The False Equivalence of Academic Freedom and Free Speech: Defending Academic Integrity in the Age of White Supremacy, Colonial Nostalgia, and Anti-Intellectualism," *ACME: An International E-Journal for Critical Geographies* (2018), 253.
22 Joan Robinson, *Economic Philosophy* (1962), 46.
23 Walter Rodney, Angela Davis, et. al., *How Europe Underdeveloped Africa* (2018).
24 Robin Grier, "Colonial Legacies and Economic Growth," *Public Choice* (1999).
25 Tirthankar Roy, *The Economic History of India, 1857-1947* (2011).
26 James Feyrer and Bruce Sacerdote, "Colonialism and Modern Income: Islands as Natural Experiments," *Review Of Economics And Statistics* (2009).

27 James Stacey Taylor, "The Case Against the Case for Colonialism," *International Journal of Applied Philosophy* (2018), 28.
28 Leander Heldring and James Robinson, "Colonialism and Economic Development in Africa," in Carol Lancaster, Nicolas Van de Walle, eds., *The Oxford Handbook of the Politics of Development* (2018).
29 Melissa Dell and Benjamin Olken, "The Development Effects of the Extractive Colonial Economy: The Dutch Cultivation System in Java," *The Review of Economic Studies* (2020).
30 Brandon Kendhammer, "A controversial article praises colonialism. But colonialism's real legacy was ugly," *Washington Post*, September 19, 2017.
31 Matthew Lange, "British Colonial Legacies and Political Development," *World Development* (2004); Matthew Lange, *Lineages of Despotism and Development: British Colonialism and State Power* (2009).
32 Lange, "British Colonial Legacies," 917.
33 Ibid., 921.
34 Moses Ochonu, *Colonial Meltdown: Northern Nigeria in the Great Depression* (2009).
35 Ibid., 4.
36 James Stacey Taylor, "The Case Against the Case for Colonialism," *International Journal of Applied Philosophy* (2018), 23, 24.
37 Crawford Young, *The African Colonial State in Comparative Perspective* (1994); Crawford Young, "The Heritage of Colonialism," in John Harbeson, Donald Rothchild, eds., *Africa in World Politics: Constructing Political and Economic Order* (2016).
38 Taylor, "The Case Against the Case for Colonialism," 22, 23.
39 Brandon and Sarkar, 78.
40 Marlous Waijenburg and Ewout Frankema, "Structural Impediments to African Growth? New Evidence from Real Wages in British Africa, 1880-1965," *The Journal of Economic History* (2011).
41 Vijay Prashad, "Marks of Capital: Colonialism and the Sweepers of Delhi," *International Review of Social History* (1995).
42 Ian Kerr, "On the Move: Circulating Labor in Pre-Colonial, Colonial, and Post-Colonial India," *International Review of Social History* (2006), 88-89, 106.
43 Bruce Gilley, "How Junk Citations Have Discredited the Academy," *Minding the Campus* (5 parts), March 2023.
44 Philip Ball, "Paper Trail Reveals References Go Unread by Citing Authors," *Nature* (2002).
45 Wayne Booth, Gregory Colomb, and Joseph Williams, *The Craft of Research*, 3rd ed. (2008), 87.
46 Benjamin Lawrance, Emily Osborn, and Richard Roberts, "Introduction," in Benjamin Lawrance, Emily Osborn, Richard Roberts, eds., *Intermediaries, Interpreters, and Clerks: African Employees in the Making of Colonial Africa* (2006), 7.
47 Brandon Kendhammer, "A controversial article praises colonialism. But colonialism's real legacy was ugly," *Washington Post*, September 19, 2017.
48 Waijenburg and Frankema, 921.
49 Maya Berinzon and Ryan Briggs, "Legal Families Without the Laws: The Fading of Colonial Law in French West Africa," *The American Journal of Comparative Law* (2016).
50 Frederick Cooper, *Decolonization and African Society: The Labor Question in French and British Africa* (1996), 7.
51 Daron Acemoglu, Simon Johnson, and James Robinson, "Reversal of Fortune: Geography and Institutions in the Making of the Modern World Income Distribution," *The*

Quarterly Journal of Economics (2002), 1263.
52 Jan Vansina, "Deep-down Time: Political Tradition in Central Africa," *History in Africa* (1989), 344.
53 Raymond Buell, *The Native Problem in Africa* (1928).
54 Ibid., 568, 570, 573.
55 Arthur Scott, "Review of The Native Problem in Africa," *American Journal of Sociology* (1929).
56 Klein, 46.
57 Gabriele Cappelli and Joerg Baten, "The Evolution of Human Capital in Africa, 1730 – 1970: A Colonial Legacy?" *Centre for Economic Policy Research Discussion Papers* (2016).
58 Alexander Moradi, "Towards an Objective Account of Nutrition and Health in Colonial Kenya: A Study of Stature in African Army Recruits and Civilians, 1880–1980," *The Journal of Economic History* (2009): 746, 719, 720.
59 Rosella Calvi and Federico Mantovanelli, "Long-Term Effects of Access to Health Care: Medical Missions in Colonial India," *Journal of Development Economics* (2018).
60 Herschel Grossman, Murat Iyigun, "Population Increase and the End of Colonialism," *Economica* (1997).
61 Klein, 39.
62 Tom Young, "The Gilley 'Debate,'" *The Journal of Modern African Studies* (2019).
63 Klein, 43, 44.
64 Ola Olsson, On the Democratic Legacy of Colonialism," *Journal of Comparative Economics* (2009).
65 Jacob Hariri, "The Autocratic Legacy of Early Statehood," *American Political Science Review* (2012).
66 MacWilliam, 13.
67 Camille Lefebvre, *Frontières de sable, frontières de papier. Histoire de territoires et de frontières, du jihad de Sokoto à la colonisation française du Niger, XIXe-XXe siècles* (2015).
68 Camille Lefebvre, "We Have Tailored Africa: French Colonialism and the 'Artificiality' of Africa's Borders in the Interwar Period," *Journal of Historical Geography* (2011), 199, 201.
69 Taylor, "The Case Against the Case," 23.
70 Lefebvre, "We Have Tailored Africa," 199, 202.
71 Khan, "The Case Against 'The Case for Colonialism.'"
72 G. Allana, *Pakistan Movement: Historical Documents* (1977).
73 Latika Chaudhary, Jared Rubin, Sriya Iyer, and Anand Shrivastava, "Culture and Colonial Legacy: Evidence from Public Goods Games," *Journal of Economic Behavior & Organization* (2020)..
74 Peter Uvin, "Ethnicity and Power in Burundi and Rwanda: Different Paths to Mass Violence," *Comparative Politics* (1999), 254.
75 Boku Tache and Gufu Oba, "Policy-Driven Inter-Ethnic Conflicts in Southern Ethiopia," *Review of African Political Economy* (2009); Kidane Mengisteab, "Ethiopia's Ethnic-Based Federalism: 10 Years after," *African Issues* (2001).
76 Bruce Gilley, I*n Defense of German Colonialism: And How its Critics Empowered Nazis, Communists and the Enemies of the West* (2022), Chapter 3.
77 Suzanne Kuss, *German Colonial Wars and the Context of Military Violence* (2017), 74, 47.
78 Gilley, *In Defense of German Colonialism*, 50-58.

79 Taylor, "The Case Against the Case," 21.
80 Ken Lees, *Mau Mau Interrogator* (2019); Lee Boldeman, *Mau Mau Whitewash, Britain Slandered: A Critique of the Revisionist Account of Mau Mau* (2021); Eric Louw, "Mau-Mauing History and Truth," *Quadrant Magazine*, October 1, 2021.
81 Brandon & Sarkar, 80.
82 David Leonard and Scott Strauss, *Africa's Stalled Development: International Causes and Cures* (2003).
83 Ibid., 59.
84 Ibid.
85 Jack Paine, "Ethnic Violence in Africa: Destructive Legacies of Pre-Colonial States," *International Organization* (2019).
86 Klein, 39.
87 Ibid., 49.
88 Gary King, Christopher Murray, Joshua Salomon, and Ajay Tandon, "Enhancing the Validity and Cross-Cultural Comparability of Measurement in Survey Research," *American Political Science Review* (2004).
89 Klein, 42.
90 Khan, "The Case Against 'The Case for Colonialism.'"
91 Suzanne Miers and Martin Klein, "Introduction," in Suzanne Miers, Martin Klein, eds., *Slavery and Colonial Rule in Africa* (1999), 2, 5.
92 Nathan Nunn and Leonard Wantchekon, "The Slave Trade and the Origins of Mistrust in Africa," *NBER Working Papers* (2009), 25.
93 Nathan Nunn and Leonard Wantchekon, "The Slave Trade and the Origins of Mistrust in Africa," *American Economic Review* (2011), 3229, 3234.
94 Ibid.
95 Chistopher Bayly, "Indigenous And Colonial Origins Of Comparative Economic Development: The Case of Colonial India And Africa," *World Bank Policy Research Working Papers* (2008), 26.
96 Brandon and Sarkar, 93.
97 Mike Davis, *Late Victorian Holocausts: El Niño Famines and the Making of the Third World* (2001); V. Smil, "The Shadow of Doughts' Deaths," *Science* (2001).
98 Abernethy, 403.
99 Khan, "The Case Against 'The Case for Colonialism.'"
100 See also Philip Bowcock, *Last Guardians: Crown Service in Sudan, Northern Rhodesia, and Britain* (2016)
101 S.G. Cheah, "The Case for British Colonialism in Malaya," Online Essay (2018).
102 David Van Reybrouck, *Congo: The Epic History of a People* (2014), 255.
103 Brandon and Sarkar, 83.
104 "PSU-AAUP Condemns Professor Bruce Gilley's 'procolonialism' Platform," PSU-AAUP, Press Release, 2021.
105 Mary Felice Smith, *Baba of Karo: A Woman of the Muslim Hausa* (1954), 67.
106 Paul Bjerk, "Commentary: 'The Case for Colonialism,'" *Institute for the Study of Western Civilization*, Texas Tech University (2018).
107 Bruce Gilley, "The Meaning and Measure of State Legitimacy: Results for 72 Countries," *European Journal of Political Research* (2009).
108 Klein, 41.
109 Ronald Robinson, "Non-European Foundations of European Imperialism: Sketch for a Theory of Collaboration," in Roger Owen, Bob. Sutcliffe, eds., *Studies in the Theory of Imperialism* (1972).

110 Tanja Bührer, Flavio Eichmann, Stig Förster, and Benedikt Stuchtey, *Cooperation and Empire: Local Realities of Global Processes* (2017), 4.
111 Bührer et al., 6, 12.
112 Michael Hechter, *Alien Rule* (2013), 141.
113 Taylor, "The Case Against the Case for Colonialism," 25.
114 Bruce Gilley, "Chinua Achebe on the positive legacies of colonialism," *African Affairs* (2016).
115 Patrice Lumumba, *Congo, My Country* (1962), 12, 13.
116 James Stacey Taylor, "Foreign Rule and Colonial Fictions," *CATO Unbound*, October 13, 2017, 26.
117 Catherine Hoskyns, *The Congo Since Independence* (1965).
118 Catherine Hoskyns, "Review of Congo, My Country," *International Affairs* (1962), 129-130.
119 Klein, 39.
120 Tom Young, "The Gilley 'debate,'" *The Journal of Modern African Studies* (2019), 332.
121 Klein, 49.
122 Robert Bates, *Prosperity and Violence: The Political Economy of Development* (2001).
123 Robert Bates, *When Things Fell Apart: State Failure in Late-Century Africa* (2008).
124 Martin Lynn, *The British Empire in the 1950s: Retreat or Revival?* (2008).
125 Berny Sèbe, "From Post-Colonialism to Cosmopolitan Nation-Building? British and French Imperial Heroes in Twenty-First-Century Africa," *The Journal of Imperial and Commonwealth History* (2014).
126 Berny Sèbe, "The Case Against Historical Anachronism," *CATO Unbound*, October 11, 2017.
127 Berny Sèbe, "How Birmingham research into cultures of empire feeds into worldwide debates about colonialism," *Modern Languages News*, University of Birmingham, December 22, 2017.
128 Khan, "The Case Against 'The Case for Colonialism.'"
129 Amardo Rodriguez, "A Case Against Colonialism," *Postcolonial Studies* (2018), 258.
130 MacWilliam, 22.
131 Rosemary Galli, "Capitalist Agriculture and the Colonial State in Portuguese Guinea, 1926-1974," *African Economic History* (1995).
132 Patrick Chabal, "National Liberation in Portuguese Guinea, 1956-1974," *African Affairs* (1991).
133 Sultana, 232, 237, 238, 248.
134 Bruce Gilley, "An Academic Responds to His Cancellers," *The American Conservative*, October 9, 2020.
135 Hamid Dabashi, "Moral Paralysis in American Academia: On 'Civilised' Scholars and Their Liberal Defence of Immoral Hate Mongering," *AlJazeera.com*, September 28, 2017.
136 Kanika Batra, "Protest letter against 'The Case for Colonialism,'" Texas Tech University, November 26, 2018. https://web.pdx.edu/~gilleyb/TexasTech_DisinviteDemand.pdf.
137 "PSU-AAUP Condemns Professor Bruce Gilley's 'procolonialism' Platform," PSU-AAUP, Press Release, 2021.
138 Michael Bérubé and Jennifer Ruth, *It's Not Free Speech: Race, Democracy, and the Future of Academic Freedom* (2022).
139 Tanya Lyons, "Decolonising African Studies—The Politics of Publishing," *Austral-*

asian Review of African Studies (2018), 7.

CHAPTER FIVE

Is It Shameful to Defend Colonialism?*

"How does it feel to be so despised that applicants who have been associated with you need to make clarifying statements?"

That was the question posed to me in an intemperate email in 2018 by a former graduate student in political science whom I taught at Portland State University, writing to me from his doctoral program in geography to declare his censure of my article, "The Case for Colonialism," and to shame me with the revelation that in applying for academic jobs in the United States, where he will be expected to become a steward of the institutions of a free society, he was taking special care to declare that my deviationist thinking—which he noted in his email had caused several of his students to "cry" in his office—was "utterly ignorant" because it failed to take into account the views of "black Marxists" and "Third World feminists," and that he was declaring in those applications that he was "not in solidarity" with me; meaning, I suppose, that I stood outside the circle of what the communists used to call "the people" and that, as he wrote in a separate blog post about the "violence" of my intellectual viewpoints, my role should be to "sit down and shut up" and await the day of justice "when the leftists finally have some disciplinary power in political science to make it less disciplined," and the big payoff: "to challenge the capitalist, imperial/colonial oppression of black and brown people," which, as a black Nigerian female friend of mine who works in northern Nigeria on education and is an actually existing Third

* An earlier version of this chapter was given at the National Association of Scholars conference "Disgrace: Shame, Punishment, and Redemption in American Higher Education," Chapman University, January 11 and 12, 2019, Orange, California.

World female wrote in an essay, is a position that is a "bilious personification of anti-intellectualism," notwithstanding the pretensions of my very white, male, well-fed, and lifetime Westcoast U.S. resident correspondent, whom, I later learned, used to be a professional trombonist.

I have nothing against trombonists. Some of my best friends have been friends with trombonists. Nor, for that matter, am I particularly exercised when strange people in the academy tilt at windmills. But I am concerned when this sort of scolding language on questions of mainstream and common concern starts to show up in American society at large. It makes me wonder if shaming culture over violations of political correctness in American higher education has escaped from the asylum, so to speak, and become a sort of generally acceptable, or at least not unacceptable, way of dealing with pluralism. My correspondent has since washed up in Budapest, so this particular shamer has been exported. Still, it makes you wonder.

In 2018, the *New York Times* ran a lengthy essay by the virulently anti-Western Indian journalist Pankaj Mishra (who prefers to live in London) in which he declared that anyone who took a positive view of colonialism was part of a "white suicide cult." Moreover, Mishra wrote, yours truly was one of those "panicky white bros" worried about the decline of the West ("white power"). I was, moreover, a "busy recycler of Western supremacism" who had "promptly shot to martyrdom in the far-right constellation as a victim of politically correct criticism" after the withdrawal of my article.[1] Be reminded that this is the *New York Times*, not *The Black Panther Daily*. Even the very liberal residents in my tony Portland neighborhood expressed puzzlement about Mishra's screed.

None of us, I suppose, is inherently interested when dime-a-dozen South Asian radicals, who secretly wish they had been born white, try to shame into silence those they disagree with. Nor when Woke professors do likewise. At the end of the day, literary and intellectual culture is a marginal part of American society, thank goodness. But we do have an interest in how our children and our professionals are being prepared for the world around them. I see the pitter-patter of assaults on freedom and vigorous debate in our institutions of higher education (and in our former newspapers of record) as a reasonable thing to worry about and inquire into because of evidence that it is spreading to the mainstream.

Much of the inquiry into cancel culture in higher education has centered on overtly coercive forms of censorship—no-platforming, protests, structural censorship through faculty hiring and promotion, institutions of investigation and punishment such as diversity offices, and to be sure, in my case, overt coercion was present. Most notably, the credible death threats against the editors of the *Third World Quarterly* is what led to the withdrawal of my article with my consent.

French settlers in Algeria admire a new monument to French colonization, 1947. Credit: Robert L. Pendleton Collection, University of Wisconsin-Milwaukee Libraries

But the soft weapon of shame is an underappreciated part of the armory of the assault on freedom and truth. Shame, and the resulting guilt and disgrace, is a form of normative rather than material punishment. While this represents psychological rather than material coercion, it is no less effective. It operates not through brute facts, such as fear for one's life or an inability to make it onto the podium, but through constructed narratives about the shameful behavior of the accused. Most usefully, as Frye argues about the Internet age, shame can be scaled up faster and better than coercion.[2]

In my case, it was important for the shamers to establish a narrative about my various transgressions. In particular: (1) that my article had not passed peer review and I had somehow cajoled or bribed my way into print; (2) that my article was intended as click-bait to boost my citations count for professional gain or it was intended as a spectacle to draw attention to myself; and finally (3) that the investigation into me launched by my university's Diversity Office (after students who at first demanded I be punished for expressing the case for colonialism were coached instead to file a complaint claiming that I was a racist or graded girls harder) showed—on the theory of "where there's smoke, there's fire"—that I must be an deviant human being and thus my article, by association, was a deviant article.

The weapon of shaming depends on the vulnerability of the target to being shamed. My first response to the global shame mob was of that sort. I apologized, asked the journal to retract the article, and begged pardon. It took me a few days to stand up and declare that I was not ashamed, and that the shame was on those who joined the mob and on those who had not opposed it.

Like coercion, shame usually operates in the background via what social theorists call "virtual causation." The mere expectation that one's behavior will trigger coercion or shaming has the intended effect of modifying one's behavior without the censors ever lifting a finger. Since there are no visible acts of censorship—whether coercive or normative—the censors claim it is much ado about nothing. This tends to entrench the censorship because of the lack of a sensory experience for society in seeing someone being silenced via coercion or shaming, what is known as an "availability heuristic." Without an availability heuristic that the brain can summon, the motivations in society to do anything about it are reduced.

In some sense, then, the greatest achievement of "The Case for Colonialism" debacle was to provide a vivid and memorable availability heuristic for concerned citizens about the serious decline in academic and more general speech freedoms in Western societies. A doctoral student in social work at my home university who claims native American ancestry sent me the following email after my original essay was published: "I dont [sic] need to say more about your maniscript [sic], except that its [sic] gatbage [sic] scholarship, you are a garbage humsm [sic] being and a white supremacist. You owe the Indigenous people of this land an apology for your exsitance [sic]." She added a Chinook war cry at the end of the email for good measure. I could have pursued student misconduct charges against her, but merely asked our administrators to have a chat with her about grown up behavior.

In such ways, millions of citizens were given a dramatic reminder that thousands of academics and researchers are probably silencing themselves because of the virtual causation of shaming culture operating silently to narrow the range of acceptable debate. Even my friend the trombonist, via my reporting of his correspondence, has played his little part in this achievement.

Mao Maoing the Flak Catchers

The theme of public shaming is particularly resonant to me because of my research into communist political campaigns, in particular those with which I am familiar in Mao's China. Contemporary intellectual shame and purge movements, like those in Maoist China, rely heavily on the idea of an "ideological error" and a resultant label of "deviationist" thinking. This brings about the unfortunate separation of the error-prone individual from "the people." No longer being a person, their liquidation becomes necessary. The public shaming rituals that precede such punishments provide the vivid dramatization of what awaits others silly enough to stray from the orthodoxy.

I use the term "Maoist" advisedly because actually existing Maoism killed more people than any other political movement in world history. The modern shamers threaten only professional death. But their repertoire is a brass rubbing taken from the tomb of Mao. People often assume that overt coercion was the main mode of revolutionary rule in Russia and China. True enough, the gulags and labor camps, as well as the ranks of "model workers" given special rewards by the party, attest to the wide use of coercion, both negative and positive. But shaming was cheaper and more effective—why liquidate the enemies of the people when they could be shamed into leaping from the balcony? And, from a normative approbation perspective, why waste time and money handing out benefits to the virtuous if you can convince most people to simply feel good about themselves by cleaving closely to the Party line?

Most memorable in Mao's China was the Cultural Revolution, a purification movement intended to crush political opponents through recourse to ideological struggle. The identification of right-deviationists would purge the Party of incorrect thinking and invigorate the ranks. Ambitious cadres were given a way to signal their virtue and loyalty to the cause. Not surprisingly, the most aggressive agents were the Red Guards, teenagers and university-aged youth for whom participation in the purges was both fun and a quick route to the top. They ran the "shaming festivals" where deviationists were shamed by having their hair cut, their heads bowed, and their thought crimes read aloud for all to hear. But the real agents of the Cultural Revolution were the higher ups in the Party who, rather than standing up, sat silent or mouthed support.

The parallels between Maoist anti-deviationist movements and contemporary "social justice" movements in American higher education are striking. The repurposing of the state to pursue class struggle rather than govern effectively is paralleled by the repurposing of the university to pursue social justice rather than truth. The sudden privileging of poor peasant associations, like the sudden privileging of campus identity (or affinity) groups over other student groups, is the mobilizing of the movement. Once peasant status—like contemporary "marginalized" identity—becomes the currency of the realm, others must be shoehorned into those roles in order to play a part in the movement. Mao called soldiers "peasants in battle fatigue" while progressive administrators, faculty, and students are invited to be "allies," credentialing them for participation in campus shaming and censorship.

Mao guided the movements with "work teams" and "central leading groups" sent from the top, no different from the Diversity Office or Institutional Review Board investigations of today. The error-prone were invited to correct their ways through struggle sessions, self-criticism, hysterical declarations of loyalty to Mao, and rustication to learn from the peasants—parallels found in today's remedial cultural competency training, "awareness of whiteness" seminars, mandatory diversity statements, and service-based learning.

Hyping the threat was central because this legitimated shaming. The Party warned about "fascism," which needed to be nipped in the bud; thus, any suggestion of moderation or centrism was appalling, and part of the problem itself. Most of all, was the focus on the unbearable suffering, interminable victimization, and ineluctable exclusion of the "people"—the carefully curated construction of party ideologues—paralleled in today's bogus term "marginalized groups."

Meanwhile in Lubbock

Do we worry too much about where this is heading? A litmus test for me came in 2018 when I gave a talk entitled "The Case for Colonialism" at Texas Tech University. The talk was kept low profile until the weekend before, when it was announced on the university's events site. A mob of 23 faculty members signed a letter to the university president protesting the talk and demanding that it be cancelled. They also, rather eccentrically, demanded an official statement that "there is no case for colonialism."[3] My talk, the faculty letter wrote, "sends a clear message that the university does not value decolonial and postcolonial perspectives." This was rather like saying that a talk on monetarism in the economics department shows the university does not value Keynesianism. Having alternative ideas debated on campus was dangerous, according to the faculty letter, because "we don't need our students thinking ideas advocating colonialism are valid."

One might shrug the shoulders and say that 23 out of 1,563 full-time faculty—17 of whom are in the English Department—does not a mob make. But it is always the vocal minority, not the silent majority, that carries the day. This is what happened in my case. The craven joint reply of the university president and provost was bizarre and disheartening: I should not have been invited, they wrote, because my article had been "discredited," because my talk was "objectionable and potentially harmful," and...wait for it... because the president and provost of a major public university had decided "emphatically" that "there is no case for colonialism."[4] I supposed that the following weeks would bring forth a geyser of presidential decrees from Lubbock on controversial academic questions—no case that Ming dynasty seafarer Cheng He had reached Africa, no case for mind-body separation, no case for multiple-authorship approaches to Shakespeare, no case for the low nitrogen hypothesis of the sun's chemical composition. Dear me, the Office of the President at Texas Tech could certainly set the world to rights with a stream of edicts on controversial issues.

Actually, we turned the tables on the mob by inviting one of the faculty signatories—a historian—to join me on stage, refute my talk with his best arguments, and then engage in a civilized debate. You can watch it on YouTube.[5] It was wonderful. Everyone was pleased, except for the university provost who rather sheepishly sat at the back and then slunk out of the room without introducing himself, perhaps feeling rather foolish about his capitulation to crackpots in the English department. Shame on the university president and provost of Texas Tech, and shame on the silent faculty who did not stand up to the 23 thugs of the letter.

Soumission

So if that was a litmus test, the news is not good, and we are correct to be worried. I have often thought about the 2015 bestselling novel *Soumission* (*Submission*) by the French writer Michel Houellebecq. It tells the story of a French professor who, bored with the comforts of Western society, submits to the blandishments of Islamic fundamentalists who have come to power in a coalition government and ends up debasing his university. The focus is not on the radicals who demand submission but on the moderates who submit.

The faculty protest mob at Texas Tech was led by another dime-a-dozen South Asian radical, English professor Kanika Batra. She is a self-described postcolonial queer activist from Delhi making her splash in the academic world with books like *Worlding Postcolonial Sexualities: Archives, Activism, and Anterior Counterpublics*. The submission to her demands by the university president and provost, a mathematician and food scientist respectively, came too late to cancel the talk. They made some hollow protestations about being bound by the First Amendment. But a submission it was. The redacted section of their letter reads: "Had input been received from the academicians who have expertise in this area, we believe that an invitation to Dr. Gilley to speak on this subject would not have been extended." In other words, if postcolonial queer theorists in the English department who specialize in anterior counterpublics had been consulted, their views would have carried the day.

What, you might wonder, is a major American public university thinking when it submits to the blandishments of radicals completely unrooted in the Western liberal tradition and whose life work is to tear down that tradition? And what, you might ask, is the next generation of leaders in this country being taught in terms of how to engage with different viewpoints and to steward the institutions of a free society?

It can be stopped. In the case of the Cultural Revolution, the underlying pressures for a change came from the silent majority, through widespread popular disgust and rejection of the radicals who had seized the commanding heights. The initiative was taken by those in authority who were outside of the morass. The movement was stopped without any score-settling. The new leaders simply said they were taking the country in a new direction.

For us, change must begin with the everyday public—the parents, the alumni, the taxpayers, and the employers—who are fed up with the mis-education of our youth. We cannot expect university leaders or faculty to be the agents of change because they are part of the problem. Change needs to be initiated by Boards of Trustees, state legislators, state education commissions, alumni associations, broad and strategic coordination of like-minded organizations like the National Association of Scholars, and, yes, courts. Finally, the process needs to be guided by an overwhelming toleration and liberalism—the purpose is not to shame or purge but to reinvigorate pluralism and the search for truth by putting the zealots back in their places.

Endnotes:

1 Pankaj Mishra, "The Religion of Whiteness Becomes a Suicide Cult," *New York Times*, August 30, 2018.
2 Harrison Frye "The Problem of Public Shaming," *Journal of Political Philosophy* (2022).
3 See the letter at: https://web.pdx.edu/~gilleyb/TexasTech_DisinviteDemand.pdf.
4 See the response at: https://web.pdx.edu/~gilleyb/TexasTech_PresidentialDecreeon-Colonialism_Redacted.pdf.
5 "Bruce Gilley Lecture with Commentary by Paul Bjerk," Institute for Western Civilization, Texas Tech University, https://youtu.be/doZXhC3rFfI.

PART II

Episodes of Colonialism

CHAPTER SIX

African Civilization and The Premature Termination of Colonialism*

THIS CHAPTER IS about the sociology and development of Africa. It assumes that ideas and the way they shape cultures and societies through development and norm shifts are the engine room of civilization, although they are not the same thing. Civilization is the culmination of these changes and includes institutionalized forms of art, government, economic behavior, religious practice, and memory.

I define Africa as sub-Saharan Africa because of the civilizational fault line between the Islamic North African region and the sub-Saharan region. In assuming the existence of a (sub-Saharan) African civilization, this paper sides with the Afrocentrists in the academy—especially the Senegalese anthropologist Cheikh Anta Diop[1]—as well as with international relations realists—famously Samuel Huntington—who insist that there is such a thing as a distinct African civilization. As many scholars of the politics of Africa have noted, the patterns of African development, especially its politics, are strikingly similar in contrast to other regions. There must be a common underlying civilization in the region that explains this pattern, whatever variations we can find at the ground level.

I make four points. First, African civilization represents the starkest contrast with Western civilization compared to any other. Second, the difference lies not just in fundamental social and ethical assump-

* An earlier version of this essay was presented at the National Association of Scholars regional conference "What is Western Civilization?", Phoenix, February 10, 2018.

tions but also in the developmental gap, which means that we do not really know what a modernized African civilization would look like and how it would compare to the West. Third, the colonial encounter was the most significant and important opportunity for Africa to modernize its civilization and development, and thus, its premature termination was a tragedy for Africa. Fourth, the world badly needs Africa to develop a modernized African civilization but at present the prospects for that remain bleak.

In a well-known essay of 1992, the Cameroonian economist Daniel Etounga-Manguelle argued[2] that the main features of the common culture that defined African civilization were: (1) a high degree of fatalism, irrationalism and belief in magic; (2) a communitarianism that suffocates individual initiative; (3) a focus on the past and present, not on the future; (4) a disregard for economic realities and planning; and (5) an excessive concentration of authority and power in one individual—the so-called "big man ruler"—who will often claim to have magical powers.

These five features represent an almost perfect contrast to the five dimensions that the French philosopher Philippe Nemo argued were the key aspects of Western civilization,[3] namely: (a) Greek ideals of individual liberty, reason, and science; (b) Roman ideals of law and humanism; (c) Judeo-Christian biblical notions of ethics, empathy, and progress against evil (echoed in Rachel Fulton Brown's argument[4] that the reading of Psalms is what led to empathy for others); (d) the Papal call to action and responsibility in human affairs, which created the idea of a universal and secular civic space (echoed in Larry Siedentop's view in *Inventing the Individual*[5] of the central role of medieval canon law); and (e) the Enlightenment discovery of the attractions of pluralism, tolerance, democracy, and political equality.

So when we look at Etounga-Manguelle's description of Africa, it presents a perfect contrast to the West, as defined by Nemo. African irrationalism contrasts with Greek reason. African communitarianism contrasts with Roman humanism. The African focus on the past and present contrasts with the Biblical belief in progress. The African disregard for economic realities contrasts with the Papal call to action and responsibility. The African concentration of authority contrasts with Enlightenment pluralism.

The fact that Europe conquered Africa rather than the other way around reflected mainly Europe's developmental advances rather than its civilizational superiority, which existed long before major imperial advances. Indeed, nineteenth century (mostly male) romantics in the West believed that African civilization (along with Native American and Polynesian life) was superior to that of the West precisely because it remained grounded in longstanding, primitive ideals of community, tradition, authority, place, and imagination.

Yet the post-colonial record in Africa, which represented a reversion to African ideals, has discredited the notion that African civilization was ever desirable, either inherently or in terms of its functional contribution to human development. That is why Etounga-Manguelle titled his 1991 article (then book), "Does Africa Need a Cultural Adjustment Program?" He had formulated this question in 1985 while attending Harvard Business School, where he learned about the importance of corporate cultures to financial success. Surely, he reasoned, this must be true of societies and nations as well. Hence, his call for "cultural transformation" in Africa.[6]

The dilemma was not how to Westernize Africa. For instance, Asia has made striking advances without a strong commitment to individual liberty, humanism, or pluralism and democracy. Rather the dilemma was how to modernize African civilization so that a modern African civilization could emerge just as a modern Asian civilization has emerged today. This is where Africa presents a puzzle. What happened to its modernizers: where were its Suhartos, its Park Chung Hees, its Deng Xiaopings, or Lee Kuan-Yews?

The answer was that even if modernizers existed in private life, when they came into power, their beliefs and actions changed. To understand this unique African tragedy, we need to turn to another well-known essay, this one published in 1975 by the Nigerian sociologist Peter Ekeh, entitled "Colonialism and the Two Publics in Africa." In it, Ekeh noted that post-colonial Africa was characterized by a disconnect between the ideals of private life and those of public life. Of course, such disconnects were not unique to Africa. The first identification of such a disconnect was Banfield's discussion of amoral private behavior in southern Italian villages in his 1958 book, *The Moral Basis of a Backward Society*.[7] Communist systems were similarly notorious for the disconnect between the selfless, patriotic public sphere and the dog-eat-dog, radically uncivil private one.

But in these examples, a moral public sphere had been established, even if it failed to supervene on every aspect of private society. The difference in Africa, Ekeh argued, was that it was in the private realm where morality existed and in the public realm where it was absent. The expectations of public life in Africa were to rob, loot, break rules, and abandon any ethical commitments formed in private life. The striking deterioration of South Africa under president Jacob Zuma from 2009 to 2018, where the corruption was in full view and yet he remained president with much support, is the most obvious recent example of this. Zuma was "doing the right thing" by looting the state and using its resources to reward his supporters. In taking part in public life, "duties ... are de-emphasized while rights are squeezed out of the civic public with the amorality of an artful dodger," Ekeh wrote. Corruption flourished among civil servants, who were seen as "smart fellows" when they had their hands in the till. Only once you receded into private life did African cultural norms take hold, according to Ekeh. When Zuma's successor, Cyril Ramaphosa, was found to have stashed $580,000 in cash inside a couch cushion at his ranch, the response of his ruling African National Congress was a shrug of the shoulders.

Where Ekeh got things wrong was in assuming that the moral private sphere that lay waiting in the wings was somehow suited to modern conditions. Yet, as Etounga-Manguelle's description showed, the African civilization of the private sphere was no more suited to modern conditions than the amoral politics it replaced. Democracy may have brought to power a more sophisticated set of "big man rulers" with more popular support. But the "morality" they brought with them was the morality of a small-scale society. This private morality was little more than primitive face-to-face solidarity mechanisms designed for survival.

Goran Hyden, the great African politics scholar, noted that the egregiously bad public behavior of Africa's leaders reflected this underlying sociology of institutions that were "embedded" in face-to-face relationships. That is what made private life in Africa the place of morality because inclusion in a group is based on acceptance of its moral obligations. These are first and foremost moral communities, led by a "big man" who is less interested in territorial control than social control.

For Hyden, the reason that Africa's private morality remained primitive was developmental, or material. African societies never went through a developmental period in which people started to conceive of themselves as belonging to a "disembedded" public where one could depend on the impersonal market and the rational and predictable rules of an impersonal legal system to survive. There was no equivalent of Ming Dynasty commercialism in China or the municipal life of medieval Europe. This is simply an unavoidable tragedy of Africa's late development.

The result, wrote Hyden, was that leaders came to power who still thought like tribal chiefs. They saw their main duty as staying in power and gathering adherents, not delivering on public promises—what he called seamanship rather than navigation.[8] Leaders like Yoweri Museveni, who seized power in 1986 in Uganda with much promise of reform, slowly colonized the public sphere with a "big man ruler" identity, complete with magic-based ethics, neo-patrimonial spoils for supporters, and communal appeals to discredit the opposition.

A Catholic mission teacher in Portuguese Mozambique, 1950.
Credit: Widener Library, Harvard University

Africa thus had a choice of two types of political regime, both rotten. After independence, and with the inducements of the Cold War, Africa was ruled by amoral despotisms that reflected the lack of morality in the public sphere. They lacked a firm basis in African culture and were more akin to Ekeh's notion of the lawless and short-term criminals who loot quickly before being ousted by the next "national movement." After the Cold War, came the rise of electoral regimes. These reflected moral populisms, the entry of private African morality into the public sphere. This private morality was wholly unsuited to the modern world, and no less lawless and destructive. The irruption of premodern African morality into the public sphere simply made things worse,

This simple analysis then allows us to see why Africa is a tragedy. In essence, it has faced a triple challenge since the wave of political independence in the 1950s and 1960s: (1) how to modernize the basic features of its pre-modern cultures, as outlined by Etounga-Manguelle; (2) how to extend those norms into the public sphere, as noted by Ekeh and turn this into a modern civilization; and (3) how to simultaneously attain the expansion of economic wealth that has empirically always been associated with these cultural and civilizational transformations.[9]

Here is where I want to bring in the role of colonialism. Ekeh argued that the origins of the disconnect between public and private spheres in Africa was the national resistance to colonial rule that portrayed the colonial public sphere as the enemy of African culture and civilization. Once you encouraged the idea that the public sphere was to be attacked and looted, you could not just turn off the idea at independence. "The irony of it all," wrote Ekeh, "is that the ordinary African took the principles involved in such [anti-colonial] activities quite seriously." They continued to see the public realm as a vile area where morality was not required even after independence.

If this were true, then one would suppose that after 50 to 60 years—which is two generations—this separation would have broken down since today's Africans have no personal memories of colonialism. Let's not forget that Robert Mugabe was seen as uniquely suited to lead Africa into the future when he came to power in Zimbabwe in 1980 because he had never been tainted by involvement in colonial (or anti-colonial) politics.

But even if Ekeh was right about the 1970s, his argument about the problems of the public sphere has weakened. The problem now is that the public sphere reflects the private sphere all too well. Cold War regimes embedded in an amoral public sphere have been replaced by electoral regimes embedded in a premodern private sphere. The reality now is that it is no longer the harmful legacies of anti-colonialism that are holding Africa back. Rather, it is the underlying, unreformed African culture that colonialism was unable to change. Relative to the challenge, colonialism in Africa was far too short-lived and unobtrusive.

Colonialism offered to Africa an intensive, accelerated course in a cultural modernization, economic development, and public sector articulation—the social, economic, and political requirements for a modern civilization. When we look at colonial experiences in the 1920s, 1930s, and 1940s, it is a time of amazing optimism and flourishing. The triple challenge is being met against all expectations. As the Nigeria novelist Chinua Achebe, born in 1930, recalled of that period: "The pace of change in Nigeria from the 1940s was incredible. I am not just talking about the rate of development, with villages transforming into towns, or the coming of modern comforts, such as electricity or running water or modes of transportation, but more of a sense that we were standing figuratively and literally at the dawn of a new era."[10]

The Afro-centric Diop was in Paris from 1946 to 1960 studying under various French luminaries in the arts and sciences, where he developed the idea of an African civilization. His later claim that colonialism had subverted African national consciousness is absurd: rather it created the conditions for African consciousness to emerge by linking people like himself to a civilization that could nurture and facilitate such a formulation.

Etounga-Manguelle argued, like Hyden, that the problem with colonialism was not that it disrupted Africa's cultures (and thus its civilization) too much but that it disrupted them too little. Or, colonialism was not given the time it needed to bring about the triple transformation: sustained economic growth, cultural modernization (the private sphere), and civic construction (the public sphere). The countries fortunate enough to have post-independence leaders who clung tenaciously to that colonial vision after independence—Botswana, Kenya, and Senegal, for instance—managed to survive the onslaught of Afrocentrism much better than those that venerated "authentic" anti-colonial leaders—Congo, Ghana, Guinea-Bissau, pretty much everywhere else.

Outside of Africa, this much-needed triple transformation has been happening in the "creative Third World" that replaces the "protest Third World" of the past.[11] But Africa remains the slowest to cast off the self-wounding anti-colonial identity. The tragedy of Africa's encounter with modernity via colonialism, as Jeffery Herbst argued,[12] was that colonialism was too short-lived and too unobtrusive. World War II and then a wave of anti-colonial agitation supported by a cynical Soviet Union, an ever-puerile India, and a relatively naïve United States caused these successful colonial experiments to be prematurely terminated. Colonialism ended not because of local "resistance" but because of Western "resignation"—the rapidity and simultaneity of decolonization gives lie to the romantic ideal that local resistance movements had anything to do with it.

In Africa, there was not even a remnant of colonialism like Hong Kong to stimulate reforms. Well, there was one: apartheid South Africa. It served as one model of a modernized African state. Over 100,000 black Africans a year applied to migrate to apartheid South Africa during the 1980s. (Tell that to today's college students and black studies dons and you get a blank stare.)[13] But black nationalists paid attention only to the white rulers, not to the black middle class—Africa's first—that was emerging there. The slide backwards in South Africa since the end of apartheid is a reminder of how deeply entrenched Africa's pre-modern, embedded institutions are because they outlasted the nearly century-long experiment of Boer colonialism.

This has serious costs. Within weeks or months after colonial rule ended, African societies unraveled into primordial structures, and the state collapsed along with civic life. The examples are too numerous and tragic to recount. In South Africa, for example, about 35% of households continue to use solid fuels (coal, firewood, dung, paraffin) for cooking and heating. The health costs of using these without proper methods are steep—2,500 lives lost per year. In 1998, the bureaucracy proposed a new policy to make solid fuels safe. But the policy was ignored by politicians because they saw solid fuels as symbolic of the apartheid era when only whites had access to electricity. Politicians refused to fund programs for this "symbol of oppression," wrote Njirambo Matinga and colleagues.[14] Imagine if apartheid police mowed down 2,500 black protestors per year. Anti-colonial politicians have been doing this for over a decade with impunity, and this is only in the very obscure realm of solid fuels use.

So where does that leave us in thinking about African culture and civilization? If the classical Western tradition is anything, it is universally accessible and deployable. Indeed, the mastery and deployment of the Western classics by African and African-American writers and activists is deeply underappreciated, as the Elon University professor of law and the humanities Eric Hairston showed in his 2013 book *The Ebony Column: Classics, Civilization, and the African American*.

But to be honest, things do not look good for a fourth African renaissance at present (the previous three were declared in the late 19th century, the early 1960s, and the early 1990s). South Africa under Jacob Zuma made a catastrophic great leap backward and one-time hopefuls like Museveni are "hippos" rolling about in the mud of African "big man ruler" tradition. The "cheetahs" who would lead African culture and civilization into the modern era—these are the terms used by the Ghanaian economist George Ayittey[15]—are nowhere to be found. Even Liberia, once hopeful under Ellen Sirleaf Johnson, later elected a former soccer star as president with a vice president who was the wife of Charles Taylor, the grossly incompetent tyrant who led the country into a civil war.

We need more civilizations because Western civilization as a best practice always needs challengers that may bring new practices. Sir Alan Burns, a long-time British colonial official who was governor of the Gold Coast (Ghana) in the late 1940s, was typical of the colonial viewpoint on Africa. Far more than Africans themselves, he hoped for the emergence of a modern African consciousness, as well as national consciousnesses. To this end, he not only funded and supported efforts to write the history of what became Ghana, but he also lent his own hand. His *History of Nigeria* was the standard reference on the country until well into the 1970s. The colonialists documented the languages, saved and studied the art treasures, delineated the ethnic patterns, and extolled the ancient virtues of African civilization. They were the true African nationalists and their ouster set Africa back by a century or more. As Burns wrote: "There is no reason why, in the future, if they are given a fair chance economically and socially, [Africans] should not advance in civilization and culture, and contribute their undoubted qualities to a world which has not yet reached perfection under white domination."[16] We are still waiting for those contributions to land.

Endnotes:

1 Cheikh Anta Diop, *The Cultural Unity of Black Africa: The Domains of Patriarchy and of Matriarchy in Classical Antiquity* (1978).
2 Daniel Etounga Manguellé, *Cent Ans D'aliénation* (1985); *L'afrique a-t-Elle Besoin d'un Programme D'ajustement Culturel?* (1992).
3 Philippe Nemo, *Qu'est-Ce Que L'occident?* (2004); *What Is the West?* (2006).
4 Rachel Fulton Brown, *Mary and the Art of Prayer: The Hours of the Virgin in Medieval Christian Life and Thought* (2017).
5 Larry Siedentop, *Inventing the Individual: The Origins of Western Liberalism* (2014).
6 Daniel Etounga Manguellé, *Vers Une Société Responsable: Le Cas De L'afrique* (2009).
7 Edward Banfield, *The Moral Basis of a Backward Society* (1958).
8 Goran Hyden, *African Politics in Comparative Perspective* (2006).
9 Ronald Inglehart and Christian Welzel, *Modernization, Cultural Change, and Democracy: The Human Development Sequence* (2005).
10 Chinua Achebe, *There Was a Country: A Personal History of Biafra* (2012), 39.
11 Bruce Gilley, "The Challenge of the Creative Third World, *Third World Quarterly* (2015).
12 Jeffrey Herbst, *States and Power in Africa: Comparative Lessons in Authority and Control* (2000).
13 Aurelia Segatti, "Reforming South African Immigration Policy in the Post-Apartheid Period (1990–2010)," in Aurelia Segatti, & Loren Landau (eds.), *Contemporary Migration to South Africa* (2011), 39-40.
14 Margaret Njirambo Matinga, Joy Clancy, and Harold Annegarn, "Explaining the Non-Implementation of Health-Improving Policies Related to Solid Fuels Use in South Africa," *Energy Policy* (2014), 68, 53-59.
15 George Ayittey, *Africa in Chaos* (1998).
16 Sir Alan Burns, *Colour Prejudice, with Particular Reference to the Relationship between Whites and Negroes* (1948), 136.

CHAPTER SEVEN

The Case for Colonialism in the Middle East

IN 2020, AFTER a warehouse explosion destroyed the Port of Beirut in Lebanon, an online petition began circulating in the country requesting a return to French rule. "We believe Lebanon should go back under the French mandate in order to establish a clean and durable governance," the petition stated.[1] Within the first day, it attracted sixty thousand signatures.

The petition was an appeal for a return to the short-lived French "mandate" over the former Ottoman province granted by the League of Nations after World War I. The purpose of the mandate was for the French to "render administrative advice and assistance to the population" as well as "such steps as it may think best to ensure the development of the natural resources of the said territory." Under French rule, agriculture was expanded, a stable administration created, and social relations balanced, especially in comparison to the tumult resulting from the mandate of adjoining Syria. Even for critical scholars, the facts of Lebanon's success under the French mandate are hard to ignore.

The Lebanese historian Fawwaz Traboulsi wrote: "Beirut port, confirmed as the principal port of the Syrian interior, was enlarged and modernized, a second dock was constructed and the city, provided with an airport, progressed to become a center for international communication. According to a new urban plan, the city was re-centered around Place de l'Étoile, designed on the model of that of the French capital, and the Parliament and a new business quarter were inaugurated there on the occasion of the French Colonial Exposition of 1921. These projects contributed to the development of a tertiary sector dominated by a merchant/financial bourgeoisie, which was becoming more and more embedded into the mandate system. This was supplemented by the expansion of education, another mandate policy, which helped create a middle class destined for liberal professions and the bureaucracy."[2]

A constitution of 1926 prepared the way for self-government. Internal self-rule was initiated in 1936. To maintain local support after driving German and Vichy France forces out in 1941, Free France pre-emptively declared Lebanon an independent state in 1943.

After the war, independent Lebanon slowly deteriorated, leading to the outbreak of protracted civil war in 1975. When French president Emmanuel Macron visited the wreck of a country in 2020, the same week that the petition was launched, he promised "a new political pact" to drag Lebanon out of its morass. This would include German control of the airport, United Nations control of security, International Monetary Fund control of public finances, and French proconsular leadership to bring it all together. The organizers of the petition declared victory.

Middle East commentators expressed alarm at the explicitly colonial relationship being proposed. "Foreign forces are eager to kick around a concept of the country's external management…Ideas of colonialism are still resilient and might be applied to modern conditions," wrote an Azeri analyst.[3] But the Lebanon petition is a reminder that the once unthinkable is no longer so in the context of dire prospects for human well-being in Lebanon, not to mention the West Bank–Gaza, Yemen, Syria, Afghanistan, and Libya. The same revival of discussions of colonialism may figure in future chaotic transitions in Iran, Morocco, and Algeria.

As the critical commentator above suggests, any renewed form of colonial management in the Middle East would look profoundly different from the colonialism of the nineteenth and twentieth centuries. Still, the justifications and forms it would take are already becoming clear. Since colonialism remains as much a dirty word in the Middle East as it is in Africa, it is worth clearing the air about the colonial past and what a colonial future might look like.

Colonial History in the Middle East

The twenty-three countries of the Middle East region, defined broadly as an area stretching from Mauritania to Pakistan, experienced on average fifty years of European colonial rule during the high tide of classical colonialism in the nineteenth and twentieth centuries (64 years if we count only those 18 countries that were actually colonized). Of these 23, eleven came under British rule (11.5 if we count the southern part of contemporary Yemen), six under French rule, and one (Libya) under Italian rule—each for different periods. The region also has a diverse cross section of five noncolonized contemporary countries: Turkey, Saudi Arabia, Iran, Afghanistan, and most of what became Yemen. These five provide useful counterfactuals to colonial rule.

Using the blunt measure of number of years spent under nineteenth and twentieth century Western colonialism, there is only a slightly positive relationship to the equally blunt measure of development of contemporary income levels (a correlation of r=0.22—see Figure 7.1). The region displays almost as many long-colonized states that are underdeveloped today (Pakistan) and non-colonized states that are modestly developed (Turkey), as it does colonized and developed (U.A.E.) and non-colonized and undeveloped (Afghanistan).

Figure 7.1: Colonialism and Development in the Middle East

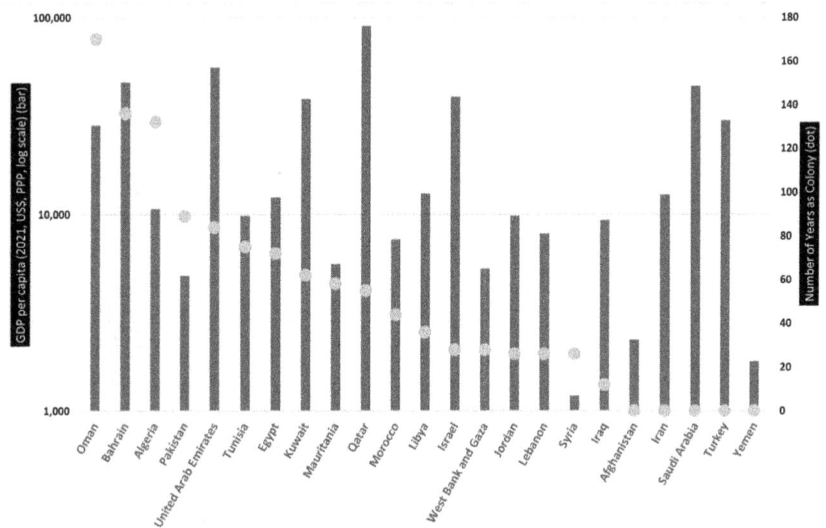

Correlation between gross domestic product (GDP) per capita, expressed as purchasing power parity (PPP), in US dollars, and number of years spent under colonial rule among the twenty-three nations of the Middle East. Sources: International Monetary Fund, Author calculations.

There is a more significant correlation (r=0.43) between years spent under Western colonialism and the present state of the rule of law (see Figure 7.2). But again, the variations are great—with long-colonized countries like Algeria being more lawless and non-colonized countries like Saudi Arabia being relatively law abiding. One would hesitate to draw firm conclusions from this data.

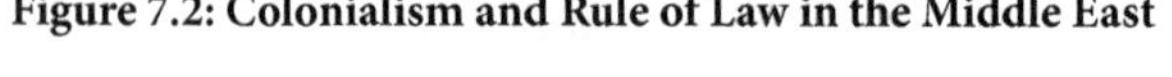

Figure 7.2: Colonialism and Rule of Law in the Middle East

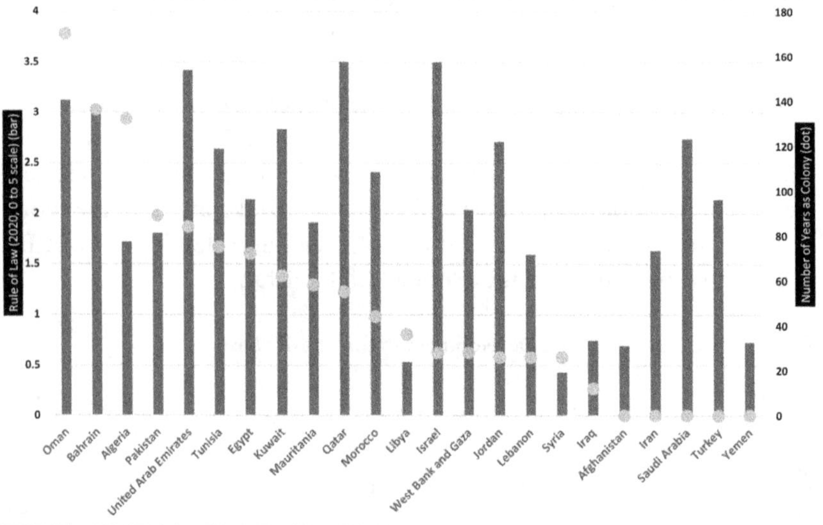

Correlation between measure of rule of law and number of years spent under colonial rule among the twenty-three nations of the Middle East. Sources: World Bank Governance Indicators, Author calculations.

Making general statements about Western colonialism in the Middle East is also confounded by the different circumstances under which it appeared: of the eighteen colonized cases, six (Israel, Palestine, Syria, Jordan, Iraq, and Lebanon) resulted from the collapse of Ottoman rule during World War I, while at the other end of the spectrum, three (Oman, Algeria, and Bahrain) predated the era of modern colonialism in the early 1800s. There is, in addition, the unavoidable question of how to treat contemporary Iraq and Afghanistan, which experienced eight and twenty years, respectively, of US-led occupation in the early twenty-first century.

A prudent analyst might refrain from making any general statements about "colonialism and the Middle East." The circumstances and patterns of the colonial encounter vary so widely that one is forced to reckon with 23 different case histories. Indeed, the most reasonable conclusion, from a cursory glance, is that the colonial encounter, in whatever guise and intensity, is more or less irrelevant to the contemporary Middle East as a general statement. It would appear to be no more important as a determinative structural factor than, say, the distance of the capital city from Mecca (which, it turns out, is negatively correlated to contemporary income levels at a reasonably interesting level of r=-0.39).

Melani Cammett, for example, after considering various explanations of the region's lagging economic development, rejects the importance of colonialism *per se* in favor of a more historically dynamic account of how precolonial and colonial legacies were variously acted upon by the critical agency of postcolonial elites in the region to shape varying outcomes through distinctive forms of government-business ties. As she notes concerning structural determinism, "A single framework cannot explain the diverse cross-national economic trajectories because the region includes countries with widely variable natural resource and human capital endowments, while state institutions and state-society relations have evolved differently in countries with distinct levels and experiences of colonial rule and postcolonial state- and nation-building."[4]

Blame Colonialism

Such carefully designed empirical studies tend to undermine broad theoretical claims. This has not prevented many scholars from making precisely such broad claims about "colonialism and the Middle East." Almost without exception, these individuals insist that colonialism was the critical structural fact that explains *all* bad outcomes in the region today. Since contemporary social science rarely discovers iron laws that are not subject to boundary conditions and whose causal effects do not change over time, colonialism is something of a social science unicorn if these claims are to be believed.

For instance, Mark Fathi Massoud argues that the rise of Islamic extremism in the region is a result of the sidelining of *sharia* law under colonial rule.[5] While the decision to continue with secular legal systems was made by postcolonial rulers, he argues, the ineluctable structural tendencies for this were laid by colonialists. The result: "Muslim-majority countries stunted the democratic potential of *sharia* by rejecting it as a mainstream legal concept in the 1950s and 1960s, leaving *sharia* in the hands of extremists."[6] That his article contains the phrase "blame colonialism" reflects a remarkable lack of intellectual maturation in the Islamic world for over half a century, transporting us back to the days of soap-box revolutionaries in the casbah. By definition, his theory could not account for Islamic extremism in non-colonized Saudi Arabia, Afghanistan, Iran, Turkey, or Yemen. This is a rather significant deficiency, since it implies the need to discover the explanation for Islamic extremism in those countries and then to see if that explanation works better for the former colonial countries as well, something Massoud fails to do. Without engaging in an extended critique of the logic and evidence that Massoud deploys, one might ask why political agency was so surprisingly reduced in this one domain in countries where political agency over all other matters was (tragically) so great; and, second, whether there is a single example of a country ruled by *sharia* law that has been actually democratic.

Moreover, if the claims were true, then those countries with more colonialism presumably would have less *sharia* law today. In fact, the correlation of the Islamic nature of the constitution to years of colonial rule (which should be strongly negative on Massoud's theory) is virtually nil at r=-0.17.[7] It is true that the two states that have the most Islamic constitutions, Iran and Saudi Arabia, were never colonized. It is also true that countries that were colonized by the secularizing French see relatively lower levels of Islamization than countries that were colonized by the British. But in general, colonialism tells us nothing about the ability of postcolonial rulers to shape their nations. Pakistan and Bahrain were heavily colonized and yet have created strongly Islamic constitutions while Turkey and Jordan, freed of any intensive colonial period, nonetheless have more secular constitutions. There is also some debate about whether secular states are necessarily at odds with *sharia* law: Western countries are the most consistent with Islam, according to the work of Hossein Askari.[8]

The large canvas approach of "blame colonialism" was given academic respectability by Edward Said's 1978 *Orientalism*, a study of the European cultural encounter with the Middle East and South Asia that has been used as a template by students of Middle East politics as well. Said had very little to say about the actual practices of colonial governance. Since colonialism was obviously evil, his interest was more in the causes of that evil. His answer was Orientalist thinking that "embodies a systematic discipline" that "fatally tend[s] towards the systematic accumulation of human beings and territories."[9] Quite apart from distorting the humane and diverse content of Orientalism, as Ibn Warraq retorted,

Said offered Middle East societies "a kind of comfort and absolution in being told that none of your problems are of your making, that you do not have to accept any responsibility for the ills besetting your society. It is all the fault of the West, of infidels."[10] Said's main legacy seems to have been to emasculate a previously empirical and well-grounded Middle East intellectual tradition and replace it with an effete, wounded intellectualism. This is reflected in Hamid Dabashi's updating of Frantz Fanon for the contemporary Middle East, *Brown Skin, White Masks*, or in a 2016 offering from Université Internationale de Rabat with the meaningless title, *Decentering Patterns of Otherness: Towards an Asymmetrical Transcendence of Identity in Postcolonial MENA.*[11]

The modern Middle East has lagged behind the rest of the world in terms of not just development, but also democracy. From a gap of 0.90 in 1977 on the six-point Freedom House scale (a modest shortfall of 15%), its divergence in average levels of democracy from the rest of the world grew steadily to a yawning 2.4 (40%) in 1997 and has only slightly closed since then (see Figure 7.3). In effect, the "third wave" of democratization (beginning in 1974) bypassed the region altogether, and the region continues to play catch-up.

Figure 7.3: Democracy in the Middle East

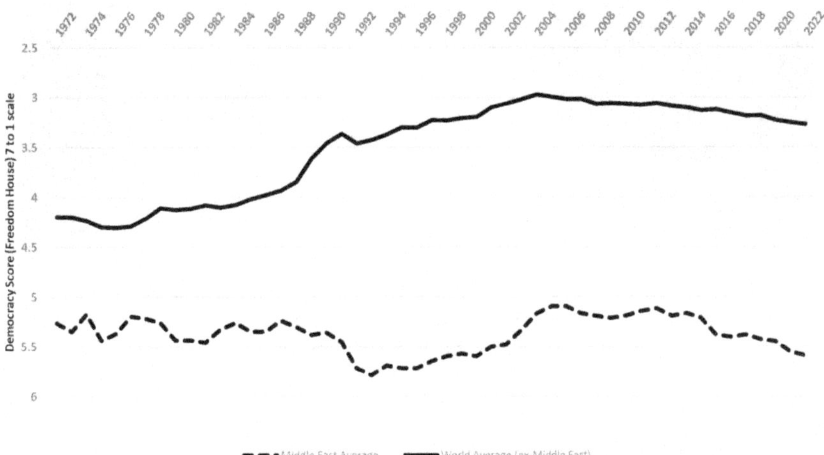

Freedom House combined average rating (7 low to 1 high) for democracy among countries of the Middle East, compared with the rest of the world, 1972–2022. Source: Freedom House: Freedom in the World.

Not surprisingly, the anticolonial tradition in Middle East studies departments has pinned the blame for democratic collapse not on post-colonial despots or on the unreformed patriarchal tradition of Islam in the region, but on colonialism. In a 2021 book, Elizabeth Thompson claims that Britain and France "stole" democracy from Syria and Lebanon in 1920 by accepting League of Nations mandates, fatally undermining their urges to self-government.[12] Colonialism in the Middle East was thus "a crime against humanity" and but for it, these two countries would be flourishing liberal democracies today. Radical Islam is, in her telling, the fault of the West. Thompson promises to "slay the demons" of colonial apologetics about the Middle East and debunk the stubborn belief that Arabs are in any way responsible for their own fates since 1920.

Arrival of a film projection bus in a village in colonial Algeria, late 1950s. Credit: Institut de recherches et d'études sur les mondes arabes et musulmans, CNRS/Aix Marseille Université.

Colonial Violence

As with democratic and economic collapse in the Middle East, critics of colonialism often blame the ongoing insurgencies in the region on the counterinsurgency campaigns waged by colonial authorities. This is further evidence of the "violence" at the heart of Western colonialism whose legacies have persisted to the present. The critics never bother with standard scientific questions: How do we define violence? What level of violence in defense of political order would be normal in such a situation? What level of violence would have obtained absent colonial rule? What degree of force was proportionate to the security threat? What level of violence ensued following the end of the colonial period? The total absence of such considerations is evidence of the stiff gale of irrationalism and decadence in scholarship on colonialism in the Middle East.

To take one prominent example, Harvard historian Caroline Elkins writes of the British counter-insurgency campaign against a protest movement that erupted in Egypt in 1919 as a signal case of her "legacy of violence" thesis.[13] The landed nobleman and former justice minister and deputy speaker of the colonial legislature whose arrest prompted the protests in Cairo, Saad Zaghlul, enjoyed "widespread support," she insists. Zaghlul's demand at Versailles for an Egyptian takeover of Sudan was a virtuous act of anti-colonialism. The British forces sent to protect railroad and telegraph lines "razed villages and imposed collective punishments." By the time order was restored, "three thousand Egyptians were dead." The only reason the British administration began talks on self-government, she argues, is that it "could ill afford multiple costly conflicts in the empire and needed to negotiate its way toward stability rather than relying entirely on costly sustained repression."

Every single sentence of her description is false. While a carnival of protest did erupt in Cairo in response to Zaghlul's arrest, the peasants were protesting post-war inflation and food shortages, not the arrest. They merely took advantage of the chaos in the capital to raid rural granaries and cut off railroad shipments.[14] Zaghlul's demand for Sudan was not a benevolent act of liberation but a proto-fascist gambit for "living space," one that Egyptian nationalists would pursue directly with Hitler during the next war. The 1919 "revolution" had little to do with colonialism *per se*. The only truly anti-colonial protests were in Cairo, and the British mostly ignored them. British forces were concentrated in the rural areas to protect railroads, telegraphs, and agricultural facilities. Despite threating to raze the closest village to any sabotaged facilities, the British never did this unless they were first attacked. For instance, at a rail break near the village of Shobak on March 30, 1919, the British approached the village seeking supplies and were fired upon. Thereafter, they cleared the village, arrested and shot the five leaders, and burned the village to the ground. A lengthy inquiry was carried out that eventually caused the head of the operation to lose his command.[15] In other instances, the British did not hesitate to defend critical facilities like train stations and granaries when under attack. At Saida-Zenab station on April 9, 1919, for instance, the Essex Regiment fired into a mob that was rushing the building, leaving ten dead.

An inter-war study of the entire 1919 conflict by a British officer concluded that the British response was wholly apt and always proportionate: "With the exception of those cases in which a definite attack which had to be repelled was made, there was little loss of life."[16] Simeon Shoul's later research concurs with the official British account. He reached a slightly *lower* figure than the official British count of 800 Egyptians killed, tallying 748 Egyptian dead and 29 British forces dead.[17] After the rebellion, the British continued with their long-standing talks on constitutional development which had begun with their entry into Egypt in 1882.

Elkins cannot judge whether the 1919 counter-insurgency campaign was justified because the answer for her is always: No. She cannot judge whether the British use of force was proportionate to the threat because the answer for her is always: No. She cannot judge whether specific acts of reprisal against villages near railroads that had been sabotaged were proportionate because the answer for her is always: No. And she cannot judge whether the final agreement announced in 1922 suitably balanced the demands of the nationalist elite, the needs of the common man, and the interests of the British because, again, the answer for her is always: No. As such, she has nothing meaningful to say about this episode. The only meaning is: Caroline Elkins hates the British empire. She could have reduced her entire 900-page book to just six words.

In stark contrast to the carefully calibrated and always accountable use of violence in Egypt during the British colonial period, the country was wracked by waves of heedless mass arrests and killings from the moment of its independence in 1952. Egypt's military killed at least 817 protestors at a sit-in at Rab'a al-Adawiya Square in Cairo in a single volley of fire in 2013. As a Human Right Watch report noted: "Using armored personnel carriers (APCs), bulldozers, ground forces, and snipers, police and army personnel attacked the makeshift protest encampment, where demonstrators, including women and children, had been camped out for over 45 days, and opened fire on the protesters."[18] Has independent Egypt been more violent towards Egyptians than colonial Egypt?

Contemporary anti-colonial critics avert their eyes from the bloodshed of post-colonial regimes because it does not excite their passions. Mere black and brown people being killed by other black and brown people. A shrug of the shoulders. The only history that stirs mainstream scholars to action is the idea of white men with upturned mustaches and pith hats making pompous statements about the need for order. Everything that comes afterward is a "legacy of colonialism."

Case Studies

In any case, whatever the probabilistic or "tendency" arguments about European colonialism and bad outcomes, it is easy to find one or two cases that show it is not an iron-clad law. The colony at Aden (in today's Yemen) and its surrounding protectorate, for example, was a whole-cloth creation of the British. The same is true of Israel, which is a pure creation of British imperialism. Without the British presence there in World War I, there would be no mandate, no Balfour Declaration, no Jewish homeland, and no independence in 1947. As with Aden, it is difficult to argue that this successful British colony, which attracted an insurgency from hostile groups on its periphery, was thereby the *cause* of slow development and a weak rule of law in those peripheral areas, whatever the justness of their complaints against the British colonial creation. The case of Jordan, for instance, shows that the Arab areas of the West Bank and Gaza were likely to be significantly less developed and less lawful with or without a separate Israel.

A better case to cite in refuting the "colonialism is bad" arguments are the stately emirates. It is surely a tragedy of the modern Middle East that the British were unable to find a similar sheikh to hold onto Aden as they found to continue sound administration in the United Arab Emirates. Appeals at the United Nations for a continuation of British rule by Adenese sultans like Muhammad Farid al Aulaqi fell on deaf ears. Another sheikh who defended British rule, Ahmad Abbad al-Sharif, died at age 90 in 2021, after a lifetime of political scheming to stay on the right side of the incumbents of the moment.

Critics may respond that these small states should not hold equal analytic weight to the "big eight" of Pakistan, Egypt, Turkey, Iran, Algeria, Iraq, Morocco, and Saudi Arabia, which together account for 80 percent of the region's population. Here again, however, care is advised. Only four of these—Pakistan, Egypt, Algeria, and Morocco—have a significant colonial history. These four account for 49 percent of the region's population and attract an inordinate amount of attention from anti-colonial scholars, especially scholars of Egypt and Algeria. By contrast, the other four—Turkey, Iran, Iraq, and Saudi Arabia—should, by this measure, be modern miracles showing the benefits of not being colonized. That may explain why most anticolonial scholarship on these countries centers on nonfalsifiable claims of "neocolonialism" made on the basis of political and economic ties to the West.

Pro-Colonialism

Against the fierce gale of anti-colonialism in Middle East studies, there has been a wispy breeze of pro-colonial arguments. The most interesting of these have been made by people of the left. Marx, mainly in newspaper articles, expressed a belief in the progressive role of colonialism in breaking down feudal social orders. The "tragical couplet" of backward societies and avaricious capitalism, he predicted, would lay the foundations for communist utopia. Colonialism was "the unconscious tool of history."[19] These views found expression in leftist writers on the Middle East who, in Said's view, were unconsciously captured by the "omnicompetent definitions" of Orientalism despite their otherwise humane instincts, and who went all in for colonialism.[20]

The Spanish writer and republican activist Aurora Bertrana, to take another example, wrote an impassioned plea for more intensive Spanish colonialism in Morocco after visiting the protectorate in 1935. She noted the continued low status of women, and bemoaned "our incurable incapacity for colonial administration," contrasting it unfavorably with French rule in Morocco.[21] The title of her 1936 book, *Sensual and Fanatical Morocco*, is enough to send a modern academic to the fainting couch. Bertrana is today scolded by postmodern professors for "perpetuating Orientalist stereotypes" and of having "a colonial gaze." Yet her arguments resound strongly among liberals and democrats in contemporary Morocco.[22]

The greatest traitor to the Left on matters colonial in the Middle East is without doubt Albert Memmi, whose about-face on the issue caused a minor storm. In a 1957 essay, issued in English in 1965 as "The Colonizer and the Colonized," Memmi described the impossible relations between outsiders like himself—a Tunisian Jew—and rising nationalists in the colonies. It was heralded, in the words of a reviewer of a 2003 re-issue, "first and foremost as a documentary expression of the human catastrophe which colonialism truly was."[23] Well, perhaps.

But Memmi's follow-up book with the nearly symmetrical title *Decolonization and the Decolonized* suggested life had not been half bad under colonialism. His book was a catalogue of folly and collapse once those nationalists took power. He now admitted to "a sense of remorse" for his earlier "lack of perspective."[24] The academy was enraged by Memmi's "reactionary turn" and never forgave him for shifting the blame from the colonizers to the colonized.

French-language research is considerably cleaved in half between the reliably anti-colonial establishment of the academic sinecures and the doughty pro-colonial amateur historians, many of them descendants of the *pieds noirs*, a million or so descendants of White settlers to mostly Algeria who moved to France after Algerian independence. They publish a steady stream of pro-colonial accounts of French rule in North Africa, having early on established countercultural publishing enterprises that bypass the ideological gatekeeping role performed by mainstream academic publishers.[25]

In 2023, for example, the independent scholar Driss Ghali published *Une contre-histoire de la colonisation française* (*An Alternative History of French Colonialism*) with a special emphasis on his native Morocco, as well as on French Tunisia and Algeria. "It is true that my parents and grandparents experienced colonial oppression," he wrote, "but my ancestors before them suffered from the anguish of underdevelopment." France had set in place the foundations for successful societies in North Africa, only to see their work destroyed by post-colonial governments. While these governments labored under a "blame colonialism" mentality, the former colonies of French Indo-China have leapt ahead by embracing globalization and good governance. "My father never thought of asking for reparations from France or of attributing his difficulties to her."

One exception to the steady anti-colonial *diktat* of the French academy was the University of Paris scholar, Daniel Lefeuvre, whose 2006 *Pour en Finir Avec la Repentance Coloniale* (or *Against Colonial Guilt*) built upon his earlier work on Algeria to declare that French rule in the north of Africa had been the only lifeline to save the country from the misery and starvation it later descended into.[26] Rapid population growth was for Lefeuvre the main challenge for Algeria, as he outlined in his 1997 *Chère Algérie: La France et Sa Colonie, 1930-1962* (or *Dear Algeria: France and Her Colony, 1930-1962*), and this is what had made it susceptible to nationalist propaganda.[27] The problem of French colonial rule, he argued, was that it was not up to the task of civilizing Algeria, a word he does not place in the usual quotation marks as a sign of intellectual sophistication and knowing cynicism.

From the likes of Bertrana, Ghali, Memmi, and Lefeuvre emerges a pro-colonial argument for the Middle East, which would go as follows: taking account of pre-colonial stagnation under Ottoman, caliphate, or warlord rule, and controlling for the particular challenges arising from Islamist tendencies, oil, and geography, historical colonialism played a mostly positive role in development in the Middle East. Absent that colonial encounter, Middle East countries today would be poorer, more autocratic, and less socially developed than they are. Those that were not colonized at all would more likely than not have better outcomes today if they had experienced colonial rule.

Whatever the historical debate, any attempt to revive colonial modes of governance would, of course, face a stiff headwind in the contemporary Middle East. The opposition to any renewed form of colonialism comes from both Left and Right.

On the left, the argument is simple: Colonialism was evil and harmful, so why would we revive such a practice? As mentioned, the evidence for this is scanty, but the argument is politically powerful. The semi-democratic government of Tunisia, for instance, has been trying to draw back tourists by refurbishing its colonial sites and centers. This effort has won them a good scolding from postmodern professors in the West who do not need to worry about where their next meal is coming from. "There exists a lucrative market for tourism based on nostalgia that perpetuates Orientalist views cultivated during the colonial era," scolds Daniel Coslett of Drexel University in the United States. The renovations "have arguably had the effect of reinforcing the longstanding colonialist duality of juxtaposed 'old' and 'new' city wherein 'traditional' Tunisian culture is fetishized for visitors within the medina [older area of narrow streets], while modernity and global integration are stressed without." While insisting that he does not want to rush to judgment, Coslett cannot resist rushing to judgment, reductively explaining that any participation in the global economy is essentially a continuation of colonialism. The sites "represent just a few examples of Tunisia's participation in a globalizing tourism economy that arguably reinforce the neocolonialist agendas of the [European Union] and other Western powers, as well as general internationalist interests."[28] That this tourism might generate needed revenue to pay for life-saving health and other public services appears not to enter into the Coslett's calculations.

Standing up to the anti-colonial criticisms of the Left is easy because they are so cliché. The more significant challenge may be standing up to anti-globalists of the right who see the sovereign state as inviolable and national interests as necessarily excluding foreign assistance. The deeply entrenched European ideal of sovereign modern states overseen by Weberian bureaucracies is one that is more popular today outside of Europe than within. Even if the reality of Middle East governments reflects the sovereignty of despots rather than of the people, and the states are more often failed than modern, still the ideal holds sway.

One justificatory approach may be to recenter analysis on legitimate forms of alien rule, whatever the form. As the Lebanon case illustrates, foreign participation in domestic governance structures may generate more legitimate rule than the current model. This is particularly the case if we consider non-Western governments that might play this role, since a strong undercurrent of specifically anti-Western (as opposed to anti-colonial) sentiment continues to animate much of the region.

The sort of "new political pacts" being forged by the UAE and Saudi Arabia for southern Yemen, and as suggested by France for Lebanon, with a clear colonial character provide models for how other Middle East countries could be rebuilt. The "public face" needs to be a trusted power, and this in turn creates the conditions in which Western governments, militaries, and businesses, as well as the resource-poor United Nations system, can operate.

Syria, Libya, and Afghanistan present the most obvious cases in need of a colonial governance structure. These would entail central roles for Turkey, Egypt, and Pakistan, respectively, in the reconstruction of these countries, just as Saudi Arabia and the UAE are the natural quarterbacks for the rebuilding of Yemen. One little-noted aspect of the Abraham Accords between Israel and other Middle East states may be the creation of an alliance that, unlike the Arab League, is committed to regional stability, good governance, and modernization, the very heart of the colonial enterprise. Deciding "who" will colonize and "why," after all, remains the most urgent issue for any colonial strategy, because, far more than the issue of the consent of the colonized, the issue of the willingness of the colonizer to expend precious resources on the well-being of alien peoples looms large.

It is notable that the United States, despite having a footprint in the Middle East that bespeaks its global power and responsibilities, is not a likely actor in any colonial-style partnerships in the Middle East in future. To Tony Badran's question of whether the US even needs a policy on Lebanon, we might add a more general question of whether the US needs a policy for failed states in the region beyond those that comport with its security and economic interests.[29] Brief colonial periods—a virtual UN mandate in Afghanistan that lasted 20 years and a more traditional eight-year colonial occupation of Iraq—are far briefer than the average 64-year colonial imprint for the eighteen Middle East countries that experienced Western colonial rule in the nineteenth and twentieth centuries. While portrayed by critics as examples of "endless war," both protectorates experienced large month-to-month variations in levels of internal conflict not inconsistent with many colonial episodes of the past. The reason that colonialism was drawn into such varying contexts in every region of the world, after all, was the universal existence of premodern social patterns characterized by weak political organization, endemic civil conflict, and vicious developmental cycles.

At present, it is unlikely that the United States will be a player in reviving new forms of governance in the Middle East. It will, however, almost certainly be called upon to support those forms that emerge, and to do so will require some intellectual background to the colonial experience in the region as a whole.

Endnotes:

1 The petition can be viewed online at AVAZZ.org, https://secure.avaaz.org/community_petitions/en/emanuel_macron_place_lebanon_under_french_mandate_for_the_next_10_years_/.

2 Fawwaz Traboulsi, *A History of Modern Lebanon* (2012), 92.

3 Teymur Atayev, "Blown Up Lebanon," *Turan Information Agency*, August 15, 2020.

4 Melani Cammett, "Development and Underdevelopment in the Middle East and North Africa," in Carol Lancaster and Nicolas van de Walle, eds., *The Oxford Handbook of the Politics of Development* (2018), 597.

5 Mark Fathi Massoud, "How an Islamic State Rejected Islamic Law," *American Journal of Comparative Law* (2018).

6 Mark Fathi Massoud, "Don't Blame Sharia for Islamic Extremism—Blame Colonialism," *The Conversation*, April 8, 2019.

7 Dawood Ahmed and Moamen Gouda, "Measuring Constitutional Islamization: The Islamic Constitutions Index," *Hastings International and Comparative Law Review* (2015).

8 Hossein Askari and Hossein Mohammadkhan, *Islamicity Indices: The Seed for Change* (2016).

9 Edward Said, *Orientalism* (1978), 123.

10 Ibn Warraq, *Defending the West: A Critique of Edward Said's Orientalism* (2007), 246.

11 Hamid Dabashi, *Brown Skin, White Masks* (2011); Najib Mokhtari and Aomar Boum, *Decentering Patterns of Otherness: Towards an Asymmetrical Transcendence of Identity in Postcolonial MENA* (2016).

12 Elizabeth Thompson, *How the West Stole Democracy from the Arabs* (2021).

13 Caroline Elkins, *Legacy of Violence: A History of the British Empire* (2022), 143-144.

14 Ellis Goldberg, "Peasants in Revolt: Egypt 1919," *International Journal of Middle East Studies* (1992).

15 James Kitchen, "Violence in Defence of Empire: The British Army and the 1919 Egyptian Revolution," *Journal of Modern European History* (2015).

16 Charles Gwynn, *Imperial Policing* (1934), 79.

17 Simeon Shoul, "Soldiers, Riots, and Aid to the Civil Power, in India, Egypt and Palestine, 1919–1939," University of London, Department of History, Doctoral Dissertation (2006), 71.

18 Human Rights Watch, *All According to Plan: The Rab'a Massacre and Mass Killings of Protesters in Egypt* (2014).

19 Karl Marx and Friedrich Engels, *On Colonialism: Articles from the New York Tribune and Other Writings* (1972), 216, 41.

20 Said, *Orientalism*, 156

21 Aurora Bertrana, *Marruecos sensual y fanático* [*Sensual and fanatical Morocco*], translated by Rajae El Khamso and Fernando García Martín (2009), 76.

22 Monica Lindsay-Perez, "Anticolonial Colonialism: Aurora Bertrana's *El Marroc Sensual i Fanàtic* and the Shortcomings of 'Anticolonial' Spanish Republican Feminism in the 1930s," *Journal of Middle East Women's Studies* (2019), 337, 339.

23 Patrick Chabal, "Review of The Colonizer and the Colonized," *Development in Practice* (2004), 716.

24 Albert Memmi, *Decolonization and the Decolonized*, translated by Robert Bononno (2006), 67.

25 For instance, see the *La librarie pied-noir*, http://www.librairie-pied-noir.com.
26 Daniel Lefeuvre, *Pour en Finir Avec la Repentance Coloniale* (2006).
27 Daniel Lefeuvre, *Chère Algérie: La France et Sa Colonie (1930-1962)* (1997).
28 Daniel Coslett, "Preservation and Tourism in Tunisia: On the Colonial Past in the Neocolonial Present," *Journal of North African Studies* (2020), 737, 742.
29 Tony Badran, "Does The US Need a Lebanon Policy?," *The Caravan* (Hoover Institution), December 8, 2020.

CHAPTER EIGHT

Why European Colonialism Was Right*

In the final episode of the British television comedy *Blackadder*, aired in 1989, the eponymous Edmund Blackadder (the vehicle for the comic wit of actor Rowan Atkinson) stands in the trenches on the Western Front in 1917 preparing to lead his men into a fatal assault on the German position. Captain Blackadder comments wearily: "Millions have died, but our troops have advanced no further than an asthmatic ant with some heavy shopping." This stirs a debate among his troops on how the war started. Lieutenant George posits: "The war started because of the vile Hun and his villainous empire-building." Blackadder delivers his famous rebuke: "George, the British Empire at present covers a quarter of the globe, while the German Empire consists of a small sausage factory in Tanganiki. I hardly think that we can be entirely absolved of blame on the imperialistic front."

In the eyes of contemporary critics, no European colonial power can be entirely absolved of blame on the imperialistic front. The practice itself was patently unethical, in their minds, because it always meant the illegitimate imposition of rule by the white man over the colored man. This robbed him of self-determination. This "distinctive procedural wrong"—the act itself was wrong—meant that no amount of good works could justify it.[1] The heroic assumption, of course, is that coherent, self-governing communities in which members consented to be ruled, existed before the white man, or would have emerged absent colonialism. The contemporary evidence from today's China, Iran, Sau-

* An earlier version of this chapter was presented at the conference "Ethics & Empire IV: The Modern Period", Christ Church College, University of Oxford, 30 June - 1 July 2022.

di Arabia, Ethiopia, Thailand, and Nepal is supposed to be a ringing endorsements of the just and legitimate orders that would have emerged absent colonialism.

Even if there was nothing wrong *per se* with one group extending its power over another and settling on its land, the critics continue, European colonialism always had terrible results. Exploitation, violence, racism, famine, and oppression were widespread, not to mention a lot of prurient photographs of brown breasts, the exclusion of the colonized from colonial drinks clubs, and colonial names in plant nomenclature. This genre of argument has more or less defined the whole intellectual outlook of South Asians, and their arguments about how Britain allegedly ruined Mother India.[2] These bad outcomes render any attempt at justification futile, they continue. Since there is extensive documentation of a lot of bad stuff under colonialism, colonialism must have been wrong. There is no need to engage in all the messy work of scientific history: conceptualization, measurement, control variables, counterfactuals, case selection, and so on. Boring. Please tell us another comforting bedtime story about how The White Man made our life miserable.

Even countries like Switzerland or Sweden, or latterly the United States, that did not have colonies cannot escape blame on the imperialistic front. They were accessories to the crime. "A group of feminist researchers" had come up with the idea that not being a colonial power meant that a country had in fact been a colonial power. The failure of these non-colonial countries to embrace mass immigration from Africa and the Islamic world showed that they had internalized colonial racism just like former colonial powers, according to these critics. Scientific endeavors like wrist-watches and vaccines created "knowledge orders that rely on a Eurocentric 'universal truth,'" a cardinal colonial wrong. The "international capitalist enterprises" of such countries had a colonial character when examined from the perspective of Leninist theory. Most unforgivably, they "used missionary activities to spread the idea that Christianity and the West were superior." The fact that this major insight from the group of feminist researchers had been "marginalized" in mainstream society was further evidence that it must be true because marginalizing was what colonialism did.[3]

What's more, the indictment continues, these colonial evils were no oversight. They reflected a horror at the heart of the West itself. A true ethical reckoning would admit that the problem was not Western colonialism but the West itself, premised on the triple evil of Christianity, capitalism, and Caucasianness.[4] Had the world been left to the tender mercies of Islam or African fetish priests, and then put under socialist management with white people scattered to the winds, life would have been better. That a lot of black and brown people continue to jostle to live in the West with its Christianity, capitalism, and Caucasians is merely an act of mercy to rid it of these ills.

Thus the debate on the ethics of European colonialism is nothing less than a debate on the ethics of the West itself. Since colonialism was evil, on this account, the West is evil. The only remaining work to be done is to liquidate Western countries through mass immigration, reparations, and the erasure of white culture. That the resulting polities are unlikely to be liberal, wealthy, or stable is merely comeuppance for colonial crimes. Authentically decolonized societies will replace the unbearable trauma once known as Western civilization. The thought leaders in the academy coming up with these political manifestos need not fear for their own lives, since they will be long gone. And they have stopped breeding (to fight climate change), so they have no concerns about the well-being of their progeny either.

That, in a nutshell, is where the debate on the ethics of European colonialism has descended in the contemporary academy and, by extension, in much of the educated public. With rare exceptions, no scholar dares to lay out an ethical justification for colonialism that might be put alongside its empirical record. So it is useful to bring some reality back to the confused philosophers and feminist researchers of the academy to show why European colonialism was right when it began and right throughout its tenure. In turn, it is a reminder of the fundamental rightness of the West and of its constituent aspects.

Germany as Exemplar

The ethics of European colonialism are best approached by taking a case study of a particular episode and evaluating it based on some logical and measurable standard. The example of the German colonial empire in Africa and Asia is a good case study because of its compact and short-lived nature. German colonialism was not just ethical in conception and in nature, but also in practice. In turn, the German example, because it was typical of the European colonial model, can be used to judge European colonialism as a whole. Writ large, German colonialism was a noble validation of the liberal heart of the West, and why it is Best.

I am, in one respect, entirely in agreement with establishment scholars of German colonialism. I believe that German colonialism can be judged as a whole and without much need for exceptions or doubts. Like many of them, I also believe that the German colonial experience is a good basis on which to judge European colonialism as a whole. I depart from them only in my complete disavowal of every aspect of their conclusions. Almost without exception, in their view, German colonialism was unethical by definition and unethical in its operation, and this in turn shows the evil at the heart of the European colonial adventure which showed its true face with the rise of the Nazis.

The most prominent advocate of the view that German colonialism was always, everywhere, and in an extreme degree, unethical, the University of Hamburg's Jürgen Zimmerer, has put it this way: "Colonialism is violence and it is a crime against humanity."[5] The only tasks these historians set themselves are the documentation of horrors and the literary panache with which they can deliver the moral verdict. A 2019 book of essays in Germany given the ironic title *The Colonialism Debate,* for instance, contains "debate" only on the questions of whether German colonialism was inherently evil or evil only in practice; whether the evil was really extreme or just extreme; and whether Germany should immediately and unconditionally hand over billions of euros, denounce itself before those it previously oppressed, and empty its museums and libraries of any offensive works or, on the "conservative" side, spread out those necessary acts of penance to ensure they achieve the desired self-loathing and liquidation of the German nation.[6] This reminds me of "debates" in Mao's China about whether the capitalist West would collapse in 10 years or, on the "conservative" view, in 20 years.

The blanket condemnation of German (and other European) colonialism is the shared moral lens of 99% of scholars of German colonialism. These establishment scholars deny the possibility of any person of *compos mentis* holding views to the contrary, and they vigorously organize themselves to ensure that no dissent arises. The Humboldt University historian Andreas Eckert refers to pro-colonial utterances in the academy as "flights of fancy." Thus, he worries that "even high-powered historians are not protected from flights of fancy,"[7] citing Wehler's point that "critics of forced labor in the colonies never offer feasible alternatives" to the provision of government services[8] and Flaig's point that European colonialism in Africa "opened up the possibility of new paths after a 1,000-year history of bloody violence and genocide."[9] In similar mode, in 2020, Hubertus Büschel of the University of Kassel urged new efforts to quash dissent and achieve Leninist-style unified thinking in the academy on colonial issues: "The long road to a 'common' colonial history (*'gemeinsamen' Kolonialgeschichte*) becomes a little easier if those who want the same thing, and stand up for the same thing, work together—and not against each other."[10] This reflects a more general insistence in the academy that colonial history should be shut down: "There is no need for further research to 'finally discover the historical truth' about colonialism," wrote the Belgian historian Guy Vanthemsche of Vrije Universiteit Brussel (VUB).[11]

I allow the possibility that perhaps 1% of scholars in Germany on this issue may harbor dissenting views because, in addition to the old warhorses who are protected from the Woke mobs by their age, there are a few frightened young scholars out there who dissent from the crushing orthodoxy of their ogre professors. A young Ph.D. student in German studies at an American university teaching a course on German colonialism recently wrote to me: "I wanted to reach out and ask if you had any suggestions for good articles about the history of German colonialism that are not marred by undue political biases. I want to make sure students get a full picture and thus would like to assign some solid historical texts, regardless of the persuasion." In the German academy, such an act of pedagogical daring would be a refuse-chute straight into the professional dumpster.

An undergraduate student from Germany studying at another American university wrote this about my positive view of German colonialism: "I have always expressed similar view points at my school in Germany and at college here as well, but teachers usually, especially in Germany, told me to not speak about colonialism in even a partially positive way."

Even a few scholars whom I invited to blurb my book on German colonialism demurred with responses (to cite the words of one of Germany's best-known scholars whose work is relatively balanced) "for reasons that I am sure you understand." Another potential participant in a conference on this paper, in this case an academic in the UK, replied to my invitation as follows: "In an ideal world, I would be able to debate this consequence-free in any given context, but I think you appreciate that we are far from such a world and there are real professional dangers to an independent historian like myself appearing in the context of the conference, almost independent of what I actually end up saying." The *omertà* of the academy on questions colonial is more strictly enforced than its counterpart in Sicily.

Having succeeded in eliminating any debate from their ranks, the scholars of German colonialism have turned their guns on society at large. Here, the task is more difficult, as the University of Exeter's Richard Toyne writes wearily about pro-colonial essays that circulate in the media: "There are ordinary people who share and like the articles and perpetuate the tropes, either in conversation or in social media." For Toyne, this outrageous spectacle of ordinary people having the affrontery to read and share articles that they find compelling, and then to have conversations about them, without first consulting the Index of Approved Thoughts compiled by postcolonial scholars like himself is "the problem of colonial history" that scholars have set themselves to correct. As Zimmerer says of my book *In Defense of German Colonialism*:[12] "There have quite recently been attempts by the Far Right to reintroduce the balance sheet approach to the understanding of colonialism, or to provide an outright 'defense of German colonialism', as a new publication announces...We are witnessing a resurgence of voices, which are working on a collective (national) narrative, in which the 'civilizing mission' is reaffirmed, and with that the superior role of the erstwhile missionary, namely the German government itself."[13]

Note, in passing, the supercilious off-hand reference to "the balance sheet approach," as if mere mention of this will send correct-thinking people into paroxysms of outrage. Academics like Zimmerer have not the faintest idea about what cost-benefit analysis is, or how it is applied in policy analysis. Its main purpose is to elucidate the implications of different scope, weighting, and valuation strategies in policy analysis mainly for the purpose of stress-testing hypotheses and double-checking other methods. As I wrote: "One main challenge of [colonial] research is to properly enumerate the things that matter and then to assign them weights, weights that presumably varied with time and place."[14] As Abernethy wrote of the intellectual value of the cost-benefit approach, there is at minimum a plausible aggregation strategy under which "the case for colonialism is strong."[15]

I cite all this in order make an epistemological point: given the very high costs of dissent from the reigning anti-colonial orthodoxy in the German academy and more generally on questions of European colonialism, the knowledge generated since this terror began around 1960 is, by definition, suspect and should be assumed to be mostly false. I might end my whole argument there. Given the tainted conditions in which the "scholarship" of the academy seeking to show the unethical basis of colonialism was created, we are left with the burden of proof on the shoulders of the critics. There is no reason to suppose that any of their research, except by fluke, would withstand scientific conditions of scrutiny given the ideological hothouse in which it has been raised. Thus I fully endorse the statement by the University of Marburg professor Benedikt Stuchtey that "what Gilley and others are doing is a new chapter in the perception of the colonial past."[16]

The High Ethical Standards of German Colonialism

As Blackadder avers, the German colonial empire was indeed little more than a sausage factory when compared to the British, or even French empires. Even at its greatest extent, it was at best a large industrial estate. In 1913, it ruled 12.5 million people, about 2% of the European colonial total or 7% of the ex-Raj total. As with all European colonial empires, there was a "big part" and then all the rest. In the German case, the big part was German East Africa (later British Tanganyika, mostly today's Tanzania as well as Rwanda and Burundi), accounting for 7.7 million people in 1913, or 57% of the "people-years" (number of people times number of years) of German colonialism. This was quite a large sausage factory. The next biggest part was German Cameroon (today's Cameroon), with 30% of the colonial people-years. The rest was made up little bits: German Togo (mostly today's Togo with one small part in Ghana) at 8%, the two Pacific colonies of New Guinea and Samoa (today's Marshall Islands, Nauru, Palau, Samoa, and Solomon Islands) at 3%, and two small holdings of 1% each at Jiaozhou (better known as Qingdao) in China and a tiny enclave in German Southwest Africa (today's Namibia).

These colonies all came into being sometime in the 1880s or early 1890s, and they all came to an abrupt end as German holdings at the Treaty of Versailles in 1919. German colonialism is thus unique in being a late arrival and an early departure from modern European colonial project. Although German historians have predictably carved it up into an impossible complexity of phases, places, purposes and results, it is better understood as a piece—a 30-year experiment in overseas rule. As such, it is ripe for ethical analysis *tout court*.

To make plain my profound scholarly dissent from the reigning and strictly policed anti-colonial orthodoxy, let me state for the record the view that I will elaborate here: German colonialism was both inherently ethical, as well as ethical in practice, in every place where it was found. It arose from natural processes of human endeavor, violated no formal or informal laws in doing so, and found a ready welcome in all places. Its initiation through the Berlin conferences marked it as ethical from the start because of the moral compass established by the Berlin agreements. It brought untold security and peace to formerly conflict-prone territories, generated rapid gains in health and material well-being, initiated the documentation and celebration of local cultures, created pathways to accountability and self-government, freed hundreds of thousands of slaves, and protected women and minorities from exploitation. The absence of economic gains for Germany itself might be called an ethical failure for the German taxpayer, but one of minor significance. In all these ways, German colonialism was ethical and legitimate not just from an objective viewpoint, but also from the subjective viewpoints of the colonized. German colonial subjects worked and fought vigorously for German colonial rulers, and protested loudly when they were replaced by other alien rulers after World War I. The combination of rule-following, justificatory ethics, and consent-based rule that characterized the German colonial experience marks it as a high-point of the European colonial achievement.

The analysis that follows bears close resemblance to the similar studies of other episodes of European colonialism by the Belgian historian Jean Stengers[17] and the Stanford political scientist David Abernethy[18] in making the following five main points which, although related, need not be accepted together.

First, European civilization, of which Germany was an exemplar, was superior to any of the civilizations that it colonized in terms of its ability to organize a society in ways that would lead to justice and human flourishing. It is, therefore, *ipso facto* the case that any European country that had the means and the will to establish its rule in any other place would *by definition* make that place better off unless the establishment of colonial rule was somehow premised on an explicit renunciation of its own domestic norms, institutions, and policies—if, in other words, it set sail with an explicit *mission barbare* in the formulation or implementation of its colonial rule. This was never the case in the post-Napoleonic phase of European colonialism. In this way, there is an *ex ante* deductive case for the ethical justification of European colonialism.

Secondly, European colonial expansion was inevitable given the large developmental gap that emerged compared to all other areas and given the strong pull factors drawing European powers into various places. Empire is not just unremarkable in world history, but especially unremarkable in this case. If there is anything remarkable, it is how little colonialism German pursued until very late—especially given its undisputed stature as the center of Oriental studies (contra Edward Said's theory that Oriental studies caused colonialism) and being the second largest economy in Europe (contra Lenin's theory that capitalism caused colonialism). This means that the relevant counterfactual on which all critique of the specific actions and policies of European colonialism must be based is rule by another colonial power or rule by some alliance of domestic imperialists armed with Western weapons and mercenaries. In all cases, the colonized areas would have experienced massive shifts in economic activity, new infectious diseases, a communications revolution, the breakdown of traditional society, and much else. Even though this is not a particularly novel claim, it is repeatedly ignored by colonial critics because it would force them to think like adults rather than enraged teenagers.

Third, European colonial expansion was justified because it is anachronistic to say that overseas expansion violated nations or sovereignties or rules that did not exist. A typical phrase from critics—uttered for instance by Kenya's UN ambassador in 2022—was that European countries set up colonies with "no regard to the ancient nations that they cleaved apart." Calling internecine and inter-tribal warfare "ancient nations" is a stretch. Even if there were coherent nations with sovereign borders and institutions of governance at work (none of which is true), they themselves did not recognize limits on their own ability to colonize other nations. As Fisch wrote: "Strictly speaking, the colonial acquisition of Africa needed no justification. The Europeans had the necessary strength and, even within Europe, the right of conquest was widely accepted both in theory and state practice."[19] Accounts of the European arrival usually suggest a sort of "here are the latest rulers" shrug of the shoulders from local peoples. As the eminent Hermann Hiery noted, Germany's Pacific expansion "conformed completely to indigenous behavior" insofar as the Germans conquered their rivals and became the strongest tribe, demanding fealty from others.[20] Absent German rule on most islands, the alternative was a powerful clan or break-off faction of the current chief, with all the blood-letting that typically ensued.

Fourth, European colonialism delivered positive results. Objective measures of the colonial impact show that places that were colonized earlier, more intensely, held for longer, and whose post-colonial rulers more strongly affirmed the colonial legacy are better off today by all measures of development. This provides an *ex post* inductive case for the ethical justification of European colonialism. I have produced a lengthy bibliography that brings this research together in one place.[21] The only point to add is that the objective benefits of German rule were generally widely noted by other colonial powers until they needed to justify what one British diplomat called the "shabby annexations" of Versailles.[22]

Finally, European colonialism enjoyed local consent and was locally legitimate. The points (1) to (4) above were recognized as such by colonial subjects, who treated colonial states as subjectively legitimate and undertook voluntary acts of consent to colonial rule. It is, of course, possible in theory that a people might treat as legitimate a regime that is barbaric, illegal, avoidable, and harmful. Indeed, most German scholars have responded to the obvious evidence of subjective legitimacy with charges of "false consciousness" among the colonized. For other anti-colonial scholars, expressions of support or acts of consent were merely instrumental, a feigned compliance intended to reap self-interested rewards rather than a moral verdict on the regime. These claims often reach absurd levels.

The Askari soldiers who fought for German rule in East Africa, for instance, often went months without payment (given only IOUs written up on the spot) and without a single German officer in charge. Many years later, in 1953, the German commander in East Africa, Paul Emil von Lettow-Vorbeck, returned to redeem all the IOUs, with interest. He was welcomed by surviving Askaris sporting their German-era medals who greeted him with their old marching song *Heia Safari!*

When World War I ended, over 6,000 native soldiers and 12,000 other natives along with 117 chiefs from German Cameroon and their entourages chose to leave the colony with the 95 surviving German officers. The delegation marched into neutral Spanish Guinea (today's Equatorial Guinea).[23] While cooling their heels on the island of Fernando Po, the 117 chiefs petitioned the King of Spain to intervene to reestablish German rule in Cameroon. "We hope soon to return with the German government. This love and loyalty is unchanged. We have only one wish: to join the German government to return to Cameroon."[24]

Of the five points above, the first—about the superiority of European civilization—carries extra weight because of its epistemological implications. A key dimension of European civilization is its self-critical tradition. To carry the logic, as members of liberal society, we participate in such critiques since this is the heart of the Western tradition—the self-critical, contentious, free speaking, and Christian natural rights traditions that elevate the moral and material well-being of the individual above all else.[25] So, to make the point sharply: the very fact that we sit in a conference room in Oxford debating "the ethics of European colonialism" is evidence that European colonialism was ethical. We make the point all too well. Let me assure you that there are no conferences in China on ethics of Qing imperialism, no conferences in India on the ethics of the subjugation of Goa, no conferences in Pakistan on the failed subjugation of what became Bangladesh, no conferences in Turkey on the ethics of the Ottomans, no conferences in Oklahoma on the ethics of Comanche empire, no conferences in Saudi Arabia on the ethics of Arab expansion, and no conferences in Africa on the ethics of Bantu or Buganda or Fulani expansion.

Having stated these assumptions, then, the "ethical analysis of European colonialism" becomes a very different project from what is normally assumed in the academy. European colonialism was a *de facto* "good thing", in the same way that we view the establishment of the modern state, the market economy, and the emergence of modern society as "good things." Therefore, to Lu's point[26] that both the international system and Western societies helped create permissive "structural" conditions for colonialism to happen, I differ only in the valence of my response: plaudits and awards should be given to those enabling forces.

The key question to ask about German colonialism is whether there are any reasons to suppose that it was an outlier from the standard patterns of rule by European powers in the overseas areas. Was there some *mission barbare* that emerged from Berlin in which a European country somehow went abroad in fundamental violation of, indeed with intentional malice towards, its liberal ethics at home? Second, was there some catastrophic failure grounded in gross negligence or willful neglect that rendered the colonial encounter either objectively harmful or subjectively illegitimate in practice?

The Spirit of Berlin

German colonialism, unlike that of other colonial powers, began with an explicit, and multi-national commitment, to ethical behavior. This is what I have called the "Spirit of Berlin"[27] that emerged from the Berlin conference of 1884-1885. While the immediate issues of the conference were the Congo and West Africa, as well as free trade, the broader question was on what basis territorial claims could be justified. The Spirit of Berlin was embodied in two principles. First, colonial powers, whatever else they did, had a responsibility to improve the lives of native populations. European powers, the agreement stated, should be "preoccupied with the means of increasing the moral and material wellbeing of the indigenous populations."[28] When a colony was established, the powers "engage themselves to watch over the conservation of the indigenous populations and the amelioration of their moral and material conditions of existence." That included putting an end to slavery and the slave trade. It also meant supporting religious, scientific, and charitable endeavors to bring the "advantages of civilization." Bismarck praised the "careful solicitude" the European powers showed towards colonial subjects. A British delegate noted that "humanitarian considerations have occupied a prominent place in the discussions."[29] Native uplift was now an explicit rather than implicit promise of colonialism.[30] Words only. But words that would create norms, and norms that would shape behavior.

The second principle insisted that any colonial claim needed to be backed up by "the existence of an authority sufficient to cause acquired rights to be respected." Merely planting the flag or signing a treaty with local chiefs for a box of cigars was no longer enough. Colonialism required governance so that "new occupations ... may be considered as effective." This was later known as the principle of "effective occupation." With this idea, Bismarck introduced the expectation that colonialism was not mere claim-staking or resource development—even if those things were still better than no colonialism at all. Rather, as with his newly-created Germany, political institutions needed to provide the means to deliver the end of good governance. The effective occupation principle applied at first only to coastal areas since the powers did not want to set off conflicts over border demarcations in inland areas.[31] But as mapping of the inland proceeded in subsequent years, it crept willy-nilly into the bush as well. It "became the instrument for sanctioning and formalizing colonial occupation even in the African hinterland," noted a legal historian.[32]

Thus German colonialism, more than any other, set sail with an explicit *mission civilatrice* that closely tied its external policies to its domestic norms, institutions, and policies. Given point (1) above, this makes its structural nature *by definition* ethical.

Operational Questions

Was there anything about the implementation of the Spirit of Berlin by Germany that created conditions that were predictably or obviously likely to result in gross negligence or willful neglect that would render the policy on net harmful for the colonized? At first, Bismarck wanted colonialism on the cheap. "Clerks from the trading houses, not

German generals," would handle the functions of government.[33] It did not take long for this plan to fall to pieces as new colonial governments wired to Berlin requesting funds to establish "effective occupation." Bismarck could not refuse since that principle was of his own making. Nonetheless, the gap between initial plans and later revisions of plans opened a period of between five and ten years in every colony where governance was too limited and thus opened the way for abuses that violated the first principle of the Spirit of Berlin.

The German colonial port of Qingdao in 1897. Credit: Bundesarchiv.

We should pause to note the nature of this ethical critique: that there was *not enough colonialism*. Critics of colonialism who frequently speak out of both sides of their mouths—colonialists were evil when they did x and also evil when they failed to do x—have no grounds for assailing Berlin for not colonizing intensely enough if their view is that colonialism itself was evil. This is especially the case where the counterfactual to German rule was precisely the sort of "colonialism on the cheap" seen under trading companies (as in the German Pacific) or vaguely supported settler groups (as in German Southwest Africa and German East Africa).

Here, is it important to debunk the popular myth of a genocide against the Herero peoples in German Southwest Africa between 1904 and 1907. One academic referred to "the undisputed 1904 genocide of the Herero people" in which "three-quarters of the entire Herero population (60,000 out of a population of 80,000), as well as half of the Nama people, were killed, either in battle or due to harsh conditions imposed by German troops."[34] This is nonsense, every word of it. The decline in the enumerated populations of *all* groups in that colony between a census issued in 1904 and another in 1911 of roughly 50% is mainly indicative of weaker census capacity, more dispersed populations, declines in fertility, and out-migration following the very real (and justified) German counter-insurgency campaign against an explicitly anti-German genocidal insurgency led by Herero leader Samuel Maherero.[35] What battle losses and population deaths resulted from the German campaign, whether numbering in the hundreds or thousands (certainly not 60,000), emerged unintentionally and contingently in the unpredictable desert conditions of that conflict. In the words of Susanne Kuss, the German counter-insurgency strategy "emerged entirely independently of any conscious decision for or against a strategy of concerted racial genocide."[36]

There are several historians who have called out the nonsense of the "genocide" claim.[37] The work of Brigitte Lau, for instance, caused gasps from the German academic establishment because, following the truth, she reached conclusions that differed from the genocide narrative.[38] "Those whose interventions are taken up today in quarters one would not want to suspect they mean to associate with," warned one scholar darkly about Lau's work, "still have an obligation to at least pause and reflect on the potential, if unintended consequences of their interventions—even if, in the case of Brigitte Lau at least, such appropriations run clearly counter to the intention of her life work."[39] In other words, even though her work is factual, those facts need to be suppressed for the greater glory of anti-colonial ideology.

The initial condition of "limited colonialism" in all German colonies raises some ethical issues because of the slow pace at which security, health, education, and the rule of law were established. After that, the operation of German colonialism was usually described as typical of other European colonialism. Germany acted as a typical colonial power in terms of the institutionalization, organization, governance, and administration of its colonies. As two German scholars concluded: "The imperialists, including the Germans, provided peace, settled rule, an expanded trade area, infrastructure, bureaucracy, a tax system—the essentials of a modern state which would rule over a wider swath of territory than would have obtained if African and Pacific ethnic rivalries had been allowed to persist." Faced with similar circumstances, they wrote, "Germans acted much like their French and British imperial counterparts."[40]

Thus the ethical issues are about optimization of pathways to good outcomes. Here we find ourselves in the well-trodden territory of ethical critique of particular individuals, governments, and policy choices. Did German colonialism suffer from an unconscionably large number of policy failures, individual acts of misbehavior, or failed governing systems? Far from it. Indeed, right up to 1914, Germany was gaining wide admiration, especially in Britain, for the remarkable achievements of its short colonial era. As late as January 1914, the director of Germany's main colonial training school was in London being praised by his British counterparts. "German[y] is throwing herself into the unfamiliar task of colonial policy with characteristic thoroughness and energy," commented the venerable architect of Britain's southern Africa policy, Lord Milner, "and it would be a great mistake to think we have nothing to learn from their experiences."[41] As an eminent American historian wrote: "If an opinion poll had been taken in England before August, 1914, the result probably would have been that the Germans were regarded as better colonial rulers than any others except the British."[42]

Undaunted, German scholars dig away in the garden searching for delicious bones of colonial misdoing. For instance, Rebekka Habermas of Georg August University of Göttingen wrote a book called *Scandal in Togo: A Chapter of German Colonial Rule* concerning an allegation of misconduct made in 1906 about a young German district officer named Georg ("Geo") Schmidt. The book documents the story of Schmidt's alleged rape of a Togolese girl. She had been force-married to a Togolese man at a young age, who then apparently rented her out to Schmidt on weekends. The allegation (against Schmidt for rape, but not against the Togolese man for polygamy and pimping) was lodged by a local Catholic missionary. It was taken up by the Berlin press and investigated by the Reichstag, and led to the filing of formal criminal charges. Schmidt was tried and acquitted but then removed from his position by the governor.

Habermas called her book "micro-history" which, by definition, does not tell us anything in general about German colonialism. This is especially the case when the example has been chosen because it is a "scandal." If anything, we should assume that a scandal is a scandal because it is not typical. But let us assume that we can learn something about German colonial history from this incident. What do we learn? That German colonial rule by the early 20th century had reached impressive standards of governance. Even in the hands of a dedicated anti-colonial ideologue, the Schmidt story provides a ringing endorsement of German colonial rule. The people of Togo, who under their pre-colonial rulers had been systematically raped, murdered, plundered, and enslaved, experienced under German rule a brief moment in which a single alleged rape by a single official became the subject of a wide-ranging national inquiry, public debate, court trial, and ultimately professional sanction. If only the people of Togo could have enjoyed anything like German rule before or after!

To take another example, much has been made of the case of Heinrich Leist, acting governor of German Cameroon. In 1893, Leist came into conflict over pay and work conditions with native soldiers from the region of Dahomey. After they tried to kill him, Leist whipped their wives and arrested the conspirators, hanging several of them. After an official investigation, he was charged with brutality for the whippings. He was tried in Potsdam, found guilty, and removed from his position. Legislators debated the case in the Reichstag and introduced a new legal code to manage labor relations in the colonies.

What should an intelligent person make of this case? Certainly, they should not take their cue from German academics, who fly into a rage with cries of misogyny, racism, and exploitation. These great minds make no effort to imagine what it was like for a lone German official in a remote station to bring security and development to a region long plagued by tribal warfare and human carnage. In addition to his governing duties, Leist was patron of the local nursing association that cared for rescued black slave children. He also, unusually, offered free medical services to all black staff lucky enough to work for the German authorities. More pointedly, the Dahomey soldiers who rebelled had been purchased by a German explorer from a local chief who planned to use them in a human sacrifice ritual. Their fate under German colonialism was *by definition* better than under tribal rule. How many Dahomey women and slave children would have been beaten, whipped, and left to die by fellow Africans absent German colonial rule? Was the overall trend of justice under the Germans improving or getting worse?

During the Leist trial, one Reichstag critic brandished the hippo leather whip that Leist had borrowed from the natives to flog the women. Why did the natives have hippo leather whips? Because corporal punishment was widely practiced in West African society for theft, infidelity, and unpaid debts. The use of flogging, as in Europe not long before, was considered more humane and effective than other forms of punishment. Most criminals could not pay fines while prison was considered a luxury because of the food and bedding. Flogging as a form of punishment had been abolished in Germany itself only in 1871. In fact, everything about the Leist case sounds a ringing endorsement of German dominion. If this is the "dark side," then there is clearly a marvel awaiting discovery.

Legitimacy

I take the most important ethical question when discussing particular governments, individual officials, policy choices, and administrative acts to be whether the given political object holds and exercises political authority in a "rightful" or legitimate manner. The best judges of that are those subject to that political authority. Like Burke, I am skeptical of the metaphysicians, alchemists, and Doctors of the Rights of Man who presume to sit in the comfort of their studies in the West casting down thunderbolts of ethical condemnation on the alleged injustices of the past.

I follow Beetham[43] in believing that the considered judgements of those subject to any political object have a default assumption of being correct. This does not rule out external ethical critique, indeed Beetham believed that philosophical critique was a key empirical tool because it stress-tested the assumptions and replayed the ethical debates that were operative in any given political system. Properly done, it could show which were weaker and which more likely to succumb to popular revolts. But ultimately, "legitimacy in action" was to be judged from the behavior of those subject to the political object, not philosophers in the universities.

Like Morris, I reason that there is no *a priori* reason why a colonial governing system should be less legitimate than an indigenous one.[44] Quite the opposite, in fact. A colonial governing system headed by a European state, which was always more law-bound, accountable, and liberal than any indigenous governing system, was *a priori* more likely to be legitimate by creating the conditions for legitimacy to arise among its subjects (social consciousness, social trust, universal norms, etc.)

Beetham seminally defined the concept of legitimacy as inhering in three distinct but complementary dimensions. These were *legality*, meaning, adhering to rules and procedures, in other words, the "legalness" of political authority that was the original meaning of the term legitimacy (the Latin *legitimatus*, or made legal); *consent*, meaning enjoying the expressed, behavioral consent of the political subjects as evident in their relatively voluntary actions that invest political authority with public recognition and active compliance; and *justification*, meaning, conforming in both operation and outcomes to the shared ethical norms and expectations of those who are subject to the rule, often described in the sociology literature as a "congruence" of state values and social values.

These three dimensions of our modern understanding of "rightfulness" or "legitimacy" are to me the appropriate basis on which to judge the ethics of European colonialism. I will briefly apply them to the German case.

Legality

At the time of German colonial expansion from roughly 1884 to 1899, there were no legal prohibitions in national or international law against territorial expansion, quite the opposite, in fact. The Duala, Herero, Dahomian, Ngoni, Samoan, and Qing cultures that the Germans displaced recognized no legal or procedural restraints on their own expansion. In policy terms, the roll-out of German colonialism was probably the most legalistic of any major European power, consistent with the Prussian legal tradition that was spreading to the unified Germany itself.[45] German administrative officers took care and interest to study local legal norms and adopt the colonial ones accordingly. In Qingdao, the top German judge published two books on Chinese jurisprudence and its integration into colonial rule.[46] Again, it is true that lawless rule by local chiefs and native officers was a common complaint because of the sparse German presence on the ground—just 79 European administrative staff for all of German East Africa in 1914, for instance, a territory of 7.5 million souls.[47] The period of improvement, dating from around 1907, was one in which an increased German administrative presence was being built. Indeed, the thick legality in which the Germans carried out their colonial rule—detailed regulations and documentation of flogging punishments, for example, or extended trials for administrative misconduct in several celebrated cases—became fodder for the ideological scolds of the academy who could pore over the records to allege the evils of German colonialism.

Attention to context and accuracy also undermines the claims made by Firth and others about the flogging of workers in the German Pacific. As in criminal justice, floggings were first used by the government offices and state companies to compel workers to fulfill their contracts but then reduced under formal German rule. In 1912, in the district of Rabaul, the center of contract workers, 128 floggings were administered with an average of 7 strokes of the cane (the legal maximum being 15). In all cases, a doctor was present and the details carefully recorded. At the time, the total contract workforce in the Rabaul area was 18,000. In other words, far less than one percent of the workforce drew a flogging in that year (the last for which records exist). The governor called the use of floggings "brutal and immoral," and a raging debate gripped the final years of the colony over the ethics, law, and legitimacy of the practice.

The carefully compiled statistics on punishments in German East Africa likewise suggest not just a rule-following management of criminal justice but also its light touch (Figure 8.1).

Figure 8.1: Criminal Punishments in German East Africa (1911-12)[48]

Punishment	Number of People	Per 1,000 people
Execution	16	0.002
Prison (over 6 mos.)	1,127	0.15
Prison (under 6 mos.)	10,718	1.42
Flogging	5,944	0.79
Fines	3,518	0.47

Another hotly contested issue of legality is the German use of forced labor. One must distinguish here between the ideal and the practice. The ideal is perfectly defensible. Colonial government projects and services needed to be funded and taxation was impractical. Moreover, a key element of development was labor force participation. Mandatory labor in lieu of the payment of taxes served both purposes and was historically the norm throughout empires. So, when critics describe German colonies as "slave states" because they imposed a mandatory annual labor requirement, they are challenging the very idea of mandatory labor, not its practice. Since that idea was more than ethical, the challenge fails.

In practice, there was the predictable train of petty abuses. African chiefs, for instance, often sent their slaves to perform the duties and then sent them back several times under different names. In German New Guinea, the few instances of forcible labor recruitment outside of the annual limits, Sack noted, were rare compared to the 37,000 voluntarily recruited in the last five years of that colony alone. If this is "the ugliest side" of German rule in the Pacific, as Hiery insists, then German rule was remarkably humane.[49]

Consent

Native consent to the initial founding and subsequent operation of German colonial government was enthusiastic and explicit. In 1888, for example, the Germans annexed the remote island of Nauru which had been engaged in a devastating civil war for a decade. It had been prompted by a dispute at a ceremonial feast where, in a quarrel over some coconut oil, the wrong man was shot with an old horse pistol.[50] The war threatened to extinguish the native people, estimated at 1,300 when the Germans arrived, and so the German annexation was a life-saver. About 800 weapons were confiscated after the 12 chiefs of the island were put under house arrest in a copra shed (for drying coconut). The weapons secured (along with all stores of alcohol), the chiefs were released. The traditional head chief was then reinstalled, and the islanders turned from tribal vendettas to copra and later phosphate mining. Whatever the cavils of later critics, Hiery notes, "there is much evidence of local support for German policy," and there was no "conservative-traditional opposition movement…in favor of blood feuding and the like."[51]

In the post-colonial era of independence, when elected or military governments ruled, the German era came to be seen as a golden age of consent. In 1971, Papua New Guinea adopted a national flag showing the German colors black-red-gold with a bird-of-paradise, a symbol introduced by the Germans, which also appeared in the new coat of arms similar to the coat of arms designed by the legendary German governor Wilhelm Solf. In 1991, the Federated States of Micronesia replaced their previous national anthem (adopted in 1976) with the old German national song, *Ich hab mich ergeben*, leaving the melody unchanged and making the first stanza a more or less literal English translation of the German original.

In other cases, while German colonialism represented a threat to some native power-holders, it enjoyed the consent of those living under their oppression. The 1905-1907 Maji Maji insurgency in German East

Africa, for instance, was led by Ngoni warlords trying to hold together their tyrannies over local people. Tanzanian scholars Eginald Mihanjo, Director of Studies at the National Defense College of Tanzania and Oswald Masebo, Chair of the Department of History at the University of Dar es Salaam, noted that the Ngoni warlords were vicious militarists who plundered and killed lesser tribes until the Germans stepped in to establish order. "The emergence of a younger generation that included Christian converts, Western educated youths, well-traveled traders, and even ex-slaves all becoming part of the social fabric was perceived as a challenge to their traditional authority," wrote Mihanjo and Masebo.[52] The consent of the oppressed to "colonial oppression" was plainly evident from the robust native participation in the counter-insurgency operation against the Maji Maji.

A critical aspect of consent was preparations for self-government under colonialism. The Nigerian scholar Ben Azikiwe wrote in 1931 of German, French, and British colonies (with a poise and intelligence that is scarcely imaginable today) that in place of what he called the Spirit of Berlin's "ethics of aggressive altruism" should be forged a "constructive ethics of imperialism." This would put preparations for self-government and a more collaborative approach to development at the center: The "responsibility of trusteeship is not fully discharged in securing justice to the natives," he wrote. "If the natives will eventually become a dominant factor in the administration of their own native land, and if their colonial rulers are really honest and sincere, their material and moral advancement must be fostered by positive measures" towards self-government. He concluded: "It is desirable from the standpoint of universal order for the stronger races to rule or guide the weaker ones, provided the rulers will act merely as guides—on a reciprocal basis of exploitation for development—and provided the ruling power is willing to surrender its colonial suzerainty when the subject feels that he is fledged for political independence."[53] No less than in British colonies, the Germans managed this consent-based legitimacy with explicit preparations for self-government.

Justification

German colonialism was generally seen by other European states as more "pro-native" in its justification (especially as memorialized in the Spirit of Berlin) and subsequent operation than those of other European colonial powers. The justificatory debates in Germany and in the colonies were intense—especially among Reichstag members who made use of their control of the annual colonial budget to apply intense scrutiny to colonial affairs.

Figure 8.2: Living standards relative to Germany before (1890), during (1890-1920), and after (1920-2020) German colonial rule (GDP per capita as % of German GDP per capita)

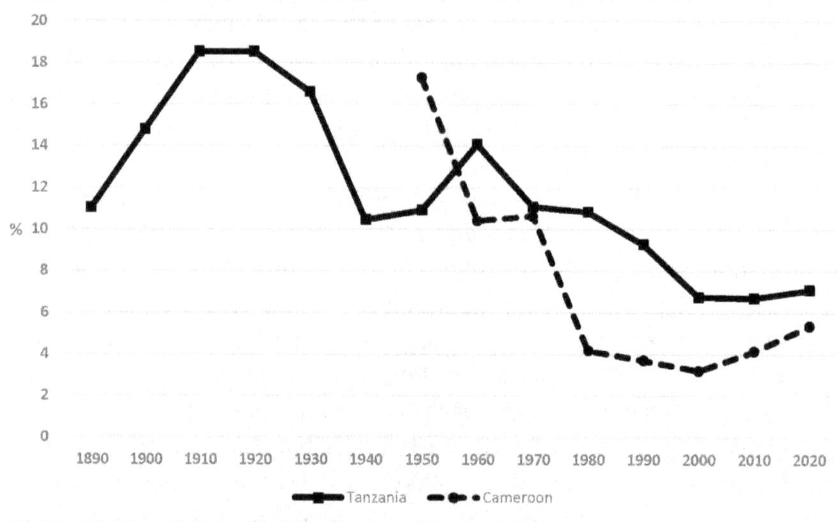

Sources: For 1890 to 1910, based on Broadberry and Gardner (2022); For 1920 to 1940: Real wages in Tanzania from Klocke (2022), Figure 4.6, compared to Maddison Project real GDP per capita in Germany calibrated to Maddison Project 1950 ratio of GDP per capita in both countries; For 1950: Maddison Project Database 2010; For 1960 and 1970: Penn World Table Version 10.0; For 1980 to 2020: IMF World Economic Outlook Database.

The most powerful justificatory ethic of German colonialism—the congruence of core values between the ruling system and those held by the population—was development. Nothing really can come close in terms of a powerful justificatory ethic. Cavil all you want about hippo whip floggings, exclusive colonial clubs, and unchaste photographs of African breasts, the overwhelming justification of German rule was provided by its being a way to attach very poor areas to the engine of a modern industrial economy through which extensive human flourishing became possible. This fact is dull, bloodless, and absolutely central. Nothing else really matters.

We can estimate income gains for German colonies in Africa using the Broadberry and Gardner estimates for colonial South Africa and Kenya. These show that the colonies narrowed the gap in their income levels compared to the UK by an average of seven and a half percentage points between 1885 and 1910, which was one of the strongest periods of colonial growth in Africa.[54] There is no reason to suppose that German East Africa was any different, indeed contemporary accounts express surprise at the rapid development there compared to British colonies. If so, then, assuming no changes between the 1910 and 1920 figures due to the war, the growth in German East Africa would also have narrowed its income gap to the home country by a similar figure of 7.5 percentage points. That would put living standards at 19% of German living standards by 1920, this in a society that a generation earlier had been in the Stone Age. Calibrating backwards from the 1920 figures allows us to present the entire period relative to German income levels (Figure 8.2).

When the Germans took over East Africa, there was no cash economy to speak of because the Anglo-German abolition of slavery had devastated agricultural production. During the German colonial period, the standard of living in its colonies was converging sharply on the German economy, as would be expected from the integration of the colonial areas into a major industrial economy. As Klocke wrote: "Colonial rule served to mobilize many of these resources in the first place, creating cash-earning opportunities, and facilitating a wide range of new economic activities. It thus initiated a series of important structural changes that have been observed in nearly all colonial economies. These include increased market penetration, a higher degree of monetization of the economy, the introduction of new crops, an increased commercialization of agriculture, the expansion of infrastructure, the expansion of wage labor, the establishment of a national administration, and the creation of a system of Western education."[55]

This trend was reversed under a League of Nations mandate from 1919 to independence around 1960, with the exception of the final decade of mandate rule. It then continued to decline after independence. In other words, developmental outcomes have never again reached their levels of the German colonial period.

From this standpoint, the consequential justification of the German colonial record is excellent. This objective development created opportunities for subjective betterment which generated legitimacy. It is notable, for instance, that one of the first things that native communities in the Pacific did with their savings from copra and phosphate production was to build a community church. Next would often come a highly decorative community canoe. External critics might decry this use of funds, but it was self-evidently a valued result of German colonialism to these communities—a congruence between the values being promoted by the German colonial system and the values inherent in the local communities.

Conclusion

European colonialism was ethical and beneficial, as shown by the German case. As the preeminent cultural and economic power of Europe (rivalled only by Britain), it is surprising that the German colonial experience was so modest. It is also a tragedy. No country was able to scale-up life-saving governance infrastructure at the speed of the Germans, and no country enjoyed such long-lasting goodwill among the colonized. In 1938, a Yale historian published the results of his fieldwork in the 1920s in the former German Cameroon, noting that "wherever I went, I heard natives praise the excellent German administration."[56]

Stripped of its colonies at Versailles, Germany became embittered. "The only colonial power that professed the idea of solidarity with practically all of the consequences of that word," wrote the German economist and colonial advocate Arthur Dix in 1926, "is the one that paid the price for its attitude by losing all of its colonies."[57]

In place of its liberal colonial identity came an illiberal and viciously anti-colonial identity in the Nazi/Communist alliance of inter-war Germany. Europe would be the first victim of this vicious new ideology. The colonial British, fighting alongside millions of colonial subjects, defeated Nazism despite Hitler making common cause with anti-colonialists from India, Palestine, Egypt, Iran, and Iraq (similar to how his Japanese fascist allies were setting up anti-colonial movements in Malaya, Burma, and the Dutch East Indies).

But fascism did not die in 1945. Instead, it was exported to European colonies with consequences no less dire—especially under the "fascist anti-colonialism" of the Afro-Caribbean psychiatrist Frantz Fanon.[58] The colonized were soon decolonized into the hands of indigenous tyrants promising to cleanse the fatherland of the alien element. Prominent Nazis were hired by the Egyptian madman Gamal Nasser to foment anti-colonial uprisings throughout the Middle East.[59]

After colonialism retreated from the Third World, fascism took root again in its original home: the totalitarian circles of the West where extreme right and left were indistinguishable. Calls to "decolonize" life in the West were made by radicals who hoped to replace the liberty and equality of liberal democracy with race-based hierarchies and spoils systems. The West is still trying to recover its colonial identity under ongoing assaults from the inherent illiberalism of anti-colonial ideology. The stakes are no less than they were in the past.

Endnotes:

1 Lea Ypi, " What's Wrong with Colonialism," *Philosophy & Public Affairs* (2013); Margaret Moore, "The Taking of Territory and the Wrongs of Colonialism," *Journal of Political Philosophy* (2019); Massimo Renzo, "Why Colonialism Is Wrong," *Current Legal Problems* (2019).

2 Kanaiyalal Maneklal Munshi, *The Ruin that Britain Wrought* (1946).

3 Patricia Purtschert, Francesca Falk, and Barbara Lüthi, "Switzerland and 'Colonialism without Colonies': Reflections on the Status of Colonial Outsiders," *Interventions: International Journal of Postcolonial Studies* (2016), 289-291.

4 Terence Ranger, "Christianity, Capitalism and Empire: The State of the Debate," *Transformation* (2006).

5 Richard Toyne, "German Colonialism: Suppressed Memories: A CIGH Interview with Jürgen Zimmerer," University of Exeter, *Center for International and Global History Forum*, July 9, 2021.

6 Olaf Zimmermann and Theo Geißler (eds.) *Kolonialismus-Debatte: Bestandsaufnahme und Konsequenzen* [*The Colonialism Debate: Assessment and Consequences*] (2019).

7 Andreas Eckert, "Rechtfertigung und Legitimation von Kolonialismus" ["Justification and Legitimation of Colonialism,"], October 23, 2012.

8 Hans-Ulrich Wehler, "Transnationale Geschichte: Der neue Königsweg historischer Forschung?" ["Transnational history: The New Silver Bullet in Historical Research?"], in Gunilla Bude et al. (eds.), *Transnationale Geschichte. Themen, Tendenzen und Theorien* [*Transnational History. Themes, Tendencies and Theories*] (2006), 170.

9 Egon Flaig, *Weltgeschichte der Sklaverei* [*A World History of Slavery*] (2009), 214.

10 Hubertus Büschel, "Ehrerbietung gegenüber den Opfern" ["Deference to the victims"], *Der Tagesspiegel*, October 18, 2020.

11 Guy Vanthemsche, "'It's Time to Finally Discover the Historical Truth': How Belgium Deals With Its Colonial Past," *The Low Countries*, April 16, 2019.

12 Bruce Gilley, *In Defense of German Colonialism: And How its Critics Empowered Nazis, Communists, and the Enemies of the West* (2022).

13 Toyne, "German Colonialism: Suppressed Memories".

14 Bruce Gilley, "The Case for Colonialism," *Academic Questions* (2018).

15 David Abernethy, *The Dynamics of Global Dominance: European Overseas Empires, 1415–1980* (2000), 403.

16 Benedikt Stuchtey, *Das Schwierige Erbe Des Kolonialismus: Die europäische Debatte über den Umgang mit den kolonialen Vergangenheiten* [*The Difficult Legacy of Colonialism: The European Debate on Dealing with the Colonial Past*] (2020), 4.

17 Jean Stengers, "Les malaises de l'histoire coloniale" "[The problems of colonial history"] in *Congo: Mythes & Réalities* [*Congo: Myths and Realities*] (2020), 310.

18 Abernethy, *The Dynamics of Global Dominance.*

19 Jorg Fisch, "Africa as Terra Nullius: The Berlin Conference and International Law," in Stig Forster et. al. (eds.), *Bismarck, Europe and Africa: The Berlin Africa Conference, 1884–1885, and the Onset of Partition* (1988), 360.

20 Hermann Hiery, *Fa'a Siamani: Germany in Micronesia, New Guinea, and Samoa 1884-1914* (2020), 74.

21 Bruce Gilley, *Contributions of Western Colonialism to Human Flourishing: A Research Bibliography*, Version 3.0 (2020), DOI: 10.13140/RG.2.2.16960.56328

22 William Harbutt Dawson, "Introduction" in Heinrich Schnee, *German Colonization: Past and Future* (1926).
23 Jacqueline de Vries, "Cameroonian Schutztruppe Soldiers in Spanish-Ruled Fernando Po During the First World War: A 'Menace to the Peace'?," *War & Society* (2018).
24 Hans Poeschel, *Die Koloniale Frage im Frieden von Versailles* [*Colonial Questions at Versailles*] (1920), 242-243.
25 Larry Siedentop, *Inventing the Individual: The Origins of Western Liberalism* (2017); Joseph Henrich, *The WEIRDest People in the World: How the West Became Psychologically Peculiar and Particularly Prosperous* (2020).
26 Catherine Lu, "Colonialism as Structural Injustice: Historical Responsibility and Contemporary Redress," *Journal of Political Philosophy* (2011).
27 Gilley, *In Defense of German Colonialism*, 25-40.
28 "General Act of the Conference of Berlin Concerning the Congo," *American Journal of International Law* (1909).
29 Great Britain, National Archives, PRO30/29, "Malet to Granville", Februry 21, 1885.
30 Thomas Pakenham, *The Scramble for Africa* (1991), 254.
31 Geoffrey de Courcel, "The Berlin Act" in Stig Forster et. al. (eds.), *Bismarck, Europe and Africa: The Berlin Africa Conference, 1884–1885, and the Onset of Partition* (1988), 255.
32 Imanual Geiss, "Free Trade, Internationalization of the Congo Basin, and the Principle of Effective Occupation," in Stig Forster et. al. (eds.), *Bismarck, Europe and Africa: The Berlin Africa Conference, 1884–1885, and the Onset of Partition* (1988), 271.
33 Steven Press, *Rogue Empires: Contracts and Conmen in Europe's Scramble for Africa* (2017), 153, 159.
34 Lu, "Colonialism as Structural Injustice," 265.
35 Gilley, *In Defense of German Colonialism*, 41-58.
36 Susanne Kuss, *German Colonial Wars and the Context of Military Violence* (2017), 74, 47.
37 Hinrich Schneider-Waterberg, *Der Wahrheit eine Gasse: Anmerkungen zum Kolonialkrieg in Deutsch-Südwestafrika 1904* [*A Path to Truth: Notes on the Colonial War in German South West Africa 1904*] (2008); Andreas Eckl, *"S'ist ein übles Land hier": zur Historiographie eines umstrittenen Kolonialkrieges* [*"It's A Bad Country Here": On the Historiography of a Controversial Colonial War*] (2005); Claus Nordbruch, *Völkermord an den Herero in Deutsch-Südwestafrika?: Widerlegung einer Lüge* [*Genocide of the Herero in German South West Africa? Refuting a Lie*] (2006)
38 Brigitte Lau, *History and Historiography* (1995).
39 Reinhart Kössler, "Entangled History and Politics: Negotiating the Past Between Namibia and Germany," *Journal of Contemporary African Studies* (2008), 322.
40 Arthur Knoll and Hermann Hiery (eds.), *The German Colonial Experience* (2010), 495, vii.
41 "German Colonial Policy," *The Times* (London), January 14, 1914.
42 William Rogers Louis, *Great Britain and Germany's Lost Colonies, 1914-1919* (1967), 3.
43 David Beetham, *The Legitimation of Power* (1990).
44 Christopher Morris, "What's Wrong With Imperialism?" *Social Philosophy & Policy* (2006).
45 Die Landes-Gesetzgebung des Deutsch-Ostafrikanischen [German East Africa, Legislative Assembly], *Schutzgebiets: systematische Zusammenstellung der in Deutsch-Ostafrika geltenden Gesetze, Verordnungen, usw.* [*Systematic compilation of the laws, regula-*

tions, etc. applicable in German East Africa], July 24, 1911.

46 Georg Crusen, "Die rechtliche Stellung der Chinesen in Kiautschou" ["The Legal Status of the Chinese in Jiaozhou]," *Zeitschrift für Kolonialrecht* (1913); "Moderne Gedanken im Chinesenstrafrecht des Kiautschougebietes" ["Modern Thoughts on the Chinese Criminal Law of Jiaozhou]," *Mitteilungen der Internationalen Kriminalistischen Vereinigung* (1914).

47 Great Britain, Colonial Office, Report to the League of Nations on the Administration of Tanganyika. (1921), 32.

48 Great Britain, Naval Intelligence Division, *A Handbook of German East Africa* (1920), 21.

49 Hiery, *Fa'a Siamani*, 77, 150, 75.

50 Nancy Viviani, *Nauru: Phosphate and Political Progress* (1970), 15, 22-23.

51 Hiery, *Fa'a Siamani*, 74.

52 Eginald Mihanjo and Oswald Masebo, "Maji Maji War, Ngoni Warlords, and Militarism in Southern Tanzania: A Revisionist View of Nationalist History," *Journal of African Military History* (2017), 63.

53 Ben Azikiwe, "Ethics of Colonial Imperialism," *Journal of Negro History* (1931), 306, 307, 296, 307.

54 Stephen Broadberry and Leigh Gardner, "Economic growth in Sub-Saharan Africa, 1885–2008: Evidence from Eight Countries," *Explorations in Economic History* (2022). The numbers are a 10 percentage point narrowing from 16% to 26% of the UK level for South Africa and a five percentage point narrowing from 9% to 14% of the UK level for Kenya from 1885 to 1910.

55 Sascha Klocke, *Land, Labour, Legacies: Long-term Trends in Inequality and Living Standards in Tanzania, c. 1920-2020*, Department of Economic History, Lund University, Doctoral Thesis, 2022, 61.

56 Harry Rudin, *Germans in the Cameroon, 1884-1914* (1938), 419.

57 Arthur Dix, *Was Deutschland an seinen Kolonien verlor* [*What Germany Lost In its Colonies*] (1926), 14; *Schluss mit 'Europa': Ein Wegweiser durch Weltgeschichte zu Weltpolitik* [*The End of "Europe": A Guide Through World History and Politics*] (1928).

58 Egon Flaig, "Faschistoider 'Antikolonialismus' Frantz Fanon" ("The Fascist Anti-Colonialism of Frantz Fanon") in *Die Niederlage Der Politischen Vernunft* (*The Defeat of Political Reason*) (2017).

59 Joel Fishman, "The Postwar Career of Nazi Ideologue, Johann von Leers, aka Omar Amin, the 'First Ranking German' in Nasser's Egypt," *Jewish Political Studies Review* (2014).

CHAPTER NINE

In Defense of King Léopold's Congo

SINCE 1998, the idea of the Congo has been closely linked in the Western imagination to the book *King Leopold's Ghost* by the American journalist Adam Hochschild. The book is widely assigned in high schools and colleges, and it regularly tops best-seller lists in colonial, African, and Western history. Hochschild has become a sort of king of the Congo, or at least of its history. The book is lazily cited by reputable scholars in their footnotes any time they wish to assert that it is "well known" and "beyond doubt" that sinister men in Europe wrought havoc in Africa over a century ago. Any discussion of the Congo, or of European colonialism more generally, invariably begins with the question: "Have you read *King Leopold's Ghost*?"

I have read it. And I can declare that it is a vast hoax, full of distortions and errors both numerous and grave. Some people might view "King Hochschild's Hoax," as we might call it, as an empowering fable for modern Africans at the expense of the white man. But its debilitating effects on Africa, and on the Congo in particular, make the opposite more nearly the case. It is a callous and negligent chicotte (hippo whip) lash on the backs of all black Africans, narcissistic guilt porn for white liberals at the expense of the African. The Congolese lawyer Marcel Yabili calls it "the greatest falsification in modern history," a compliment of sorts, I suppose.[1]

Hochschild's book is a history of the private domain of the Belgian King Léopold II in the Congo river basin that was founded in 1885 and then handed over to the Belgian government in 1908. The book alternates between diabolical accounts of Léopold and hagiographic accounts of three of his critics, the British campaigner Edmund Morel, the

British diplomat Roger Casement, and the black American missionary William Sheppard. The narrative style is dark and conspiratorial, from the initial plans for the domain to its final dissolution. All along, Hochschild's aim is to elevate the story into one of the greatest evils ever perpetrated by the West upon the Rest.

There have been two documentary films about Hochschild's fable, both travesties of art as well as of fact. But the worst is yet to come. A dramatized Hollywood version by the American directors Ben Affleck and Martin Scorsese, co-produced with the late singer and activist Harry Belafonte, has been in development since 2019. The history of the Congo might have survived one gut punch from California (Hochschild did his research entirely at libraries in the state and teaches at Berkeley), but once Hollywood weighs in on the matter, history, as such, will be impossible. Before that happens, let's set the record straight and end this most malicious form of imperial plunder.

The first and biggest deceit at the heart of *King Leopold's Ghost* is the attempt to equate Léopold's "État Indépendant du Congo," or EIC (long mistranslated as the Congo Free State), with Western colonialism.[2] Yet the EIC was a short-term solution to the absence of colonial government in the Congo river basin. The deal was simple: Léopold was to open the area to trade and eliminate endemic Arab slave empires and African tribal wars. In return, he hoped to bring glory to the Belgian people for having done what no other European ruler dared (one in three Europeans who travelled to the Congo died, usually of illness), namely to lay the foundations of a modern state via private means. The EIC had nothing to do with the Belgian government. To the extent that limited abuses and misrule occurred in some parts of his domain (discussed below), this was a direct result of its not being controlled by a European state. As no less than Edmund Morel insisted (not quoted by Hochschild): "Let us refrain from referring to the Congo as a Belgian colony, let us avoid writing of 'Belgian misrule.'"[3]

European colonies were governed by and accountable to the institutions of a liberal state at home. That was the fundamental structural fact of a European colony, meaning the characteristic that explains its behavior. This fundamental fact was absent from the EIC. This explains its evolution and eventual takeover by Belgium. The EIC was a second-best solution to the absence of colonialism. Hochschild will have none of it because his intention all along was to use his tale as an indictment of European colonialism ("A Story of Greed, Terror, and Heroism in Colonial Africa" as the subtitle put it). Yet a fevered ideological agenda does not collapse a valid conceptual distinction.

In a pattern of misrepresentation that is repeated on other issues, Hochschild at first admits that the EIC was no colony and then proceeds to say the opposite for the entirety of the book. The fiefdom "was shared in no way with the Belgian government" which "had no legal authority over [Léopold] as ruler of the Congo," he alerts readers. Yet not only the subtitle of the book but laced throughout are constant smears against European colonialism. The book shows "colonial brutality" and "the wrongs of colonial rule" resulting from the "logical consequence of the very idea of colonialism."[4]

This distortion is no mere technicality. Rather, it is the central lie of *King Leopold's Ghost.* The freelance EIC had at peak just 1,500 administrative officers and about 19,000 police and soldiers for an area one third the size of the continental United States. As such, it exerted virtually no control over most areas, which were in the hands either of Arab slave-traders and African warlords, or of native soldiers nominally in the employ of the EIC or Belgian concession companies without a white man for a hundred miles. Hochschild's description of the EIC as "totalitarian" is bizarre, as is his claim that Léopold exerted a "framework of control…across his enormous realm."[5] If only this were true.

That is why Congo reformers like Morel, much to the annoyance of Hochschild, advocated either German or British colonization of the area. Morel's view, according to Hochschild, speaking *ex cathedra* from the hallowed seat of Modern California, "seems surprising to us today" and was among his "faults" and "political limitations."[6] Quite the opposite. The moment the Belgians colonized the Congo in 1908, a miraculous improvement was noted on all fronts. Seeking to debunk colonialism, Hochschild's book points to the opposite conclusion. This is the first and biggest lie at the heart of *King Leopold's Ghost.*

From 1908 until the Belgians were forced out by an unholy alliance of Western radicals and rootless native men in 1960, the Congo was a place that European people took their families for vacations. The South African author Alan Paton, no friend of colonialism, would look back wistfully in his posthumously published autobiography of 1988 on a trip he took with his family in 1957, wondering if perhaps his own anti-colonial advocacy had been a mistake:

> Can one take such a journey [to Congo] today? Are there such hotels today? I cannot speak with authority, but I would doubt it. The roads and hotels and public services of the Congo were, if one may

> call them so, gifts from Belgium. Today Zaire lives under a dictator, and has, like most African countries, a crippling foreign debt. Colonial rule brought to this vast country its usual gifts of curses and blessings. The undoing of colonial rule brought its further gifts of curses and blessings. Which were worse, the curses of the doing or those of the undoing? Which were better, the blessings of the doing or of the undoing? These are not questions which permit rational inquiry. The passions and emotions that are aroused by their very asking make rational inquiry impossible. I can only conclude that Dorrie and I and our sons and daughters-in-law were given the privilege of making one of the great journeys of the world, at a time [1957] when it was possible to make it.[7]

The second, but more visible, untruth is the claim that for 23 years, EIC officials throughout the territory sponsored violent actions such as chopping off hands to force natives to collect rubber, leaving millions dead in a horror that should be directly compared to the Holocaust. There are about a dozen little cheats here, one embedded in the other like Russian nesting dolls.

Here are the facts. By 1891, six years into the attempt to build the EIC, the whole project was on the verge of bankruptcy. It would have been easy for Léopold to raise revenues by sanctioning imports of liquor that could be taxed or by levying fees on the number of huts in each village, both of which would have caused harms to the native population. A truly "greedy" king, as Hochschild repeatedly calls him, had many fiscal options that Léopold did not exercise. Instead, he did what most other colonial governments, and many post-colonial ones in Africa did: he imposed a labor requirement in lieu of taxes. In a small part of the upper Congo river area, he declared an EIC monopoly over "natural products," including rubber and ivory, that could be harvested as part of the labor requirement to pay for the territory's government. From 1896 to 1904, an EIC company and two private companies operated in this area, which covered about 15% of the territory and held about a fifth of the population. The resulting rubber revenues temporarily saved the EIC, but only until rubber prices collapsed in 1906. Still, the preservation of the EIC meant the preservation of its life-saving interventions against disease, tribal war, slavery, and grinding poverty that had bedeviled the region since recorded time.

The rubber quotas imposed on natives in this 15% of the territory were enforced by native soldiers working for the companies or for the EIC itself. In many areas, the rubber came with ease and the natives prospered. The rubber station at Irengi, for instance, was known for its bulging stores and hospitable locals, whose women spent a lot of time making bracelets and where "no one ever misses a meal" noted the EIC soldier Georges Bricusse in his memoirs.[8] Elsewhere, however, absent direct supervision, and with the difficulties of meeting quotas greater, some native soldiers engaged in abusive behavior to force the collection. Bricusse noted these areas as well, especially where locals had sabotaged rubber stations and then fled to the French Congo to the north. In rare cases, native soldiers kidnapped women or killed men to exact revenge. When they fell into skirmishes, they sometimes followed long-standing Arab and African traditions by cutting off the hands or feet of the fallen as trophies, or to show that the bullets they fired had been used in battle. How many locals died in these frays is unclear, but the confirmed cases might put the figure at about 10,000, a terrible number.

The abuses were first reported by an American missionary in *The Times of London* in 1895.[9] It quickly brought Léopold's censure: "If there are these abuses in the Congo, we must stop them," he warned EIC officials in 1896. "If they continue, it will be the end of the state."[10] For the next ten years, reforming the Congo's rubber industry absorbed an inordinate amount of attention in the British and American press and legislatures, not to mention within Belgium and the EIC itself, leading to formal Belgian colonization in 1908.

Hochschild thus takes a very limited, unintentional, unforeseen, and perhaps unavoidable problem of native-on-native conflict over rubber harvesting and blows it up into a "forgotten Holocaust" to quote the subtitle given to the French edition of his book. Inside this great invention are many more perfidious Russian dolls.

First, in what might charitably be described as a puzzling instance of creative editing, Hochschild takes the testimony of an EIC officer against rubber harvesting and turns it into a call for rubber atrocities. This little dodge forms a cornerstone of his argument that chopped hands for rubber was "deliberate policy" and "officially sanctioned."[11] The speaker is Charles Lemaire, who was the first commissioner of the Equator district and whose memoirs are held at the University of Ghent. The original quotation reads:

> Lors qu'il fut question de caoutchouc, je m'y refusai et écrivis au Gouvernement: "Pour faire du caoutchouc dans le district de l'Équateur, (où nulle preparation n'avait été faite), il faudra couper des mains, des nez et des oreilles, et je ne sache pas que nous ayons

> chassé les bandits arabes pour nous substituer à eux.[12]

My own translation would render it:

> As soon as the rubber question was raised, I stood firmly in opposition and wrote to the government: "We will have to be cutting off hands, noses, and ears if we intend to collect rubber in the Équator district (where no preparations had been made). And I don't think we drove away the Arab bandits in order to take their place."

As even the anti-Léopold historian Daniel Vangroenweghe noted, Lemaire, like most EIC officials, was unwilling and unable to pursue a systematic rubber harvest: "He didn't have the time and he understood that it would not work without the use of force."[13] Hochschild, however, creatively edits the quotation to say the opposite:

> As soon as it was a question of rubber, I wrote to the government, "To gather rubber in the district...one must cut off hands, noses and ears."[14]

Hochschild subsequently recognized this "misleading" quotation, said he was sorry, and asked that it be corrected for future editions.[15] Still, this is such a reckless act of dishonesty that one can only marvel.

Let's proceed to the next cheat. Most memorably for readers, Hochschild reprints staged photographs taken by the English missionary Alice Harris-Seeley and supplied to the anti-Léopold campaign through the English missionary John Weeks. The great irony of these photos—a man being whipped ("The chicotte in use"), a woman held by two soldiers ("Women hostages, held under guard in order to force their husbands to go into the rain forest to gather wild rubber")—is that many were staged recreations of earlier staged recreations of the first "Congo reform" movement of the 1880s that drew attention to these Islamic practices in order to urge colonization. An illustration of a white trader counting the lashes being meted out to a black man under *sharia* law graced the cover of the *Le Moniteur du Congo* in June 5, 1885, before the EIC was formed. The magazine criticized this "civilization in the Congo" in order to urge reform. In Hochschild's hands, staged photos of pre-colonial barbaric customs became staged photos of "colonial violence."

The missionaries knew that showing these fake photos at "lantern shows" in community halls in Britain won more attention and donations than their detailed accounts of cannibalism and sleeping sickness ravaging their areas. Hochschild does not tell the reader that the photographs are staged, nor does he explain that the photographs of people with severed hands were victims of gangrene, tribal vendettas, or cannibalism having nothing to do with rubber.

He was careful to avoid reprinting some of the most widespread photos that were later shown to be fakes but which circulate on the Internet to this day: a boy named Epondo who lost his right hand in an accident but whose photo was used by the reformers to illustrate "the war for rubber;" and, most notoriously, two women sitting in a village making clay pots taken in 1892 that was repurposed for Seeley's shows in 1904 with the pots turned into skulls to illustrate widespread cannibalism that Léopold had failed to eliminate.[16]

Hochschild cannot resist reprinting the most famous fake photo of all, a man whom Seeley got to sit on the veranda of her mission station with a severed hand and foot before him. We don't know whose hand and foot these were. But it does not matter. Hochschild has even faked the original fake. The original caption given by Morel reads:

> Sala of Wala and remains of his five year old daughter; both wife and child were eaten by king's soldiers at a cannibal feast.[17]

Until Hochschild, no one had suggested that the girl or her mother were killed for rubber, only that the EIC had failed to control the eating habits of its citizens. Hochschild, however, captions the photo thus:

> Nsala, of the district of Wala, looking at the severed hand and foot of his five-year-old daughter, Boali, a victim of the Anglo-Belgian India Rubber Company (A.B.I.R.) militia.[18]

This is like saying someone killed by a person who works for Boeing is "a victim of the Boeing labor union." It is chicanery, plain and simple.

Third, as a self-proclaimed human rights activist, Hochschild can be forgiven for his economic illiteracy. But since it is the keystone that begins his tale, it is another fib worth correcting. The EIC's large trade surplus (more physical goods going out than coming in) was because virtually none of the revenue from the goods sold in Europe was sent back to pay for labor, which was "paid for" as a fulfillment of the EIC labor obligation. Instead, the revenue paid for European administration, infrastructure, and trade services in the Congo as well as profits that were parked in Belgium (an overall payments deficit). For Hochschild to claim that Africans were getting "little or nothing" for the goods they produced because fewer goods were being sent to Africa displays a stunning economic ignorance.[19] It is like saying that the empty container ships returning to China from today's port of Long Beach show that China's workers are being paid "little or nothing."

A Belgian military advisor to the newly-independent Congo government, 1961. Within months, the country would plunge into civil war. Credit: Harrison Forman Collection, University of Wisconsin-Milwaukee Libraries

Hoschild insists that Léopold's drive for profits in the Congo showed that he was insincere about the promise to eliminate slavery and open the region to trade and transport. But how precisely does Hochschild propose that the latter should be funded? Generous donations from Belgians? Even if funded by such "foreign aid," why would that be preferable to a creating a viable market economy for the Congolese? Hochschild is either willfully ignorant of the need for things to be paid for, or intentionally obtuse about what the Congo undertaking demanded.

Fourth, the big headline of the book, a whopper really, is Hochschild's claim that the population of the Congo fell by 50% or 10 million on Léopold's watch. The EIC, he claims, engaged in "mass murder" of "genocidal proportions" due to its drive for rubber profits. The EIC engaged in "mass murder on a vast scale" that constituted "one of the great mass killings of recent history."[20]

The damage to historical truth caused by this claim is immense. It has been repeated and cited so many times that any attempt to expose it is invariably caught in a sticky goo of more people who cite it like a mammoth in a tar pit. It's not just Internet hacks. In a 2020 paper, two scholars at the National Bureau of Economic Research open a paper on the legacies of the rubber concessions with the statement: "An estimated 10 million people, approximately half of the population of Congo, died between 1880 and 1920."[21] A United Nations document expands the fallacy, while adding the bizarre claim that the alleged depopulation was a result of outright murder: "It is believed that 17 to 25 million Congolese persons were killed by colonial agents and authorities during the colonial period."[22] The former cites Hochschild while the latter cites the rap sheets of the anti-Léopold campaign of the 1900s that Hochschild accepted uncritically.

How did approximately 10,000 people killed in skirmishes between the EIC police and natives in a small portion of the territory over a 20-year period mushroom into 10 million dead (25 million according to the UN), "mass murder on a vast scale" and "a forgotten Holocaust"?

Hochschild was highly motivated from the start to "find" a Léopoldian genocide because, as he notes, his project began by reading the American humorist Mark Twain's claim that eight to ten million people had died at the hands of the EIC. Hochschild's only scholarly source was an off-hand remark by the Belgian ethnographer Jan Vansina that, as discussed in Chapter 4, was a misquotation of an earlier study that cited such high figures in order to point out that they had no basis in fact and were almost certainly false. Vansina misquoted a Harvard study that rejected a claim of 50% decline made by a report of the Permanent Committee for the Protection of the Natives of 1919.

In any case, Vansina later rejected his earlier conclusion. In his 2010 book on the Kuba people, *Being Colonized*, Vansina said he was "misled" about population decline.[23] Rubber and military operations by the EIC were negligible factors, he now admitted. Disease was the main factor driving population down, brought by both Arab and Western incursions into Central Africa as well as by Congolese travelling farther afield. His earlier "50% decline" claim was an "erroneous conclusion." The Kuba population had been artificially swelled by the importation of slave women before and in the early years of the EIC. These women were serially raped to boost the population, which peaked in 1899. In 1910 all slaves were freed by the Belgians, so the population plummeted since most fled. Porters returning from the Great War introduced new diseases, pushing the population lower still. "The Kuba population was actually rising rather than falling during the first two decades of the colonial era," he concluded. "The decline began with the [EIC] conquest in 1900 and then continued to 1919." Conflicts with EIC contributed only a small fraction to the estimated population decline by 1919 of 25%, perhaps a fifth. Most resulted from local diseases and slave emancipation, followed by global epidemics from the Great War.

Hochschild subsequently cited two other authorities to defend his claim.[24] One is the demographer Léon de St. Moulin who assayed the 50% decline possibility in 1990.[25] But Hochschild fails to mention that Moulin, like the later Vansina, believed that the EIC and rubber had nothing to do with it. The causes for Moulin were, in order, sleeping sickness, smallpox, Spanish flu, and venereal diseases. Moulin did not *even mention* the EIC or rubber. Like the later Vansina, he recognized that these were footnotes in the demographic history of the Congo.

Hochschild also later cited for his claims the Congolese historian Isidore Ndaywel è Nziem. His various utterances in editions of his national history of the Congo ("13 million killed," "5 to 10 million killed") are hard to keep track of. Initially, the starting year for his assertions was 1880 (five years before the EIC was founded and ten years before any rubber harvesting) and then the end year was moved to 1930 (22 years after the EIC). A later edition, without explanation, moved up the starting date to 1885. Ndaywel cited no data or methods. All three editions of his book merely cited Moulin.[26] It is notable that in a lengthy essay on the EIC published in *L'Histoire* in 2020, Ndaywel no longer makes any specific population claims, asserting only that the effects of the EIC were "worse than grim" ("*plus que macabres*").[27] In the end, Ndaywel is not credible. His works are published by the Royal Museum for Central Africa in Belgium because he is black. This helps them to "decolonize Eurocentric narratives," which means using blacks as shadow puppets to shield their radical accounts from criticism.

By contrast, dozens of serious demographers and statisticians have concluded the overall population of the Congo was unchanged at around 8 to 10 million from 1885 to 1908. The most knowledgeable estimates suggest that any deaths attributable to the limited abuses in the rubber areas were far outweighed by deaths resulting from factors unrelated to the EIC and by the lives saved and created by the EIC's direct interventions in other respects.[28] Taken on its own, the EIC was a positive influence on the black population in the Congo because of its campaigns against slavery, endemic tribal warfare, cannibalism, and polygamous rape and torture. Infrastructure and trade brought life-saving income. The population remained unchanged only because of the persistence of endemic disease and slavery. According to Romaniuk, venereal disease alone can explain the persistence of slow population growth after 1900 when the EIC had finally brought a modicum of peace and prosperity to the region.[29]

Even if we can always agree that any life lost to senseless violence and negligent governance is always and everywhere deserving of condemnation, Léopold's regime was a monumental achievement in saving and promoting black lives. Less than one percent of the violent deaths during the EIC era had anything to do with the EIC, according to economic historian Aldwin Roes. The main cause of violent deaths was not a rubber-hungry Léopold but "an extremely violent society in which various individuals and social groups within and outside of the state apparatus committed violent acts for multiple reasons."[30]

Early explorers used population densities along rivers to infer the existence of a massive population in the interior, often to stoke interest in more funding for their endeavors.[31] Hochschild's claim of 20 million souls when the Belgians arrived is little more than pro-imperialist propaganda. The first proper sample-based census was not carried out until 1949. So demographers have to reconstruct population totals from micro-level data on food supply, settlement patterns, village counts, birth records, and the like. The most sophisticated modelling by French and Belgian demographers variously suggests a population of 8 to 11 million in 1885 (the UN Department of Economic and Social Affairs estimate is 7.91 million) and 10 to 12 million by 1908. The Belgian Jean-Paul Sanderson, using a backward projection method by age cohorts, found a slight decline, from 10.5 million in 1885 to 10 million in 1910.[32] Even this pessimistic estimated change in total population governed by changing birth and death rates over a 25-year period represents a negligible annual net decline in population. More to the point, it is more or less the same nominal decline as occurred in all other parts of Africa at the time, including the non-colonized parts.[33]

Even taking Sanderson's pessimistic estimate as correct, does this mean that Léopold's rule "killed" 500,000 people? Of course not, because, in addition to the misplaced personalization of long-term population changes, the rubber regions, as mentioned, experienced both population increases and declines. Even in the latter, such as the rubber-producing Bolobo area in the lower reaches of the Congo river, population decline was a result of the brutalities of freelance native chiefs and ended with the arrival of an EIC officer. More generally, the stability and enforced peace of the EIC caused birth rates to rise near EIC centers, such as at the Catholic mission under EIC protection at Baudouinville (today's Kirungu). Population declines were in areas outside of effective EIC control. The modest population gains caused by EIC interventions were overwhelmed by a range of wholly separate factors, which in order of importance were: the slave trade, sleeping sickness, inter-tribal warfare, other endemic diseases (smallpox, beriberi, influenza, yellow fever, pneumonia, dysentery, tuberculosis, typhoid fever, and venereal disease), cannibalism, and human sacrifice. A Canadian doctor who worked for the EIC from 1892 to 1895 reported a whole district "devoid alike of men and food" as a result of "slave-raiders in [Arab slaver] Tippu Tip's employ."[34] Yet Hochschild ascribes the abandoned villages of the Congo to the depredations of the EIC and its lust for rubber.

Hochschild in a sense knows he will be called out on this, and thus rolls out the fudge that "although outright murder was not the major cause of death" the most important determining factor of demographic trends in the entire territory was the "finding and using" of labor for rubber and other devious endeavors like building railways.[35] Again, this is simply untenable and has never been advanced by any reputable scholar. Even more, it is an insult to Congolese who fought against native tyrants and slavers alongside the EIC. As the anthropologist Michael Singleton noted: "The condition of African populations resulted primarily from the demographic strategies of those whose lives were at stake, and not from the interventions, well or ill-intentioned, of foreigners…That whites tended to blacken the situation is one thing. That 'black' was always 'beautiful' is another, and whoever claims as much risks betraying the memory of the victims of tyrants with totalitarian tendencies."[36]

Why did Hochschild put such store in plainly erroneous data about a loss of life caused by the EIC? Here we come to the horror at the heart of King Hochschild's Hoax: his attempt to equate the EIC to the Nazis and to the sacred memory of the Holocaust. Throughout the book there is a nauseating, indeed enraging, use of Holocaust and Auschwitz comparisons. In part, these reveal an insecurity about his main thesis and the knowledge that one way to silence criticism is to play on the fact that no one wants to be called a Holocaust denier. While we know "how many Jews the Nazis put to death," he menaces readers, insisting on such precision in the EIC is distasteful.[37] You have been warned!

The strategy works. In reviewing *Léopold II: Un Roi Génocidaire?*, a 2005 defense of the EIC by the Belgian historian Michel Dumoulin, the emeritus Boston University professor Edouard Bustin wrote malevolently: "Dumoulin is waging a futile—and somewhat unsavory—battle that is bound to ring like revisionist versions of the Holocaust."[38]

Another explanation for Hochschild's odious rhetorical strategy is the troubling phenomenon of "Holocaust trivialization" on the modern Left, which the Jerusalem Center for Public Affairs defines as "a tool for some ideologically or politically motivated activists to metaphorically compare phenomena they oppose" to the Holocaust.[39] Hochschild opposes colonialism, capitalism, monarchy, railways, science, barometers, and it seems, most Belgians as well. He thus engages in a pernicious example of Holocaust trivialization with this book.

The further falsehoods and distortions that make up King Hochschild's Hoax all collectively derive from the problems above. Perhaps most signally, the book is not really much about the history of the EIC at all. The central activity that justified, motivated, absorbed, and in the end defeated the EIC is missing: the battle against the Afro-Arab slave trade.[40] This extreme truncation of history is similar to the oddball strategy deployed by the Danish historian Kim Wagner in his 2019 book *Amritsar 1919: An Empire of Fear and the Making of a Massacre* which reduces the entire 89-year history of British India to a minor skirmish in a remote region that left 379 dead. Wagner's book has nothing to say about the actual history of British India, not even its governance much less its economic and social endeavors.

The rubber concessions lasted for a mere 14 years. Even the most determined scholars who try to pin the blame for all of the Congo's post-colonial woes on King Léopold struggle to find anything of importance. The two National Bureau of Economic Research scholars cited above who breezily repeated the "10 million died" claim of Hochschild, made a splash in 2020 with a statistical model that claimed to show that villages inside the former rubber concession areas had less public welfare and less public goods in 2005 than those living outside. They called the EIC concessions "one of the most important events in modern African history."[41]

Since the math is beyond most people's understanding, their paper has been cited as yet more evidence of the horrors of the Belgians and their everlasting guilt for everything wrong in the Congo. But, as so often in these studies, the scholars miss the forest for the trees. While it is true that they manage to torture their data enough to elicit as statistically relevant difference in public goods and public well-being in areas inside the former concessions versus outside, the strength of the relationship and the absolute size of these differences is minuscule. For instance, their model attributes 1.3 years less years of education to those living inside versus outside the former concession areas. Whatever the validity of that claim, it is a non-finding. At the time of their study, the average number of years of education in the Congo was 6.2 years, so their finding represented a 20% shortfall. By 2022, the average Congolese was earning nine years of education, mainly as a result of recovery from the devasting civil war of 1996 to 2002 (which explained the depressed six years total in 2005). So mere recovery from civil war added double the years that Léopold supposedly took away. How can a 14-year period of rubber concessions in an area representing 15% of what became the Congo that ended a century before the education and other social outcomes being studied possibly explain anything? Even more, how can they be "one of the most important events in modern African history?"

The authors have no idea what possible reasons might link yesterday's rubber concessions to today's slightly below average social outcomes. They venture that the concessions "undermined local institutions" and the "traditional legitimacy" of chiefs.[42] The result was that in the chaos of independent Congo, where people fell back on traditional tribal rule, those in the concession areas had less robust institutions. Fair enough. But we know that breaking down pre-colonial autocratic institutions was critical to a people's ability to achieve development, rather than being stuck in low level equilibrium survival with traditional autocrats. So from this perspective, the concession areas were a gift of the EIC to a possible modern future for the Congo precisely for the reasons that these anti-colonial scholars unwittingly show. The "blame" lies not with the Belgians who began the process of modernization, but with the Congolese leaders who stopped it.

No serious scholar argues that leaving the Congolese at the mercy of their "local institutions" was a path to development. When Léopold first sent his envoys into the region, noted Stanford historians Gann and Duignan, "much of the country was in a state of turmoil." The Swahili were pushing in from the east, the Umbundu from the south, warlords like Msiri and Kakenge had emerged, and the Chokwe and Lunda "were involved in fierce battles for supremacy."[43] The Hungarian anthropologist Emil Torday, who travelled in the Congo from 1907 to 1909, gathered oral histories of the great king of the Kuba people known as Bope Mobinji who had died in 1885.[44] The Kuba were unusual in the Congo for the accuracy of their oral histories going back at least 100 years because of the importance of such accuracy in royal rituals.[45] According to Torday, the king's violence was famous: "Whenever anyone committed an offence against the king, or his orders, the sons would attack his village, kill him, plunder the place and take his women-folk and children into slavery. His severity provoked several revolts, which were suppressed with great cruelty." During the three-day funeral rites for the king in 1885, "his grave was said to have been lined with two thousand victims." That tally was "very probably an exaggeration," Torday added, although there was no doubt that tribal customs required his son to find victims for the rites and that "personal animosity as well as political antagonism played an important part in his selection."[46] Such pre-EIC histories make Hochschild's claim that the EIC robbed the Congo of "independence and self-government" or the NBER claim of how the EIC ruined "local institutions" laughable.[47]

Again, Hochschild wearily mentions the "wide swath of terror through much of east and central Africa" caused by the Arab slave trade and the EIC efforts against it, but merely to sneer at it as "dubious" because of prior European involvement in the slave trade. He mocks the EIC's campaigns against the "dastardly" slavers, as if they are noble proto-nationalists, and he fawns over the notorious slaver Tippu Tip as "handsome, bearded, strongly built" as well as "shrewd" and "resourceful" with "administrative acumen."[48]

Belgium had no prior history in the slave trade, nor of African slaves. Léopold could fight against slavery without any hint of hypocrisy, even of the ahistorical type advanced by Hochschild. And it was slavery, not rubber operations, that contemporary observers viewed as the biggest threat to the people of the Congo. The missionary Fanny Emma Fitzgerald Guinness was allowed to visit one Arab slave fort in 1890, seeing "rows upon rows of dark nakedness, relieved here and there by the white dresses of the captors" in one pen holding 2,300 souls. She estimated that for every one slave eventually sold, seven died either in the raids, in the camps, or while being transported to the Indian Ocean.[49] In 1892, a Belgian trader and his entire caravan of six Europeans and 40 porters were beheaded by a thug controlled by the notorious slaver and warlord Msiri, who asked that their heads be returned to him to decorate his compound. The trader had tried to persuade Msiri and other local tyrants to sell their ivory to his company, which could transport it by river, thus obviating the need for slaves.

The black American missionary George Washington Williams, visiting in 1890, noted "the most revolting crimes" committed by the natives: "Human hands and feet and limbs, smoked and dried, are offered and exposed for sale in many of the native village markets. From the mouth of the Loumami-River to Stanley-Falls there are thirteen armed Arab camps; and in them I have seen many skulls of murdered slaves pendant from poles and over these camps floating their blood-red flag."[50] Oddly, Hochschild quotes Williams' testimony against native practices to criticize the EIC for being insufficiently vigorous in its attempts to govern the territory. Heads I win, tails you lose.

As this logical slip implies, a justifiably proportionate response to the scourge of the slave trade required keen efforts by the EIC to recruit and feed soldiers, clear villages in areas prone to slave raids, establish military and governance posts, and pursue slave armies to the death. "Accommodating the Arab slave traders would be a crime," wrote the EIC captain, and later Great War hero, Jules Alphonse Jacques in 1892.[51]

Tacking his boat back in the direction of the EIC being too vigorous, Hochschild transposes EIC efforts *against slavery* into cruel efforts *for rubber*. The reader is lured into believing that every conflict he documents is about the drive for rubber not the drive against slavery (or inter-tribal vendettas). One of many egregious examples will have to suffice.

Hochschild describes the EIC official Léon Fiévez as a "sadist" who "terrorized" the rubber-rich Équator district where he was commissioner.[52] His source is the George Bricusse mentioned above. Bricusse lasted only three years in the Congo before dying of either typhoid or malaria, a common occurrence for the EIC where the *annual* mortality rate for European soldiers was 20%. In the 1894 incident recalled, Fiévez is recounting to Bricusse his desperate attempts to feed his soldiers while battling slave lords in the area. There is *no mention* of rubber because this particular place had little of it. The slaving business, on the other hand, is flourishing and Bricusse notes its devastation everywhere. Fiévez had arrived a few days earlier and held parlay with local chiefs. They had agreed to supply his soldiers with food for payment. They then reneged and fled into the forest. Fiévez sent his troops in pursuit and, in the ensuing fight, 100 of the chiefs' soldiers were killed. After that, the chiefs made good on their promise.

"In the face of their manifest ill will, I do battle with them," Fiévez explains to Bricusse. "One example was enough: one hundred heads cut off and there have been plenty of supplies at the station ever since."[53] Hochschild has redacted the cause of the battle and implies that the "them" are hapless villagers who failed to turn over rubber. He has also removed the context. Fiévez is correct that these hundred battle fatalities saved the lives of his 500 troops who are on the verge of starvation. More generally, these 500 troops are eliminating noxious practices that are taking thousands of lives every year in the district. As Fiévez explains in the intervening sentence (removed by Hochschild): "Slavery still occurs on a vast scale. However, it is very difficult to eradicate it. Certain populations even unearth corpses and eat them. Sacrifices still take place on the death of a chief or on the advice of witch doctors."

Hochschild's editorial motives are clear. He wants to set up the next quotation from Fiévez: "My goal is ultimately humanitarian." We are supposed to roll our eyes with knowing derision. If we know the full story, we will feel manipulated by Hochschild instead. Fiévez was a humanitarian it turns out, and his actions were justified. Take the Fiévez example and multiply it by two dozen and you have a good idea of how King Hochschild's Hoax operates.

This, then, is the essence of the case against Hochschild, but I must hasten to point out three additional aspects of the blarney that is *King Leopold's Ghost*, which, while less central, are more revealing for the dark arts being practiced.

Hochschild is at pains to convince the reader that anyone opposing the EIC was good, whether brutal slave trader, inveterate cannibal, fetish priest, or ethnic-cleansing warlord. His treatment of the 1895 rebellion by native soldiers at a military camp named Luluabourg in the southern savannah strains to portray the rebels as noble savages pining for freedom and a return to peaceful pastoral life. In his telling, the Belgian commander Mathieu Pelzer was a "bully" who "used his fists" and thus got his comeuppance at breakfast with a knife to the throat.[54] Actually, Pelzer had nothing to do with it. The rebels were former soldiers for a black slave king. The EIC had brought them to the southern camp to reintegrate them as government soldiers. But their loss of royal prerogatives to whore, steal, and maim caused them to rebel. The group never exceeded 300 (Hochschild speculates that it reached 2,500) and petered out in the northern jungles in 1897, a rag-tag criminal gang gone to seed.

This egregious example of "Belgians bad, natives good" is the conceptual foundation of King Hochschild's Hoax. And it bleeds into what is, for most readers, the enduring imaginative impact of the book—to have put a nasty Belgian face onto Mistah Kurtz, the phantom who draws Marlow's steamboat up the Congo river in Joseph Conrad's 1902 novella *Heart of Darkness*. Like generations of English professors, Hochschild has entirely mistaken the point of the book as an indictment of colonialism, which is difficult to square with its openly pro-colonial declarations and the fact of the "adoring" natives who surround the deceased Kurtz.

Conrad spent six months working for a cargo company in the EIC in 1890, three weeks of it aboard a steamship travelling up river to today's Kisangani. There is no mention of rubber in the novel because Conrad was there five years before rubber cultivation began. Kurtz is an ivory trader. So whatever sources Conrad was using when he began work on *Heart of Darkness* in 1898, his personal experiences would at most have added some color and context. Hochschild will have none of it, insisting that Conrad "saw the beginnings of the frenzy of plunder and death" over rubber which he then "recorded" in *Heart of Darkness*. The brutalities by whites in the 1979 film *Apocalypse Now* was inspired by the novel, Hochschild avers, because Conrad "had seen it all, a century earlier, in the Congo."[55]

In another example of creative chronology, Hochschild's cites a threat in a private letter that he believes was the inspiration for Kurtz's famous scrawl "Exterminate all the brutes!"[56] The off-hand remark—"Inform the natives that if they cut another [rubber] vine I will exterminate them to the last man!"—was made in a private letter to a subordinate by Jules Alphonse Jacques who, after three years in the anti-slavery campaigns served as district commissioner in the rubber area of Lac Léopold II (1895-1898). But it was made public only in 1906 during a Belgian legislative debate, a fact that the diligent reader will discover by perusing the footnote that Hochschild gives to Morel's *West African Mail* of March 16, 1906. In addition to Jacques never being accused of any such violence, despite his frustrations, the outburst could not, by definition, be a source for a book published in 1902.[57]

Mere quibbling, you say. The main point is that Conrad realistically described the terrible things done by Belgians in the Congo. Hochschild certainly wishes this was Conrad's purpose. He repeats an old theory that Kurtz was based on the EIC officer Léon Rom whom Conrad "may have met" in 1890 and "almost certainly" read about in 1898.[58] Visitors noted that Rom's garden was decorated with polished skulls buried in the ground, the garden gnomes of the Congolese which Rom's staff presumably installed following local tradition in order to inspire awe for their boss. But polished skulls buried in the ground is not the "signal feature" of Kurtz's compound, as Hochschild claims. Rather, it is freshly severed "heads on the stakes" that "seemed to sleep at the top of that pole." As the British scholar Johan Adam Warodell notes, none of the "exclusively European prototypes" for Kurtz advanced by Woke professors and historians like Hochschild displayed freshly severed heads on poles. By contrast, dozens of accounts of African warlords and slavers in the Congo published before 1898 described rotting heads on poles—"a wide-reaching area marked by a grass fence, tied to high poles, which at the very top were decorated with grinning, decomposing skulls" as one 1888 account had it.[59]

Far from being "one of the most scathing indictments of [European] imperialism in all literature," as Hochschild declares it, *Heart of Darkness* is one of the most scathing indictments of the absence of European imperialism in all literature. Kurtz is a symbol of the pre-colonial horrors of the Congo, horrors that the EIC, however fitfully, was bringing to an end.

Disagree if you like, and feel free to consult the extensive archives and records left behind, which provide constant fodder for the global industry of EIC critics. Hochschild repeats the urban legend that Léopold burned all the EIC documents, going "to extraordinary lengths to try to erase potentially incriminating evidence."[60] Quite the opposite: Léopold was proud of the EIC and went to extraordinary lengths to leave behind an extensive record. The testimony of his military aide that Hochschild cites about "burning the State archives" and turning "most of the Congo state records to ash" was a misunderstanding: what the aide saw burning were ruined and unreadable papers among the thousands of documents that came back in crates from the Congo in 1908. Léopold even left behind 14 trunks filled with his personal letters and financial statements. Everything was carefully catalogued in "a vast room that looked like a post office," the aide recalled.[61] Some of it went missing in the turmoil of World War II before resurfacing in the basement of a house in 1983.[62] As recently as 2022, researchers at the Royal Museum for Central Africa brought out a new book based on the EIC archives.[63]

Still, one wonders if Léopold should have burned all the EIC archives given the malicious craft practiced by Hochschild and others like him. For all our modernist beliefs in truth, evidence, logic, and fairness, perhaps we have reached a point of no return in the writing of history where modern progressives attack the historical record with malice aforethought, leaving us stupider than we were before this movement took shape in the 1960s (when the 20-something Hochschild was at the barricades protesting Vietnam and all the rest).

But No! It is for future generations to re-colonize history using the precious intellectual resources of the Enlightenment. Until then, we do well to fight the progressive warlords like Hochschild who enslave formerly colonized peoples in distorted victimization narratives that rob them of agency, all the while keeping the white man front and center.

Endnotes:

1 Marcel Yabili, *The Greatest Fake News of All Time: Leopold II, The Genius and Builder King of Lumumba* (2021), 230.

2 General facts about the EIC in this chapter are mostly from four sources: Jean Stengers and Jan Vansina, "King Leopold's Congo, 1886–1908," in Roland Oliver and G. N. Sanderson (eds.) *The Cambridge History of Africa* (1985); David van Reybrouck, *Congo: The Epic History of a People* (2014); Lewis Gann and Peter Duignan, *Rulers of Belgian Africa, 1884-1914* (1979); and Guido De Weerd, *The Congo Free State: In Search of the Historical Truth* (2017).

3 Edmund Morel, *Red Rubber: The Story of the Rubber Slave Trade Flourishing on the Congo in the Year of Grace 1906* (1906, 1970 edition), 137.

4 Adam Hochschild, *King Leopold's Ghost: A Story of Greed, Terror, and Heroism in Colonial Africa* (1998, 2006 edition), hereafter KLG, 87, 258, 4, 198, 212.

5 KLG 34, 123.

6 KLG 257, 210, 212.

7 Alan Paton, *Journey Continued* (1988), 174.

8 Pierre Marcel Salmon, *Les Carnets de Campagne de Georges Bricusse* [*The Notebooks of the Campaign of Georges Bricusse*] (1966), 35.

9 "The Congo Free State," *The Times*, 18 November 1895. .

10 Jean Stengers, *Congo: Mythes & Réalités* [*Congo: Myth and Reality*], (1989, 2020 edition), 118.

11 KLG 165, 278.

12 Daniel Vangroenweghe, "Charles Lemaire à l'Équateur: Son Journal Inédit, 1891-1895" ["Charles Lemaire in Equator Province: His Unedited Journal, 1891-1895"], *Annales Aequatoria* (1986), 14.

13 Daniel Vangroenweghe, *Du Sang Sur les Lianes: Léopold II et Son Congo* [*Blood on the Vines: Léopold II and His Congo*] (1986, 2010 edition), 52.

14 KLG 165.

15 Adam Hochschild, "Response to Bruce Gilley," *The American Conservative*, May 27, 2023.

16 Marcel Yabili, *Le Livre Blanc* (2023), 66-67.

17 Morel, *Red Rubber*, 33.

18 KLG 246.

19 KLG 2.

20 KLG 233, 283, 225, 283, 3.

21 Sara Lowes and Eduardo Montero, "Concessions, Violence, and Indirect Rule: Evidence from the Congo Free State," *NBER Working Papers*, No. 27893 (2020), 1.

22 United Nations, Office of the High Commissioner of Human Rights, *Visit to Belgium: Report of the Working Group of Experts on People of African Descent*, A/HRC/42/59/Add.1, 14 August 2019, 3.

23 Jan Vansina, *Being Colonized: The Kuba Experience in Rural Congo, 1880–1960* (2010), 145-147.

24 Adam Hochschild, "Response to Bruce Gilley," *The American Conservative*, May 27, 2023.

25 Léon de St. Moulin, "What is Known of the Demographic History of Zaïre Since 1885?" in Bruce Fetter (ed.) *Demography from Scanty Evidence: Central Africa in the Colonial Era* (1990).

26 Isidore Ndaywel è Nziem, *Histoire du Zaïre* (1997), n.p.; *Histoire Générale du Congo* (2009), 125; *Nouvelle Histoire du Congo* (2008), 319.
27 Isidore Ndaywel è Nziem, "Congo: l'État Privé du Roi des Belges," *L'Histoire* (2020), 43.
28 Bruce Fetter (ed.), *Demography from Scanty Evidence: Central Africa in the Colonial Era* (1990).
29 Anatole Romaniuk, "Demography of the Democratic Republic of the Congo During the Colonial Mercantile Regime, 1885-1940: A Case of Depopulation Due to Infertility of Pathological Origin" (2013).
30 Aldwin Roes, "Towards a History of Mass Violence in the Etat Indépendant du Congo, 1885–1908," *South African Historical Journal* (2010).
31 Bruce Fetter, "Decoding and Interpreting African Census Data: Vital Evidence from an Unsavory Witness," *Cahiers d'Études Africaines* (1987).
32 Jean-Paul Sanderson, "Le Congo belge entre mythe et réalité: Une analyse du discours démographique colonial" ["The Myth and Reality of the Belgian Congo: The Colonial Demographic Discourse"], *Population* (2000); Jean-Paul Sanderson, *La démographie du Congo sous la colonisation belge* [*Congo's Demography Under Belgian Colonization*], Department of Political and Social Sciences, Doctoral Dissertation, Université Catholique de Louvain (2010); and Jean-Paul Sanderson, *Démographie coloniale congolaise. Entre spéculation, idéologie, et reconstruction historique* [*Congo's Colonial Demography: Speculation, Ideology, and Reconstruction*] (2018).
33 Guy Vantemsche, *Congo-De impact van de kolonie op België* [*Congo: The Impact of the Colony on Belgium*] (2007), 34-35.
34 Sidney Hinde, "Three Years' Travel in the Congo Free State," *The Geographical Journal* (1895), 430.
35 KLG 226, 225.
36 Michael Singleton, "Pratiques ancestrales et la démographie de l'Afrique noire précoloniale" ["Ancestral Practices and the Demography of Pre-Colonial Black Africa"], *Anthropos* (2005), 69, 64.
37 KLG 225.
38 Michel Dumoulin, *Léopold II: un roi génocidaire?* [*Léopold II: A Genocidal King?*] (2005); Edouard Bustin, "Review of Léopold II, un roi génocidaire?," *International Journal of African Historical Studies* (2006), 540.
39 Manfred Gerstenfeld, "Holocaust Trivialization," *Jerusalem Center for Public Affairs*, April 9, 2008.
40 Mario Draper, "The Force Publique's Campaigns in the Congo-Arab War, 1892-1894," *Small Wars & Insurgencies* (2019).
41 Lowes and Montero, "Concessions, Violence, and Indirect Rule," 4, 5.
42 Lowes and Montero, "Concessions, Violence, and Indirect Rule," 22.
43 Gann and Duignan, *Rulers of Belgian Africa*, 109.
44 Emil Torday, Thomas Athol Joyce, and Norman Hardy, *Notes Ethnographiques Sur Les Peuples Communément Appelés Bakuba* (1911).
45 E. Sidney Hartland, "On the Evidential Value of the Historical Traditions of the Baganda and Bushongo," *Folklore* (1914).
46 Emil Torday, *On the Trail of the Bushongo* (1925), 172, 177.
47 KLG 257.
48 KLG 27, 131, 130.
49 Fanny Guinness, *The New World of Central Africa* (1890), 125-126.
50 George Washington Williams, *A Report Upon the Congo-State and Country, to the*

President of the Republic of the United States of America (1890), 13.
51 Guido De Weerd, *The Congo Free State*, 268.
52 KLG 166.
53 Salmon, *Les Carnets de Campagne de Georges Bricusse*, 56.
54 KLG 127-8.
55 Adam Hochschild "Léopold's Congo: A Holocaust We Have Yet to Comprehend," *Chronicle of Higher Education*, May 12, 2000.
56 KLG 229.
57 Marjan Dewulf and André Gysel, *Alphonse Jacques de Dixmude: historische interpretatie van een omstreden figuur* [*Alphonse Jacques de Dixmude: A Historical Interpretation of a Controversial Figure*] (2016).
58 KLG 145.
59 Johan Adam Warodell, "A New Prototype for Kurtz in 'Heart of Darkness,'" *Conradiana* (2015).
60 KLG 294.
61 Gustave Stinglhamber and Paul Dresse, *Léopold II au travail* [*Léopold II At Work*] (1945), 52-53; Works based on the EIC archives include Royal Belgian Colonial Institute, *Biographie Coloniale Belge* [*Belgian Colonial Biography*], 9 vols (1948-2015); and Emile Banning, *Mémoires politiques et diplomatiques: Comment fut fondé le Congo belge* [*Diplomatic and Political Memories: The Founding of the Belgian Congo*] (1927).
62 Olivier Defrance, "The Goffinet archives shed light on Belgium's colonial past," *King Baudouin Foundation* (2021).
63 Patricia Van Schuylenbergh and Mathilde Leduc-Grimaldi (eds.), *The Congo Free State: What Could Archives Tell Us?* (2022).

CHAPTER TEN

Malaya and the Low Point of Colonial History Writing

Hating the British Empire is nothing new. Indeed, it has been the primary occupation of the academy since about 1970. Not without exceptions, of course. The prolific British historian Jeremy Black's *Imperial Legacies* of 2019 reminded readers of the British Empire's political and social benefits to subject peoples. The very naughty economic historian Tirthankar Roy of the London School of Economics has obstinately pursued empirical inquiries, such as his *An Economic History of India 1707–1857*, showing the economic benefits and strong local support for colonialism in the granddaddy of them all, British India. Nonetheless, every hint of dissent from the academy's jealously guarded anti-colonial orthodoxy elicits hysterical reactions from the guardians.

In the United States, the temple is guarded by many Ivy League professors who are shielded from scrutiny by the country's own anti-colonial tradition. Of these, none are more vigilant than Harvard's Caroline Elkins. Unchastened by criticisms of *Imperial Reckoning*, her bizarre 2010 defense of the murderous Mau Mau movement in colonial Kenya, and of her participation in a nuisance lawsuit by "survivors" of the apt British response that was widely supported by Kenyans, she applies the lather to the British Empire as a whole in her 2022 *Legacy of Violence: A History of the British Empire*. The good news for the young historian is that, taken together, her two books may well represent the nadir of the interminable fall of objective colonial history.

For half a century—from black Marxist Walter Rodney's economically illiterate and shambolic *How Europe Underdeveloped Africa* of 1972 to Elkins' 2022 *Legacy of Violence*—the Western academy was gripped by a moral panic over the alleged crimes of European colonialism. It responded with passionate atonements delivered with religious fervor. As a result, colonial history became impossible. Young scholars had to accept anti-colonial premises in order to succeed. The conditions for objective, scientific research—notably the possibility of differing viewpoints—were absent. Whatever claims to "careful research" were made on its behalf, colonial history was *by definition* not scientific. It became little more than a mutual admiration society.

Oddly, even as colonial history became more putrefied, the possibilities of social scientific research on colonial history expanded. Evidence of colonial benefits and legitimacy continued to accumulate outside of colonial history, particularly in economics and political science.[1] As a result, there is today a golden opportunity awaiting the aspiring scholar to rewrite essentially everything that has been published on European colonialism (with notable exceptions) in the past 50 years.

There is no better example than *Legacy of Violence* to understand the depths to which colonial history sank under the deadweight of academics like Elkins. At the outset of *Legacy of Violence*, she asserts that all use of force by colonial states was illegitimate because colonialism itself was, in her view, illegitimate. "Coercion was central to initial acts of conquest and to the maintenance of rule over non-consenting populations," she claims breezily.[2] Just 17 words, but three very serious claims. One might just as well, and with more evidentiary backing, state the opposite: *cooperation* was central to initial acts of conquest and to the maintenance of rule over *consenting* populations. Elkins is not much interested in the various native empires and tyrannies that European colonialism replaced. Nor can she explain the threadbare European presence in most colonies, which were run by and for the natives. Having in *Imperial Reckoning* wholly ignored the doughty black participation in the anti-Mau Mau counterinsurgency in Kenya, she cannot help but avert her gaze in *Legacy of Violence* from similar evidence in the empire as a whole.

Nowhere in the book does Elkins provide a definition of "violence" that could be deemed present or absent, nor any definition of justified versus nonjustified violence. We are never told what levels of response to political violence might be justified in any given situation because the answer for "illegitimate" colonial rulers for Elkins is always: None. We never hear from the natives who fought for the colonial state. We never hear from the tens of millions of native victims of criminal and terrorist movements, whether before, during, or after colonial rule. Most inexcusably for a historian, Elkins never explains her methods for data selection. We never hear any reflection on why, if the colonial rulers were engaged in such wrongdoing, they recorded it so earnestly, challenged it when it was seen as disproportionate, wrote lengthy reports on it after the fact, and then proudly deposited it in climate-controlled archives with nice tea rooms where malevolent monsters from the academy could come to perform their mean-spirited vivisections.

Elkins' pretension to theoretical innovation with a concept called "legalized lawlessness" is silly and will be quickly forgotten. As the South African scholar Eric Louw wrote, the "concept fails to convince because even her selected facts cannot hide the surfeit of evidence that Britons ran a liberal empire governed by people obsessed with the rule of law and documenting their actions."[3] The empire also did more than fight insurgencies and lock up criminals. It established human rights, documented cultures, created educational systems, built public health infrastructure, saved threatened minorities, protected the environment, reduced poverty, trained native governors, and encouraged civil society and a free press.

Even the attempt to reduce the history of warfare in the British empire to counter-insurgency campaigns is mistaken, as Louw notes. "Claiming the sort of violence associated with this type of warfare lay at the heart of British imperial governance is either a conceptualizing error on Elkins part, or a deliberately false construction," he writes, because "counterinsurgency warfare was not characteristic of conflicts across the entire British Empire, hence this genre of warfare cannot be generalized the way Elkins seeks to do."

As he notes, 19 different countries fought counter-insurgency wars during the Cold War and all more or less adopted the same methods. "It is just plain wrong to suggest this genre of warfare is a peculiarly British phenomenon or has anything to do with a specifically British style of governing or maintaining order in its empire." In her rage against the British empire, Elkins has committed a classic category mistake. In making it, she ends up defending odious movements on the grounds that any brown person shooting at the Tommies must have been on the side of justice.

Lacking either logical or empirical justification, Elkins does what lawyers do: she makes a case for "British empire = unjustified violence" and hopes that no one notices the defects. In the long course of preparing her book, Elkins was clearly never challenged about her basic methods, definitions, and data. The colonial history eco-system in which she worked is too hermetically sealed to allow for differing viewpoints. Instead, she set about her task of sedulously torturing the archives. It's a pity because, as a result, none of the research of *Legacy of Violence* is worth a penny. A mean-spirited suspicion coats each and every artifact she unearths. She is wholly unreliable as a reporter, and future scholars will have to return to every document she cites knowing that she cherished their inability to talk back.

The head-spinning catalog of distortions and moralizing that follows demands sustained critique. One example will have to suffice: her treatment of the British counter-insurgency campaign against a communist rebellion in Malaya.

The Malayan insurgency began under the tutelage of Moscow in 1930. Despite the external support, the British were at first willing to entertain the movement as a legitimate domestic political actor. Its trade union operated freely throughout the 1930s and its armed units were integrated into the British effort in World War II. After the war, its troops were given pensions. The Malayan Communist Party was allowed to contest elections, and its leader was awarded the Order of the British Empire. But with the urging of the soon-to-be-established communist government in Beijing, it resumed armed attacks in 1948. From the start, then, the so-called "Malayan Emergency" was not a local insurgency at all. Moscow and Beijing wanted the Communist Party of Malaya to be the spearhead of their push into Southeast Asia, moving next into Thailand and then Indonesia. From the resumption of violence in 1948 until the movement was finally crushed in 1960, it killed 8,000 Malayan civilians and police.

The reason the insurgency failed is that ordinary Malayans (as well as Thais and Indonesians) had no desire to live under communist rule, especially given evidence of the turmoil and terror coming out of the communist movement in Vietnam. "We coerced the people too much," said one political organizer, Liew Thian Choy.[4] His view was repeated by senior communist organizer Lam Swee in his 1951 pamphlet *My Accusation* that carried the subtitle *Written Against the Blind Struggle of the Communist Party.*

Elkins portrays the Beijing-backed rebels as heralds of a progressive native vision that was tragically thwarted by the cruel and reactionary British. If not for the unjustified colonial repression, she insists, the peoples of Southeast Asia would have prospered under the gentle rule of the Comintern. If only the British had treated the communists as a legitimate political party with aspirations to rule, the story goes, these places would be more democratic and more prosperous today. She describes the communist insurgency as "anti-imperialist" and as "waging a war for national liberation," a rather difficult claim to square with its external direction from Moscow and Beijing. The insurgency, Elkins rhapsodizes, sought "freedom and human dignity," presumably of the sort known in Mao's China, whose "New Democracy" it promised to replicate. The communists gained "traction" in Malay society, she asserts, because the British could offer only "social crises, homelessness, disease, and semistarvation." The British response, she assays, was merely an attempt "to reassert colonial control in Malaya with its own form of liberal imperial harshness." The 300,000 Malays, Chinese, and Indians who took part in the fight against communism were not thinking people but playthings of colonial manipulation. The British practice of "brutalizing individuals and communities," not fears of communist terror, caused the insurgency to collapse.[5]

The problem for this "people's movement" was that "the people" wanted nothing to do with it. The Malay communist movement was 90% Chinese in a country whose population was only 38% Chinese. Even the Chinese population mostly opposed it. The insurgency spread terror by executing both "traitors" who worked for the government as well as "backward elements" who refused to go along with the communist program. Styling itself the voice of the peasant, it destroyed peasant livelihoods by sabotage of tin and rubber plantations. In 1950, after villagers of Simpang Tiga in northwestern Perak state refused to comply with orders from the communists, a squad of goons burned the village to the ground. Among the hundreds of communist atrocities reported by police in 1952, the peak of the insurgency, was a Chinese farmer and his wife hacked to death with a machete and their eight-year old daughter thrown into the flames of their burning hut. Another young Chinese girl had a nail driven through her skull in Perak. At Kampar, a terrorist heaved a grenade into a crowd watching a circus, killing five people.

But Elkins is not really interested in the preferences and actions of brown people, or their suffering at the hands of anti-colonial criminals. Her gaze is ever-centered on The White Man. As with the black "loyalists" who fought against and ran the anti-Mau Mau campaign in Kenya, she erases from history the 41,000 native policemen and 250,000 native auxiliaries who signed up to combat the communist insurgency in Malaya. Instead, she attributes magical powers to the British governor, Henry Gurney, who, in her telling, oversaw "a police state" with the alarming ability to arrest criminals, levy fines, and impose "the death sentence for a range of offenses," including terrorism. The large number of Malayans who voluntarily fought for the campaign were mere pawns shuffled around by the British who were "throwing massive weight behind the forces of law and order." The British wanted to cling to Malaya "for economic resources" such as tin and rubber, not to save the people from communism.[6] Odd that one of Gurney's major policies was the creation of a pan-ethnic Independence of Malaya Party. Clever!

By contrast, she waxes poetic about the leader of the insurgency, known as Chin Peng (actually, his name was Ong Boon Hua), who was a freedom fighter in her telling. In fact, Ong's domestic support was nil beyond a small band of Chinese radicals, who, as he later wrote in his memoirs, were motivated by "Chinese patriotism" and "international socialism."[7] Even the sympathetic scholar Anthony Stockwell admits that "his conversion—or perhaps his drift—to communism was less a visceral reaction to colonial exploitation than a romantic yearning of a Chinese patriot 'to die for my motherland, a land I had never visited.'"[8] This had zero appeal to the Malay, Indian, and Chinese communities in the colony. In addition to enjoying freedoms under the British, all of these groups were deeply religious (Muslim, Hindu, and Buddhist respectively), an issue that Elkins never mentions because religion is an annoying opiate that her romantic socialist guerillas were intent on stamping out. Even Stockwell admits ruefully that Ong's "predominantly Chinese guerrilla force was largely divorced from the bulk of the Malay peasantry" and "failed to develop a national, non-communal appeal."[9]

As to "legalized lawlessness" one is hard-pressed to interpret the British response as anything other than nauseatingly law-bound, even to the point of absurdity. In 1952, for instance, one Lee Meng was charged with being in possession of a grenade and condemned to death under Emergency Regulations. The first trial was declared flawed by a colonial judge. Convicted in a second trial, his lawyers appealed to the Federal Court of Appeal which upheld in a split decision. After a further appeal to the British Privy Council failed, the Sultan of Perak in whose state the trials took place, exercised his own authority and commuted the sentence to life in prison.[10]

The relish for terrorism in Elkins' writing is clear. Ong's jungle fighters ambushed Gurney's car north of Kuala Lumpur in 1951. Gurney died in a hail of bullets, drawing fire from his driver and wife. They hid in a culvert with his dead body until help arrived. "Dead in one of the empire's remote, roadside gutters," in the enthusiastic telling of Elkins. He had it coming, after all. A "trademark mustache punctuated his ever-present scowl." The day of his assassination, he was heading for "a weekend of colonial leisure" in a "Rolls-Royce" with "crown insignia." Presumably, the graduate students gathered on the library floor for Colonial Horrors Story Hour with Teacher Caroline are expected to gasp with each salacious detail. Levying fines! A mustachioed scowl! Colonial leisure! (Whatever that is).[11] In 1959, native police tracked down the ambush leader, Siu Mah, to a cave near Ipoh and shot him dead. Dead in a muddy cave filled with the filth of global communism. Such a view is at least more redolent of the views of ordinary Malayans.

Communist flags and caps found at a guerrilla camp by British forces and their Malay scout during the counter-insurgency. Credit: Imperial War Museums.

While the British were keen to negotiate a settlement with the communists, the local Malays, Indians, and Chinese in the colony wanted nothing to do with them. When the insurgents briefly came out of the jungle in 1955 claiming they wanted to talk peace, the Malay chief minister Tunku Abdul Rahman said No. "It was a big juicy red apple but Rahman was shrewd enough to realize that it was poisoned," wrote the architect of the British counter-insurgency strategy, Sir Robert Thompson.[12] The insincere communist approach to the peace deal signed in Vietnam a year earlier would prove him right.

Instead, the British focused on sapping communist support through "New Villages" that would protect locals from communist terror and deny recruits and supplies to the insurgents. It worked well and became the basis of the "hearts and minds" approach to counter-insurgency. The 423 villages were strictly run according to published rules in order to avoid any perception of arbitrary administration or favoritism. The 500,000 mostly Chinese migrants who moved into the villages gained land rights for the first time and proved loyal to the British cause.

Contemporary academics work up the New Villages into a Wagnerian drama of repression and control, ignoring their success and legitimacy with the residents. The insurgency's membership, which had peaked at 8,000 in 1952, collapsed by 1957. Monthly attacks fell from 100 to 20. As one military strategist wrote: "The evidence suggests that the main lesson to be drawn from the British practice of counterinsurgency is that physical control of the contested segment of the population is essential."[13]

Ong was eventually exfiltrated to Beijing via North Vietnam in 1960 as his movement collapsed into ideological schism and Stalinist purges. For Elkins, it is a great pity that his movement did not succeed. Were Elkins to ask a Malaysian or Singaporean today, she would find those poor ex-subjects still laboring under the silly "colonial" idea that not being taken over by a communist tyranny was a good thing. A leader of Malaya from the Indian community who would become independent Malaysia's ambassador to the United Nations, Radhakrishna Ramani, said at the time of Gurney's death: "This should not merely be the end of another great man. This must be the beginning of a renewed determination to steel our hearts and strengthen our hands to end such dastardly crimes forever, and with the greatest possible speed."[14] Ramani represented the people of Malaya. Ong did not. You won't find Ramani mentioned in Elkins' book. She is too busy relishing the thought of Gurney's riddled corpse lying in a colonial gutter.

While the French lost the stomach to defeat communism in Southeast Asia, the British took it head on. Thompson was justifiably proud of how the British saved Malaysia and Singapore from collectivization and terror. He was called upon by the Americans to help them in Vietnam in 1964. His advice: focus on a defensive war to build up a South Vietnam that is "free, united, independent, politically stable and economically expanding" rather than an offensive one to drive the insurgents out of the country. His advice was not heeded despite an attempt to replicate the New Villages program there. South Vietnam would exist today as a flourishing riposte to a Stalinist North Vietnam if it had been.

Historians of colonialism like Elkins always end their tales of colonial oppression at independence. This allows them to ignore the fact that postcolonial leaders in places like Malaysia, Singapore, Thailand, and Indonesia carried on the same policies as their colonial rulers (or, as in Africa, abandoned them with disastrous results for "freedom and human dignity"). In Malaysia, the communists restarted their insurgency in 1968. Again, there was no local support. They finally gave up in 1989. Malaysia's rulers rejected an appeal to replace the National Monument (Tugu Negara) in Kuala Lumpur with one that included a communist figure in the heroic tableau. The "Malaya Red Square" the insurgents dreamed of at the heart of a Democratic People's Republic of Malaya never came into being. Today's Malaysians and Singaporeans can thank the British.

Fellow Harvard historian Jill Lepore blurbs *Legacy of Violence* as being "carefully researched," while Stanford historian Priya Satia, awed by the "staggering research," blurbs the "fearless brilliance and prodigious skill in the historical craft" of the author. Like Elkins, Lepore and Satia think of history as source material for their ideological crusades. History has thus become a branch of literary theory, scouring the past for source material with which to engage in Victorian moralizing encrusted in dense jargon about "othering" and "controlling the body."

In the final chapter of *Legacy of Violence*, Elkins lets her mask slip with a full-press political commentary on modern Britain. It is a country with a "configuration of white power" that includes such monstrosities as the Royal Institute of International Affairs (which she misnames the "Royal Institute of Foreign Affairs") and a referendum mandate to leave the European Union. There are odes to Black Lives Matter and an analysis of the Iraq War. For good measure, she voices her opposition to "monarchy, hierarchy, and racial exclusion." Hierarchy? This intellectual incontinence is apparently what happens when a Pulitzer Prize is awarded.

Not to leave out her American readers, and in a kind of crescendo intended to alert the audience to cue for their standing ovation, we get attacks on former president Donald Trump, all forms of policing, and the idea of sovereign borders. The timpani begins with an ode to Meghan, the Duchess of Sussex, and then, the concert cymbals crash with an insistence that her extreme political views must be imposed "sometimes peacefully and other times forcefully."

Aspiring young historians are supposed to get the message. Any hopes of a career in colonial history will require submission to extreme anti-colonial dogma, sometimes peacefully and other times forcefully. Are you on your feet? So am I, barreling for the exits. I hope those committed to objective history will remain and seize the stage, whether peacefully or forcefully.

Endnotes:

1 For a summary see Bruce Gilley, "Contributions of Western Colonialism to Human Flourishing: A Research Bibliography", Version 4 (2023).
2 Caroline Elkins, *Legacy of Violence: A History of the British Empire* (2022) [hereafter LOV], 22.
3 P. Eric Louw, "Colonialism: Taking the Good with the Bad," *Academic Questions* (2022).
4 Karl Hack, "'Iron Claws on Malaya': The Historiography of the Malayan Emergency," *Journal of Southeast Asian Studies* (1999), 103-4.
5 LOV 470, 466, 460, 461, 457, 538.
6 LOV 466, 466, 468, 473.
7 Anthony Stockwell, "Chin Peng and the Struggle for Malaya," *Journal of the Royal Asiatic Society* (2006), 295.
8 Stockwell, "Chin Peng," 280.
9 Stockwell, "Chin Peng," 288, 289.
10 Stockwell, "Chin Peng," 291.
11 LOV 511.
12 Robert Thompson, "Squaring the Error," *Foreign Affairs* (1968), 447.
13 Wade Markel, "Draining the Swamp: The British Strategy of Population Control," *The US Army War College Quarterly: Parameters* (2006), 36.
14 "Guerrillas Murder High Commissioner in Malaya," *The Canberra Times*, October 8, 1951.

CHAPTER ELEVEN

Colonial Yemen, Post-Colonial Yemen

THE SOUTHERN END of the Arabian peninsula has been at war with itself for two centuries. When the latest round of civil conflict erupted in 2014, humanitarian organizations rushed to send food aid to refugees through the port of Aden. It had been the second busiest port in the world after New York when part of a British colony.[1] But the deterioration of the facility since the British were forced out in 1967 meant that the food aid was mostly stranded and went to waste.

As a case study in the triumph of colonialism and the tragedy of decolonization, the former British colony in what is today Yemen is unrivalled. What today might have been a relatively stable and prosperous Arab country alongside neighboring Oman and the emirate states of the Persian Gulf is instead a cauldron of human suffering. Post-colonialism, an attitude that spurns the colonial past and envisions some anti-Western notion of modernity, is blinkered at the best of times. In the case of Yemen, it is a cruel joke.

The port of Aden that anchored the British colony eventually known as the Federation of South Arabia came into British hands as a ship refueling station in 1839. A representative of the British East India company had been stationed here from 1821 under strict orders to make peace with the local tribes. It was the first addition to the British empire under the young Queen Victoria. The Ottomans had moved to nearby Mocha because they preferred the coffee there and were tired of ruling rebellious Arabs near Aden. The nearby Sultan of Lahej put up a half-hearted protest at British annexation. But he was reconciled with the promise of an annual stipend and many honorifics. His power and prestige grew under British protection and the beginnings of a legalized sultanate emerged.

An attack on the port by an inland Arab tribe, the Abdalis, led to another settlement with another annual stipend in 1843. As one historian notes: "The greatly increased demand in Aden for the produce that the Abdalis raised, as well as the extra merchandise passing through their territory, on which a treaty with England enabled the chief to levy 2 per cent *ad valorem* duty, made him far more affluent than his neighbours and secure against a coalition of needy and adverse tribes eager to appropriate his property and prosperity." Another tribe, the Hawshabis, "supplied Aden's markets with flour and grain" and were, as a result, also "well-disposed towards the English."[2]

Despite Ottoman attempts to tempt tribes away from the British, the colonial sphere of influence grew as the tribes under its protection prospered. The population of Aden itself soared from just 600 in 1839 to 25,000 by 1844. The opening of the Suez Canal in 1869 ignited Aden's importance as a transit hub and in-migration accelerated.

While critics of colonialism sometimes point to pre-colonial systems of rule as evidence that colonialists "imposed" their own system, in Aden there was a sparse population (600 fishermen living in huts) and no system of rule. As with other places created by the British, like Hong Kong, Singapore, Freetown, and Barbados, there is by definition no alternative to colonial history here. Whoever replaced the British would, by definition, be another alien ruler, local or otherwise. Most of the pre-modern social connections of the Aden area were with present-day Eritrea and Ethiopia under Byzantine influence, followed by Persian and Ottoman conquest.

British rule in Aden was a magnet for Arab migrants who "self-colonized" by fleeing Arab tyrannies in the inland. The only fear among the locals was that the British would not stay.[3] Fortunately, they did, signing treaties with 90 sheikhs, sultans, emirs, sharifs, and naibs in the hinterland and expanding the port colony of just 75 square miles into a larger protectorate in southern Arabia of 112,000 square miles.[4] A cosmopolitan "Adenese" identity emerged that included Jews, Muslim Indians, Arabs, Iranians, and Somalis, all of whom spoke Arabic as a *lingua franca*.[5] The modernist French poet Arthur Rimbaud moved to Aden in 1880 to work for a French coffee trader and ran a café that was a center of intellectual life.[6]

When a British traveller passed through in 1892, he marvelled at "the gay thronging crowd of many nationalities all bent on their several businesses" including Arabs, Jews, Greeks, Somalis, Turks, and Indians.[7] In 1914, Turkey agreed to a formal border delimiting the Ottoman empire to the north from the British colony of the south. After the Ottoman collapse, the boundary was recognized in a status quo agreement of 1934 with the chaotic new Kingdom of Yemen of the north, pending final negotiations. Thousands more Arabs fled independent Yemen for the human flourishing of colonial Aden.

In 1936, the British brokered a truce among three of the major tribes of the eastern part of the protectorate. It required 1,300 signatures. "This is perhaps a record for a peace treaty, and it shows how disunited the country was that so many signatures should be necessary," commented the British resident advisor in 1938. With the truce, roads and airfields were built, educational and agricultural extension services introduced, and imports boomed. "Little more than a year ago every tribesman in the country carried his rifle with him, even to walk across the street," the advisor noted. "Blood feuds were widespread and the ordinary Arab traveler went in fear of his life. Even travelers by car had to take escorts with them from village to village. Now, however, it is comparatively rare to see a tribesman carrying a rifle."[8]

The port of Aden had 80,000 residents by 1946. A 1951 treaty with Yemen promised to conclude the boundary talks, but by this point Yemen was little more than a criminal state. It preyed on the wealth and stability of the British colony, arming rebels and destroying infrastructure while casually killing Arabs working on water and road projects. In 1954, British Petroleum opened a refinery in Aden, which drew thousands more Arabs from Yemen.[9]

The British were careful to balance the needs of economic development with cultural change. The rapid expansion of roads in the 1950s, for instance, threatened the livelihoods of Bedouin camel operators. In the eastern region headquartered at the port of Mukalla, "it was decreed that a traveler may transport only a certain specified poundage by truck if camels are available for the rest of his load," observed a British expert on Islamic law. A native official would visit Bedouin camps in the morning to ascertain the number of camels available for transport to the interior. After that, he would approve trucking requests.[10]

As development proceeded, London outlined plans for "a considerable degree of internal self-government" for the Federation of South Arabia, including Aden, while promising not to abandon the place to the tender mercies of the north.[11] Envious of the colony's success and facing domestic unrest, the Iman of Yemen declared himself "liberator" of the colony and scourge of the British imperialists. As the London *Times* observed in 1954: "The growing prosperity and increased security enjoyed by the sheikhdoms in the Protectorate contrast all too favorably with the failure of the medieval regime in the Yemen to provide even a modicum of sound administration."[12] By 1962, the north was in civil war after the Iman was overthrown. The population of the port of Aden reached 150,000 by 1965, while another half million lived in the surrounding protectorate.[13]

Nationalist Egypt soon replaced Yemen as the main backer of rebel attacks on the British colony. In a 2017 BBC television mini-series on the final days of Aden, *Last Post*, an arrogant rebel leader tells a British diplomat: "I want my country back." But the "country" the insurgents laid claim to was a creation of the British. It had not been "taken" from anyone. Nor was it "theirs." Most of them were Yemeni migrants and Egyptian mercenaries. The pro-British sultans in the colony bitterly opposed these self-styled liberators who wanted to replace the moderate and liberal administration of the British with a northern tyranny. The Adenese sultan Muhammad Farid al Aulaqi travelled to the United Nations to beg for the support of British rule in order to save the region from collapse.[14]

The final three years of the colony from 1965 to 1967 were characterized by a doughty British counter-insurgency campaign. A key resource for the British was intelligence gathered from captured insurgents. The chief of staff for Middle East Land Forces remarked: "Pretty well all our information comes from interrogation." Other senior British officials concurred. Without interrogation, security forces would have "virtually no forewarning against terrorism or information on its development," said the governor, Richard Turnbull. The commander in chief of Middle East Command stressed that "unhindered operation of the interrogation center in Aden is critical to all our operations." Any interference with the center "would result in a very sharp deterioration of the security situation" that would lead to "a more sophisticated and determined form of terrorism."[15]

The information obtained from insurgents was vital to saving the livelihoods of the colony's 650,000 people. Coercive interrogation was justified, and it was used. The Swedish branch of Amnesty International launched an investigation into the plight of captured insurgents, even as the organization had nothing to say about the deaths of hundreds of innocent Arabs from the terrorist campaign. When Amnesty went public with its findings in 1966, the *New York Times* crowed in delight: "Britain has been embarrassed by the actions of a Swedish doctor."

A British soldier in Aden ten months before colonial rule collapsed. Credit: National Archives (UK)

Facing censure in the West, the British agreed to allow Red Cross doctors to examine every insurgent sent for questioning. While the doctors filled out neat reports with scolding remarks on bruised cheeks and rope burns from hoods, a monstrous gang of terrorists was moving closer to control of the whole colony, ushering in 80 years of human rights catastrophe. By early 1967, with intelligence collection effectively impossible, Britain started to lose the war. Attacks and bombings rose from a dozen a month in late 1966 to a hundred a month and then a thousand a month by mid-1967. Insurgents set off a bomb in the home of the Adenese chief minister, Abdul Mackawee, killing him and his three sons. A local British official wrote to the Foreign Office: "Amnesty International have succeeded in carrying [Egypt's] objective of destroying our only major source of operational intelligence nearer to achievement than ever before."[16]

Washington knew perfectly well what was happening but said nothing. The US was keen to avoid the appearance of conspiring with the "imperial taint" of British colonialism. Allowing the "imperial taint" of Cairo, Moscow, and Beijing was less damaging, and certainly excited no haughty editorials in the *New York Times*.[17] The National Liberation Front (NLF) was neither national nor liberating. When its political chief declared himself the rightful ruler of the colony in 1967, the London *Times* reported, he "sat beneath a portrait of President Nasser [of Egypt], 'the leader of all the Arabs', and the walls were plastered with revolutionary slogans or quotations from Che Guevara."[18] The *New York Times* wrote without apparent irony or misgiving: "Everyone wanted to wipe out the traces of 128 years of British presence."[19] A veritable Boston Tea Party with promises of a young and flourishing liberal nation to come. As the NLF moved closer to capturing the colony, it split into factions. The streets of Aden were soon a cross-fire of gunfights among rebels as much as against the British. After defending a shrinking perimeter, 3,500 British troops evacuated on November 29, 1967.

The critics of empire averted their gaze the moment the Brits were sent packing. For the Western media, the history of the 650,000 people in Aden and vicinity ended on November 29, 1967. After all, it might disturb their readers to know that the stately procession towards freedom and self-determination had turned into a wreck. It took just four months before the NLF-ruled South Yemen suffered its first coup. In 1968, the head of Aden security forces fled to North Yemen and joined the rebels. In 1970, the former prime minister went before the firing squad, followed by the Chief Justice.

After snickering at the hasty departure of the Brits and admiring the post-independence celebrations, a pall of silence fell upon the *New York Times*. There is one article in 1968 with a loving mention of the "revolutionary dynamism" of South Yemen followed by a surprised article on the "lack of progress" towards human betterment.[20] Then comes a ten-year silence, punctuated by only a brief mention that South Yemen had been included in the United Nations' list of countries in a "starvation belt."

Academics mimic this naïve progressivism and ladle loving attention over the post-1967 regime. Its socialist tendencies were sure to make a "positive contribution" to human welfare, as one labor historian writes. "The radical Left elements of the NLF in the new republic definitively broke with 'petty bourgeois' Nasserism and sought a revolutionary state run by democratic councils of 'workers, poor peasants and partisans.'...There was an important visit to China for NLF training in 1967. One of the brigades of the new regular army was named Che Guevara, reflecting the inspiration of the revolution in Cuba."[21] That the facts on the ground showed a clear immiseration of the "workers and peasants" appears irrelevant to such scholars, a technicality that in no way discredited their high ideals.

When a London *Times* reporter visited Aden in 1972, it was a ghost town. "No longer do tourists throng among the Arab and Indian shops huddled near the waterfront under the shadow of Mount Jebel Shamsan. Their stocks of cut-price cameras, tape-recorders and watches remain unsold. The only customers are a few visiting seamen," he noted. "The once hustling harbor is almost still. The lighters lie moored in long, sad lines waiting for custom. The little boats which used to ferry tourists from liners to the ships are totally neglected."[22]

Amnesty International, which had whipped up world public opinion with its reports of bruised cheeks and cold showers under the British, issued a grim report on human rights for South Yemen for 1976:

> The issues of particular concern to Amnesty International include: wide-scale arrests or disappearances of suspected political opponents or criminal offenders and/or their relatives; large scale detention without trial; the use of torture for eliciting information or confessions (in some cases this has resulted in death); use of the death penalty for a wide range of political and economic offences, its extra-judicial use and the death in custody of political prisoners ... Arrests are seldom announced officially, so it is impossible to give an accurate figure for the present number of political prisoners. But the total probably fluctuates between about 2,000 to 10,000 (out of a population of about 1.5 million) ... There now appears to be no organized political opposition in the country, but within the NLF, the sole political party, those suspected of disloyalty to the government are liable to arrest. Since suspect members of the party are considered a particularly serious threat, their treat-

> ment can be more severe and their sentences, if they are tried, may be heavier … A lawyer, Tawfiq 'Az'azi, reportedly was kidnapped from his home in 1972 after refusing to convict and sentence some political detainees and ordering their release because he claimed they had committed no offence under the penal code. He has not been seen or heard of since … In 1972 there were reports of four groups of political prisoners (66 in all) killed during transfer from one prison to another "while trying to escape." Many of those killed were members of the former government and ruling class, and it is alleged that these killings were part of government policy to eliminate such leading tribal figures … During 1974 up to 150 prisoners were reported to have disappeared from Al Mansura prison. One of them may have been Muhammad bin Abdullah bin Awadh Al Aulaqi, formerly minister of finance in the federal government, who in 1968 was sentenced to 15 years imprisonment on charges of high treason and feudalism.[23]

In 1978, the Soviet Union installed a Marxist regime. It soon had all the trimmings of a Soviet satellite state: starvation, East German police, and high-sounding resolutions on the rights of women. The first president went to the firing squad. The collapse of the Soviet global system led to a hasty unification with North Yemen in 1990. Things got worse. Civil wars erupted with tick-tock regularity in 1994, 2004, and 2014.

From unification in 1990 to 2023, the average income of a Yemeni citizen fell by 45% to just $1,800, using the purchasing power measure of exchange rates used by the international community.[24] The 32 million people of today's Yemen are heirs of a people who have become steadily poorer and more prone to violence and early death under Arab nationalism and decolonization. It is no small irony that global wake-up call about the string of failed post-colonial states across the greater Middle East (stretching from Morocco to Pakistan) began with the bombing of a U.S. warship that was refueling at Aden in 2000.

The need for some external force to create order in Yemen eventually brought regional powers into play. In 2016, the United Arab Emirates ousted al-Qaeda from the eastern port city of Mukalla and instituted what in other contexts would be described as a colonial regime, known as the Southern Transitional Council. The rebuilding of Mukalla drew upon the broad Hadhramaut diaspora in the region. The UAE built hospitals and schools in the city and, along with the Saudis, provided oil grants to power electrical plants. A small American military presence at its airport provided security alongside Saudi and British forces deployed elsewhere in the former southern republic. In 2021, shipping company Maersk reopened regular service to Mukalla in a partnership with the UAE's Port of Salalah, now marketing itself as the "gateway to Yemen," the way the British used to market Aden. The Southern Transitional Council eventually ceded Mukalla to the formal government backed by Saudi Arabia, moving its headquarters to Aden.

Today, the most poignant reminders of the British era are the graves of the working class British soldiers who did an impossible job with bravery and fortitude to defend the colony in its final years. A handful of the graves of the 214 British soldiers killed there between 1955 and 1967 are found in the aptly named Silent Valley Cemetery on a small peninsula west of Aden. The graves are tended with care by the local population. The surviving British veterans of the campaign retreated to their regimental redoubts in Britain, ignored and scorned as cogs of empire. A lieutenant of the Argyll and Sutherland Highlanders, Colin Mitchel, known as "Mad Mitch" for his daring capture of a rebel stronghold in Aden in 1967, died in 1996 unrecognized by the British military for his valor.

The rise and fall of colonial Yemen, like the rise and fall of colonial Hong Kong (see Conclusion), is an unambiguous example of the case for colonialism. But it remains stuck in the public imagination as a lost cause. The BBC cancelled a planned second season of *The Last Post* in 2018 amidst a growing moral panic in Britain about the need to be more anti-colonial.

Perhaps someday, Mad Mitch will be given his due honors, and the British will be brought back to rebuild the military and police in Yemen. Their first post should be at Aden.

Endnotes:

1 Robert Stookey, *South Yemen: A Marxist Republic in Yemen* (1982), 77.
2 Caesar Farah, *The Sultan's Yemen: Nineteenth-Century Challenges to Ottoman Rule* (2002), 122, 124.
3 J. P. Malcolmson, "Account of Aden," *Journal of the Royal Asiatic Society* (1846).
4 Brian Lapping, *End of Empire* (1985), 280.
5 A. S. Bujra, "Urban Elites and Colonialism: The Nationalist Elites of Aden and South Arabia," *Middle Eastern Studies* (1970), 192.
6 Lucine Taminian, "Rimbaud's House in Aden, Yemen: Giving Voice(s) to the Silent Poet," *Cultural Anthropology* (1998).
7 Walter Harris, *A Journey Through the Yemen and Some General Remarks Upon That Country* (1893), 124.
8 William Harold Ingrams, "The Exploration of the Aden Protectorate," *Geographical Review* (1938), 649-650.
9 Ronald Hyam, *Britain's Declining Empire: The Road to Decolonisation, 1918–1968* (2007), 289.
10 Herbert Liebesny, "Administration and Legal Development in Arabia: Aden Colony and Protectorate," *Middle East Journal* (1955), 394.
11 Lapping, *End of Empire*, 283; Hyam, *Britain's Declining Empire*, 288; Bujra, "Urban Elites and Colonialism," 190.
12 "Frontier raiders," *The Times* (London), July 16, 1954.
13 Lapping, *End of Empire*, 290; Bujra, "Urban Elites and Colonialism," 191.
14 Lapping, *End of Empire*, 292.
15 Brian Drohan, *Brutality in an Age of Human Rights: Activism and Counterinsurgency at the End of the British Empire* (2017), 115, 132.
16 Drohan, *Brutality in an Age of Human Rights*, 136.
17 Tore Petersen, "Anglo-American relations over Aden and the United Arab Emirates, 1967-71," *Middle Eastern Studies* (2017).
18 Nicholas Herbert, "Aden NLF demand to Britain," *The Times* (London), November 9, 1967.
19 "In Aden, It's Goodbye to Britain," *The New York Times*, December 3, 1967.
20 Dana Adams Schmidt, "Royalists in Yemen Move to Mount New Drive in 6-Year War," *The New York Times*, March 15, 1968; Eric Page, "After 10 Months, Southern Yemen Has Made Little Progress," *The New York Times*, September 22, 1968.
21 John Chalcraft, "Migration and Popular Protest in the Arabian Peninsula and the Gulf in the 1950s and 1960s," *International Labor and Working-Class History* (2011), 35.
22 Nicholas Ashford, "The ghost port of Aden plans for time when the Canal is reopened," *The Times* (London), January 1, 1971.
23 Amnesty International, *Briefing: People's Democratic Republic of Yemen* (1976).
24 International Monetary Fund, *World Economic Outlook Database* (2023).

PART III

Colonialism in the United States and Canada

CHAPTER TWELVE

The Good Fortune of Being Enslaved in America

THE YEAR 1619 was one of terrible cruelty in the world. In Europe, the French king imprisoned his mother in a rural chateau and had her tortured in conditions described as no better than in the Bastille. The horrific Thirty Years' War began in Central Europe: before it ended, it would take eight million lives and reduce the population of parts of Germany and France by over half. The bubonic plague was sweeping India and millions were dying from epidemics and border wars in Ming China, both places ruled by decadent god-kings that saw mass death as a natural part of the cosmic order. In the Americas, the governor of British Bermuda was replaced after having a man hanged for stealing a piece of cheese.

My own Scottish forebears were being rounded up by the king for duties in New Scotland (Nova Scotia). The king preferred to settle this new colony with ne'er-do-wells, criminals, and "Brownists"—Protestant followers of Robert Browne, the same radicals who would people the Mayflower in 1620. Most died in the 1620s from freezing, starvation, or scurvy. The expedition leader described the latter condition in a 1629 letter as "a nasty and lazy disease with swelling of feet, legs, and thighs, with shoots the colour of the rainbow, with sores falling off the hair, a canine appetite, even til death much discontent."[1] Further down the North American coast, "20. and odd Negroes" were put ashore at Jamestown, slaves stolen from a Portuguese ship that had loaded them at Angola in southwest Africa.

For all such groups—Bohemian rebels, Bastille prisoners, Chinese and Indian serfs, Caribbean settlers, Scottish malcontents, and African slaves—life was nasty, brutish, and short around the year 1619. The Reformation was only a century old and had yet to achieve its moral revolution in the world. The Industrial Revolution, through which capitalism generated unprecedented human welfare, was over a century away. None of us would choose to have belonged to any of these groups: canapés and an honest Grenache at Versailles for me, please. But if one were forced to make a choice, a plausible argument could be made for the good fortune of the "20. and odd Negroes," not just compared to the other unfortunates but also compared to the millions of slaves of African and Arab owners that they left behind.

The Jamestown 20-odd were likely part of the plunder from a war a year earlier between the dominant Ndongo kingdom in Angola and a Portuguese-led alliance of African rivals, dissidents, and mercenaries.[2] While slaves were always part of war plunder in Africa, most slaves in Africa were a result of market transactions not war. The Jesuit chronicler Pero Rodrigues wrote in 1594 that the number of "slaves taken in war are nothing compared to those bought at *feiras* [markets], at these *feiras* the kings and lords and all Ethiopia [i.e., east Africa] sell slaves."[3] Those who ended up in Jamestown were headed for the Caribbean and would otherwise have ended up in east Africa or the Middle East.

The Spanish and Portuguese believed they were doing African slaves a favor by rescuing them from cruel local tyrannies and that they would fare better as slaves under Christian masters, their souls saved. Hence the hasty baptism of slaves about to be shipped from Angola, including probably those who ended up in Jamestown in 1619. The glimmer of a push for equality and emancipation from the ethical resources of Western civilization was already present on those beaches.

None of this made their enslavement "right." But then little of what happened to the wretched of the earth in that era was "right" by contemporary standards. There is a historical bait and switch when contemporary critics charge Europeans with all sorts of modern crimes: stealing land, owning slaves, shooting lions. These charges appeal to norms and expectations that emerged later from Western civilization itself, and only from Western civilization. Stealing land, owning slaves, and slaying wildlife were, after all, the national sports of pre-European contact African, Arab, and native American cultures.

Mary Grabar, in her critical response to *The 1619 Project* of the *New York Times*, notes that slavery was so common and presumed normal through the period leading up to the American Revolution that it is better to see free wage labor as unusual, as well as the astounding assertion of human equality in the Declaration of Independence. "Though it is hard for us to imagine a worse fate than slavery as it existed in North America, slaves in other societies sometimes faced even worse prospects, such as the possibility of being used as human sacrifices."[4]

In the event, the life chances of those enslaved under the British empire improved markedly compared to what they would have been in Africa even as freemen, and certainly compared to other slave colonies in the Americas. Within a flourishing capitalist system, the value put on slaves meant that slave owners had every interest in keeping them healthy. That is why black slaves in the United States were healthier than most people in Europe, and indeed healthier than poor whites in the United States itself. By their 17th birthday, American male slaves were taller than "the working classes of England, the poor of Italy, students in Habsburg military schools, the middle class of Stuttgart, German peasants, and factory workers in Russia. As adults they also exceeded the aristocrats of Stuttgart, Moscow middle school pupils, and were… less than one inch below the nonlaboring classes in England." By their 18th birthday, American female slaves "exceeded Boston women of American or Irish parents, factory workers in England or Russia, and the upper class in Italy."[5] It is also why U.S. slave population expanded more rapidly than elsewhere through natural increase. Elsewhere in the Americas, the slave problem resolved itself when imports declined because slaves were worked to death.

Just as a beneficent act may have evil consequences, an evil act may have beneficial consequences. And when there is no feasible pathway to those beneficial consequences other than through the initial act of evil, we might think again about the nature of the evil itself. Would the alternative act of virtue, consigning the slaves that the Europeans came across in Africa to a short and benighted life in the jungle, have been so virtuous after all?

Such consequentialist or utilitarian arguments for slavery were of course standard fare for the slave states of what became the Confederacy and their argument for an expansion of slavery to the Western territories that precipitated the Civil War. Defenders like Thomas Cooper placed slavery within a progressive, populist, and democratic conception of legitimacy. For these thinkers, there was no "first best" of free, healthy, safe, prosperous, and self-directing citizenship for the legacy slaves of early republican America (slave imports ended in 1808), only a set of second-best alternatives. "The poor have a right that their comforts should be carefully considered; and that is a bad government that neglects it," he wrote. In this paternalistic conservative tone, he rejected virtue-signaling statements of rights such as the "dangerous abstractions of abolitionism and other ill-supported theories of social reform."[6] The startling and rapid descent of the French Caribbean colony of Saint-Domingue into misery and turmoil after a rebellion against slavery in 1791 and then independence as Haiti in 1804 was a widely cited example of what awaited black America if there were sudden emancipation from slavery.

The problem for such utilitarian or consequentialist arguments was that they could not keep up with reality. No doubt, the 388,000 black souls eventually delivered to the shores of America as slaves suffered a great evil in their capture and removal. No doubt, as well, their utilitarian welfare, and certainly that of their descendants was markedly better than what it would otherwise have been. Absent plantation slavery, there would have been no pathway to the massive human betterment for black Africans that awaited them in America. But the moment they had the good fortune of being incorporated into a republic with high ideals about human liberty and equality was the moment that the utilitarian calculus began to shift against their continued enslavement.

The Jamestown 20-odd were dropped into a particularly idealistic part of the West, where Protestant notions of emancipation and the equality of men would develop faster than elsewhere. As time passed, the moral revolution against slavery that began in Britain would sweep the United States. From 1619 until the British abolition of the slave trade in 1807, the moral revolution was building. Slave traders were increasingly held accountable for the humane treatment of their slaves and their legal rights. Where else would there have been such a protracted legal process as at Newport, Rhode Island in 1791 for a captain accused of throwing a slave woman overboard because her smallpox threatened to kill everyone on his ship? The case went on for five years before a lengthy opinion acquitted him on the grounds of emergency measures.[7] All this for a single slave woman. Nowhere else in the world, certainly not in Africa, was human life treated as so precious.

The American founding came before there was a widespread view of slavery being inconsistent with liberal equality, even though the Founding Fathers recognized at the start that the two were in conflict. "All men are created equal" of 1776 was recognized as a promise that would bind. Black slaves immediately embraced the founding ideals, electing their own "Negro kings" in New England, remonstrating with masters to allow them to buy their freedom, and frequently using the court system to assert their rights. None of that would have been possible in Africa, which is why they took pride in being "founders" of America.[8]

Slave children rescued by the British navy from an Arab dhow off East Africa, 1868. Credit: National Archives (UK).

The moral awakening against slavery took place in the West, not in Africa, and certainly not in the Islamic world. Throughout Africa, the British used antislavery treaties as the basis of their influence. A full 10 percent of British naval resources were assigned to anti-slaving duties in the Atlantic and Indian oceans in the 1840s. Brazil and then the U.S. joined in the abolition of slavery, and then in the latter half of the 19th century the abolition spread to Africa.

That is why the more significant assertion that "All men are created equal" came at Gettysburg in 1863 after the Union armies had lost 360,000 soldiers to the cause of emancipation, essentially one soldier killed for every one of the 388,000 African slaves brought to the United States. If there was a blood debt to be paid by white America for the importation of African slaves, it was fully discharged by this eye-for-an-eye sacrifice in the Civil War.

Some critics discount the British and American efforts to abolish slavery during the 19th century on the grounds of their earlier involvement, arguing, in essence, that it should be compared to burning a fellow's house down and then volunteering to rebuild it. That is a false analogy because it assumes an intentional and acknowledged wrong is committed in the first place. Slavery was not of that sort—the moral revolution came after, not before. A better analogy would be a slum lord who, having provided housing to the destitute becomes a major advocate and funder of affordable housing programs and legal reforms to make evictions more difficult and raise standards for low-income housing. The growth of a new moral outlook brings about the change. Is this not to be praised?

The slaves brought to the United States were a tiny sliver (about 3%) of the trans-Atlantic slave trade but they created a uniquely African-American culture that would attract generations of voluntary migrants from Africa, which totaled 2.6 million from 1820 to 2022. In other words, of all the Africans who have come to the United States, seven times more have come voluntarily than as slaves. Black America is today composed mainly of the descendants of Africans who came to the United States of their own accord. To speak of "the legacies of slavery" as shaping the fate of this entire population is to engage in a Promethean act of French structuralism: nothing for blacks is every contingent or even causal, on this view. Everything is enmeshed in a vast structural system of oppression from which there is no escape because it constitutes the very logic or language of black existence in America. It is demeaning and false.

Today, being black in America is one of the best outcomes for a black person globally. In no other society in the world, do blacks have such a high standard of living, not even close. Blacks in Canada also have an average income approximately 70% of the national average, as they do in other Western countries that never had slavery like Belgium. To be black in America is, historically speaking, to have hit the jackpot. For those who came ashore at Jamestown and in the centuries that followed, being enslaved under the British empire was about as good as it got. If your fate was to be African, then being enslaved under the British empire gave you and your descendants a better shot at a decent life than they would have had even as freemen in Africa.

When the *Washington Post* sent a black reporter, Keith Richburg, to be its correspondent in Africa in 1991, the expectation was that readers would be given an "Afro-centric" perspective on the continent. Richburg would have none of it. After three years in Africa, he declared himself an American through-and-through, and one grateful for his ancestors' unwilling enslavement.

> I was in Africa, birth place of my ancestor, standing at the edge of a river not as an African but as an American journalist—a mere spectator—watching the bloated bodies of black Africans cascading over a waterfall. And that's when I thought about how, if things had been different, I might have been one of them—or might have met some similarly anonymous fate in one of the countless ongoing civil wars or tribal clashes on this brutal continent. And so I thank God my ancestor survived that voyage…We are told by some supposedly enlightened black leaders that white America owes us something because they brought our ancestors over as slaves...So excuse me if I sound cynical, jaded. I'm beaten down, and I'll admit it. And it's Africa that has made me this way. I feel for her suffering, I empathize with her pain, and now, from afar, I still recoil in horror whenever I see yet another television picture of another tribal slaughter, another refugee crisis. But most of all I think: Thank God my ancestor got out, because, now, I am not one of them. In short, thank God that I am an American.[9]

Richburg's testament was about individual betterment. But to be enslaved by the British empire was also to be an agent of broader moral change. The black abolitionists understood the inconsistency of slavery with American values, which is why they participated so manfully in the American Revolution and in the Civil War. When the black poet James Weldon Johnson celebrated 50 years of emancipation in 1913, he extolled his people's journey "From heathen kraals and jungle dens, To freedmen, freemen, sons of God, Americans and Citizens." As citizens, black Americans had been part of that great American story: "We've lived within a mighty age; And we have helped to write a line, On history's most wondrous page." Guilt? Blame? Reparations? Johnson was having none of it. Black Americans were both fortunate and ennobled by their American story. Why would a group conceive of itself in any other way? Why would it willfully impose upon itself, especially its children, a tale of woe and oppression, robbing itself of its heroism *alongside*, rather than against, white America?

With the British empire on the side of anti-slavery, more good was done for the global elimination of the slave trade than would ever have happened had the British not become involved in the trade. In historical perspective, the only thing worse for black lives in general than British and American slavery would have been its absence.

One wonders then why *The 1619 Project*—an invitation to history—became such a boorish rejection of history. Instead of insight and empowerment, it became an exercise in Soviet-style historiography. In this version, rather than all history leading to the workers' paradise, all history leads to eternal and indelible black victimization. It is fake history, propaganda, and utter nonsense.

When the state of Florida revised its grade school curriculum for African-American history in 2023, it included several inconvenient truths: slavery was long "utilized in Asian, European and African cultures" as well as among indigenous peoples in the Americas; the Europeans merely came into contact with "systematic slave trading in Africa;" the fate of slaves should be compared to the fate of "indentured servants" in Europe (like my forebears in Scotland) and to the caste slaves of India; the American republic was in a constant frenzy of "judicial and legislative actions" with regard to slavery because of its incongruence with notions of individual freedom and equality; American slaves "developed skills which, in some instances, could be applied for their personal benefit;" white people and Christian churches were central to the abolition movement; black slaves in the U.S. were far better off than their unfortunate counterparts in Central and South America; post-emancipation blacks became better off because of the diligent efforts of whites to realize the promises of the republic; and so on.

This was merely to state the obvious, even though it caused a furore. But not even Florida's historically-grounded approach, nor any of the critics of *The 1619 Project*, have challenged the main premise of the unique American ideology about slavery: that it was our nation's great sin, an error in our founding. In his critical response, for instance, Peter Wood noted that while slaves in the United States actually lived quite well compared to freemen and certainly compared to those left behind in Africa, "these qualifications convince no one that slavery was a positive good" because "the radical denial of one person's individual freedom by another." The "brute fact of such oppression," he continues, renders any counter-arguments null and void.[10] But the African slaves had *already* been radically denied their freedom by their African enslavers. The "oppression" they faced on the trans-Atlantic crossing and in the U.S. was less than what they faced in Africa, even as freemen.

Imagine if in 1619 the Portuguese had erected a little wooden stand on the beaches of what became Angola with a sign that read: "Seeking volunteers for passage to America. Life as a slave on plantation. Possibility of manumission or emancipation. Inquire within." Over the next few centuries leading to the ban on slave imports in 1808, the wooden stand remained, later staffed by British and then American slavers. Are we to believe that less than six people per day from all of Africa (roughly 388,000 people up to 1808) would have signed up? After all, voluntarily putting oneself into slavery was widespread in Africa at the time. So-called *adihyifunafu* in today's Ghana were voluntary slaves who sought the protection of a wealthy or powerful family when they fell on hard times. At other times, "parents who could not maintain their children sold some of them to obtain the means of survival." In other parts of Africa, people regularly sold themselves into slavery and remained in the same household for life, even when offered the chance to buy their freedom.[11]

America's great sin was not slavery. It was to have called slavery its great sin. This characteristically American attempt to arrogate for the "City on a Hill" a holy degree of sinfulness, guilt, and contrition will not stand. Doing so dehistoricizes the historical norm of slavery. It imposes a moral calculus of oppressor/oppressed onto every white/black relationship. It is the ultimate grand narrative, the ultimate French structural system. It has left the U.S. caught in a Sisyphean struggle against its history, unable to move on even as other former slave nations did so. Slavery was not a great sin, just an ordinary one. It was common enough and was naturally delegitimated as alternatives became available.

Search in vain for any American intellectual, even a conservative one, to say as much. For plain talk, we need to turn to a brewer. Back in 1984, a scion of the Coors company, William Coors, told black business owners in a private talk: "One of the best things they (slave traders) did for you is to drag your ancestors over here in chains."[12] Coors denied this particular phrasing, and the newspaper apologized. But even in the 1980s, speaking truth was on the ropes. The company coughed up $650 million in reparations for his remarks in the form of payoffs to black and Hispanic community groups.

Asked by the *Los Angeles Times* to recant in 1988, Coors carried on. "I said: 'This is a great country, and regardless of how we got here, we all ought to be glad we're here.'...And then, I extended it to the blacks. I said: 'You ought to be so delighted you're here . . . your ancestors for the most part were dragged over here in chains . . . none of us can tolerate the concept of slavery, but that act in itself got you here, so they did you a favor!'…And, even if blacks didn't originally get here of their own volition, they've still cashed in on the same boundless opportunity…I mean, I just don't see Jesse Jackson, or any of these other blacks, making any mass exodus back to Africa, do you?"[13]

Coors knew more about the history of the failed "Back to Africa" movement than he let on. It failed because life was better in America than in Africa. Even as a trickle of high-profile oddballs show up in Africa claiming to have escaped the unbearable fate of being black in America, millions of African blacks are desperate to board crammed vessels for the United States. If blacks did not think their life was better in America than anywhere else, more would own passports and would, over time, have migrated to other places, such as Guyana, Liberia, Haiti, or Sierra Leone.

Yet even as their actions bespeak an appreciation of life in America, their community leaders feed them a mother's milk of helplessness and incapacity. A catwalk of supermodels parading the latest fashion in eternal black victimization—from Malcolm X to Ta-Nehisi Coates—continues to set the style. This reinforces the social and psychological crisis of black America, which is now inextricably linked to the absence of historical memory, quite a feat for a group whose radical luminaries espouse attention to history.

Distortionary tales of white guilt and black virtue have become a recreational drug for white liberals as well, suggesting that as time goes by, historical understanding becomes ever more degraded. The fate of too many of those who followed the Jamestown 20-odd was to be caught in a web of self-pity, apples tied to the branch rather than being allowed to fall freely as Frederick Douglass warned. Perhaps I would have preferred scurvy in Nova Scotia after all.

Endnotes:

1 N.E.S. Griffiths and John Reid, "New Evidence on New Scotland, 1629," *The William and Mary Quarterly* (1992), 502.
2 Engel Sluiter, "New Light on the '20. and Odd Negroes' Arriving in Virginia, August 1619," *The William and Mary Quarterly* (1997).
3 John Thornton, "The African Experience of the '20. and Odd Negroes' Arriving in Virginia in 1619," *The William and Mary Quarterly* (1998), 425.
4 Mary Grabar, *Debunking The 1619 Project: Exposing the Plan to Divide America* (2021), 82.
5 Richard Steckel, "A Peculiar Population: The Nutrition, Health, and Mortality of American Slaves from Childhood to Maturity," *Journal of Economic History* (1986), 728.
6 Daniel Kilbride, "Slavery and Utilitarianism: Thomas Cooper and the Mind of the Old South," *Journal of Southern History* (1993), 479, 483.
7 Leonardo Marques, "Slave Trading in a New World: The Strategies of North American Slave Traders in the Age of Abolition," *Journal of the Early Republic* (2012).
8 David Hackett Fischer, *African Founders: How Enslaved People Expanded American Ideals* (2022).
9 Keith Richburg, *Out Of America: A Black Man Confronts Africa* (1997), xxi.
10 Peter Wood, *1620: A Critical Response to the 1619 Project* (2020), 42-43.
11 Kwabena Adu-Boahen, "The Impact of European Presence on Slavery in the Sixteenth to Eighteenth-Century Gold Coast," *Transactions of the Historical Society of Ghana* (2012), 178; A. E. M. Gibson, "Slavery in Western Africa," *Journal of the Royal African Society* (1903), 21-22.
12 "Coors Says Statements Misrepresented," United Press International, February 25, 1984.
13 Bella Stumbo, "Brewing Controversy: Coors Clan: Doing It Their Way," *Los Angeles Times*, September 18, 1988.

CHAPTER THIRTEEN

Erasing White Settlers with Fake Indian Rocks

For the last several decades, the history of Anglo-settlement countries has been under a revisionary assault from forces broadly described as cleaving to a vision of "indigeneity." Despite being formed by British colonialism and given systems of language, writing, order, prosperity, and civilized debate (including debate on the colonial past) by British colonialism, these countries were now described in purely indigenous terms. The white national founders were out. The natives were in. A vast skein of academic and popular histories arose to assert that it had always been so. The white man had crashed into this history like a fiery meteorite. Despite all the destruction and mayhem of the white cosmic body, the history as such remained indigenous, even to the present. Going beyond the anti-Western rage of the "settler-colonial" paradigm, these new indigenous histories denied the importance of the colonial settler altogether.

It began in New Zealand in the 1990s when Māori activists began to demand payments from the government for alleged violations of the country's founding treaty. This led to a rethinking of the country as Māori first and British only by regrettable accident. As the spoils of being Māori rose, the number of people claiming to be Māori doubled to 900,000 between 1991 and 2022. When I visited the country in 2015, the makeover was complete. The country was being called "the land of the long white cloud" or Aotearoa. The only mention of British colonial history in the national museum in the capital Wellington had been relegated to a lobby outside the bathrooms. The Pax Britannica of 1840 that ended a brutal 30-years of inter-tribal warfare on the islands was now dismissed as a white annoyance to a peaceable and spiritual people.[1]

Australia was not far behind. Having previously erased the name New Holland used for more a century after the island's discovery by the Dutch, white Australians were all too happy to erase their own colonial term of Australia with any number of alternatives. The problem was that the various aboriginal groups in the country had different stories and histories. Stuck with the name Australia, the country nevertheless was hard at work by the 2000s removing its known history in favor of fables. It was lustily called "the colonial boomerang," a violent weapon that came spinning back to decapitate the white man.

Racing to catch up was Canada, seeking a post-Christian and post-British identity amidst rising ethnic pluralism. Enter Turtle Island, the new name for Canada. The term first appeared in an 1833 manuscript put together by a Moravian missionary in Indiana who recorded it as being used by a Delaware (or Lenni Lenape) tribe of the Algonquian peoples.[2] It was not heard much again until hippies and beatniks in 1970s America started to use it while writing their LSD-fueled poetry. Recognizing the brand value, it began cropping up in the oral histories of dozens of native groups in Canada and the United States, claiming it had been their term for the land "since time immemorial." By the 2010s, Turtle Island (North) was in a renaming and rewriting fervor, erasing its white colonial history with the enthusiasm of Moravian missionaries.

The United States remained the lone hold-out among Anglo settlement countries, refusing to expunge its actual history in favor of an child's tale of native spiritualism. Books like *Rethinking Settler Colonialism* from Manchester University Press in 2006 left the United States out entirely due to its reactionary failure to comply. But the trend was pushing hard. In his 2023 book, *The Rediscovery of America: Native Peoples and the Unmaking of U.S. History*, Yale University professor Ned Blackhawk dismissed the idea that "the United States evolved from its British settlements." Like Houdini, he promised audiences that he would miraculously escape from "the framework of European discovery" in writing his history. Instead, he would emerge from those confines totally free of the white man, having shown "the centrality of Native Americans…to every century of U.S. historical development."[3]

Of course, it is always possible for historians to emphasize certain groups, trends, or aspects of the human activity in a geographic area as their favored interpretation. They may favor it on empirical, ideological, or aesthetic grounds. It is up to others to decide whose interpretations are most valid, useful, or appealing. Dr. Blackhawk was merely exercising his freedom to "focus on" that which pleased him. Search for books with "...and the making of America" in the title and you will find a delightful litany of Dr. Blackhawks each with their favorite "focus" including: civic charity, the Louisiana Purchase, Daniel Boone, Catholic nuns, anti-communism, Chicago, Methodists, baseball, federalism, magazines, Muslims, the military, lawyers from Pittsburgh, and the river crossing known today as the Master Sergeant Stanley W. Talbot Memorial Bridge.

But one stricture that has usually constrained such interpretations is a fidelity to more-or-less known facts. Even an indigenous history of the United States, after all, will not gain many adherents if it makes no reference to empirical claims grounded in shared standards of validity. Dr. Blackhawk refers to the need for "reliable information" in erasing the white man from his history of the United States. While he tells us nothing about how he evaluated and selected "reliable information," at least, there is a pretense of keeping history separate from story-telling.

Today, the pretense is falling. The white man's way of thinking has itself come in for revisionary assault. After all, doesn't it merely reinforce the thing that the determined indigenous interpretation is seeking to overturn? One thus finds today a major attempt to "decolonize" the very methods of history so that unverified "oral traditions" and such are given equal status to verified facts. Indigenous "ways of knowing" are in. "Western" science is out.

Nowhere is this more evident than in the bizarre phenomenon of "ceremonial stone landscape" (CSL) activism in contemporary America. This movement seeks to have stone piles left behind by early American farmers redesignated as pre-European spiritual temples built by Indians. For our guide to this movement, we can do no better than Dr. Timothy Ives, formerly Principal Archaeologist of the Rhode Island Historical Preservation and Heritage Commission.

A little background. Timothy Ives is a mild-mannered scholar, one of those well-meaning and educated people of the political Left who finally snapped under the accumulating psychological burdens of identity politics in his practice area. He gained a Ph.D. in anthropology in 2010 from the University of Connecticut and after two fruitless years on the academic job market ("too white," he was told), settled for a position with the Rhode Island commission. There he began to push back on CSL activism with a series of articles that made plain his view that the vast majority of these "sacred sites" were in fact debris left by early white farmers.[4]

The condemnation from local activists was swift and severe. His own boss coined the term "redneck archaeologists" to not-very-subtly refer to the likes of Ives who were refusing to be stampeded into the acceptance of the CSL claims. At that point, Ives faced a clear choice. Should he recant of his research, beg forgiveness from Indian communities, and remake himself as a crusader against white settler-colonialism? As he noted in his coming-out article of 2018: "If my answer to any of these questions was Yes, I would not be writing this article."[5]

Ives then expanded upon the article for his 2021 book *Stones of Contention*, a work so lucid and unsparing in its criticism of the ceremonial stone landscape movement that one might have guessed (correctly) that he was planning to take leave of the ideological constraints of working in the public sector. As of this writing, he is a private archaeology consultant. In *Stones of Contention*, Ives exposed the academic fraud and political larceny of the CSL movement. It is a warning.

While there are a few well-recognized Indian ceremonial stone or cave sites in New England, most of the sites that would have existed before European settlement are long gone. Until the 1970s, the only people who thought otherwise of the region's varied natural and man-made stone structures were fantasists who attributed them not to the Indians, but to Vikings, Knights Templar, Irish monks, or the lost Tribe of Israel.

Enter "disco-era America," as Ives describes it. The founding myth of the ceremonial stone landscape movement was handed down by two old white men: James Mavor, a retired oceanographer who had claimed in a 1969 book, Voyage to Atlantis, to have discovered the mythic water kingdom; and Byron Dix, a retired engineer who believed there were secret codes in megalith sites in Great Britain. Mavor and Dix set about "discovering" the secrets of what we now know to be farmer rock piles throughout New England, reinterpreting them as sacred Indian sites that revealed magical kingdoms of the past. Irish monks were out, native Indians were in. The over-eager minds of Mavor and Dix "discovered no shortage of 'standing stones,' astronomically aligned 'stone rows,' and calendric 'stone circles' throughout New England's forests," Ives writes. Their 1989 book, *Manitou: The Sacred Landscape of New England's Native Civilization,* let loose an army of white retirees who set out from their subdivisions into the newly-enchanted forests of New England, there to reveal all manner of stone piles left by magical Indians that might, perhaps, extend their lives or cure their arthritis.

If you doubt the enthusiasm of this movement or the willingness of members to imagine every rock pile as a sacred Indian site, I suggest spending some time browsing the various Facebook pages where they share their discoveries, such as "Celebrating the Ceremonial Stone Landscapes of Turtle Island," "Indigenous Ceremonial Stone Landscape Protection," and "North East's Historical Stone Sites Investigations and Explorations Group" as well as the many web sites such as rockpiles.blogspot.com and stonestructures.org. After enough time, you will find yourself lured into the self-confirming wisdom of the enthusiasts. They have discovered a fairytale land that the grumpy grown-ups refuse to acknowledge. The more that the grown-ups tell them to come inside for dinner, the more they cling to their make-believe world.

Boys and men clearing stones from a field in Red Hook, New York, 1930s. Credit: Community Service Society of New York Collection, Columbia University Libraries.

The whole thing, with very few exceptions, is nonsense "growing on an old compost of American Romanticism infused with the individualistic, exploratory spirit of the New Age," Ives writes. *Manitou* was a case study, notes Ives, of "how two well-educated scientists cast off the shackles of disciplined rationality to indulge the pursuit of a consensus-based ideological vision."

The movement could not have succeeded without the supporting roles played by four other groups. Lest you assume that CSL activism is mainly an Indian endeavor, much of Ives' book is taken up with other actors. The Indians have only walk-on roles to legitimate and then receive payment for CSL victories.

The first to join the movement were the academic archaeologists who by the 1980s saw their purpose not as advancing truth but as redressing perceived historical injustices. The academics were primarily focused on themselves, staring into the mirror wracked by guilt about their "colonial gaze" and determined to make restitution by "unmasking" systemic racism at the heart of their field with its "Eurocentric" reliance on facts and logic. That these academics were pandering to romanticism concocted by old white men who could not get a tee-off time did not devalue the cause.

Running scared closely behind the academics came local, state, and federal authorities, who, being handmaids of the people, would do just about anything to avoid controversy. They also needed to get stuff done: "Federally regulated projects with broad public interest that need to follow a tight schedule present money trees worth shaking," Ives notes of the "mitigations" offered to local tribes and antiquarian groups to ease the pain of development. "What town officials are going to publicly disagree with Indian representatives bearing accusations of racism and religious oppression?"

Slower to recognize the bounty of the CSL movement came local NIMBYs (not in my backyard) looking for a politically powerful weapon to prevent land development. These residents discovered "the Indian Rock Defense." It is now a time-tested strategy for land-use lawyers in the region. Some rock or shell formations even appeared of a sudden in lands slated for development. Proposed solar farms are a favorite target of NIMBYs who resort to the Indian Rock Defense, making the CSL movement an accessory to the fossil fuel industry.

Ives documents one triumph of NIMBYism now known as the Manitou Hassannash Preserve in Rhode Island. The site was slated for development when NIMBYs demanded a survey. Tribal leaders were bussed in to declare, after a seemly pause for divination, that they had recovered the memories of the sacred stone sites. The antiquarians then moved in with their cameras and self-published manuscripts. A consultancy of antiquarians and graduate students was hired to write an official report. Photos were taken of rock piles at winter solstice, suggesting a celestial purpose. Even with evidence staring the researchers in the face, they insisted on ancient origins. One large boulder had "rounded drill holes…[which] are typically the result of the 'plug-and-feathers' method of quarrying and splitting stone, a technique developed around 1830," the report observed. "However, the documentation of this detail is not intended to suggest a date of construction of this feature."

The clincher came at a public forum in 2017 when Paul Loether, then Keeper of the National Register of Historic Places, delivered himself of the statement that "my ancestors were New England farmers and they didn't build these structures." As Ives notes: "If everyone knew what their ancestors did and did not do, the fields of archaeology and history would not exist." Nonetheless, it was a watershed. The town and state rallied to the cause, and tribal elders came back to bless the stones. Since then, many little old ladies have been making videos providing their own Indian spiritual interpretations of the rock piles in the preserve. Ives has no doubt these stones are field clearing debris from white farmers: "This is why I do not read fiction. Life provides enough surprises."

Of course, the "network of middle class whites overindulging in an Indian cultural fetish" that constitutes the CSL movement could not have succeeded without the moral warrant provided by the fourth group: self-identified Indians. At first, the Indians brushed off the claims. But timing is everything. Disco-era America was also a time when Indian revitalization was taking shape. "Parade Float Indians" turned into "Angry Indians." The CSL movement presented an opportunity for cash, to be sure. But the main draw, as Ives notes, was cultural and thus political.

Culturally, the hard truth is, as Ives shows, that Indians are basically extinct as an identifiable genetic group. In the face of cultural loss brought about by the encounter with the modern world and the increasingly bizarre ways that people claim Indian heritage, CSL activism provided a new rallying point. "Indian racial paranoia" came full force to the defense of the CSL movement.

As life came to imitate art, the fanciful "sacred sites" discovered by old white men became actual sacred sites divined by Indian leaders. One old white man in Massachusetts claimed extrasensory powers as a result of training under a "Cherokee medicine woman." One of his discoveries was then "sacralized" by local Indians who put four clusters of quahog shells on the site, wampum money in today's terms. This "proved" that the site was still in use as a ceremonial place and thus must have been since time immemorial. Any expert who dared to challenge the claim by suggesting the sites were field debris left by farmers was charged with "failing to become enlightened." As Ives wrote in his original article: "CSL activism compels white citizenry, stigmatized by their association with settler colonialism and racism, to choose between reclaiming their moral authority, by signaling support, or renewing their moral bankruptcy in a narrative about Native American cultural survival."

Keeping this cultural glue together requires a lot of additives from Indian participants. Attempts to solicit greater information from them are invariably met with the insistence that non-disclosure agreements were reached with their ancestors. Suggestions to excavate sites are denied because this would amount to desecration, not because it might reveal farm refuse from around 1830 rather than crystals or skeletons from 2000 B.C. Ives refers to a "decolonial divorce settlement" that has left these sites and many others off-limits to professional inquiry.

CSL thus goes one step beyond the normal practice in contemporary archaeology whereby professional archaeologists discover an Indian site and its meaning before calling in Indians to announce that the Indians, using their decolonized methodologies, have discovered the site and used their ancient wisdom (if tribal rules allow) to fill in the clueless archaeologists hidebound in their "Western" methods. In the case of CSL, we have professional archaeologists consciously submitting to a false interpretation to avoid the serious charge of "taking a non-spiritual position." Thus "from the moral high ground of an indigenous warriors rebelling against the settler colonial state" the Indian activists "rally others to join their cause."

In one of this book's many shafts of light, Ives questions whether the Indian leaders know the harm they are inflicting on their communities. The lesson that money must be earned through productive work and interaction with others five days a week is a lesson that pertains also to "most of the Indian adults inhabiting New England," he reminds us. Whatever the feel-good effect of the gravy train of "mitigations" and "cultural anger" for Indians, the CSL movement is devastating to their productive capacities. "Would such beliefs inspire them to passionately pursue their talents, to recognize the full horizon of opportunities before them, and to demand nothing less from themselves than excellence? Or might this vision conspire…from the deepest recesses of their own hearts, whispering a ready alibi against the pursuit of their full potential?"

Of course, as with all movements founded on ideological conformity, the various factions in the CSL movement soon erupted into vicious division. One of the most volatile relationships is between the antiquarians and the Indians. While the academic archaeologists are fully socialized into allowing their research to be stolen by Indians and claimed as their own, the amateur antiquarians are less generous. Ives documents one fissure that erupted in 2018 when one of the antiquarians complained of the "fake history" being offered by the Indians about his own fake discoveries. It was "an ironic circularity, that of a radical revisionist of ancient Indian history experiencing an allergic reaction to the perceived filtering" of his work. "This situation also presents a rare, if not unique, political unicorn – a white settler colonist suggesting that a local Indian has appropriated his ideas and then erased him from history."

The CSL interpretations also invariably contradict one another, setting off internal disputes of interpretation. Sometimes the sites are called burial grounds, then memory piles, then ritual sites, then sacred sites. One site was apparently located in a place that ancient Indian prognosticators predicted correctly would be the future right-of-way for a high voltage transmission line, thus placed "so they could turbo-charge their visions using its electromagnetic field." A hilltop site declared on one interpretation to be an ancient Indian place of "vision quests," meanwhile, is made up of jagged boulders set in angular ridges that the ancients apparently dragged up the hill by unknown means. Ignoring the better scientific explanation of hilltop erosion patterns, Ives notes, "I believe the first things those Indians would have envisioned was a more comfortable place to sit."

A great virtue of this book which recommends it to a broad readership is that Ives every once in a while climbs out of the excavation pit to remind readers that a lot more is at stake than piles of rocks. The reason why a disco-era America conspiracy theory was swept up into mainstream political advocacy, he reminds readers, was the dark shadow cast upon the West's intellectual canvas by the emergence of "cultural Marxism." As Ives nicely summarizes, cultural Marxism was the outgrowth of the anti-empirical Frankfurt School that viewed the role of a scholar as "social critic without the need to validate any of his claims." The Frankfurt School took the stale Marxist concepts of class and exploitation and vastly expanded the repertoire of identity groups and forms of oppression. It has contributed so much collective political psychosis to the West that one might have wished Allied bombardiers had diverted from Dresden. "Essentially, ceremonial stone landscape activism represents a regional front where the standard of Cultural Marxism has advanced," Ives writes in battlefield analogy. That these acts might have "collateral effects" on Indian lives is never entertained. The "categorical association of archaeology with settler colonialism and racism hangs in the memosphere, as does a vision of Indian victims joined by morally outraged defenders."

This requires believers to "hold faith in a matrix of intertemporal abstractions," in this case, about "the heritability of settler colonial guilt." Thus, to fight for a reinterpretation of those stone piles as sacred Indian sites is not just to join the Marxist fight against "oppression" but also, and here is the post-Marxist move, to indulge in "a quasi-religious awakening."

There is an unmentioned theme in this book that is nonetheless well-documented by Ives, indeed it forms the core of the discussion. This is the willful erasure of the traditions and histories of early New England farmers by the CSL movement. Ives goes to great lengths to provide documentary evidence from contemporary newspapers, memoirs, and almanacs, as well as scientific site studies, about the common practice of heaping exposed stones in piles in the middle of fields in early America. In "old Yankee taxonomy," the heavier stones which framed the walls of so-called stone corrals were called "two-handers" while the smaller stones thrown into the middle were "one-handers." Other times, the structures were built around large rocks exposed by "melt-out till," the rocks left by glaciers that melted in place.

The practice of piling stones was a topic of raging debate in early America because the experts thought the farmers should remove the stones altogether rather than just pushing them into piles. The farmers resisted calls to cart the stones away, often using stone piling as a chore for children and other times hoping to sell the stones when needed for nearby roads. The piles "embodied the pragmatism of hill farmers," Ives writes, citing sources like the *Carlisle Mosquito* and the *Green Mountain Freeman*. He is probably the only active scholar in the United States interested in the stone-heaping practices of early American farmers.[6]

Other sites represent cellar holes from farmhouses long gone. The whole history of farm abandonment as new areas were opened up in the West is an important part of the American story. It explains why these stone piles or cellar holes are mostly found in wooded areas because the trees grew back after the farms were abandoned. When excavated by excitable graduate students hoping to find Indian ceremonial items, they always reveal, instead, rusting barrel hoops, bricks, and farm detritus from "just beyond the edge of social memory."

So the stone piles represent culture, traditions, family histories, and early American understandings of agriculture. Ives cites all this to establish the clear evidence that these are not Indian spiritual sites. But we might note that to misrepresent them in this way is to engage in a terrible act of cultural erasure and appropriation. Ives calls this "social amnesia" about early New England families. As he wrote in the original article: "Opinions that many of the same structures were likely built by farmers only a few generations ago for purposes such as land clearing, field division, and livestock enclosure are rejected as the sophistry of a settler colonial state."

In CSL circles, he adds in the book, "the notion of historic farmers leaving heaps of stones in their fields is a white supremacist myth." One leading academic advocate calls the insistence that these really are just old farmsteads an ugly attempt to "purify the land" of Indian spirituality. That this movement directly mimics the "violence" and "erasure" of those it assails cannot escape attention.

Not all these farmers were white either. Free blacks and many Indians took to the plough, and the finest stone piles invariably were those left by Indian farmers because they had been taught by settler-colonial English stonemasons. Irony of irony, the Indian activists are erasing fellow Indians from memory. The Indians, write Ives, "forget their own relatively recent historic agriculture practices."

This erasure is not just social, it is also governmental. Ives makes several references to official reports that have been deep-sixed by tribes who do not want information on the agricultural origins of the piles to be known to the public. Of the best-documented report that has been disappeared by the government, he writes: "Data potentially threatening to the ceremonial stone landscape vision are quietly cleared, like unwanted stones, from the intellectual field."

Since poor settlers in early America are not the *plate du jour* of our Woke republic, they can be easily disparaged, erased, and forgotten. Even better, the facts of their past can be censored and new fake data fabricated in its place. The scandal of this scandal is that it is completely in the open. Ives has continued to document it, to little avail.[7]

While Ives concentrates on the CSL movement in New England, there is no shortage of activists re-interpreting stone features across the United States as ancient sites of sacred Indian ceremonies. In 2000, for instance, Indian tribes in Oregon demanded that the American Museum of Natural History in New York return to them a 15.5 ton meteorite found near Portland in 1902. They claimed it was a spirit rock that traveled from the moon whose water, found in cavities, their ancestors had used for medicinal and military purposes (even though it was almost entirely buried when found). The Willamette Meteorite is the largest ever found in the United States and the sixth-largest in the world, so much was at stake. Funny thing, the Indian stories were first told in support of the claim of the original white prospector to keep it against the wishes of the land owner. A wealthy white philanthropist bought the rock in 1904 and donated it to the museum to save it from being melted down for its iron. Putting aside the veracity of the original Indian stories, it seemed pretty rich to demand the rock for themselves. In the end, a deal was reached that gives the tribes special access to the museum hall for sacred ceremonies once a year.

Again, what is erased by this deal between the scientists and the tribes is the quite remarkable story of the white settler who found and excavated the meteorite, a Welshman named Ellis Hughes. The story of how he dragged the meteorite to his house three quarters of a mile away is the stuff of legend, real and well-documented.[8] But these ingenious and industrious white settlers who founded modern America are today the least likely to get a hearing from the intellectual establishment. There is no mention of Ellis Hughes in the American Museum of Natural History documentation, which is all about science and tribal mythology. Hughes has been erased, a "mere" prospector who "merely" found and recognized the meteorite and "merely" brought it to the world's attention.

One would expect that Ives' thorough debunking of the CSL movement would give it pause. In his own delightful phrase, Ives has been busy "unsettling decolonial landscapes."[9] Not on your life. Since the publication of Ives' book, the movement has gained strength. Ives is now the poster-child for the evils of settler colonialism engaging in cultural genocide with its nonsense about facts and data. In 2023, no less than the University of Arizona Press published a new collection written by CSL activists and Woke archaeologists who "present overwhelming evidence in the form of oral tradition, historic documentation, ethnographies, and archaeological research that these important sites created and used by Indigenous peoples are deserving of protection."[10] Ives jokingly refers to this new book, *Our Hidden Landscapes*, as the New Testament to complement the Old Testament of *Manitou*.

All of the parties to this betrayal of truth and fairness in pursuit of ill-defined "justice" and "preservation" deserve a chapter of shame. The mostly old, white, male antiquarians with too much time on their hands should have thought more about the consequences of launching half-baked conspiracies into the Internet. The Indian tribes, whatever rationality is attributed to their shake downs, should have seen the long-term harms of perpetuating the victimhood narrative especially when it is based on such gross abuses of history. The spirit-seeking white activists seeking moral redemption for the heritability of their white guilt should have got woke to the narcissistic and demeaning nature of their "allyship"—using Indians as stage props for their passion play and in the process stigmatizing Indian culture as some premodern form of nature worship. The local politicians and state and federal authorities who rolled over in the name of "cultural sensitivity" should have had a more public service-oriented perspective to their jobs. And of course the NIMBYs who used the Indian Rock Defense as a last-gasp to preserve their wooded views might have reflected on the Kantian imperative that asks people to act only in ways that reflect generalizable principles of good behavior.

Perhaps the greatest censure should be reserved for the academics who betrayed their professional duty to seek truth. After all, in a free and pluralistic society, there is nothing wrong *per se* with participation in a delusion. If there were, there would be nobody attending Buffalo Sabres games. But the academic vocation is one that demands a rigorous pursuit of truth. The falsity of the academics is that they have quite openly eschewed their calling in favor of ideological activism.

Ives, in his gentle humor writing in a time of pandemic, suspects that "I will enjoy a special envelope of social distancing in many settings for years to come." Yet his social ostracism began long before, alluded to vaguely in the small communities of New England as "the redneck archaeologist." Whatever brickbats to come, Ives writes that he would rather face them than "feel complicit in a silence with far-reaching negative implications" about the grubby exchange that constitutes the CSL movement: "As you have probably guessed by now, I find cheap political bargains disgusting."

How much easier, he muses, if he were to issue a gushing statement of white guilt and a soaring promise to "let the landscapes speak" unencumbered by fact or logic. He would also need to declare that he is "in a committed relationship with" a tribal historic preservation office. In time, he might find himself "secretly hallucinating below power lines." At last, "redemption would be mine." He would be able to "certify [his] reformation" by joining the moral panic over charges of belittling Indian heritage.

That he refuses to do so makes him a hero in my book. His praise for the rare Indian leaders who refuse to be stampeded into CSL nonsense might as well apply to him: "More power to them in an age when the simple act of declining to get on the racial rhetoric train presents a modest form of public heroism."

That example, in the end, is one that Ives wants us to follow. He wants us to ignore rather than engage those suffering from Indian racial paranoia or fetish. Instead, we should stay centered on finding the truth. "Well-intentioned people in prolonged contact with them may find that they have allowed themselves, as have I, to have become needlessly reinvested in race constructions in a way they did not see coming." His final appeal is to "unlearn race," the core concept on which CSL depends. With time, the CSL movement could be ignored and a scientific approach to the past restored: "Life is too precious to spend as a projection of someone else's imagination."

Endnotes:

1 Ron Crosby, *Musket Wars: A History of Inter-Iwi Conflict, 1806-1845* (2017).
2 Jordan Paper, "The Post-Contact Origin of an American Indian High God," *American Indian Quarterly* (1983).
3 Ned Blackhawk, *The Rediscovery of America: Native Peoples and the Unmaking of U.S. History* (2023), 1, 6, 3, 8.
4 Timothy Ives, "Remembering Stone Piles in New England," *Northeast Anthropology* (2013); "Romance, Redemption, and Ceremonial Stone Landscapes," *Bulletin of the Archaeological Society of Connecticut* (2015); "Cairnfields in New England's Forgotten Pastures," *Archaeology of Eastern North America* (2015).
5 Timothy Ives, "The Hunt for Redneck Archaeology: Disentangling 'White Guilt', Ceremonial Stone Landscape Activism, and Professional Archaeology in New England," *Northeast Anthropology* (2018).
6 Timothy Ives, "Historical Accounts of Forgotten Stone-Heaping Practices on Nineteenth-Century Hill Farms," *Northeast Historical Archaeology* (2020).
7 Timothy Ives, "Legends of Rock: Are New England's Stone Heaps Native Americans' Sacred Ruins?" *The Spectator World*, January, 2022.
8 Henry Ward, "The Willamette Meteorite," *Scientific American*, July 9, 1904.
9 Timothy Ives, "Unsettling a Decolonial Landscape," *Annual Meeting of the American Anthropological Association* (2022).
10 Lucianne Lavin and Elaine Thomas (eds.), *Our Hidden Landscapes: Indigenous Stone Ceremonial Sites in Eastern North America* (2023).

CHAPTER FOURTEEN

Defending the British Empire on the Canadian Prairies

There is a delightful irony when a priest tells the secular laity to be less confident in its moral dogmas. Nigel Biggar, professor of theology at Oxford, is that priest, and in 2023, he posted his theses about the British empire (including the empire in Canada) on the door of the High Church of Anti-Colonial Ideology. His book, *Colonialism: A Moral Reckoning*, set out eight theses about what we might call the global expansion of the kingdom of Wessex, a remnant of the Roman empire that was overrun by the Danes and then the Normans before emerging as a rather successful unified state called the United Kingdom.

I will dwell here on his treatment of one episode of the British empire in the Canadian prairies. But it is useful to place this in the context of his overall thesis. Biggar is not precise about which phase of the British empire he has in mind. Most of his discussion covers not the first phase that began with Ireland in 1603 and Bermuda in 1609 (and which would include Canada and the United States), but the grander, post-Napoleonic second phase that began with the Cape of Good Hope (1814), Singapore (1819), and Burma (1824). The eight theses are in any case backward-looking evaluations rather than chronological assessments, so they cover the whole four centuries ending with the surrender of Hong Kong (1997).

The eight theses are as follows: The British empire was based on admirable motives even if, like all human affairs, it often suffered from vices; that anti-slavery, far more than slavery, was a central thrust of

British imperial policy; that a justified belief in the superiority of British civilization, a belief shared by most natives, sometimes bled into an unjustified sense of racial superiority (but this was mainly among the working classes, and it was less common than the caste racism in India or the inter-tribal racism in Africa or among indigenous peoples in the Americas); that disease, far more than land acquisition, is what rendered many native populations weakened by European settlement (and state-led land acquisition was the best alternative to what would otherwise have been an unholy scramble with no legal remedies for the natives); that efforts at cultural uplift for the natives were based on anti-racist and humanitarian motives, none of which either in intention or in practice can be glibly called "genocide;" that colonialism brought a necessary and inevitable economic shift from subsistence and plunder economies to markets, wage labor, and capitalism which delivered more economic well-being than would have arrived in these places otherwise; that colonial governments were heavily dependent on native support and participation, sowing the seeds of national consciousness and self-government; and, finally, that the use of force by colonial governments was usually justified and proportionate to the violent threats from unrepresentative insurgencies.

In the eight chapters documenting each thesis, Biggar takes up the moral critique of empire and the key events that have been used to justify that critique. Like a patient man of the collar providing pastoral care for the spiritually afflicted, he offers those trapped in the "Hate the British Empire" narrative a way out that is both empirically and ethically sound. If you are interested in the familiar debates on Cecil Rhodes, for instance, or the Mau Mau insurgency in Kenya, Biggar makes sure to cover the ground. He also offers a delightful debunking of the myth of the "Amritsar Massacre" (not the one in 1984 that killed 1,500, or the Sikh death squads in Amritsar that killed thousands of Muslims during Partition of 1947, but the one involving a frightened British brigade in 1919 that killed 379). Biggar's relegation to a footnote of his response to the specious claims of the Danish-British historian Kim Wagner that the 1919 skirmish reflected a violent and racist "essence" of the British empire is appropriate.[1] "Literally peripheral," Biggar writes. After all, he explains, even the most generous reading of Wagner's thesis would find that it applies only in the chaotic conditions of frontier areas, not in the core areas.

Let's turn to Biggar's response to claims of "ethnic cleansing" and "displacement" lodged against the government of Sir John A. Macdonald by University of Regina health studies professor James Daschuk in his 2013 book, *Clearing the Plains.*[2] The charges relate to the Macdonald government's handling of the Canadian prairie famine from 1878 to 1883. Biggar shows that Daschuk's criticisms are specious. The Canadian government responded with alacrity and shipped huge amounts of food to Indians who were starving as a result of tuberculosis, a winter drought, and the decline of the bison population. It asked that healthy Indians who could be useful on planned Indian farms should work for their rations. Indeed, it worried that too many Indians wanted to work on the farms and that it would run out of employment.

The Canadian government response was sufficient to prevent blood-letting among the Indians that would have resulted from what Daschuk coyly refers to in his book as "traditional means of acquiring wealth" (i.e., stealing). As Biggar shows, the supposedly evil statement by Macdonald in the House of Commons in 1882 that Daschuk and other critics have cited—"[W]e are doing all we can, by refusing food until the Indians are on the verge of starvation, to reduce the expense"—is mangled by being taken out of context. The "all we can" referred to attempts to stretch the available rations to cover as many of the starving as possible given supply constraints. It also referred to the desperate sense in the government that the Indians needed to be coaxed from their stupor to ensure they survived the coming winter. Making the food conditional on wage labor was not a devious scheme for genocide but a well-reasoned plan to give the Indians a basis for future survival. Per capita spending on famine relief by the government was "comparable with white working class household" income at the time, according to an analysis by the former Director of the Centre of Canadian Studies at the University of Edinburgh, Ged Martin. The response was "impressive and humane."[3] In all, 45 Indians died in this "genocide" according to a count by Patrice Dutil in *The Dorchester Review* cited by Biggar.[4] As Biggar notes: "No, that is not a typographical error."

The treaty Indians whose lives were at risk in the prairie famine expressed appreciation for the government response. Not that the likes of Daschuk would allow the opinions of those whose lives were at stake to get in the way of his Grand Narrative. He opens his book with the assertion that "racism among policy makers and members of mainstream society was the key factor in creating the gap in health outcomes" between Indians and the rest of Canadian society. Nothing to do with the Stone Age level of development among Indians when the Europeans arrived. Nothing to do with the disease and warfare that scattered their numbers.

Nothing to do with the welfare dependency and victimization narratives thrust upon them by later Canadian leftists—the narrative that Biggar's book challenges. No, none of that. White racism all the way down!

My only complaint about Biggar's treatment of such episodes in the history of the British empire is that he is not nearly critical enough of the clergy in the High Church of Anti-Colonial Ideology. Biggar is merciful in his gentle remonstrance with Daschuk. He accepts many of their anti-colonial critiques too readily. It is that old British tick: the need to be sensible, dear fellow. Biggar sometimes sounds like a country parson eager to avoid a summons to tea with the Bishop. Even a reformer, after all, has to keep his living in the Church. As a result, his deference to some of the claims of anti-colonial doctrine is delivered with too much apology for my Puritan tastes.

In his description of the prairie famine, for instance, he cites Daschuk himself (whose claims of genocide he has just shown to be ludicrous) that the Indian farming program was "hastily contrived" and an "abysmal failure." All this haste and failure, avers Biggar, raises the possibility of "culpable negligence" by the Macdonald government, a very rum thing. Why is Daschuk suddenly a pillar of reason and objectivity? When the famine began, there were no railroads and no food supply systems to deliver rations to the prairies. In addition, the Indians were still mostly nomadic, so to find everyone would require sending the Mounties to chase them about the plains. Macdonald tripled government (i.e., white taxpayer) spending on Indians, making it the third largest program expense in the federal budget. The Indian farming program began in 1878 required instructors, seeds, and tools for the 17,000 Indians scattered across an area seven times larger than the entire United Kingdom. Seventeen farming outreach agencies were established as well as two model government farms and provision stations. But without railways and with starvation preventing work, the results were meager. The farm instructors spent most of their time distributing rations, according to Sarah Carter's 1990 book, *Lost Harvests: Prairie Indian Reserve Farmers and Government Policy*. Most important, no one yet knew how to farm in the Canadian prairies. White settlers were having just as much difficulty surviving as the Indians. "Farming at this time in the [Northwest] Territories was a dubious, precarious undertaking for anyone, even an experienced Ontario farmer," Carter wrote in her book. "It was not to be for a decade and more that suitable techniques for dryland farming were discovered through trial and error and the work of the experimental farms."[5]

Also read, if you will, Carter's account in the same book of the travails of James Scott, the appointed Indian farm instructor for Touchwood Hills near today's Punnichy, Saskatchewan. Scott left his wife and seven children in Brampton in June 1879 and arrived in late August, a journey of 2,500 km (roughly Lisbon to Berlin for the reference of our European friends). Most of his equipment had gone missing, his oxen were near-death, and his companions had scattered. Creating viable farms in this area was the work of a generation, but Scott lasted only two years. One Indian chief hoarded the farm equipment he was given for use by his own family. Other Indians insisted that Scott buy his supplies only from them. Farm tools arrived missing parts. Land thought to be arable turned out to be barren. And so on. The program was ended in 1884, a noble experiment that failed.

Other charges laid by Daschuk include the complaint that many of the tools broke. Since he studies only Indians, he automatically assumes this was some dark racist conspiracy. I dare him to read Nellie McClung's account of a faulty wheat binder in her memoirs, *Clearing in the West*, after her family arrived in Manitoba in 1880. "The story of that binder is a story of grief and the other [people's] binders were no better. Everything went wrong, someone was on the road to Brandon nearly every night, for the parts left with the blacksmith were not sufficient... It seemed that we had replaced every part on the binder that could possibly break."[6]

Poor old Nellie McClung has since been downgraded from a noble woman and suffragette to yet another evil tool of British settler colonialism by no less than the same Sarah Carter whose earlier work was less infected by the Woke moral panic of our age. In her 2016 book with the University of Manitoba Press, *Imperial Plots: Women, Land, and the Spadework of British Colonialism on the Canadian Prairies*, Carter accuses McClung of a cardinal sin: she "expressed deep pride in and admiration for the British Empire." Further, as a young girl brought to Manitoba to eke out a living, Carter charges, McClung was "complicit in the enterprise of dispossessing Indigenous people."[7] Dispossessing them, that is, of the illusion that their people and culture stood any chance of survival in the modern world without a bold and accelerated program of uplift and integration; and, along with other colonial-minded women pioneers in the Canadian prairies, expressing unbridled support for the residential schools for Indians that were requested by Indian elders and filled with Indian children sent by their parents who recognized their value. ("They too were the children of Mother Britannia, but they were in need of a stern but kindly guardian," in Carter's sneering account.) As an alumnus of Nellie McClung Elementary School in Calgary, I can only say that the derision of Carter's book has raised dear Nellie in my esteem immensely.

Carter and Daschuk are emblematic of the lunatic turn in the writing of colonial history. They should be called out for what they are, not coddled. To return to Biggar's too-easy charge of possible "culpable negligence" in the Macdonald government's response, it is as off-base as the narratives he challenges. "Hastily contrived?" Of course, the Indian farms were hastily contrived: a famine was underway and winter was coming (a term that in Canada has a very different meaning than the gentle rains of England in January). "Abysmal failure?" By what possible reasonable standard of expectations in the context? Biggar later told an online Canadian magazine that "the delivery of that government relief was clearly deficient. The American firm contracted to deliver food on the Prairies was corrupt and government agencies also failed."[8] Corrupt? Failed? This sounds like a lot of moral posturing of the sort one hears on the BBC from people trying to sound reasonable. Methinks the specter of the Bishop's summons to tea weighs too heavily on the writing of our reforming Oxford parson.

Another instance of Biggar being too sensible by half comes in his chapter on economic development under colonialism. After dousing claims of "economic drain" and "de-industrialization," especially with respect to India, he "sensibly" avers that "greed, racial contempt, the abuse of superior power and consequent injustice...deserve our indignation and moral condemnation." Yet he offers no examples of greed, racism, or abuses of power that might rouse our indignation and condemnation. No doubt, the clergy in the High Church of Anti-Colonial Ideology would hasten to offer examples, the sorts of false flag operations used to raise a moral panic and stampede the impressionable minds of the learning public into the burning of some witches. Alas, greed, racism, and abuses of power can be found in every human society (Yes, children, even in First Nations, black, lesbian, and matriarchal societies). To rouse more than our normal corrective sympathies, to rouse us to Indignation and Condemnation, would require those injustices to be enduring, intensive, and baked into the system, as well as unforeseen and avoidable. Were greed, racism, and abuses of power such a systemic feature of British colonialism? Can we find official regulations in British colonial governance that stated that "Administrative officials shall be hired based on their greed, racism, and ability to abuse their power"? Of course not. Our sensible parson doth concede too much. These attempts to sound balanced come across as rhetorical, offered for good measure, in hopes of avoiding tea with the Bishop (who was probably put up to it by his wife, she more fearful than he).

All this is history, but what of the present? In each chapter, Biggar pitches the argument into the present, which may interest readers more. Telling non-whites that they do not need to adapt and integrate into white society because they are now free to "decolonize" their lives is a recipe for their continued failure and misery. An equity agenda that denies human equality will shortly lead to a Great Leap Backwards to an illiberal society. The use of force by a liberal state is justified and necessary to preserve human well-being: start calling it "oppression" and demanding a "decolonized" police force and you will very quickly see blood-letting that takes mostly non-white lives. Finally, the art of self-government, so painstakingly built up under the British, survived or failed after independence depending on how long it had been given to take root (too short in most African colonies) and whether the post-colonial elites made the effort to uphold it or destroy it. What made Anglo-settlement countries such a stunning success despite their geographical dispersion was their firm adherence to the rule of law, constitutionalism, property rights, and civic virtues (even in "revolutionary" America). In our era, he notes, Western countries are at risk of replicating the post-colonial failures of many colonies by repudiating the Western liberal heritage, regressing like so many failed states of the Third World. "Thanks to illiberal 'cancel culture', British and other Western peoples stand in danger of losing," the democratic virtues of respecting the equal right of various viewpoints and individuals to compete for power, Biggar warns. "Cultural advantage, however hard won, can always be lost again, since what has been learned can always be forgotten."

The Eight Theses of Father Nigel Biggar may prompt the Church to reform but so far they have prompted only angry outbursts. When the book was published in 2023, the *Globe & Mail* invited Biggar to write an essay making his case on Victoria Day. After he submitted the essay, Toronto experienced "a change in editorial priorities" and cancelled it. It was published in *TheHub.ca* instead, and attracted wide attention.[9] Then, Biggar appeared on the Jordan Peterson podcast for Victoria Day, racking up 200,000 views in the first week.[10] So who really cares anymore what the old Marxists and young gender studies graduates in the editorial offices of the *Globe & Mail* think anymore? They have lost the game. So have the indigenous studies professors at the University of Regina.

As Martin Luther wrote: "That person whom no one disturbs does not have peace." Biggar can enjoy the deep peace of knowing that he has lanced the Babylon of fake colonial history. May he be continually disturbed.

Endnotes:

1 Kim Wagner, *Amritsar 1919: An Empire of Fear and the Making of a Massacre* (2019).
2 James Daschuk, *Clearing the Plains: Disease, Politics of Starvation, and the Loss of Aboriginal Life* (2013).
3 Ged Martin, *The Department of Indian Affairs in the Dominion of Canada Budget*, 1882, gedmartin.net (n.d) .
4 Patrice Dutil, "Not Guilty: Sir John A. Macdonald & the Genocide Fetish," *The Dorchester Review*, January 14, 2021.
5 Sarah Carter, *Lost Harvests: Prairie Indian Reserve Farmers and Government Policy* (1990), 94.
6 Nellie McClung, *Clearing in the West: My Own Story* (1935), 129.
7 Sarah Carter, *Imperial Plots: Women, Land, and the Spadework of British Colonialism on the Canadian Prairies* (2016), 321, 17.
8 Peter Shawn Taylor, "Reckoning with Canada's Colonial Past: In Conversation with Nigel Biggar," *C2C Journal*, April 6, 2023.
9 Nigel Biggar, "Was the British Empire Evil?," *TheHub.ca*, May 22, 2023
10 "Separating Good from Evil in the British Empire", Jordan Peterson Podcast (2023), Episode 359.

PART IV

Voices of the Colonized

CHAPTER FIFTEEN

Africa's Chinua Achebe on the Positive Legacies of Colonialism

In 2012, a year before his death at age 82, the best-known of African writers, Chinua Achebe, published a mournful recollection of the Biafra war that nearly tore his native Nigeria apart between 1967 and 1970.[1] Given Achebe's stature and late demise, the book, *There Was a Country*, attracted more than the usual number of reviews, most of them paying homage to the man and his legacy. While the book is mainly a personal memoir of war, it is also a longer meditation on the history of Nigeria and the reasons for its weakness as a state and nation. Achebe's arguments about the failures of the country's political leaders are familiar ones. However, what is surprising is that Achebe also argues that a key reason for the weakness of the Nigerian state is that it repudiated too much of the colonial legacy inherited from the British. A man best known for his anti-colonial views claimed in his final work that colonialism in the lower Niger river area left legacies that remain both beneficial and relevant, alongside its harmful ones.

Perhaps more surprising, no one seems to have noticed. Virtually all of the reviewers of *There Was a Country*, ignored or downplayed Achebe's murmurings about a revalorization of British colonialism, reaffirming his identity as an anti-colonial hero.[2] This suggests there is more at stake with this book than the final thoughts of a man who insisted that his intention was "not to provide all the answers but to raise questions, and perhaps to cause a few headaches in the process."[3] Rather, the book has provided an unexpected lesson in the paradigmatic status of anti-colonial thinking in African affairs and its implications for state building and national identity.

While Achebe was a critic of the forms that the colonial encounter often took, he also believed that the challenge of modernity put to Africa by colonialism was a healthy one. Moreover, while he decried the ways that colonialism disempowered African societies, he believed that re-empowerment required embracing, not spurning, many of the same forms of governance practiced under colonialism—educational, administrative, and social. In other words, Achebe's work is a reminder that amidst the theorizing on pathways and sources of state capacity in Africa, scholars have overlooked the most obvious one: the colonial legacy itself. At a time when arguments for "going with the grain"[4] or "developmental neo-patrimonialism"[5] have revitalized discussions of indigeneity as the best approach to state-building in Africa, reclaiming Achebe's views on the positive aspects of the colonial legacy could not be more important.

This chapter proceeds in four stages. The first summarizes Achebe's reputation as a paradigmatic critic of the colonial legacy in the context of contemporary debates on state-building and nation formation. The second takes up Achebe's positions on colonialism in *There Was a Country* and the third considers whether these positions represented a decisive break with his earlier ones. The fourth section considers the paradigmatic implications of a more nuanced understanding of Achebe's views and its relevance for contemporary research on political development and state-building in Africa.

Research on state-building in Africa has moved between institutional, developmental, and social aspects. What all of these approaches generally share is a view that colonialism had a malign effect. In this view, state structures and policies put in place by European rulers destroyed indigenous forms of rule, developmental trajectories, and social arrangements, creating perverse incentives that stymied progress. Nations cobbled together by cartographers lacked coherence, while the resistance to the colonial state carried over into an aversion to the public sphere itself, except as an object of plunder. The policy implication of this view was summed up by the Guinea-Bissau nationalist Amilcar Cabral who said: "It is our opinion that it is necessary to totally destroy, to break, to reduce to ash all aspects of the colonial state in our country in order to make everything possible for our people."[6]

As a result, Africanists have been particularly averse to policy solutions that seem embedded in the colonial past, preferring instead to resuscitate indigenous solutions. Kelsall's "going with the grain" approach, for instance, explicitly repudiates the "imported ideological, legal and governmental system founded on a strong separation between public and private that has never existed in Africa," replacing it with an "opaque" system of Big Man rulers delivering resources through "personalized clientelistic networks."[7] Crook and Booth argue for the efficacy of governance that is "informalised and penetrated by local arrangements and pay-offs, deals and political clientelism" in contrast to "Northern" notions of governance.[8]

Of all the iconic figures in this anti-colonial approach to political, economic, and social change in Africa, none perhaps is more important than Chinua Achebe. His 1958 book, *Things Fall Apart*, has been widely cited to affirm the depredations of colonialism as the central fact of Africa. The European, the main African character declares in the novel, "has put a knife on the things that held us together and we have fallen apart."[9]

Anti-colonial interpretations of *Things Fall Apart* have dominated discussions of the book since its publication.[10] It has been cited to show that colonialism "destabilized societies working out their destinies along peculiar paths of existence."[11] A 2011 book reaffirms this enduring interpretation: "Achebe created a narrative that placed the African at the historic center of the colonial encounter, with the imperialistic Europeans as the usurping outsiders, whose intervention brings about cataclysmic upheaval for the traditional African civilization being colonized." [12]Merely typing "Achebe" into an Internet search will deliver a barrage of anti-colonial material.

To be sure, throughout his long and distinguished career, Achebe held views critical of colonialism. His 1974 essay, "Colonialist Criticism," originally a lecture given to American scholars, accused European writers, especially Joseph Conrad, of representing Africa in ways that justified plunder and subjugation.[13] Shortly thereafter, he chastised the British writer Iris Andreski for concluding from fieldwork in Nigeria that colonial rule had made the world safer for African women, a finding which was out of step with the radical anti-colonial ethos of the 1970s.[14] "Nigerians were taken out of our history and dumped into somebody else's history" by colonialism, Achebe told an interviewer in 1980.[15] In a 1988 interview with the American journalist Bill Moyers, Achebe described colonialism as "the most extreme form of totalitarianism."[16] This theme of colonialism as disrupting the habits and traditions of self-rule resulting in weak states was a consistent one throughout his life. In 2003, he told an interviewer: "We were considerably damaged by colonial rule…Colonial rule means that power, initiative is taken away from you by somebody else who makes your decisions. If that goes on long enough, beyond one generation, then the habit of self-rule is forgotten."[17]

In these respects, Achebe was critical of the illegitimacy and the disempowering nature of the colonial encounter. From such remarks, grew his reputation as perhaps the greatest pantheonic figure articulating an anti-colonial perspective on African state building.[18] His books were interpreted by Wren as showing that "colonial authority replaced tradition in governance" and "intensified ethnic conflict" with the result being "a decisive weakening of the power of the community to control private behavior."[19]

As a result, his subsequent fictional indictments of post-colonial Nigeria—especially *A Man of the People*[20] and *Anthills of the Savannah*[21] —were interpreted as blaming not the postcolonial leadership but colonialism. His "negation of independence," as Udumukwu called it,[22] was a negation of the idea that Nigeria had actually achieved independence from "neo-colonial" forces. For Gagiano, while Achebe insisted that "the disastrous state of many parts of the continent resulted largely from local faults and failures" these "could not be disentangled from exertions of political and economic power from the West and some of its leaders and representatives, whether during colonial or neo-colonial times."[23]

When Achebe died, this identity was re-emphasized in virtually every obituary, especially those published in Africa. Achebe, wrote Chiakwelu, "judiciously and categorically rejected colonialism in all its forms. Achebe stuck out his neck and went after the source of many African problems which is chiefly colonialism."[24] He was described (approvingly) as a "revolutionary" and a "true red" for his anti-colonial fervor.[25] Kawu wrote that "the whole sweep of anti-colonial struggle provided the backdrop for the great oeuvre."[26]

One might summarize the critical aspects of Achebe's views on colonialism along two dimensions: politically, it represented an illegitimate and disempowering form of rule that set bad precedents for being undemocratic and manipulative; socially, it institutionalized forms of ethnic hierarchy and division that undermined community. If this constituted the totality of Achebe's views on colonialism, then state-builders should follow Cabral's advice and reject the colonial legacy in all its forms. Yet throughout his life, Achebe also expressed a multitude of positive views on the political and social consequences of colonialism. The place to begin the excavation of these views is *There Was a Country*.

At the beginning of *There Was a Country*, the reader finds several anti-colonial claims. The European scramble for Africa, Achebe writes on the opening page, "did violence to Africa's ancient societies and resulted in tension-prone modern states." The breakdown of Nigeria's young democracy was caused by the "tragic colonial manipulation" of the British during the founding regional (1956) and federal (1959) elections.[27] In these places, the book seems to conform to the orthodox expectations of Achebe as an anti-colonial writer; but they do not reflect the dominant tone of the book, which, far more than previous works, articulates a positive view of colonialism and thus a more nuanced view of the reasons for the travails of post-colonial Nigeria.

For a start, Achebe is far more frank than in previous works about his voluntary self-colonization (the near-universal phenomena of indigenous peoples migrating closer to areas of more intensive colonization). "My father had a lot of praise for the missionaries and their message and so do I. I am a prime beneficiary of the education that the missionaries made a major component of their enterprise."[28] He attended Government College in remote Umuahia for secondary school because "its status as a 'government college' set up by the colonial government, reassured my parents."[29] The educational system met their high expectations: "As a group, these schools were better endowed financially, had excellent amenities, and were staffed with first-rate teachers, custodians, instructors, cooks and librarians. Of course today, under Nigerian control, these schools have fallen into disrepair and are nothing like they were in their heyday."[30] Later, he wins a full scholarship to a new university for West Africa set up by the British. "I grew up at a time when the colonial educational infrastructure celebrated hard work and high achievement and so did our families and communities...As a young man, surrounded by all this excitement, it seemed as if the British were planning surprises for me at every turn, including the construction of a new university!"[31]

The sense of optimism and progress brought by the late British colonial period is palpable. Achebe notes that his generation was a "very lucky one" and "my luck was actually quite extraordinary:"

> The pace of change in Nigeria from the 1940s was incredible. I am not just talking about the rate of development, with villages transforming into towns, or the coming of modern comforts, such as electricity or running water or modes of transportation, but more of a sense that we were standing figuratively and literally at the

> dawn of a new era.[32]

Later, he recalls feeling that "The possibilities for us were endless, at least so it seemed at the time. Nigeria was enveloped by a certain assurance of an unbridled destiny, of an overwhelming excitement about life's promise, unburdened by any knowledge of providence's intended destination."[33] In other words, the Nigeria that Achebe remembers was not one where things were falling apart. Rather, as Chambers comments, it was one where "things were coming together."[34] More broadly, Achebe at several points engages in an explicit revalorization of the colonial period. The most explicit is prefaced with the breath-drawing phrase: "Here is a piece of heresy." He continues:

> The British governed their colony of Nigeria with considerable care. There was a very highly competent cadre of government officials imbued with a high level of knowledge of how to run a country. This was not something that the British achieved only in Nigeria; they were able to manage this on a bigger scale in India and Australia. The British had the experience of governing and doing it competently. I am not justifying colonialism. But it is important to face the fact that British colonies were, more or less, expertly run.[35]

Several concrete illustrations are then offered. One is of taking a lengthy car trip from Lagos to Ibadan to visit friends and then driving on to Asaba to visit relatives. "There was a distinct order during this time," he recalls. "One was not consumed by fear of abduction or armed robbery."[36] In another, Achebe recalls how the publication of *Things Fall Apart* was made possible because of the mentoring of a British English professor, the recommendation of a sympathetic English editor (Alan Hill), the risk-taking of a major British publisher (Heinemann), and the good offices of a friend from the BBC. His greatest praise is reserved for a more prosaic ally: the British postal system, through which he sent the sole copy of the manuscript in 1956 for typing and editing in London:

> One had a great deal of confidence and faith in the British system that we had grown up in, a confidence and faith in British institutions. One trusted that things would get where they were sent; postal theft, tampering, or loss of documents were unheard-of. Today [in Nigeria], one would not even contemplate sending off materials of importance so readily, either abroad or even locally, by mail.[37]

While *There Was a Country* is primarily about the Biafran war, not British colonialism, the two cannot be separated. Achebe's judgment of British colonialism depends on constructing a feasible counterfactual of how the historically rivalrous peoples of the lower Niger river basin would have proceeded amidst the pressures of globalization and modernity either without colonialism or with an even longer colonial period. His long meditation on the causes of the war provides a grisly benchmark for constructing such counterfactuals. The thing that has fallen apart is not Nigerian society but colonial rule.

British prime minister Harold Macmillan in Nigeria nine months before independence. Credit: National Archives (UK).

The book, then, presents a contrast between attempts by the British to form a coherent political community and functioning state among the disparate peoples of what became Nigeria and the rushed termination of that project by what Herbst has called the "UN decolonization machine."[38] British rule, Achebe writes, was a "great success" in northern and western Nigeria although "far more challenging to implement" in the eastern Igbo homeland.[39] Even decolonization was orderly: "There was a certain preparation that the British had undertaken in her colonies. So as the handover time came, it was done with great precision."[40]

In other words, the book might have been titled *There Was a Colony*. What Achebe shows through the Biafran war, with its one to three million dead, is that there was no county, not a Biafra and certainly not a Nigeria, only a colony trying to create a country. Decolonization thrust this nascent political community into self-rule long before there was a reasonable chance of success. What is important about Achebe's "articulation of the unsayable," as the Malawian scholar Mpalive-Hangson Msiska calls it,[41] is not the superficial point that the British governed Nigeria better than the Nigerians, rather it is that the British project of a lengthy tutelage of state and community formation in the lower Niger river basin was a more viable route to modernity than the rushed "national liberation" that ensued.

Achebe probably overstates the role of the Igbo in this process: "The original idea of one Nigeria was pressed by the leaders and intellectuals from the Eastern region. With all their shortcomings, they had this idea to build the country as one."[42] After all, the idea of Nigeria began with the British amalgamation of north and south in 1914. Still, the bigger point is that Achebe is now affirming the "colonial" project of forging a united Nigeria. Msiska is the only reviewer who has noticed this and thus his analysis is worth highlighting:

> From the perspective of the postcolonial moment, Achebe views the colonial national formation as a more efficient and ordered society...This revalorization of the colonial period by an ardent nationalist may seem a contradiction in terms. However, it may be understood as a rhetorical device for highlighting the extent to which postcolonial Nigeria has fallen below the expectations of decolonization. So his quest for a return to the colonial moment is not to colonial rule as such, but to the forms of governmentality that ensured a measure of an ordered community. It is the *colonial national formation as a habitable community* that is one of the countries the memoir seeks to recover... Achebe counter-identifies with the dominant nationalist critique of colonialism.[43]

Whether such a habitable community would have been forthcoming in the absence of British colonialism is the great silence left by Msiska. But at least he identifies what is at stake in Achebe's final book: a late-in-life reckoning with the imperatives of state formation and political community that would have descended on the lower Niger basin with or without Lord Lugard.

Achebe, then, in this final work completes the circle of a lifetime's attempts to render the complexity of colonialism's legacies. In 1975 he described *Things Fall Apart* as "an act of atonement with my past, the ritual return and homage of a prodigal son."[44] In that work, he was atoning for his voluntary self-colonization as a youth. With *There Was a Country*, Achebe undertakes an equal and opposite act of atonement. Now he atones for 50 years of anti-colonial agitation and perhaps excessive idealization of the non-colonized Nigerian counterfactual. This is then the ritual return and homage to colonial rule. From this final vantage point, Achebe views Nigeria as anti-colonial in a bad sense. It has magnified the vices while eschewing the virtues of colonialism.

Diamond argued in 1989 that Achebe had moved away from revolutionary anti-colonialism (the need for revolution in order to combat the colonial legacy) to embrace liberal anti-colonialism (the need for democracy in order to combat the colonial legacy) with his scathing critiques of "revolutionary" Nigeria.[45] But in this final work, Achebe adds another, more dramatic, shift. Here he shifts from liberal anti-colonialism to *liberal pro-colonialism*—the need for democracy in order to reclaim the positive aspects of the colonial legacy. One could even suggest a further "heresy:" at times in this final work, Achebe the Igbo "traditionalist" as Diala called him,[46] embraces elements of conservative pro-colonialism with his frequent praise of British-era elitism, law and order, religion, and benign paternalism. Irrespective of how nuanced his views on colonialism had become by the time of his death, one thing is clear: these final words represent a significant complexification of a figure often singularly understood as a revolutionary anti-colonialist.

Achebe's late-in-life revalorization of colonialism suggests that we revisit his earlier writings and comments. When we do, we find that despite the relentless thrust of anti-colonial interpretations that grew up around the man after 1958, his complex views of colonialism were evident from the start.

The place to see this first is in *Things Fall Apart*. The book has often been criticized as going too easy on the colonialists, even for having "gone so far" as to suggest that the education and development brought by colonialism was a welcome intrusion into Igbo society.[47] The title came from Yeats. The modern world is presented as alluring and puzzling rather than evil. Indeed, the book was first interpreted as pro-colonial.[48] Achebe was arguing that the Igbo were bound to have a difficult encounter with modernity with or without colonialism and that the colonial manner in which it came helped them to hold together.[49] The colonial encounter as portrayed in the book, Wehrs argued, "sets in motion a productive dynamic…of a more just society."[50]

For these reasons, some anti-colonial writers have been scathing, calling *Things Fall Apart* complicit and approving of colonialism.[51] As three Pakistani scholars wrote: "The colonialist culture and ideology are presented as better alternatives. No resistance is portrayed to either the colonialists or their ideology. The narrative reinforces the superiority of the colonialist culture. *Things Fall Apart* cannot be categorized as a literature of resistance."[52]

A French hospital for children during the Biafra War in Nigeria. Credit: Getty Images.

Achebe's second novel, *No Longer at Ease*,[53] has a distinctly twee feeling. Achebe evinces nostalgia for the departing colonialists in the witty repartee on Graham Greene, the tennis and drinks at the British Council, and the careful civil service rules on leave and car purchases with which the protagonist, Obi, has to comply. Achebe would frequently return to his admiration for Greene, whose mixed views of empire were grounded in a view of universal human weakness.[54] Achebe, an Igbo elite, was also an Anglophile, and his love of Britain's elitist administrative, educational, and literary cultures was palpable.

Writing of Achebe's third novel, *Arrow of God*,[55] Muoneke argued that Achebe "is not a fanatical opponent of colonialism" since his main concern in that novel is the follies of all rulers rather than those of British rulers in particular. Indeed, Muoneke claimed that Achebe had by this time already come to admire how the British state-building project had unintentionally created a Nigerian nationalism. This was "about the best thing that the British did, though unknowingly," Muoneke wrote of the novel.[56] While anti-colonial interpretations dominated Achebe studies throughout his life, these more complex renderings grew up on the margins. A 2009 Nigerian conference book on his work was aptly titled *Themes Fall Apart*.[57]

Revisiting his earlier works, it is clear that Achebe, like many writers of his generation, was centrally concerned with colonialism. But it was the ideas and issues raised by colonialism, not its material impact, that he believed were most important. Achebe understood that colonialism was the impetus for cultural and national articulation in Nigeria and that the challenges that it brought were inevitable. After all, the Yeats poem from which *Things Fall Apart* took its title describes as natural (not tragic) the decline of a culture (English culture) that cannot meet new challenges. In 1980 Achebe said:

> The Igbo culture was not destroyed by Europe. It was disturbed. It was disturbed very seriously, but this is nothing new in the world. Cultures are constantly influenced, challenged, pushed about by other cultures that may have some kind of advantage at a particular time...But as I said initially, a culture which is healthy will often survive. It will not survive exactly in the form in which it was met by the invading culture, but it will modify itself and move on...So there is a need for a culture to be alive and active and ready to adjust, ready to take challenges. A culture that fails to take challenges will die.[58]

As such, he was a vocal critic of the purifying Négritude response to colonial legacies.[59] He also resisted attempts to call him anti-Western: "I don't think it's a question of protest against Europe or simply protest against local conditions. It is a protest against the way we are handling human society," he said in 1976.[60] Or in 1981: "I am not concerned with which is better, the old or the new, the African or the European; both have possibilities, imponderables, and ambiguities."[61]

Unlike other "impact-response" historiography of the Third World that always placed the West at the center, Achebe rejected the centrality of the material or structural impact of colonialism, at least as the major explanation for post-colonial Nigeria. Ultimately, agency and choices resided with Africans not Europeans. In this sense, Achebe really did break with Eurocentric explanations of Africa in a way that anti-colonial scholars and activists did not. "I intend to take a hard look at what we in Africa are making of our independence," he said in 1967.[62] In 1980 he warned that "the Igbo people are in many ways today doing as much as, or more than, the British ever did to destroy their own culture."[63] He described 1983's *The Trouble With Nigeria* as an indictment of "the chaotic jumble of tragic and tragi-comical problems we have unleashed on ourselves in the past twenty-five years."[64]

As Nigeria's post-colonial history lengthened, Achebe returned more often to the colonial period as a contrastive lens. "Before, justice may have been fierce but it could not be bought or sold…There were titles and distinctions, but they were gained by hard work…Now all that is changed," he complained in 1962.[65] In a 1966 interview, his identification with the British nation-building project in Nigeria is clear:

> These nations were created in the first place by the intervention of the British which, I hasten to add, is not saying that the peoples comprising these nations were invented by the British…And I believe that in political and economic terms…this arbitrary creation called Nigeria holds out wonderful prospects. Yet the fact remains that Nigeria was created by the British—for their own ends. Let us give the devil his due: colonialism in Africa disrupted many things, but it did create big political units where there were small scattered ones before.[66]

His appreciation of the positive legacies of colonialism was also evident in a 1967 interview:

> I am not one of those who would say that Africa has gained nothing at all during the colonial period. I mean, this is ridiculous—we have gained a lot. But unfortunately when two cultures meet... [w]hat happens is that some of the worst elements of the old are retained and some of the worst of the new are added, and so on… But again I see this is the way life is. Every society has to grow up, every society has to learn its own lesson.[67]

Achebe, then, might be described as a complex thinker about both the positive and negative legacies of the colonial encounter as it actually occurred in Nigeria. Like other writers of the period, as May has argued, Achebe *embraced* the general challenge of modernization put to Nigerians by British colonialism.[68] In 2008, he spoke as if everyone knew this:

> I had a friend who I thought admired my work, but it turned out that he didn't. He was resentful that I did not give adequate recog-

> nition to the service, to the work, of the Europeans in Africa; he thought that they deserved better treatment. So I was disappointed, because for years I thought we agreed on that role of nationalism and the role of colonialism in our history—in my history.[69]

Achebe's self-identification with the British modernization project was also evident long before *There Was a Country*. He expressed admiration for the meritocratic elitism of British education.[70] He was not a student activist against British policies during his college days from 1948 to 1953 at University College Ibadan (affiliated with the University of London) even as nationalists rioted around him.[71] His inspiration to become a writer came from a 1939 novel by a former colonial district officer, Joyce Cary, named *Mister Johnson*.[72] The novel drew on Cary's experiences managing the strains of modernity in western Nigeria. "Every reform we brought also caused dislocations or evils of some kind; and this was inevitable," Cary recounted.[73] The novel provided a way for the young Achebe to understand similar convulsions in his own village: "Cary was good, he was sympathetic, he knew Africa," Achebe said in 1972.[74]

He especially rejected criticisms that he should not have offered his first novel to a "colonial" publisher, or more bizarre claims by Western professors that he was "obliged to write in English for a London publisher."[75] Nonsense: "Without the intervention of Alan Hill and Heinemann, many of the writers from that generation may not have found a voice," he retorted.[76]

His own life reminded him constantly of the benefits of the colonial inheritance. Despite vigorous debate on his use of English, Achebe's various attempts to have *Things Fall Apart* published in the Igbo language came to naught by the time of his death. There was no demand among Igbo readers, no mentors, no editors, no publishers, and, of course, no reliable postal service. And while Western universities showered him with honorary degrees, Lagos State University was forced to cancel his honorary degree in 1988 because of Yoruba opposition.

A car accident that left him partly crippled in 1990 occurred after he had flown back to Nigeria to intervene in a bitter leadership dispute within his Ogidi tribe. The axle of the car snapped on the ill-maintained roads, throwing him into a ditch. The British Council and British Airways facilitated his transfer to a hospital in England where he was rehabilitated.[77] Those Western systems, institutions, and organizations so despised by the anti-colonial imagination saved his life. It seems to have been a turning point. His 1993 lecture at Cambridge was entitled, "The Education of a British-Protected Child." British "protected" being a reference to the British protectorate under which he grew and to the status that was emblazoned on his first passport. Achebe invoked the term ironically since no one had asked Nigerians whether they wanted to be protected, which was at the heart of his view of colonialism's disempowering consequences. At the same time, Achebe recognized that the protectorate did indeed offer many protections that would otherwise have been missing. He called the work of colonial-era British officials in improving education and commerce "a great human story."[78] At his death, his family declined a traditional Igbo funeral, holding it instead in the Anglican church founded by his father.

Looking back at his various collections of non-fiction essays—"Morning Yet on Creation Day" (1975), "The Trouble With Nigeria" (1983), "Hopes and Impediments" (1988), "Home and Exile" (2000), and "The Education of a British-Protected Child" (2009)—there are more than occasional hints at his complex views of colonialism that would eventually be in full bloom in *There Was a Country*. In a 1973 essay, Achebe allowed that his upbringing in British schools set him at a "at a crossroads of cultures" that made him "lucky" to have books and provided a "dangerous potency."[79] A 1993 essay wonders "what prompted the British colonial administration in Nigeria...to set up two first-class boarding schools for boys" as well as a national university. These colonial undertakings offered a vision of a shared humanity "primarily in the camp of the colonized, but now and again in the ranks of the colonizer too."[80] Six months before his death, when pressed to condemn colonialism by Iranian journalists, he demurred: "The legacy of colonialism is not a simple one but one of great complexity, with contradictions—good things as well as bad."[81]

In other words, a careful observer would have seen it coming. By the time he wrote *There Was a Country*, Achebe had spent a lifetime grappling with the complex legacies of colonialism and with the counterfactual of what would have ensued without colonialism. Coming from a pantheonic figure in anti-colonial ideology, this has wider paradigmatic implications.

It is difficult to overstate the importance for studies of Nigeria and Africa, as well as the former colonial countries more generally, when a figure of the stature of Chinua Achebe ends his life by explicitly affirming his view that the colonial legacy needs to be rethought not as a simple object of resistance but as a complex history and resource that Africans should engage more seriously. Achebe cannot be recast as a supporter of colonialism, which would be a disservice to his views. Yet, he can be recast as someone who took seriously the claim that most great questions have complex answers including the question of the legacies of colonialism in Africa.

Achebe's final work ventures the view that many aspects of colonialism supported attempts to create a livable political community in the lower Niger river basin. In scientific terms, Achebe is recognizing that there is a "crisis" in research on Nigeria (and Africa generally) because of its failure to come to terms with events such as the Biafran war, which is a classic "anomaly." With the nation freed of British "oppression" and euphoric about a united Nigeria, the war should not have happened. A rival paradigm, liberal colonialism as it has been called here, might explain the anomaly: the hasty end to British rule subverted the formation of political institutions and community needed to avoid such a war and to support good governance.

Colonialism never fully measured up to the standards of today's "good governance" agenda. In many ways, it was precisely the sort of "practical hybrid" of tradition and modernity—a "developmental neo-patrimonial" state that empowers local problem-solving—that authors like Crook and Booth advocate.[82] In this sense, Achebe's views of the need to reclaim certain administrative, developmental, and meritocratic facets of colonialism, while rejecting its cultural, unaccountable, and disempowering aspects, is partly consistent. The one clear point of difference is that Achebe, in the end, still believed in the *civic* public, which recent indigenous approaches have largely abandoned in favor of an *crony* public.

Achebe, the old Igbo traditionalist, discovered in his late years the elective affinity between certain aspects of British administrative, educational, and literary culture and the hopes for a livable political community in Nigeria. Those hopes could have been realized by a selective embrace of that legacy by Nigerian elites rather than the blanket resistance that precipitated a catastrophic civil war and then decades of gargantuan misrule. Achebe is calling for a creative engagement with the colonial legacy so that its virtues can be reclaimed and its vices eschewed. National identity formation is needed, but should not entrench the dominant status of any group. Meritocracy is to be valued, but not at the expense of inclusion. Traditional ruling systems can be used but they must also be modernized. Better administration must come with better accountability. And public investment in roads and health systems should be rolled out, but only through the offices of local agency.

Research on democratic development shows that prospects improve when a society selectively draws upon the ideational resources of democratic episodes in its past. A similar logic may apply here. Prospects for state-building (as well as economic and social revival) in Africa may improve when societies selectively draw upon the ideational resources of effective state episodes in their past, in this case, their colonial pasts. Indeed, it is just such a process that Sèbe observes in several African countries. He describes how the figures of European colonialism (Livingstone in Zambia, Lugard in Nigeria, and de Brazza in Congo) are enjoying a resurgence of both official and social respect in Africa after decades of execration. The reason, he argues, is that their role as state-builders is suddenly useful and praiseworthy as the failures of post-colonial leadership lead populations to search the colonial period for a "livable political community" as Achebe did. In these countries, Sèbe notes, "national origins should no longer lie in a more or less mythical pre-colonial entity, or a glorified force liberating from the colonial yoke, but quite simply from the European founder of the colony."[83] Achebe's final appeal suggests the need for new research on these aspects of the colonial trajectory abandoned at independence.

Endnotes:

1 Chinua Achebe, *There Was A Country: A Personal History Of Biafra* (2012), Hereafter TWAC.

2 Biodun Jeyifo, "First, There Was a Country; Then There Wasn't: Reflections On Achebe's New Book," *Journal of Asian and African Studies* (2013); Ogaga Ifowodo, "Chinua Achebe: The Novelist as Revolutionary," *All Africa*, April 3, 2013; Herbert Ekwe-Ekwe, "The Achebean Restoration," *Journal of Asian and African Studies* (2013); Emmanuel Ejiogu, "Chinua Achebe On Biafra: An Elaborate Deconstruction," *Journal of Asian and African Studies* (2013).

3 TWAC 228.

4 Tim Kelsall, "Going with the Grain in African Development?" *Development Policy Review* (2008).

5 Richard Crook and David Booth, "Conclusion: Rethinking African Governance and Development," *IDS Bulletin* (2011).

6 Robin Cohen, "The State in Africa," *Review of African Political Economy* (1976), 1.

7 Kelsall, "Going with the Grain," 636.

8 Crook and Booth, "Conclusion," 99, 98.

9 Chinua Achebe, *Things Fall Apart* (1958), 125.

10 Catherine Lynette Innes, *Chinua Achebe* (1990); Herbert Ekwe-Ekwe, *African Literature in Defence of History: An Essay On China Achebe* (2001).

11 Isidore Okpewho, *Chinua Achebe's Things Fall Apart: A Casebook* (2003), 14-15.

12 David Whittaker, *Chinua Achebe's Things Fall Apart: 1958-2008* (2011), xi.

13 Chinua Achebe, *The Education of a British-Protected Child: Essays* (2009), 85-88.

14 Iris Andreski, *Old Wives' Tales: Life-Stories from Ibibioland* (1970); *Chinua Achebe, Morning Yet on Creation Day: Essays* (1975), 5.

15 Bernth Lindfors, *Conversations with Chinua Achebe* (1997), 58.

16 Bill Moyers, *Chinua Achebe: A World of Ideas* (1988).

17 Holger Ehling, "No Condition Is Permanent: An Interview With Chinua Achebe," *Publishing Research Quarterly* (2003), 55.

18 Sun-sik Kim, *Colonial and Postcolonial Discourse in the Novels of Yom Sang-Sop, Chinua Achebe, and Salman Rushdie* (2004); Romanus Okey Muoneke, *Art, Rebellion and Redemption: A Reading of the Novels of Chinua Achebe* (1994); Chima Anyadike, "The Cracks in the Wall and the Colonial Incursion: Things Fall Apart and Arrow Of God as Novels of Resistance," in Remi Raji and Oyeniyi Okunoye (eds.), *The Postcolonial Lamp: Essays in Honour of Dan Izevbaye* (2008); Raphael Njoku, "Chinua Achebe and the Development of Igbo/African Studies," in Gloria Chuku (eds.), *The Igbo Intellectual Tradition* (2013).

19 Robert Wren, *Achebe's World: The Historical and Cultural Context of the Novels of Chinua Achebe* (1980), 49, 103.

20 Chinua Achebe, *A Man of the People* (1966).

21 Chinua Achebe, *Anthills of the Savannah* (1987).

22 Onyemaechi Udumukwu, "Achebe and the Negation of Independence," *Modern Fiction Studies* (1991).

23 Annie Gagiano, "Illuminating Africa: Commemorating and Reassessing the Work of Chinua Achebe (1930-2013)," *Development and Change* (2014), 1083.

24 Emeka Chiakwelu, "Achebe's Things Fall Apart: An Agent of Change," *All Africa News*, April 8, 2013.

25 Ifowodo, "The Novelist as Revolutionary."
26 Is'haq Modibbo Kawu, "Chinua Achebe's Undying Place in Our Memories," *All Africa News*, March 28, 2013.
27 TWAC 1, 51.
28 TWAC 14.
29 TWAC 20.
30 TWAC 20.
31 TWAC 27.
32 TWAC 39.
33 TWAC 40
34 Douglas Chambers, "There Was a Country: Achebe's Final Work," *Journal of Asian and African Studies* (2013), 753.
35 TWAC 43.
36 TWAC 44.
37 TWAC 36.
38 Jeffrey Herbst, *States and Power in Africa* (2000), 257.
39 TWAC 2.
40 TWAC 44.
41 Mpalive-Hangson Msiska, "Imagined Nations and Imaginary Nigeria: Chinua Achebe's Quest for a Country," *Journal of Genocide Research* (2014), 413.
42 TWAC 51.
43 Msiska, "Imagined nations and imaginary Nigeria," 413-14, italics added.
44 Achebe, *Morning Yet on Creation Day*, 123.
45 Larry Diamond, "Fiction as Political Thought: Anthills of the Savannah by Chinua Achebe," *African Affairs* (1989).
46 Blessing Diala, "Achebe the Traditionalist: A Critical Analysis of No Longer at Ease," in Ernest Emenyonu and Iniobong Uko (eds.), *Emerging Perspectives on Chinua Achebe* (2004).
47 Willene Taylor, "Igbo and European Cultures Clash," in Louise Hawker (ed.), *Colonialism in Chinua Achebe's Things Fall Apart* (2010), 93; Wren, *Achebe's World*; Eustace Palmer, *An Introduction to the African Novel* (1972), 51-52.
48 Jago Morrison, *The Fiction of Chinua Achebe* (2007), 21.
49 Neil Ten Kortenaar, "How the Center is Made to Hold in Things Fall Apart," in Isidore Okpewho (ed.), *Chinua Achebe's Things Fall Apart: A Casebook* (2003).
50 Donald Wehrs, *Pre-Colonial Africa in Colonial African Narratives: From Ethiopia Unbound to Things Fall Apart, 1911-1958* (2008), 165.
51 Ode Ogede, *Achebe and the Politics of Representation: Form Against Itself, From Colonial Conquest and Occupation to Post-Independence Disillusionment* (2001).
52 Mamuna Ghani, Mohammad Ayub Jajja, and Irshad Hussain, "Things Fall Apart: Chinua Achebe Writes Back to the Centre," *Journal of Educational Research* (Pakistan) (2013), 104.
53 Chinua Achebe, *No Longer at Ease* (1961).
54 Lindfors, *Conversations With Chinua Achebe*, 131.
55 Chinua Achebe, *Arrow of God* (1964).
56 Muoneke, *Art, Rebellion, and Redemption*, 44, 54.
57 Joe Ushie and Denja Abdullahi, *Themes Fall Apart but the Centre Holds: 50 Seasons of Chinua Achebe's Things Fall Apart (1958-2008)* (2009).
58 Lindfors, *Conversations with Chinua Achebe*, 66-67.
59 Lindfors, *Conversations with Chinua Achebe*, 37.

60 Lindfors, *Conversations with Chinua Achebe*, 72.
61 Lindfors, *Conversations with Chinua Achebe*, 89.
62 Lindfors, *Conversations with Chinua Achebe*, 23.
63 Lindfors, *Conversations with Chinua Achebe*, 66.
64 Chinua Achebe, *The Trouble With Nigeria* (1983), 62.
65 Ohaeto Ezenwa, *Chinua Achebe: A Biography* (1997), 88.
66 G. D. Killam, *The Novels of Chinua Achebe* (1969), 4.
67 G. D. Killam, *The Novels of Chinua Achebe*, 5.
68 Brian May, *Extravagant Postcolonialism: Modernism and Modernity in Anglophone Fiction, 1958-1988* (2014).
69 Jack Mapanje and Laura Fish, "Chinua Achebe in Conversation," in David Whittaker (ed.), *Chinua Achebe's Things Fall Apart: 1958-2008* (2011), 8.
70 Lindfors, *Conversations with Chinua Achebe*, 100.
71 Phanuel Akubueze Egejuru, *Chinua Achebe: Pure and Simple: An Oral Biography* (2002), 35.
72 Joyce Cary, *Mister Johnson* (1939).
73 Chinua Achebe, *Hopes and Impediments: Selected Essays, 1965-1987* (1988), 99.
74 "An Interview with Chinua Achebe," *The Manchester Guardian*, February 28, 1972.
75 Liam Kruger, "Literary Setting and the Postcolonial City in No Longer at Ease," *Research in African Literatures* (2021), 72.
76 Nasrin Pourhamrang, "'Things Fall Apart Now More Famous than Me, says Chinua Achebe," *Daily Trust*, September 8, 2012.
77 Egejuru, *Chinua Achebe*, 78.
78 Chinua Achebe, "The Education of a 'British-Protected' Child," *Cambridge Review* (1993).
79 Achebe, *Hopes and Impediments*, 34-5.
80 Achebe, "The Education of a 'British-Protected' Child," 19, 23.
81 Pourhamrang, "'Things Fall Apart."
82 Crook and Booth, "Conclusion," 101.
83 Berny Sèbe, "From Post-Colonialism to Cosmopolitan Nation-Building? British and French Imperial Heroes in Twenty-First-Century Africa," *Journal of Imperial and Commonwealth History* (2014), 955.

CHAPTER SIXTEEN

India's V.S. Naipaul and the Reckoning With Empire

In the same month in 2018 that the Nobel laureate in literature, Vidiadhar Surajprasad (V.S.) Naipaul, passed away, the Bengali writer Neel Mukherjee wrote in the *Wall Street Journal* that "Britain has never had—and is unlikely to ever have—a systematic reckoning with its unsavory history, choosing willed oblivion instead." The oblivion in question, Mukherjee explained, concerned the "hypocrisy, venality and inhumanity of British colonialism." In place of such a reckoning, the British had wallowed in "imperial nostalgia." This had, among other things, encouraged their regretful decision to leave the European Union.[1]

Mukherjee's lines, common enough in contemporary writing on empire, were also ridiculous. Debate in the West in general and among Europeans in particular about the colonial past has been, for at least a century, nothing if not a thorough reckoning. It is difficult to imagine a historical phenomenon that has been subjected to more vigorous empirical and ethical disputation, beginning at least with the 1902 book by the British economist John Hobson entitled *Imperialism: A Study*.

Coming the same month as Naipaul's death, however, added irony to Mukherjee's post-colonial cliché. Unlike Mukherjee and legions of other critics of colonialism, Naipaul was not interested in lecturing white Europeans about their need to "reckon with empire." He was, on the other hand, deeply concerned with the lack of reckoning by the formerly colonized peoples such as Mukherjee. One might say that Naipaul's entire body of work was an attempt to encourage such a reckoning. Born of Indian immigrants in Trinidad and then settled in Britain for most of his career, Naipaul was that rare bird who reckoned with the inevitability, attractions, and benefits of colonialism, while calling out the hypocrisy of anti-colonial intellectuals who both loved and scorned empire. Naipaul's legacy is a reminder of the lack of imperial reckoning by those who consider themselves empire's victims, wallowing in anti-imperial comforts.

V.S. Naipaul in Grenada, 1983. Credit: Abbas/Magnum Photos.

Naipaul argued that European colonialism was unique in the history of empires because it was based on a "universal civilization" whose ideals applied to everyone. No other imperial expansion had been based on the premise of the fundamental equality of men, and none had undertaken anything like the civilizing mission that assumed all men had the same potential. The "White Man's Burden" was a real one and it had been undertaken with honor and success. One might add a Churchillian coda that European empire was the most hypocritical, venal, and inhumane endeavor in the history of global expansions, except for every other example.

In his 1990 talk, "Our Universal Civilization," Naipaul laid claim to being part of that liberal civilization, which he found most profoundly expressed in the American promise of life, liberty, and the pursuit of happiness. "It is an elastic idea; it fits all men. It implies a certain kind of society, a certain kind of awakened spirit...So much is contained in it: the idea of the individual, responsibility, choice, the life of the intellect, the idea of vocation and perfectibility and achievement. It is an immense human idea."[2]

The ancestral India he returned to frequently, by contrast, was based on an explicit rejection of the individual with an awakened spirit. The Hindu caste system assumed human inequality and fixity. It found its worst expression in the outdoor defecation of upper caste Hindus and the caste-specific job of cleaning up all their shit. The most famous "colonial" in India to see this, Naipaul wrote in his first book on India of 1964, *An Area of Darkness: A Discovery of India*, was Gandhi. This thoroughly Europeanized man returned from Britain and South Africa and, "judging India by the standards of Europe...saw so clearly because he was in part a colonial." Without colonialism, Gandhi would have become just another upper caste snob. His profound insights about India's backwardness "needed the straight simple vision of the West." Over time, however, Indian culture destroyed him. Gandhi's transformative "colonial vision" was slowly smothered by Brahminic smugness, "absorbed into the formless spirituality and decayed pragmatism of India." The colonial lawyer became an anti-colonial holy man, and then he was useless. "Nothing remains of Gandhi in India but this."[3] A bust in Bombay. A bumper sticker in Berkeley. Willed oblivion on a national scale.

What bothered Naipaul about anti-colonial writers, especially those from India and the Islamic world, was that, like Gandhi, they felt the allure of that same universal civilization but pretended otherwise. "The attraction existed; it was more than a need for education and skills. But the attraction wasn't admitted; and in that attraction, too humiliating for an old and proud people to admit, there lay disturbance—expressed in dandyism, mimicry, boasting, and rejection," he wrote in *Among the Believers: An Islamic Journey* of 1981. He first broached the idea of a universal civilization led by the West in that book. An Indonesian intellectual told him that the country's great Buddhist and Hindu art was "mainly something for the international community to look after." The Indonesian Muslims had looted and smashed the art until stopped by the West. Now the Western cultural foundations issued invitations and published books to document those treasures. "The international community, the universal civilization, providers of tape recorders and psychological games and higher degrees in electrical engineering; and now also guardians of Indonesian art and civilization," he wrote. The same was true in India, whose Buddhist and Hindu art had been saved by the universal civilization of the West.

Anti-colonial intellectuals were always railing against the West while also demanding visas, fellowships, green cards, remittances, and invitations. They cried "racism" when denied or turned back, all the while insisting that their own countries remain stagnant. They "appealed to the ideals of the alien civilization whose virtues they denied at home." In Iran, this emotional schizophrenia was most pronounced: "The West, or the universal civilization it leads, is emotionally rejected. It undermines; it threatens. But at the same time, it is needed for its machines, goods, medicines, warplanes, and remittances from the emigrants, the hospitals that might have a cure for calcium deficiency, the universities that will provide master's degrees in mass media. All the rejection of the West is contained within the assumption that there will always exist out there a living, creative civilization, oddly neutral, open to all to appeal to." This simultaneous embrace and rejection of Western civilization was worse than hypocrisy. It meant "ceasing to strive intellectually."[4]

Naipaul could have cited Neel Mukherjee's journey from Catholic boy's school in Calcutta, to Oxford and Cambridge, and finally to a writer's career in London (including book reviews in the daily diary of American capitalism, the *Wall Street Journal*) as emblematic of this schizophrenia. Naipaul wrote in his second book on his ancestral homeland, *India: A Wounded Civilization* of 1977, that Indian elites were always dreaming of some great leap backwards to a unified volk under "a vision of Ramraj" even as they jostled to send their children to Eton and Cambridge. He found this failed reckoning with empire everywhere in the former colonial areas. Mukherjee's declamations about the "inhumanity" of British empire and related musings on the evils of capitalism would have irked Naipaul, a dishonest separation from the universal civilization that one so intently accesses. "The whole capitalist order has a lot to answer for," Mukherjee told *Publishers' Weekly* in 2017.[5] His new book of 2024 with the portentously moralizing title, *Choice*, promised to "ask the reader to consider: should we be driven by moral values or market values?" Mukherjee's lack of reckoning is stark: Capitalism for me, socialism for the little people. Market values for me, moral values for the rest of you. Imperial delights for me, imperial reckoning for others.

Naipaul also would have recognized the lack of imperial reckoning in his much younger brother Shiva, who drank himself to death at age 40. Shiva had his brother's talent for writing, but none of his intellectual greatness. Travelling Africa, Shiva was constantly drawn to the European world—its hotels, merchants, newspapers, culture, civilization. But unlike his brother, he could not reckon with it maturely without losing his cool. He described the history of colonial Kenya as a "dismal chronicle of settler civilization" in his 1978 travelogue *North of South*. It was this dismal chronicle, he implied, not the madness of Kenya's post-colonial leadership, that explained the independent country's problems. "Who banished the African from the Highlands and confined him in overcrowded reservations? Who denied him—and the Asian—an effective political voice? Whose despoliations were the direct cause of Mau Mau?" In socialist Tanzania, Shiva again cannot take his eyes off the Europeans, one of whom muses that the country enjoyed "too little colonialism."[6] The enraged Shiva rushes to the bar to douse his fires. Eight years later he is dead, consumed by a lack of reckoning.

Naipaul's 1987 book on his own personal reckoning with empire, *The Enigma of Arrival*, was dedicated to his dead brother. It was an ode to the island nation of Britain, "with the curiosity it had awakened in me for the larger world, the idea of civilization, and the idea of antiquity." His landlord in rural Wiltshire, with all his "empire and privilege," stirred only love in Naipaul: "It was easy for me, as his tenant now, to feel goodwill in my heart for him."[7] This was a reckoning with empire at both the personal and philosophical levels. It made Naipaul a literary unicorn: a brown man recognizing the humanity of the colonial endeavor despite inevitable shortcomings while a roof's line of brown and black authors like Mukherjee squawked about their imagined traumas.

There was never any doubt for Naipaul that European empire was a positive and regenerative force, despite the contortions of the Nobel committee to describe him as a critic of colonialism. The contrasting fates of Iran and India provided the perfect diptych. "Iran never became a formal colony. Its fate was in some ways worse. When Europe, once so far away, made its presence felt, Iran dropped off the map," he argued in *Beyond Belief* of 1998, his return to the Islamic world. By contrast, "India, almost as soon as it became a British colony, began to be regenerated, began to receive the New Learning of Europe, to get the institutions that went with that learning." In Argentina, "things worked under the British" even only its informal rule, a local tells him. Then the predictable anti-imperialism and the even more predictable national collapse. Now the country offered its citizens only "hate as hope," Naipaul observed.[8]

When Naipaul lavished praise on the colonial architecture of the Raj in his third book on India, *India: A Million Mutinies Now,* of 1990, he was less interested in engineering than in soulfulness. The "porticoes and verandahs, thick walls, high ceilings, and sometimes additional upper windows or wall-openings" encompassed a range of styles, together constituting "the finest secular architecture in the sub-continent." The most humble public works building was "a complete architectural thought." Post-colonial Indian architecture, by contrast, was "more disdainful of the people it serves than British Indian architecture." The British had forged a beautiful Indian vernacular, while Indians had "built like people without a tradition."[9]

Elsewhere, on an "Islamic excursion," he visited a teacher in Pakistan who lived in a stupor, shocked by the rapid deterioration of life after colonialism but unwilling to hold the country's rulers to colonial standards. His father and grandfather had run a prosperous business in Simla catering to the British army. The petty slights of colonial rule were the only injustice they knew. Then they moved to newly-independent Pakistan and things fell apart; the economy a wreck, the neighborhood beset by crime, and the kerosene streetlights of colonial days in disrepair. "My father used to say that the British were better than these governments," he tells Naipaul. "It was not injustice in this form."[10]

Even as colonial institutions were ravaged, poverty set in, and people emigrated to the West, the anti-colonial movements in the Third World remained in power. Naipaul understood from his own upbringing in Trinidad that the nationalists survived by proclaiming racial triumph over the West. In his 1967 novel, *The Mimic Men*, a local Indian politician from a fictional Caribbean island, Ralph Singh, struggles to make sense of the anti-colonial revolution that forced him into exile. Having taken for granted the order and stability of colonial days, people like Singh came to realize that "there was no true internal source of power" without the common interests of the colonial era. The revolution contained "no force of nationalism...only the negative frenzy of a deep violation." The "success" of the anti-colonial movement was a fraud. The British had long intended to depart, and the nationalists only pretended to have a creative plan. "No one had called our bluff."

The postcolonial politician became "a prisoner of his role" as a "spokesmen for bitterness." He denounced everything the country needed: foreign investment, the rule of law, plural politics. At a public rally, Singh is convicted *in absentia* of going soft on the nationalization of sugar estates and of secretly scheming to keep the British in charge of the police. "I had joined the movement, had helped to create it, only to destroy what it stood for," the speakers charged. Singh called the revolutionary slogans "an escape from thought." No one could honestly reckon with the hard realities of running a country on sound colonial principles. "We zestfully abolished an order. We never defined our purpose." The result of this failed reckoning was a double whammy: social collapse and continued re-election of the politicians causing it. "Such was the controlled chaos we had, with such enthusiasm, brought upon ourselves." The only "public goods" available were the regular sightings of expatriate staff under the command of native leaders: "It was what these ministers offered their followers: the spectacle of the black man served by the white; the revolution we claimed to have created."[11] Hate as hope.

In Naipaul's reckoning with empire also lay a sociological insight into the inescapable reciprocity of all social interactions. Colonialism was first and foremost a voluntary and mutually-enriching encounter between the West and the Rest. To carve out instances of coercive and exploitative Western behavior was to miss the whole canvas. One might as well gather together episodes where native chiefs in Africa held colonial officials hostage in order to extract concessions and then write a history of colonialism as one of the coercion and exploitation of the West by the Rest. Progressives bent on zero-sum victim-victimizer approaches could never grasp this. But Naipaul always saw the whole canvas, as if preternaturally disinclined to fall into the intellectually lazy comforts of anti-colonialism.

In the 2001 novel, *Half a Life*, about the peripatetic life of a young man in India, Willie Chandran, the protagonist's father, complains about the Western visitors during the time of independence who had swarmed to his ashram seeking Hindu spirituality. "I gave them the run of the ashram. I introduced them to everybody," Willie's father protests after receiving a letter from one who has politely declined to help Willie escape to the West. His "house-proud" lower caste wife, whom he married in order to spite caste bigotry, plays fool and speaks the truth. Those Western visitors were part of the colonial encounter, which had given Willie's father proficiency in English and a cushy job on the local maharaja's staff. "They did a lot for you too. They gave you your business. You can't deny it."[12]

But they did deny it, over and over again, until merely to suggest that the colonial encounter was anything less than genocide was an affront. Naipaul understood the shame of being colonized. Like Willie's father, he could feel spurned and despised by the superior civilization that fed upon the carcass of Mughal rule in India. But he did not deny the benefits. "The India that will come into being at the end of the period of British rule will be better educated, more creative and full of possibility than the India of a century before;...it will have a larger idea of human association, and...out of this larger idea, and out of the encompassing humiliation of British rule, there will come to India the ideas of country and pride and historical self-analysis," he writes.[13] The "million mutinies" he espied emerging from the dead hand of socialism in India were positive, not negative, part of the colonial awakening that had begun with "The Mutiny" of 1857 that ushered in formal British rule.

Africa was a trickier proposition for Naipaul's imperial reckoning because it had so thoroughly dismantled the colonial inheritance and returned to darkness. One could not reckon with what no longer existed. In his literary masterwork, *A Bend in the River,* of 1979 and its journalistic antecedents, Naipaul described an African political elite suckled on the idea that the colonial master was to blame for the return to darkness, an infantilization of the African that generations of anti-colonial scholars abetted.

The presidential domain in the Congo under Joseph Mobutu, he writes in 1975, reflects the aimlessness of contemporary Africa. It is a fantasy that reflects only the capture of power from the Belgians in 1960, nothing more. Having "no creative plan" to build upon, the African response is to tear it all down. The nationalization of the economy is "petty and bogus," "a form of pillage" that is "short-sighted, self-wounding, and nihilistic." While anti-colonialists elsewhere have the good sense to retain bits of the colonial order, the African response is blind opposition. Independence for the Congo meant only one thing: "a dismantling of what remains of the Belgian created state."[14]

It took the creative space of fiction to turn Naipaul's harsh observations into a nightmarish vision. The narrator of *A Bend in the River* is an Indian shopkeeper, who, like Naipaul, has a synoptic viewpoint because he is neither European nor African. He is friends with the young white wife of Raymond, a white American professor who edits the African president's speeches and cheerleads his every move. They loll about in the presidential Domain, hosting visiting lecturers and extolling the postcolonial African future. "The Domain was a hoax," says the narrator. "But at the same it was real because it was full of serious men (and a few women)."

In their hearts, the Africans dream of "waking up one day as white men." But the president douses any admiration for the West, telling his people in daily radio broadcasts "to be African" by returning to traditional diets and medicine. The more they are commanded to obey the Big Man, the more they disobey. So, "men had lost or rejected the idea of an overseeing authority." Africa was "going back to its old ways with modern tools." What remained after the destruction of the colonial era would be authentic in the worst sense, a primitive and violent society led by warlords. "These men would have dealt in slaves, if there was a still a market."[15]

Naipaul often caviled about the Western progressives like Raymond who served as adjuncts to the psychosis of anti-imperialism. Whatever their claims to be fighting for justice, their motivations were ultimately self-absorbed, seeking spiritual and moral renewal by washing in the holy waters of colonial guilt. "There was a section of the expatriates who saw themselves as serving this cause," he writes in his 1994 biographical novel, *A Way in the World,* of the white presidential groupies in a fictional West African country. "Some of them even liked the idea of the shortages and austerity outside, and the disciplining of the people…it was easier for villages to be collectivized and returned to the socialism of traditional African ways." Life in the president's entourage "provided something of what ashram life or the life of the religious commune provided for others elsewhere: liberation, new rigidities, a new self-awareness and self-cherishing."

True, the fictional country was in a tailspin, but merely to suggest as much was to demonstrate an unsophisticated and racist judgement of the New Era: "There isn't only one way of measuring success, and this new man of Africa will have the satisfaction of having ruled according to his own high principles," they tell themselves. They fawn over monsters like "Lebrun," the black revolutionary from the Caribbean who is hailed as a prophet of decolonization. Lebrun flits from one revolutionary disaster to the next, "never having to live with the consequences of his action, always being free to move on." When he escapes to a coddled retirement in England, the glow of his black wisdom only grows. White progressives from the mainstream media constantly write of him as a prophet: "In the mess of Africa and the Caribbean, he was oddly pure… No one thought of calling him to account."[16]

Naipaul saw in Africa the weakening hold of the remnants of the colonial state over rival power centers. Moreover, that weakening was abetted by Western academics indulging their fetish for imperial reckoning, as in *Imperial Reckoning*, the 2005 bestseller by Harvard Professor Caroline Elkins that celebrated a genocidal native movement in colonial Kenya that the British suppressed with overwhelming native support. These Western champions of black fanatics and terrorists excused every atrocity as an act of liberation from colonial forces. They fell silent when the terrors of the Big Man or the nationalist one-party state were mentioned. Even positive reckonings with empire, such as Nigel Biggar's *Colonialism: A Moral Reckoning* of 2022, kept the focus on the colonizers, not the colonized. No one except Naipaul saw the need for a reckoning by the colonized themselves.

The colonial subjects who had migrated to the West and taken up prominent positions without any sense of self-consciousness had been particularly irritating to Naipaul. There was, for instance, the inquisitorial University of Chicago Professor of Islamic Studies, Fazlur Rahman, "sleeping safe and sound every night, protected by laws, and far away from the mischief he was wishing on his countrymen at home," Naipaul wrote.[17] Rahman fled Pakistan in 1969 after his state-sponsored project to impose an "an Islamic vision" on the legal and administrative state ran into opposition. Naipaul saw the origins of 9/11 in the Islamic world's rebellion against modernity. Rahman died peacefully in Chicago in 1988.

The furiously anti-colonial Cambridge academic Priyamvada Gopal declared in 2018 that she would no longer teach her students because the working-class college porters did not address her by her formal title (which they do not do for anyone). This highlighted Naipaul's point in *Beyond Belief*, where he described the South Asian children sent to Oxford and Cambridge as the worst sort of feudal lords. "They treated their workers and peasants like serfs. The peasants would touch the feet of the landlord in submission and greeting; it was more submission than greeting; and the landlord would not ask the peasant to rise." His interlocutor Shahbaz, "fresh from England, wanted to weep."[18] Naipaul, by contrast, was embarrassed when people in his rural community in Wiltshire treated him with deference or respect.

If universal civilization was at risk, then the best solution to decolonization in most places would have been integration, not independence. Naipaul is interviewing the exiled French scholar and former governor of Algeria, Jacques Soustelle, in 1967, but the words could be his own: "True decolonization would have come from incorporation, with equal rights and an equal advance for all. But this was rejected. It was too difficult." Instead, "France yielded to the 'idol' decolonization and the pressures of mercantile capitalism and converted the low cultures of black Africa into a *poussière* [dust] of petty dictatorships." The former colonial subjects will use up every last machine and institution until they have been destroyed. "After that, they will let the goats graze where wheat formerly grew." De Gaulle, and probably much of France, rejected the grand vision of an integrated Algeria and with it a Greater France. "The million colons [French settlers, also known as *pieds-noirs*] have left; one Algerian dictatorship has been replaced by another. Arab Algeria sinks; an idea of France has been destroyed."[19]

Naipaul was mercilessly attacked by the literary establishment for what remains the most dramatic and honest moment in his personal reckoning with the West. He is having lunch on a hotel terrace at Luxor in Egypt in 1970. Italian tourists are throwing scraps of food to the beggar children in the sand below, "thin little sand-smoothed legs frantic below swinging *jibbahs*." A hotel guard beats the children away with his camel whip but the food keeps falling and the tourists love the spectacle. So the children keep grubbing while the whip keeps lashing. Suddenly, the normally supine Naipaul rushes toward the guard. "I was shouting. I took the whip away, and threw it on the sand. He was astonished, relieved. I said, 'I will report this to Cairo.' That's it. Everyone returns to their places. The moment is over. I felt exposed, futile, and wanted only to be back at my table."[20] No righteous denunciations of the petty cruelty of the Italians. No pompous declarations about the inequalities of the global system. No jargon-ridden explanations of the hapless Egyptian guard. No wounded sense of self-esteem, pretending solidarity with the children. Naipaul was too smart for all that. He had seen too much to believe those were solutions. He had reckoned with empire.

While Naipaul spent months on the road, his rival diagnostician of the Third World, the Arab intellectual raised mainly in Egypt, Edward Said, spent most of his time in Western academic seminars. The West gave Said a professorship at a leading university and showered him with adulation for every bitter attack on the West and its degenerate society. In between his holy utterances, Said indulged his passion for Western classical music at Carnegie Hall. Naipaul, by contrast, had to earn his keep in the market economy, which freed him from becoming an institutionalized totem, or asking anyone to touch his feet.

Naipaul hoped that the end of the Cold War would cause a reckoning. Certainly, there was the beginning of what his fellow Caribbean exile, the black economist W Arthur Lewis, had called a "creative" reckoning with empire as opposed to the "protest" of the past.[21] But home truths about any former colony could not compete with the blandishments of holy men. "The British pillaged the country thoroughly; during their rule, manufactures and crafts declined. This has to be accepted," Naipaul described the mandatory doxology of India in *An Area of Darkness* (1964).[22] All the variations of this so-called "drain theory" have been thoroughly debunked by economic historians such as Tirthankar Roy of the London School of Economics.[23] But drain theory, like Bengal Famine theory and, divide and rule theory, still has to be accepted. That Shashi Tharoor, a struggling politician for a party on the skids, should become a hero to the cause with a 2016 book on colonial India carrying the Naipaulian title *An Era of Darkness* shows the enduring power of the protest identity. "For the uneducated masses, quick to respond to racial stirrings and childishly pleased with destructive gestures, the protest leader will always be a hero," Naipaul bemoaned in his return to the Caribbean book, *The Middle Passage* of 1962.[24]

For that book, Naipaul visited Martinique. "That France has here succeeded, as she has perhaps nowhere else, in her 'mission civilisatrice', there can be no doubt," he wrote plainly. Locals agreed. They have opted to remain a colony of France ever since. Yet Western undergraduates are still assigned to read the bilious anti-colonial *Discours sur le colonialisme* (1950) of the Martinique poet Aimé Césaire, and tourists arrive today at the Aimé Césaire International Airport. The creative identity for French passports. The protest identity for public monuments.

And so the mimicry of anti-imperial posturing goes on. The Nigerian social activist Kelechi Okafor, who, like Mukherjee, denounces the empire from the comfort of London, made headlines in 2018 when it was revealed that she had a white boyfriend. Her excuse: he's Polish. "There is a huge difference between going out with a white Polish man and a white English man," she explained in an essay for the BBC. The former had been "governed by outsiders." The latter had engaged in "the transatlantic slave trade or colonization" and "didn't know their true history."[25]

For the likes of Okafor or Mukherjee, it is the white English man, not the black Nigerian woman with the Polish boyfriend or the Bengali Cambridge graduate with a lectureship at Harvard, who needs an imperial reckoning. As with the Iranian intellectuals fishing for invitations to the U.S., Okafor operates on a presumption that "there will always exist out there a living, creative civilization, oddly neutral, open to all to appeal to." She simultaneously uses it, expects it, and turns on it to suit her purposes. All those white English men are, by ascription, descendants of slave-traders and colonial brutes. The "true history" she urges upon her white British readers does not reference Yoruba, Igbo and Fulani slave-trading or warfare. The black woman caught in the web of white guilt and pretending to be a voice of conscience. The Bengali novelist and the Nigerian dancer living in London and telling their English readers that they need a reckoning. With Naipaul gone, there is no one to tell them they need their own imperial reckoning.

The Tamil writer Meena Kandasamy was described in *Time* magazine as "an Indian poet, novelist and translator from Chennai" who was "currently based" in London. Her haughty attack on Naipaul in the magazine at his death declared that he "became an autonomous echo to the oppressive institutions of our time, internalizing the xenophobia and dehumanization that lay at the heart of colonialism." He was, worse, "a brilliant and tormented reactionary artist in the service of unspeakable horror."[26] Kandasamy, all 34 years of her at the time of the essay, had certainly learnt a mouthful of phrases in her graduate seminars. Her Conradian echo was quaint. There is nothing so pleasing as a clutchful of aspersions hurled at Naipaul by an anti-colonial writer "currently living in London."

Similarly, the white American scholar Rob Nixon famously accused Naipaul of "Conradian atavism."[27] Naipaul had embraced the colonial viewpoint rather than the latest jargon and ideologies from the Black Studies department, Nixon charged. A Japanese scholar disagreed, noting that Naipaul simply took the Conradian insights and ran with them, making himself a modern Conrad.[28] Nixon's view remains dominant. Naipaul is scorned and treated as an embarrassing misfire.

His final collection of essays, *The Writer and the World* (2002), was edited by Pankaj Mishra, a man celebrated as "the next Said." It was surely an irony that Naipaul would be edited by a man who embodied the failed reckoning with empire. Mishra is unhinged in his attacks on the West. He claimed in *The New Yorker* that Winston Churchill caused 9/11.[29] He is yet another South Asian writer "currently living in London" with a white lover, railing at the Raj and urging an imperial reckoning on whites.

Anti-colonial critics have never had—and on present trajectory are unlikely to ever have—a systematic reckoning with their unsavory history, choosing willed oblivion instead. Naipaul failed to bend that river. We continue to live with the consequences.

Endnotes:

1 Neel Mukherjee, "The Last Englishmen: Review: India, Everest and Empire," *Wall Street Journal*, August 23, 2018.
2 V.S. Naipaul, *The Writer and the World: Essays* (2002), 517.
3 V.S. Naipaul, *An Area of Darkness: A Discovery of India* (1964), Vintage 2002 edition, 69, 75, 84, 83.
4 V.S. Naipaul, *Among the Believers: An Islamic Journey* (1981), Vintage 1982 edition, 13, 375, 209, 101, 168.
5 Liz Thomson, "Neel Mukherjee on Displacement and Desire," *Publishers' Weekly*, November 10, 2017.
6 Shiva Naipaul, *North of South: An African Journey* (1978), 115, 302.
7 V.S. Naipaul, *The Enigma of Arrival* (1987) Vintage 1988 edition, 153, 192.
8 V.S. Naipaul, "Argentina and the Ghost of Eva Péron," (1991, 1977) in *The Writer and the World: Essays* (2002), Picador 2003 edition, 430, 398.
9 V.S. Naipaul, *India: A Million Mutinies Now* (1990), Vintage 2011 edition, 280-281.
10 V.S. Naipaul, *Beyond Belief: Islamic Excursions Amond the Converted Peoples* (1998), Vintage 1999 edition, 234, 345.
11 V.S. Naipaul, *The Mimic Men* (1967), Penguin 1969 edition, 205, 200, 203, 205, 239, 198, 198, 206, 210.
12 V.S. Naipaul, *Half a Life* (2001), Vintage 2002 edition, 33, 48.
13 V.S. Naipaul, *India: A Million Mutinies Now* (1990), Vintage 2011 edition, 395.
14 V.S. Naipaul, "A New King for the Congo: Mobutu and the Nihlism of Africa" (1975) in *The Writer and the World: Essays* (2002), Picador 2003 edition, 225.
15 V.S. Naipaul, *A Bend in the River* (1979), Picador 2002 edition, 144, 241, 246, 236, 106.
16 V.S. Naipaul, *A Way in the World* (1994), Vintage 1995 edition, 356-357, 160.
17 V.S. Naipaul, *Beyond Belief: Islamic Excursions Amond the Converted Peoples* (1998), Vintage 1999 edition, 46.
18 Ibid., 276.
19 V.S. Naipaul, "Jacques Soustelle and the Decline of the West" (1967) in *The Writer and the World: Essays* (2002), Picador 2003 edition, 308, 312.
20 V.S. Naipaul, "The Circus at Luxor," in *In A Free State* (1971), Vintage 1984 edition, 242, 243.
21 Bruce Gilley, "The Challenge of the Creative Third World," *Third World Quarterly* (2015).
22 V.S. Naipaul, *An Area of Darkness: A Discovery of India* (1964), Vintage 2002 edition, 223.
23 Tirthankar Roy, *An Economic History of India, 1707-1857* (2021); *The Economic History of India, 1857-2010* (2020); *How British Rule Changed India's Economy: The Paradox of the Raj* (2019); *A Business History of India: Enterprise and the Emergence of Capitalism from 1700* (2018).
24 V.S. Naipaul, *The Middle Passage* (1962), Penguin 1978 edition, 254.
25 Kelechi Okafor, "I'm Not Hiding My White Boyfriend," *BBC News*, August 15, 2018.
26 Meena Kandasamy, "V.S. Naipaul Leaves Behind a Formidable Body of Work—and a Troubling Legacy," *Time Magazine*, August 15, 2018.
27 Rob Nixon, *London Calling: V.S. Naipaul, Postcolonial Mandarin* (1992).
28 Asako Nakai, "Journey to the Heart of Darkness: Naipaul's 'Conradian Atavism'

Reconsidered," *The Conradian* (1998), 6.
29 Pankaj Mishra, "Exit Wounds: The Legacy of Indian Partition," *The New Yorker*, August 6, 2007.

CONCLUSION

Elegy for a Colonial Perspective

I ARRIVED IN Hong Kong in 1992 on the same day as the last governor of the British colony, Chris Patten. I arrived from China after a year of teaching English. Patten arrived from London after an unexpected snub by his parliamentary constituents in a general election. I was greeted by the Hong Kong editor of a local business magazine who was taking a chance on me. Patten was greeted by the Gurkha Rifles and an editorial in the local Beijing-run newspaper warning him against acting like Lord Soames, the last governor of Southern Rhodesia who had overseen that colony's hurried transition to democracy.[1]

Hong Kong was the third place in my life living under British sovereignty. I was born and raised in Canada, which was subject to symbolic British colonial authority until the Canada Act of 1982. I studied at Oxford from 1989 to 1991 under a Foreign and Commonwealth Office scholarship. It was Hong Kong, however, where I experienced authentic colonial rule while working as a journalist. The first five years of my 10-year stay there were the obsequies of the British empire. It left a deep impression.

British Hong Kong was like a sleek new airport in the tropics. The moment you stepped inside, all the chaos and fear of the developing world disappeared. The culture was lush and passionate, but the administration was cool and steady. People took the prosperity and freedoms of Hong Kong for granted, much as those in the West take for granted the same prosperity and freedom of their lives. It was the same dilemma identified by Nobel laureate V.S. Naipaul (see Chapter 16): not wanting to admit that the whole thing is kept together by a distinctive civilization that one so freely disparages while enjoying its fruits.

The British encouraged the illusion. They frequently insisted that Hong Kong was a testament to the vigor of the local Chinese population, most of whom had self-colonized by fleeing from China. A ridiculous claim, but one that few Hong Kongers cared to correct. Only in the very last months of empire did a small movement erupt demanding a referendum on continued British rule.

Too late by far. The Qing dynasty had given the British a 99-year lease on a vast area to the north of the colony in 1898. These "New Territories" accounted for 92% of the area of the expanded colony and a growing share of its surging population and economy over subsequent decades. Communist China recognized neither the lease on the new areas nor the earlier treaties on the original areas. It always claimed the right to retake Hong Kong at its convenience. 1997 was merely a suitable moment. Giving back only the leased areas would have been an economic and diplomatic disaster. It also would have alienated Britain's allies. As Patten later wrote: "The price that Britain would pay in terms of international opprobrium would have been too high."

Beijing would have been furious. Just as India had invaded the Portuguese colony of Goa in 1961 to rescue it from "colonial oppression" (most of the Indian residents fled to Portugal), China would have found a pretext to invade Hong Kong if London had not handed it over in one piece. The British extracted promises that Beijing would appoint a local governor and protect the capitalist economy and legal system. But from the initial agreement in 1984 until what became known as "the Great Chinese Take-Away," there was no doubt that colonialism in Hong Kong would end in 1997. As Patten quipped about the local defenses: "The only bunkers were on the golf courses."[2]

As with Goa, any attempt to fit Hong Kong into a "post-colonial" narrative fails on many levels. Hong Kong was a creation of the British. It was initially intended to give the British a way to supply the opium dens of southern China that were provisioned mainly by domestic growers in the southwest interior. The Qing dynasty wanted to ban imports not because of any moral revulsion but because of their impact on the balance of payments.[3] The British insisted on access for a mixture of economic, diplomatic, and ideological reasons.

The colony's origin as an opium trading center does not devalue its achievement. Aside from the limited incremental impact of British imports on the opium addiction problem in China, those imports may have saved the British empire as a whole.[4] If so, then this might make us think twice about the usual "moral embarrassment" and "shame" about the origins of the colony. If a little opium was what it took to bring about the rise of one of the greatest forces for human betterment in world history, then it was well worth the price. Moreover, Britain's involvement in the trade, as with its earlier involvement in the slave trade, is what eventually led to its global abolition when liberal anti-opium crusaders turned against the pernicious trade just as the Qing dynasty had given up.[5]

Hong Kong was not "colonized" since there were few people there when the British arrived except for some itinerant fishermen. The colonizers were the millions of Chinese who fled there escaping "liberation" in China. It then became a critical window that allowed China to escape from the horrors of Maoism and bring a degree of economic and social well-being to its people. As Patten obliquely summarized that history to the tone-deaf comrades from China in his farewell speech in 1997, while the colony's founding "began with events that..none of us here would wish or seek to condone," the real colonizing was done by Chinese "because of events in our own century which would today have few defenders." Given its positive effects in transforming the lives of China's billions, Hong Kong alone is sufficient to make the case for colonialism.

In the midst of the controversy over my article "The Case for Colonialism," an insightful Singaporean journalist pointed out that my views were likely shaped by my time in Hong Kong.[6] She was right. To have supported the Hong Kong people in their struggle to maintain the rule of law and a degree of freedom after 1997, she wrote, was to prefer a liberal British legacy to an illiberal Chinese one. But post-colonial theory in the West had muddled the minds of Western progressives. They got tied up in intellectual knots because supporting progressive values in Hong Kong, as in so many other former colonies that descended into chaos, war, and starvation, meant supporting the colonial legacy, which they could not abide. The result was a flaccid retreat into pansy intellectualism and irresponsibility. "Colonial modernity has produced individualistic colonial subjects who have subjectively internalized the rationalistic market norms and lack a sense of political community," assayed one Hong Kong scholar in a typical research paper. She never paused to consider whether the reason so many people fled to Hong Kong was precisely its promise of market freedoms and an escape from the loving "political community" of Maoist China.[7]

The expatriate presence had thinned considerably when I arrived. Patten appointed the first local Chinese chief secretary (head of the civil service) in 1993 and the first local financial secretary in 1995. The British presence retreated to shadowy figures from the Foreign Office who insisted that they worked for the local Gilbert & Sullivan Society.

Hong Kongers salute governor Chris Patten as he departs his official residence on the day of the handover of the colony to China in 1997. The Chinese sign reads: "Long Live Patten." Credit: Author's collection.

Patten was constantly at loggerheads with the Old China Hands in London who wanted to go gentle into that good night. Early in his term, he was honored with a scathing attack from the *People's Daily* which called him a "worthy progeny of colonialism" bent on preserving the British empire. The Hong Kong people, the *People's Daily* continued, yearned to be "not slaves of a colony but Chinese people of China."[8] Beijing did everything to live-up to the billing of The Great Chinese Take-Away. Patten's emissary was a plain-spoken Australian, Kerry McGlynn, always available on speed-dial for journalists late into the night for a sharp riposte to such calumnies: "A government spokesman said..."

Patten was a conservative and a pragmatist. Without wading into the debates on colonialism, he was confident that no other country had wound up its colonial holdings "so peacefully with such benign intent." His summary of Britain's final colonial days in previous places from Palestine to Malaya provided his roadmap to 1997: "Overall…it is not a bad story: men and women infused with the values of nineteenth century liberalism, trying to do their best, installing democracy, training civil servants, policemen, and soldiers, establishing independent courts, entrenching civil liberties."[9]

But this was not a typical decolonization. The founder-sage of independent Singapore, Lee Kuan Yew, reminded Patten privately during a stopover there on his way to Hong Kong in 1992 that his job was not to prepare Hong Kong for independence but for handover to a communist tyranny. That meant he needed to act less like a retiring colonial governor and more like an energetic politician, setting out an agenda and sticking to it no matter the cavils from Beijing. Patten noted in his diary his surprise at both the lecture and the morale-boosting accommodations during the Singapore transit, "as though we were being prepared for some great sporting competition."[10]

In 1995, I began writing for the *Far Eastern Economic Review*. It was a weekly magazine of business and politics in Asia founded in 1946 by Western traders who had fled the communist revolution in Shanghai. As a colonial magazine, the *Review* had all the trappings. Its correspondents included the man who first reported Mao's death, the man who found Pol Pot in the jungle, and the woman who was on board the airplane carrying exiled Filipino opposition leader Benigno Aquino home when he was gunned down on arrival at the Manila airport. It also had an unapologetic colonial swagger, including a humor section that made fun of mangled English in the region and an annual "Guide to Nightlife in Asia" that included tips on the best dance hall girls in Hong Kong and how to avoid taking home a beauty in Thailand who turned out to be a man. The legendary editor Derek Davies owned a Chinese junk boat that was affectionately known as "The Gin Palace." Woe betide any unsuspecting intern who thought they could join the Saturday afternoon passage from Kowloon and disembark sober.

As a *Review* correspondent, I led our coverage of the Great Chinese Take-Away. Not heeding the advice of the Beijing press when he arrived, Patten had followed Lord Soames by hastily democratizing the local legislature. This included broadening the franchise for the sector-based "functional" seats to include everyone based on their job. In addition to my geographic seat, I had a vote for the "transport and communications" sector seat, which allowed me to banter with my Chinese taxi drivers on the way to the office about who we should elect.

During an interview at his official residence in 1996, Patten told me off-the-record that he wished he could go to the polls to show his strong local support. China's strategy was to make Patten sound out-of-touch and isolated, which the local business community, fearful of the coming era, did nothing to dispel. "Just once I'd like to run in an election against Zhou Nan to let them see what the Hong Kong people think," he told me, referring to the local China representative.[11] Kerry McGlynn, sitting nearby beneath a lazily rotating ceiling fan, turned to make sure I got the message. Patten's wonderfully named personal secretary, Jenny Best, entered the room on cue to remind His Excellency of a beckoning despatch box from London. In truth, Patten was isolated, through no fault of his own. The colonial era was coming to a close, and everyone was making plans to survive under Beijing.

Since Hong Kong accounted for about 85% of the remaining population of the British empire, Patten was playing a considerable walk-on role at the end of a drama that had begun nearly four centuries before—Ireland in 1603 or Bermuda in 1609 depending on your view. He seemed perfectly happy to relish the stage. It was as if he felt called upon by the ghosts of generations of British colonial governors to cherish these fading moments. I think that is why he liked the *Review*, making a point to call on us at every press conference and granting us interviews. It was not because we mattered, but because we were owed respect. A salute to the vestiges of empire.

Patten loved those vestiges. One of the most adorable was the legendary British journalist Clare Hollingworth. She had the distinction of being the first journalist to report the outbreak of World War II while in Poland. "I'll let you hear for yourself," she famously told her editor in London, holding the telephone out the hotel window to convey the rumble of German tanks crossing the frontier. Her assignments after World War II had been a Grand Tour of decolonizing disasters: Egypt, Persia, Iraq, Palestine, Algeria, Aden, and Vietnam. Forget ceremonial Gurkhas: Clare had dug in with actual Gurkhas. In the fall of 1963, she had spent several weeks embedded with British counter-insurgency forces in the jungles of Borneo, repelling cross-border raids by Indonesian communists. "Gurkhas had created a fort on a small hill in the style of the local long houses built on bamboo stilts and corrugated iron roofs," she recalled of the assignment. "On the camp perimeter, sharpened bamboo sticks were embedded in the ground behind the outer circle of barbed wire, mines, and booby traps."[12]

Her last post was China, where she re-opened the *Daily Telegraph*'s Peking bureau in the last days of the Cultural Revolution and interviewed Mao's evil wife. Clare moved to Hong Kong in 1981 because the governor at the time, Murray MacLehose, was an old friend. MacLehose found her a job at the University of Hong Kong and a two-room flat within walking distance of the Foreign Correspondents' Club, or FCC. Like the *Review*, the FCC had been founded by Western correspondents who had fled communist China. Clare quickly became the Grand Dame of the FCC, where stories of being dug in with the Gurkhas in Borneo went a very long way at the main bar. Every day at lunch, she could be found in the dining room devouring her usual steak and glass of white wine. Her table carried a sign: "This is called Clare Hollingworth's table. Members would be advised to offer your seat if Ms. Hollingworth comes."

I was young, too young to pay sufficient respects to her during our first meeting there. A veteran newsman introduced me as someone who covered China. The unfussy legend asked me what I thought of an article in that day's *South China Morning Post* about military maneuvers in southern China. Probably training to take on the Gurkha Rifles in the wee hours of July 1, 1997, I proposed. We both laughed. Everyone loved her, including Patten. For him, she was the embodiment of the colonial order that he dared not cherish in public (he wore a business suit, never a gubernatorial costume). At receptions at Government House, Patten, and pretty much everyone else with a sense of history, turned to mush in her presence.

At the 1997 handover, the British dusted off their well-practiced Winds of Change routine. The future looked bright. Full confidence in the local population. Enduring bonds of friendship with Britain. Another heirloom of the country's imperial past given away. As one Australian headline summarized Hong Kong at the handover: "Prime location, views of China, some realignment needed."[13] Then a military tattoo, soaked by rains in this case, and Patten's departure on the Royal Yacht *Britannia*, on loan from the Queen. The ship sailed to Manila escorted by seventeen ships of the line, an even bigger armada than the one assembled at the closure of the British naval base at Singapore in 1971. Patten and his family flew back to London, "prosaically ending the British Empire in the queue for a taxi at Heathrow's Terminal Three," in his own words.[14] *Britannia* was decommissioned and sent to Scotland to become a discotheque.

By 1997, the *Review*, like the colony and the FCC, was an anachronism. It never made money for Dow Jones, which had bought it from the British in 1987. After I left Hong Kong in 2002, the magazine entered its death throes. In 2009, Dow Jones ended it (followed a few years later by the closure of the Asian edition of the *Wall Street Journal* with whom we had shared offices.) The former colony also sputtered, choked, and fell. China rather rapidly imposed its nationalist-authoritarian system on the territory—vindicating a famous *Fortune* cover story of 1995, "The Death of Hong Kong," that proved too optimistic by half. Clare Hollingworth died in Hong Kong in 2017, aged 105. The members of the FCC observed a minute's silence.

When the *Review* closed, I was asked to write a retrospective essay for the final issue. The idea of the lost colonial vision immediately sprang to mind. It was the germ of the idea that eventually became "The Case for Colonialism" and this book. My tribute was an ode to the colonial endeavor that was the *Review*. I offer it here with only minor revisions, ending, so to speak, where I began.

~

It would be easy to attribute the demise of the *Far Eastern Economic Review* to the shifting economics of the media industry. After all, hundreds of newspapers and magazines have gone down the tubes in recent years under the combined weight of the Internet and economic recession. But if that were the case, it would also be easy to identify the new and emerging outlets of authoritative Asian news and analysis that had eaten the *Review*'s bento box.

In fact, there is no such thing, on paper or online. While new academic journals on the region have sprung up, an Asiaphile in search of news on the region will be totally stumped. This is remarkable when one considers that Asia Pacific has one-third of the world's population; the proportion rises to half if South Asia is included.

For many decades, the *Review* was the magazine of record for this sprawling and diverse region. How is it that Asia has disappeared as a media proposition while the region has boomed as an economic and even political proposition? *The Economist* explained that the *Review*'s demise was a result of the increasingly specialized tastes of Asian consumers, which are better reached via local publications. But the *Review* never catered to Asia's emerging middle class, whose parents were peasants when the magazine was gathering momentum. The Asia that the *Review* supposedly lost was not the one on which it built its success. Rather, its Asia has disappeared and will not return. That was the Asia of the colonial mind—and not in a pejorative sense.

For several decades, spanning the era of late colonialism in the 1950s to the spread of intense globalization in the early 1990s, a unique cultural niche sprang up in Asia. It was a transitory and transnational community peopled by Western expats—diplomats, executives, scholars and travelers—and local Asian elites in business, government and education who were themselves products of the colonial era.

In light of the region's past and future, it is remarkable that this niche existed at all. But for a few decades, it was possible to speak of a certain epistemic community of Asia-hands and Asian elites who shared a perspective on the region's development. It was an Asia that was neither parochial nor Western, but colonial—an in-between place of mutual understanding and shared perspectives and goals. That Asia has now disappeared, like a whole continent subducted under powerful new forces of localism and globalization. With it goes the *Review*.

Perhaps what is most surprising about this period was the local audience, which was often bombastically anti-Western. Yet the likes of Jawaharlal Nehru, Lee Kuan Yew, Ferdinand Marcos and Mahathir Mohamad shared an essentially colonial mentality about their region and their countries. This mentality was one of seeing certain universals in the struggle for development and governance, while affirming certain limits relating to the cultural particularities of each place. This niche allowed the *Review* to cater to a diverse region. The British empire lorded it over many of the entrepots where the *Review* sold best—Hong Kong, Singapore, Malaysia, India. Politics was about stability, economics was about state-led growth, and business was about intricate social and cultural networks.

Amid all the jousting that the *Review* undertook in piercing the pretensions of local elites—and finding itself or its reporters in the dock in Malaysia, Singapore, Thailand, Indonesia, Vietnam and Pakistan—the magazine was essentially aligned with their perspectives on the region. Lee Kuan Yew may have hated the *Review*, but only in a narrow sense of a fraternal fight, the way that Chiang Kai-shek hated Mao Zedong. In a broader sense, they were cut from the same cloth and spoke the same language. They all saw Asia from the perspective of colonial governors, which is why they so feared democracy and its localizing impulses. When the legendary Derek Davies, editor from 1964 to 1989, died in 2002, the *New York Times*' obituary commented that he had "built the magazine into a major source of news and comment on the region despite his love-hate relationship with its prickly rulers." As time passed, the love grew but the lovers died off.

Longtime Asia correspondent Jonathan Manthorpe wrote: "The *Review* was sometimes criticized by Asian nationalists for being an English language publication, written by Western journalists, and catering to regional elites. In many ways these three qualities were some of its strengths." And those Asian nationalists knew it. It is somehow fitting that just as Dow Jones announced the demise of the *Review*, Singapore's high court upheld a 2008 defamation ruling against the magazine. It was a faint echo from the past when Asian leaders cared deeply about the perspectives of a weekly magazine run by boozy expats. Lee Kuan Yew, without a hint of irony, described the *Review* as "reputable, august and authoritative" while suing it for defamation in 1989. The Orient as a media proposition could never exist without the Orientalists. Once that essentially colonial perspective gave way to today's cacophony of local and Western perspectives, no regional magazine selling a singular perspective could survive.

To understand the cultural niche that the *Review* occupied, two British novels are essential: Graham Greene's 1956 classic, *The Quiet American,* and John le Carré's 1977 bestseller, *The Honourable Schoolboy*. Greene's novel is important because it illustrates the monstrous illusion that somehow the *Review*'s failure was a result of Americanization—in particular Dow Jones's full takeover of the magazine in 1987 and the replacement of its British editor, Philip Bowring, by a very quiet American, Gordon Crovitz, in 1992. Bowring was heir to the colonial perspective at the *Review*, which had been most fully expressed under the leadership of Davies, a former British spy in Vietnam.

In Greene's novel, the British perspective is represented by Thomas Fowler, a boozy, cynical, empathetic and well-informed British journalist covering the French wars in Vietnam. The novel leaves little doubt that we are supposed to sympathize with Fowler, who is contrasted to the quiet American, Alden Pyle, the East Coast American with transformative universal theories who does not really understand or care about the region except as a test case for bigger propositions. "Isms and ocracies. Give me facts," Fowler sniffs, "I don't take sides. I'll still be reporting whoever wins."

Bowring and others from the British wing of the *Review* frequently attributed the magazine's demise to this transition from the Fowlers to the Pyles. It is true that the takeover and makeover by Dow Jones did little to help. But the ship was already sinking because the Asia that the *Review* had catered to was disappearing. Newer Asian elites were not interested in the colonial perspective, British or American. To blame it on Pyle is to tell oneself a comforting story that the colonial perspective would have continued to attract readers in Asia. It could not. A continued Fowler ascendancy would have attracted a smaller, if more fanatically loyal, audience. In Greene's novel, Fowler's loss of his mistress, Phuong, to Pyle—as the British loss of the *Review* to Dow Jones—elicits a stream of anti-American invective from Fowler. He is at least big enough to admit that "what I hated was the future."

Michael Vatikiotis, the last great Fowler of the *Review* as editor from 2001-04, put it thus: "Increasingly, the media that survives is local and circulates in Asia's larger cities, rather than between them." Vatikiotis's idea of media catering to an increasingly Balkanized readership is echoed by others. Manthorpe lamented that the *Review* "currently has no successor...There is no publication in Asia, either on processed dead trees or the Web, that has a regional focus or authoritative voice."

But the implicit conceit is that there is some shared Asian perspective that might replace the colonial one as "authoritative" and assert itself as a media proposition for some new entrepreneur. Many have tried—local media moguls in Japan, Thailand and even Hong Kong. But they fail time and again. *Asiaweek*, the weekly magazine that tried to be the postcolonial alternative to the colonial *Review*, folded in 2001, and with much less gnashing of teeth from Asian readers. There was no "Asia for the Asians" to be had. The fact that Asia briefly had such an identity—one to which the *Review* catered admirably—was a direct and fleeting result of the colonial project of postwar development. In the future, the *Review* will be studied because it reflects the possibilities of a supranational identity in Asia that subsequent generations will find scarcely imaginable.

The colonial perspective provided the only possible authoritative outlook on the region because it alone had a sufficient breadth, liberality of spirit and insistence on minimal principles of good government that could unite elites into a common purpose. I risk the opprobrium of hundreds of Western and Western-influenced academics brandishing Edward Said's *Orientalism* to explain how the *Review* was complicit in an imperial project. So be it. Because what may replace this unique period of shared understanding created by the colonial perspective is a return to a feudalism created by the postcolonial one—each to his own castle, there to nurse grievances and secret musings.

Will Asia's elites ever develop a renewed perspective on the region to replace the colonial one—which some aspiring media outlet might serve? Might a China-centered mentality silently envelop younger minds and become the basis for new media that provides a regional perspective now missing? This future is coming. Perhaps it should not be feared. If anything threatens the integration and peace of Asia more than China's rise, it is the lack of shared values and perspectives among Asian elites. The *Review* reflected and served, perhaps even abetted, such a perspective for 40 years during its glory days. Asia needs a new regional perspective to replace it.

The history of postwar Asia is a history of Western involvement, a fact much lamented by radical professors but one through which the region's institutions and economies grew. Alongside that was a set of readers, local and expat, who were participants in this essentially colonial project. As newly democratic and developed Asian countries graduated to developed-world status, their younger generations had no need for this perspective. If they want a Western perspective they turn to coverage of Asia in Western publications. If not, they turn to their local media. The Asia of the *Review* is today found only in the Foreign Correspondents' Club of Hong Kong.

The FCC is a fitting place to end. Its main bar was a crossroads for Asia and its membership a white pages of *Review* alumni. The old cold storage building it still occupies—holding milk in early days and cadavers in World War II—is a gem of colonial architecture. Its reporter members fled from communism in China in 1949, along with a million others. *Review* journalists headed the FCC on several occasions. The Club continues as a club, but less and less as a cultural milieu.

The FCC makes several appearances in Le Carré's *The Honourable Schoolboy*, which traces the same colonial illusions as *The Quiet American* while explaining its earlier successes. Le Carré thanks "Derek Davies and his staff at the *Far Eastern Economic Review*" in the preface. The central character, old Craw, is based on Richard Hughes, Far East correspondent for the *Sunday Times* who wrote a column for the *Review* from 1971 to 1983. Hughes' 1968 book on Hong Kong, *Borrowed Place, Borrowed Time*, praised the journalistic advantages of the colony, where "information from and about China droppeth like the heavy rain of heaven." In the novel, Craw is an Australian journalist who "had covered the Communists against Chiang Kai-shek and Chiang against the Japanese and the Americans against practically everyone" and "had shaken more sand out of his shorts ... than most of them would ever walk over."

At the end of the novel, old Craw reappears at the main bar of the FCC "looking much aged and soberly dressed." Overhearing some members saying how things are changing and how the Club should change too, he stomps out, "tears pouring down his face." "'Don't change anything,' he shouts, shaking his stick in fury. 'The old order changeth not, let it all run on.'"

The assembled, younger members smile sympathetically. Old Craw contributed much. But his time is done. "'Past it,' they agreed, as the doors closed on him. 'Poor fellow.'"

Endnotes:

1 Joanna Pitman and Catherine Sampson, "Warning by Peking Overshadows Pomp as Patten is Sworn In," *The Times* (London), July 10, 1992.
2 Chris Patten, *The Hong Kong Diaries* (2022), xxiii.
3 David Bello, "The Venomous Course of Southwestern Opium: Qing Prohibition in Yunnan, Sichuan, and Guizhou in the Early Nineteenth Century," *Journal of Asian Studies* (2003).
4 Carl Trocki, *Opium, Empire and the Global Political Economy* (1999).
5 Michael C. Lazich, "American Missionaries and the Opium Trade in Nineteenth-Century China," *Journal of World History* (2006); Jon Miller & Gregory Stanczak, "Redeeming, Ruling, and Reaping: British Missionary Societies, the East India Company, and the India-to-China Opium Trade," *Journal for the Scientific Study of Religion* (2009).
6 Melissa Chen, "Why Post-Colonial Theory is Not Helping Hong Kong," *Aero Magazine* (2019).
7 Eliza Lee, "Introduction: Gender and Change in Hong Kong," in Eliza Lee (ed.), *Gender and Change in Hong Kong: Globalization, Postcolonialism, and Chinese Patriarchy* (2003), 8.
8 "China attacks Hong Kong governor," United Press International, January 27, 1994.
9 Chris Patten, *East and West: The Last Governor of Hong Kong on Power, Freedom, and the Future* (1998), Pan 1999 edition, 12.
10 Chris Patten, *The Hong Kong Diaries* (2022), 22, 21.
11 The interview, less the aside, was published as Bruce Gilley, "Standing Pat: Governor Patten Won't Bend to Tycoons' Pleas," *Far Eastern Economic Review*, May 30, 1996.
12 Clare Hollingworth, *Front Line* (1990), 202.
13 Greg Sheridan, "Prime location, views of China, some realignment needed," *The Australian*, March 11, 1997.
14 Chris Patten, *Not Quite the Diplomat: How Truths About World Affairs* (2005), Penguin 2006 edition, 60.

Printed in the USA
CPSIA information can be obtained
at www.ICGtesting.com
LVHW022304271023
762258LV00014B/56/J